TALKING HANDS

What Sign Language Reveals About the Mind

Margalit Fox

Simon & Schuster
NEW YORK LONDON TORONTO SYDNEY

Camas Public Library

SIMON & SCHUSTER
Rockefeller Center
1230 Avenue of the Americas
New York, NY 10020

Text copyright © 2007 by Margalit Fox
ASL photographs copyright © 2007 by Ivan Farkas
All rights reserved, including the right of reproduction
in whole or in part in any form.

SIMON & SCHUSTER and colophon are registered trademarks
of Simon & Schuster, Inc.

For information about special discounts for bulk purchases,
please contact Simon & Schuster Special Sales at
1-800-456-6798 or business@simonandschuster.com

Text design by Paul Dippolito

Manufactured in the United States of America

1 3 5 7 9 10 8 6 4 2

Library of Congress Cataloging-in-Publication Data
Fox, Margalit.
Talking hands : what sign language reveals about the mind / Margalit Fox.
p. cm.
Includes bibliographic references and index.
1. Sign language—Psychological aspects. 2. Psycholinguistics. I. Title.
P117.F69 2007
419—dc22 2007017624
ISBN-13: 978-0-7432-4712-2
ISBN-10: 0-7432-4712-4

To the memory of two beloved language mavens:

David Fox

Israel Wilenitz

Contents

To imagine a language means to imagine a form of life.

—LUDWIG WITTGENSTEIN,
PHILOSOPHICAL INVESTIGATIONS

TALKING HANDS

Introduction

The narrative sections of this book document a journey to a remarkable place: an isolated Middle Eastern village whose inhabitants "speak" sign language—a language unlike any other in the world, witnessed by few outsiders and never before described. For the last several years, a team of four linguists, two from the United States and two from Israel, has been working in the village, documenting this extraordinary language and, little by little, deciphering it. In the summer of 2003, I was granted the immense privilege of accompanying the team on a three-day research trip to the village. To my knowledge, I am the only journalist from outside the region who has ever been there.

From the time the linguists first set foot in the village, they have striven ferociously to protect the privacy of the people they are studying. That is their job. Before they could even begin their fieldwork, the team spent many painstaking months earning the trust of the villagers. When I first learned of the project, and broached the idea of this book, the linguists felt, with ample justification, that the presence of any newcomer, much less a journalist, had the potential to capsize their entire endeavor. Because of this, I acceded to more constraints on my reporting than I normally would. These were arrived at in the course of nearly a year of transatlantic negotiations with the team's leader, Dr. Wendy Sandler of the University of Haifa, as I sought permission to make the trip.

During my time in the village I was, by prearrangement, a mostly silent observer of the linguists as they went about their work; at no time was I allowed to interview the villagers independently. (Given the breathtaking gulf between their native language and mine, this would have been no small trick anyhow.) Although the linguists continue to make regular research trips to the village, I was permitted to go along only this once. All of the scenes described in the narrative, and all of the dialogue, I saw and heard firsthand during the course of this visit. The only exception is the tale of the larcenous mice, which I have reconstructed based on an interview with the victim. My descriptions of the history and daily life of Al-Sayyid are based on my own observations, and on interviews with members of the research team.

There were other conditions. In exchange for permission to accompany the team, I agreed to show Dr. Sandler all portions of my manuscript pertaining to Al-Sayyid. Because of the exquisite cross-cultural sensitivity their work demands, the linguists are ethically obliged—and, by extension, so am I—not to disclose certain personal details about the life and inhabitants of Al-Sayyid that they have learned in the course of their visits. In the end, I chose to show the entire manuscript to Dr. Sandler as well as to the three other linguists on her team, Drs. Irit Meir, Carol Padden and Mark Aronoff. I have welcomed their corrections on matters of fact, their clarifications of technical material, and their suggestions for avenues of further inquiry. Matters of interpretation and emphasis, however, remain mine alone, as do any residual errors.

Dr. Sandler also expressed deep concern that with the publication of my book, this insular, traditional community might be overrun with curiosity-seekers and members of the news media. In keeping with the linguists' own practice, standard for this type of anthropological research, I have changed the name of every villager mentioned in the narrative. I have also disguised the precise location of the village, along with certain other identifying details. Consider Al-Sayyid a kind of signing Brigadoon (although it is very real, and I have seen it), a place utterly impossible for any outsider to find. I trust strongly that none will try.

In one other instance in the narrative, the brief account in Chapter 7 of a scholar who is said to make scientific generalizations about a language that "only he speaks," certain identifying details have been changed to protect the individual's privacy.

In recent decades, the field of sign-language linguistics has established itself as one of the most yeasty, contentious and promising branches of cognitive science. As such, it is awash in competing scholarly opinions. In a book written for a general readership, it is impossible to give an exhaustive account of either the historical development of the discipline or its present state of affairs. What this book offers is an introduction to the linguistic study of sign language in the form of a representative cross section of the field and its preoccupations from its beginnings in the 1960s to the present day. It is a slice—one of many possible slices—of sign-language linguistics at the start of the twenty-first century, and is by no means intended to represent the field in toto. A bibliographic essay at the end of the book offers suggestions for further reading.

Some notes on usage: Anyone who writes about deafness quickly discovers that worlds of meaning, politics and identity hang on the capitalization of a single letter: the initial "d" of the word "deaf." In the United States, it is often customary to capitalize "Deaf" when referring to any self-identified member of the large cultural minority, united by common language and traditions, of people who cannot hear. (The word is lowercased when it refers strictly to the audiological condition.) After much deliberation, I have chosen to keep the word "deaf" lowercased throughout the pages of this book. My only motivation is typographic consistency, in particular as it applies to the discussions of Al-Sayyid, where capital-D concepts like "Deaf culture" and "Deaf power" are unknown by virtue of the fact that it is so utterly ordinary to be deaf there. I have, however, retained the original capitalization of the word in all quoted matter.

When one is writing about sign language, verbs of attribution also grow thorny. On a physiological level, no one "speaks" sign language, or ever "says" anything in sign. Sign languages have users. They have signers. But, technically, don't have speakers. A work of this length, however, begs for stylistic variety, and as a result, I sometimes use verbs of speech—"speak," "say," "talk"—along with their derivatives, to refer to the act of signed communication, as in the title of the book itself. These words are meant purely as loose, colloquial metaphors, to be understood much as "spoke" is in the title of the anthropologist Nora Groce's lovely book, *Everyone Here Spoke Sign Language.*

In a book about cognitive science, the terms "mind" and "brain" also pose a challenge to smooth usage. I have in general adopted the familiar "hardware-versus-software" analogy, using "brain" to refer to the physical structure within the cranial cavity and "mind" to denote the range of operations this physical structure can perform.

Talking Hands is organized into seventeen chapters. The odd-numbered chapters form the narrative of the linguists' visit to Al-Sayyid and their subsequent work deciphering its language. The even-numbered chapters chart the course of sign-language linguistics: Chapters 2 and 4 offer an introduction to the signed languages of the world, and to the aims of modern linguistics. Chapters 6 and 8 chronicle the birth of the scientific study of sign language, and examine the very special conditions that give rise to "signing villages" like Al-Sayyid. Chapters 10 and 12 describe the grammar of signed languages, focusing on the unusual means by which they build words and sentences. Chapters 14 and 16 explore the psychology of sign language—memory for signs, "slips of the hand," and so on—and what sign language has to tell us about the neurological workings of human language in the brain.

Finally, a note on sign-language transcription. Following the convention of sign-language linguistics, the English glosses for signs are printed in small capital letters: FATHER, ROOSTER, THINK. Where a single sign is glossed using two or more English words, they are linked with hyphens: YOUNGER-BROTHER, TAKE-CARE-OF, LEFT-SIDE. Compound signs are glossed with a ligature mark: THRILL⁀INFORM. Words spelled out by means of the manual alphabet are capitalized and hyphenated: W-A-T-E-R.

CHAPTER 1

In the Village of the Deaf

The house is a lighted island in a sea of gathering dark. The sun has just gone down, and the desert breeze blowing in through the large open windows is cooler now. Outside, just beyond the house, fields of yellow stubble give way to a flat expanse of sand and scrub that stretches toward the distant hills ringing the horizon. A band of vermilion hangs above the hills, and above that, the sky is an inverted bowl of deep turquoise. Across the sand, a line of shadowy forms can be seen picking its way slowly toward the house: the village camels, home for the night.

From a nearby mosque, the muezzin's call to prayer floats through the open windows. The windows have deep marble sills but no glass, for the house is barely half-finished. Right now it is little more than walls, sheer slabs of whitewashed concrete that seem to rise organically from the surface of the desert. There is no front door yet, and no front steps: you enter, perilously, by clawing your way up a steep concrete ramp coated with blown sand. Inside, the house is hollow. Its half-dozen rooms have neither doors nor windows, and underfoot, where the floor will be, is only hard-packed dirt. Garlands of electrical wires sprout from the bare white walls; a black rubber hose of indeterminate purpose snakes across the ground from room to room. That is all there is to the house so far, but its raw state suits the desert.

On this summer evening, the half-built house is alive with people. In the main room, which overlooks the hills, the owner of the house, a stocky man in an untucked plaid shirt, has set a long plastic banquet table on the earthen floor, with a dozen plastic patio chairs around it. The table is filling with food. Children materialize with platters of nuts, sunflower seeds and miniature fruit—tiny pears, nectarines and plums. A tray of small china cups is set out, and a boy of about twelve enters, carrying a brass coffeepot, blackened from use, with a graceful spout curved like a pelican's beak. He pours the coffee: thick, black, sweet and tasting of cardamom. At the other end of the table, a boy with a Thermos pours strong, sweet tea into small glasses crammed with fresh mint.

People start to take their seats. At the head of the table, the owner is joined by a group of men in their thirties and forties. Down one side of the table is a row of boys in graduated sizes, from toddlers to teenagers. More children play on the floor nearby; some very young ones, a few girls among them, peer shyly into the room from behind the door frame. At the foot of the table sits a knot of visitors. There are six of us: four scholars of linguistics, a video camera operator and me. We have all traveled great distances, some of us crossing oceans, to be in this half-finished house tonight.

The man and his family are Bedouins, and the house is at the edge of their village, Al-Sayyid. Though they live in the desert, the Bedouins of Al-Sayyid are not nomads: their people have inhabited this village, tucked into an obscure corner of what is now Israel, miles from the nearest town, for nearly two hundred years. There are no timeless figures from T. E. Lawrence here, wandering the sands in billowing robes. These Bedouins are rooted, even middle-class. Men and boys are bareheaded and dressed in Western clothing, mostly T-shirts and jeans. Families live in houses, some with indoor plumbing and vast sofas upholstered in plush. They own automobiles, computers and VCRs. But there is something even more remarkable about the Al-Sayyid Bedouins, and that is what has brought the team of scholars here this evening: a highly unusual language, spoken only in this village and never documented until now.

The house is a Babel tonight. Around the long table, six languages are in use at once, conversation spilling across conversation. There are snatches of English, mostly for my benefit. There is Hebrew: two of the linguists are from an Israeli university, and many of the men of Al-Sayyid speak it as well. There is a great deal of Arabic, the language of the home for Bedouins throughout the Middle East. But in the illuminated room, it is the other languages that catch the eye. They are signed languages, the languages of the deaf. As night engulfs the surrounding desert and the cameraman's lights throw up huge, signing shadows, it looks as though language itself has become animate, as conversations play out in grand silhouette on the whitewashed walls.

There are three signed languages going. There is American Sign Language, used by one of the visitors, a deaf linguist from California. There is Israeli Sign Language, the language of the deaf in that country, whose structure the two Israeli scholars have devoted years to analyzing. And there is a third language, the one the linguists have journeyed here to see: a signed language spoken in this village and nowhere else in the world.

The language is Al-Sayyid's genetic legacy. In this isolated traditional community, where marriage to outsiders is rare, a form of inherited deafness has been passed down from one generation to the next for the last seventy years. Of the 3,500 residents of the village today, nearly 150 are deaf, an incidence forty times that of the general population. As a result, an indigenous signed language has sprung up here, evolving among the deaf villagers as a means of communication. That can happen whenever deaf people come together. But what is so striking about the sign language of Al-Sayyid is that many hearing villagers can also speak it. It permeates every aspect of community life here, used between parents and children, husbands and wives, from sibling to sibling and neighbor to neighbor. At every hour of the day, in the houses, in the fields and in the mosque, there are people conversing in sign. In Al-Sayyid, the four linguists have encountered a veritable island of the deaf.

Their work here will occupy them for years to come, in all likelihood for the rest of their careers. They plan to observe the language, to record it, and to produce an illustrated dictionary, the first-ever documentary record of the villagers' signed communication system. But the linguists are after something even larger. Because Al-Sayyid Bedouin Sign Language has arisen entirely on its own, outside the influence of any other language, it offers a living demonstration of the "language instinct," man's inborn capacity to create language from thin air. If the linguists can decode this language—if they can isolate the formal elements that make Al-Sayyid Bedouin Sign Language *a language*—they will be in possession of a new and compelling body of evidence in the search for the ingredients essential to all language, signed and spoken. And in so doing, they will have helped illuminate one of the most fundamental aspects of what it means to be human.

Early that morning, the four linguists convened at the University of Haifa, in the lab of Dr. Wendy Sandler. An American who has lived in Israel for more than two decades, she is the director of the university's Sign Language Research Laboratory, one of the few labs of its kind in the world. Proficient in both American and Israeli Sign Languages, Wendy is the lead researcher on the Bedouin project. She is small, dark and intense.

The rest of the team crowds into the little room. There is Irit Meir, the other Israeli linguist, a colleague at the university. She has a background in English and linguistics and also speaks some Arabic, which will be useful in Al-Sayyid. A former doctoral student of Wendy's, Irit is now a colleague at the university, working alongside her analyzing Israeli Sign Language. (Her name, the Hebrew word for asphodel, a Mediterranean flower, is pronounced ih-REET.) She is the visual inverse of Wendy: tall, with sandy hair and long chiseled features.

Next to Irit is Carol Padden, a linguist in the Department of Communication at the University of California at San Diego. The only deaf member of the team, Carol is one of the country's foremost authorities on the language and culture of the American deaf community. She has dark blue eyes set close together in a pear-shaped face, hair the color of dark honey, and a wide smile. The fourth member of the team is Mark Aronoff, from Stony Brook University, on Long Island. He is an internationally renowned linguist and an old friend of mine, my adviser for two degrees in the field. He is a trifle owly (though he would not care to have me say it), graying, with bottle-thick glasses and a bristling mustache. Mark is a specialist in morphology, the study of the internal architecture of words, and has done extensive work on Semitic languages, including Hebrew and Maltese. He, Carol and I had flown from New York to Tel Aviv the day before, driving up to Haifa in a rented van that in a few hours will carry the team into the desert.

The linguists are gathered around a video monitor, reviewing material they recorded a year ago, on their first visit to Al-Sayyid. (In the local Arabic dialect, the name of the village is pronounced "es-SAYY-id.") A Bedouin woman in a headscarf appears onscreen, signing. "She's the fourth deaf daughter of five daughters," says Irit, who keeps a detailed genealogical record of each person the team videotapes. Watching the monitor, Irit spots the Bedouin sign SIT, which she demonstrates for her colleagues: two fists, held straight out in front of the body, travel downward toward the floor. It differs visibly from the Israeli sign SIT, which she demonstrates next: two flat hands, palms downward, traveling toward the floor. (The ASL sign SIT is altogether different: the curved index and middle fingers of one hand tap down onto the extended index and middle fingers of the other; the result suggests a pair of legs dangling off the edge of a seat.)

Carol asks to use Wendy's computer. Today is her father's birthday, and she wants to send a text message to his electronic pager wishing him many happy returns. Both of Carol's parents are deaf, as is her brother, and she grew up equally at home in English and ASL. Her own pager, for deaf people an indispensable tool of communication, refuses to work in Israel, and she's feeling a bit cut off—her husband, at home in California with their young daughter, is also deaf. "I should buy a phone for every country, I guess," Carol says ruefully. Carol speaks and reads lips well, with less difficulty than many deaf people have. Her speaking voice is pleasant; she sounds like someone with a slight, hard-to-place foreign accent.

The members of the team have known each other for years. Linguistics is a small community, the subfield of sign-language linguistics smaller still, with perhaps a few hundred full-time practitioners in the world. These four began working as a group several years ago, analyzing the ways in which words are formed in American and Israeli Sign Languages. In a few days, when they return from the desert, they will begin to attack the language of Al-Sayyid, scrutinizing videotapes, pointing, conjecturing, arguing, rewinding and arguing some more, as they attempt to tease out the structure of this mysterious language.

Wendy first heard about Al-Sayyid in the late 1990s. Though insular, the village was not completely unknown to outsiders. An Israeli anthropologist had been there, as had some geneticists and social service professionals. Their interests lay in the deafness itself: how it was passed from one generation to the next, how it informed social relations in the village, how education for deaf children might be improved. They paid little attention, however, to the nature of the unusual language that the condition had brought into being. When Wendy learned of the village, she knew at once she had to investigate. "I thought immediately that this would be important," she explained afterward, "because it was clearly an isolated sign language."

Over the next few years, Wendy and Irit made a series of cautious forays into Al-Sayyid, setting in motion the delicate diplomacy that is a critical part of linguistic fieldwork: explaining their intentions, hosting a day of activities at the village school, over time earning the trust of a number of the villagers. Today's visit will be only the second time the entire team has been to Al-Sayyid, and only the second time the four linguists have collected data there together. They plan to stay three days. On their first visit, the year before, they videotaped several of the villagers telling stories in sign. This time, they intend to do more narrowly focused work, administering a series of computerized tests designed to summon forth the words, phrases and sentences of this unknown language.

In Wendy's lab, Shai Davidi, the resident technician and videographer, sets a laptop computer on a desk. With his close-cropped hair, narrow black-rimmed glasses and black T-shirt, Shai lends the room a touch of downtown Manhattan. The team huddles over the laptop to watch a slide show of everyday objects that Shai has prepared for them to take into the field: this will be used to elicit the basic vocabulary of the Bedouins' signed language.

One by one, a succession of images fills the screen: *Dog* . . . *Cat* . . . *Chicken* . . . *Pear* . . . *Banana* . . . *Lemon* . . . *Pencils* . . . *Scissors* . . . *Stapler.*

"You think they have a stapler?" Carol wonders aloud, picturing daily life in the desert. "What would they be stapling?"

More images scroll by: *Chair* . . . *Wristwatch* . . . *Eyeglasses.* (Everyone laughs at this; the glasses in the picture currently reside on Shai's face.) There is a bed, a dining table and a gleaming, restaurant-quality chrome stove.

"Nice stove," says Mark, who likes fine things.

"It's from a magazine," Shai says.

The slide show is followed onscreen by a series of line drawings—people buying and selling groceries, sending and receiving a letter—which the linguists hope will elicit simple sentences with subjects, verbs and objects. "It's very hard to do 'send,'" Irit remarks in her impeccable, Israeli-accented English as the drawing flickers by. "How do you show 'send'?"

There are more drawings; some short video clips of people sitting and standing, walking forward and backward, handing each other objects and yanking them away, kicking a ball back and forth. These are designed to test the particular ways in which Al-Sayyid Bedouin Sign Language, like all signed languages, an inherently *spatial* enterprise, indicates various kinds of directional movement. Next come colors: each of the world's languages divides up the spectrum of color words in one of several characteristic ways. There are photographs of people in an array of emotional states—happy, sad, frightened, angry—and, finally, an animated cartoon of Sylvester and Tweety Bird that the Bedouin subjects will be asked to retell in sign.

Wendy closes the laptop and begins to gather the things she needs for the long trip to the desert. As the team leader, she has traditionally shouldered most of the anxiety about the project, and this visit is no exception. She is by nature thorough, meticulous, rigorous, ideal qualities for a linguist. One evening in Haifa, taking Mark and me to dinner, Wendy parked her little red car on a downtown street. She got out, locked it and began to walk away. Then she turned around. There were a couple of inches to spare between the front wheel and the curb, and the car was a few degrees shy of parallel. "Unaesthetic," she announced to no one in particular, walked back, unlocked the door, got behind the wheel and reparked.

Circumstances in the desert will be much harder to control. In the hallway across from Wendy's lab hangs a large framed poster advertising the 1999 meeting of the Israeli Association for Theoretical Linguistics, held here in Haifa. Mark is billed high up as an invited speaker, giving a talk entitled "Using Dictionaries to Study the Mental Lexicon." Farther down is a listing of a paper jointly authored by Mark, Wendy and Irit, "Universal and Particular Aspects of Sign Language Morphology." The four linguists are highly respected in their field—eminent, even—but they are mostly pen-and-paper theorists far more accustomed to dealing with language as the stuff of scientific abstraction, admittedly short on the hands-on anthropological field experience this project will entail. On their previous trip to Al-Sayyid, they were received politely, but with some wariness, and that after the careful advance work by Wendy and Irit. Nearly a year has gone by since then, and in the isolated village, a van full of strangers is bound to be an anomalous, perhaps discomforting, presence. Will the villagers still be receptive to the project? Will anyone show up for the recording sessions the linguists have painstakingly scheduled? Wendy can do little more than trust in the man who is her liaison in Al-Sayyid, a hearing villager who has undertaken to make the local arrangements.

She is also somewhat concerned about the language itself. Al-Sayyid Bedouin Sign Language is by definition an unknown quantity. Over the last few decades, other "signing villages" have occasionally come to light. Often their language turns out to be something of a disappointment, less fully developed than a linguist would hope for, more a primitive pidgin than a full-blown linguistic system. Will the signing of Al-Sayyid turn out to be a full, real language? The linguists have not yet amassed enough data to be completely certain.

What is more, although the sign language of Al-Sayyid arose in a linguistic vacuum, unaffected by other languages, the social realities of modern life, even in a remote desert community, make it impossible for it to remain that way. Over the years, many of Al-Sayyid's deaf children have been bused to special classes for the deaf in nearby towns. There, they are taught all day in spoken language—Hebrew or Arabic—accompanied by signs from Israeli Sign Language, a language utterly different from their own. They carry the signs home with them at night. The sign language of Al-Sayyid's children, the linguists have already observed, is permeated with Israeli words. The situation lends the team's work a certain immediacy: in just one generation, when the older Bedouin signers die, the unique signed language of the village, at least in its present form, may be significantly altered.

We descend to the university's underground garage to pack up the rented van. The night before, Irit loaded in boxes of china and silver-toned serving trays, gifts for the Bedouin families the team plans to visit. To these we add personal luggage for six; three laptop computers; Shai's video camera, tripods and lights; two straw hats; several very large bottles of water; and a bag of fruit. The van, a sleek blue Fiat of which Mark, the expedition driver, is inordinately proud, is not large, and it takes some careful geometry to fit everything in. In the front and rear windows the linguists place laminated placards that proclaim "Sign Language Dictionary Project" in Hebrew and Arabic.

Heading downstairs with a final armload, I pass a small framed document hanging in the hallway outside Wendy's lab, opposite the conference poster. It is the lab's mission statement, which reads, in part:

> It usually comes as a surprise to the layman to learn that nobody sat down and invented the sign languages of the deaf. Rather, these are languages that arise spontaneously, wherever deaf people have an opportunity to congregate—which tells us that they are the natural product of the human brain, just like

> spoken languages. But since these languages exist in a different physical modality, they are believed to offer us a unique window into the kind of mental system that all human language belongs to.

The team climbs into the van and, dishes chattering gently, sets out for the desert in search of the mind.

CHAPTER 2

"What Is This Wonderful Language?"

Wendy Sandler found her calling as an undergraduate. It was the mid-1970s, and she was a student at Georgetown University. Wendy had grown up "all over." Her father worked in retail, and the family moved wherever his job took him, from Cleveland to Pittsburgh to upstate New York. Even now, when she speaks English, Wendy's speech reflects these transgressed dialectal borders. After high school, Wendy decided to train for a career as an actress. She enrolled at the University of Wisconsin, later transferring to a private drama school in a tiny Michigan town, staffed incongruously with transplanted members of Britain's Royal Shakespeare Company and Royal Academy of Dramatic Art. Wendy was passionate about the theater—she still is—but grew disinclined to make a career of it and left the school after a year. She went to Israel and worked on a kibbutz, fell viscerally in love with the country, and resolved one day to live there permanently.

Returning to the United States, Wendy enrolled at Georgetown, where she chose to study linguistics. She had wanted to be an actress because she was fascinated by the complex art of human communication, so becoming a linguist seemed a logical next step. It would also be a useful calling in a multilingual country like Israel.

By this time, Wendy was in her mid-twenties, older than her classmates. With characteristic energy, she also ran the Aliyah Desk at the international headquarters of B'nai B'rith, advising people who wanted to emigrate to Israel. One day, a call came in to the B'nai B'rith office. Gallaudet College, located nearby, needed a Hebrew instructor—could someone at B'nai B'rith recommend one? They suggested Wendy, and she took the job, little realizing the decision would shape the course of her professional life for the next thirty years.

Gallaudet (a French name, pronounced American: "gal-uh-DETT") is a university for deaf people, the only one of its kind in the world. Located in Washington, D.C., it was incorporated in 1857 as the Columbia Institution for the Instruction of the Deaf, Dumb and Blind; it was later renamed for Thomas Hopkins Gallaudet (1787–1851), a Protestant minister who was a pioneer in the education of deaf people in the early nineteenth century. In 1817, Thomas Gallaudet had established the first permanent school for the deaf in the United States, in Hartford, Connecticut. The community he fostered there, a diverse group of deaf men and women from around the country brought together under one roof, played a vital role in the birth of the country's national signed language, what is known today as American Sign Language.

When Wendy came to Gallaudet College (it is now Gallaudet University), she had little familiarity with the culture of the deaf. She knew no deaf people; she did not know ASL. (The university, undeterred, put her in its two-month intensive summer course.) Her first day on campus, she sat in the student cafeteria and watched, riveted, as conversations detonated in the air around her—a hundred hands flying, slicing, brushing and pointing in elaborate rhythm. "I thought to myself, 'They are talking exactly as we do, but not with speech,'" Wendy would recall years later. "'How then? What is this wonderful language?'" She has been working to answer that question ever since. As she soon discovered, the task is like taking apart one of the most sophisticated, intricate and elegantly designed machines in the world.

At the time Wendy began her studies, the field of sign-language linguistics was barely a decade old. Until the 1960s, no one had even considered that sign languages might be "real" human languages: complex, systematic and amenable to the same kind of linguistic analysis as spoken ones. In the popular imagination, to the extent that anyone thought about it at all, a signed language was one of two things: at best, it was a word-for-word version of spoken language, simply rerouted onto the hands. At worst, it was a set of rude imitative gestures, devoid of grammar and good for discussing only the most concrete essentials of daily living. Nearly all scholars, and even many deaf people themselves, held with one or the other scenario.

In their book *Deaf in America: Voices from a Culture,* Carol Padden and her husband, the scholar Tom Humphries, quote from a widely influential text on the education of deaf children, *The Psychology of Deafness,* by Helmer Myklebust, published in 1960. The point of view Myklebust articulated, the prevailing mid-century position on sign language, would not be fully discredited until more than a decade later:

> "The manual sign language used by the deaf is an Ideographic language. . . . It is more pictorial, less symbolic. . . . Ideographic language systems, in comparison with verbal symbol systems, lack precision, subtlety, and flexibility. It is likely that Man cannot achieve his ultimate potential through an Ideographic language. . . . The manual sign language must be viewed as inferior to the verbal as a language."

Even linguistics held a dim view of sign. In *Language,* his seminal book of 1933, Leonard Bloomfield, the most eminent linguist of the first half of the twentieth century, lumped sign language together with other gestural systems and summarily dismissed them all:

> Some communities have a *gesture language* which upon occasion they use instead of speech. Such gesture languages have been observed among the lower-class Neapolitans, among Trappist monks (who have made a vow of silence), among the Indians of our western plains (where tribes of different language met in commerce and war), and among groups of deaf-mutes.
>
> It seems certain that these gesture languages are merely developments of ordinary gestures and that any and all compli-

> cated or not immediately intelligible gestures are based on the conveniences of ordinary speech.

Mime or speech? What else, if not one or the other, could sign language possibly be?

It is neither. Sign languages are very much "real" languages—as real as spoken ones. The essential difference (many linguists now believe it is the only truly significant difference) is that instead of operating acoustically, sign languages work spatially. Where spoken language transmits information by stringing sounds together into recognizable patterns, sign language does the same thing *by manipulating the movement of the hands and body in space.* Like spoken language, sign language is a complex symbolic code, beholden to grammatical rules. Like spoken language, sign language is acquired by young children in regular developmental stages. And, like spoken language, it is no pantomime.

Of course some signs are mimetic—ideographic, in Myklebust's words. All signed languages developed partly from iconic gestures, and traces of those gestures are visible today. In the ASL sign HOUSE, the two hands describe a peaked roof; CAT mimics whiskers springing from the cheek; BABY is the conventional arms-crossed rocking. Signs like these are only natural in a system that exploits the three-dimensional surround. But in fact, they account for just a small subset of words in the language, mostly nouns and verbs. If sign language were truly iconic, it would be instantly transparent to everyone who sees it, a rebus written on air. But as any hearing person who has watched a signed conversation and been quickly and irretrievably at a loss to decipher it can attest, sign language entails far more than making pictures.

The linguist Ulrike Zeshan, who is engaged in comparing the grammatical structures of dozens of the world's signed languages, nicely encapsulates the difference between sign and ordinary gesture:

> When a gesture becomes a sign, its properties change, because as a sign it forms part of the linguistic structure of the signed

> language and thus becomes subject to grammatical rules operating in the signed language.... For example, a familiar gesture for "money" in many countries consists of rubbing together the thumb and one or more fingers. In Indo-Pakistani Sign Language, the sign MONEY looks very much like this gesture. Unlike the gesture, however, the sign can be turned into a verb by adding a movement directed from the person paying to the person being paid, giving the meaning "to pay (someone)." Moreover, a number of other signs, including the sign RICH and the sign INFLATION, can be derived from the sign MONEY by changing its movement pattern. The corresponding gesture as used by hearing people in the region, of course, has none of these derivations and follows no grammatical rules.

This doesn't mean, however (as its speakers are at pains to emphasize), that ASL is "English on the hands." Artificial sign systems like this do exist, invented for pedagogical use, with stiff regimental names like "Signing Exact English." They are the native language of no one. These invented systems lack the intricately layered spatial grammar found in natural signed languages around the world. Deaf parents rarely transmit them to their deaf children. Nor are they used by deaf people to communicate among themselves. These systems have been by all accounts a profound failure in the education of deaf children, forced linguistic grafts that refuse to grow. There are persuasive cognitive reasons, linguists have discovered, that this is so.

Other sign systems have been documented as well. Among them, as Bloomfield noted, are the hand gestures of the Plains Indians, which captured the interest of eighteenth- and nineteenth-century observers, and the signs used by several monastic orders in the Middle Ages and afterward. But Bloomfield notwithstanding, these are not really languages at all. They are nothing more than simple manual ciphers, jerry-built supplements to spoken language designed for use in very particular situations. No society employs these systems as its primary means of communication; no child acquires them as a native language. They are not so much language as emergency language surrogates, manual lingua francas.

Nor is sign language equivalent to the manual alphabet, the method of spelling with the fingers familiar to anyone who has seen *The Miracle Worker.* The manual alphabet does have a place in sign language: it is used to spell out proper names, as well as "foreign" words, borrowed from spoken language, for which there are no corresponding signs. It also has enormous utility as a means of tactile communication for people who are both deaf and blind. But an alphabet is all it is, and an alphabet is not a language.

Sign languages, the ones deaf people authentically use, are neither alphabets nor mime, nor are they mirrors of spoken language. They are instead full, complex, natural languages in their own right. Both signed and spoken languages are systems of arbitrary symbols, used to communicate information. Both possess an orderly grammar and syntax, the instruction sets for assembling words, phrases and sentences. Sign languages have the same "parts of speech" as spoken languages do—nouns, verbs, adjectives and the like. They also have verbs that agree with their subjects; constellations of pronouns inflected grammatically for person and number; ways of expressing past, present and future actions. They have regional and ethnic dialects. They can be used to talk about anything spoken language can, from daily banalities to the loftiest abstractions. (Carol is known for delivering papers at academic meetings, in sign language, on abstruse points of theoretical linguistics.) There is original sign-language poetry, literature and drama. In short, signed languages can do anything spoken languages can; they simply do it manually. In the words of William C. Stokoe, the first great sign-language scholar, "Sign languages are gestural systems, although gestural systems are not necessarily sign languages."

The best-known sign language is ASL, used by a quarter- to a half-million deaf people in the United States and parts of Canada. ASL is not English. It uses vocabulary and grammatical constructions found nowhere in English. (Some linguists have compared aspects of its grammar to Japanese and Navajo.) It also employs word orders very different from those found in English. In ASL, the lines "I'm hungry. You want to get something to eat?" would be signed I HUNGRY, WANT EAT YOU, with an accompanying facial expression that indicates the signer is asking a question.

Like all signed languages studied to date, ASL displays a grammatical economy that English does not have: with a twist of the wrist or an extra revolution of the arm (for varying the spatial signal gives signed language much of its grammar), a verb can be inflected to convey a nuanced spectrum of meanings that in English requires cloddish circumlocution. Simply by adjusting the movement of the hands, the verb GIVE, for example, can be modified to mean "give to each"; "give continuously"; "give to each, that action recurring over time"; "give continuously to each in turn"; and "give continuously to each in turn, that action recurring over time." This also works for adjectives: SICK stands at the center of a linguistic paradigm that includes "to be characteristically sick"; "to get sick easily, often"; "to be sick for a long time"; "to get sick over and over again"; "to be sick for an uninterrupted period of time"; "to get sick incessantly"; "to be very sick"; and "to become fully sick." In ASL, each of these concepts is expressed with a single sign. As the pioneering sign-language linguists Ursula Bellugi and Edward S. Klima have written, "The . . . grammatical processes that have developed in American Sign Language are indigenous to the language and bear little or no mark of English."

In recent years, the speakers of this rich language have come to regard themselves not as disabled—would-be hearing people in need of repair—but, quite simply, as members of a linguistic minority, a signing archipelago in a vast American sea of speech. In the United States and a number of other countries, the deaf view themselves as a cultural minority as well: besides their language, they are vitally connected by shared history and tradition. There are deaf professional and social organizations, and deaf athletic clubs. There is deaf custom: styles of humor, of social interaction, and a deaf folkloric tradition that includes creation stories about the roots of the community itself.

In *Deaf in America,* Carol and her husband recount the childhood experience of a deaf colleague, the linguist and educator Samuel Supalla, as he first became aware of the larger culture that existed beyond the familiar deaf culture at home:

> As Sam's story went, he had never lacked for playmates; he was born into a Deaf family with several Deaf older brothers. As his interests turned to the world outside his family, he noticed a girl next door who seemed to be about his age. After a few tentative encounters, they became friends. She was a satisfactory playmate, but there was the problem of her "strangeness." He could not talk with her as he could with his older brothers and his parents. She seemed to have extreme difficulty understanding even the simplest or crudest gestures. After a few futile attempts to converse, he gave up and instead pointed when he wanted something, or simply dragged her along with him if he wanted to go somewhere. He wondered what strange affliction his friend had, but since they had developed a way to interact with each other, he was content to accommodate to her peculiar needs.
>
> One day, Sam remembers vividly, he finally understood that his friend was indeed odd. They were playing in her home, when suddenly her mother walked up to them and animatedly began to move her mouth. As if by magic, the girl picked up a dollhouse and moved it to another place. Sam was mystified and went home to ask his mother about exactly what kind of affliction the girl next door had. His mother explained that she was HEARING and because of this did not know how to SIGN; instead she and her mother TALK, they move their mouths to communicate with each other. Sam then asked if this girl and her family were the only ones "like that." His mother explained that no, in fact, nearly everyone else was like the neighbors. It was his own family that was unusual. It was a memorable moment for Sam. He remembers thinking how curious the girl next door was, and if she was HEARING, how curious HEARING people were.

Describing sign, nineteenth-century observers typically saw it as a great linguistic monolith: a single language, understood in an intuitive, childlike way (this was crucial) by deaf people around the globe. Published accounts from the period have names like *The Sign Language, The Sign Language of the Deaf and Dumb,* and *Guide to the Silent Language of the Deaf and Dumb.* "The clear implication," the linguists J. G. Kyle and Bencie Woll write, "is that there is one universal sign language." This view was shared even by educated deaf people. Ferdinand Berthier, a nineteenth-century French scholar, reformer and historian of the deaf who was deaf himself, wrote: "For centuries scholars from every country have sought after a universal language, and failed. Well, it exists all around, it is sign language." Even today, many hearing people assume without question that there exists a single universal signed language, known to deaf people the world over.

In reality, there are scores of signed languages in use across the globe—perhaps even hundreds. New ones can arise naturally, in the course of just a generation or two, wherever the deaf have the chance to come together. "Virtually any time Deaf people form a community, even a community of two, some kind of gestural system will develop," the linguist Susan Fischer has written. "If the community has historical continuity, as in the case of a school or a Deaf family, that gestural system will evolve into a language, that is, a sign language."

Scholars have documented more than a hundred signed languages around the world; there are probably many others still unrecorded. Nearly every country has its own national signed language. There is French Sign Language and British Sign Language; Spanish Sign Language and Italian Sign Language; German Sign Language, Swedish Sign Language, Danish Sign Language and Finnish Sign Language; Greek Sign Language, Turkish Sign Language, Hungarian Sign Language and Russian Sign Language; Israeli Sign Language and Saudi Arabian Sign Language; Chinese Sign Language, Taiwanese Sign Language, Hong Kong Sign Language and Thai Sign Language; Japanese Sign Language and Korean Sign Language; Australian Sign Language, New Zealand Sign Language and Indonesian

Sign Language; Québécois Sign Language, Mexican Sign Language, Chilean Sign Language and Brazilian Sign Language; Algerian Sign Language, Mozambican Sign Language, Zimbabwean Sign Language; and a great many others.

The sign language of a particular country is rarely contingent on the spoken language that surrounds it. American and British Sign Languages, though both found in English-speaking places, are mutually unintelligible. A deaf American will have an easier time understanding a deaf Frenchman: ASL is historically descended from French Sign Language. (Its antecedents still show: even today, nearly two centuries after ASL became a language in its own right, more than half its signs have French Sign cognates.) Even the manual alphabet used by deaf signers can differ from one country to another: the letters of the American manual alphabet are signed using one hand; those of the British manual alphabet are made with two hands.

While the world's sign languages may resemble one another to a degree—they can, for instance, have certain vocabulary items in common—each is fundamentally different from the next. Just as a particular sequence of sounds can mean one thing in Spoken Language A and something entirely different in Spoken Language B (*bolna* means "to ache" in Russian; in Urdu, it means "to speak"), a gesture in one signed language may have an altogether different meaning in another. The ASL verb COOK is made by clapping the hands together twice in crisp succession, first palms together, then with the top hand quickly flipped over, its back striking the palm of the lower hand. For many people the gesture calls to mind flipping a hamburger on a grill. But in Danish Sign Language, the same sequence means INTERPRET.

A gesture that is meaningful in one language may be no more than visual nonsense in another. In Hong Kong Sign Language, it is grammatically permissible to form words in the armpit: without the armpit you cannot, for instance, say WEDNESDAY. But not every sign language presses the armpit into linguistic service: ASL, for one, gets along fine without it.

Besides the differences in word order, ASL has other characteristic, and very un-English, ways of putting its sentences together. ASL has no copula—the verb "to be"—though it is able to convey the full range of states of being, past, present and future. (Many spoken languages, including Russian and Hebrew, also have no copula in the present tense.) It can often vary the movement pattern of a single sign to convey complex phrases that in English may require the piling-on of adverbs and adjectives. In short, ASL sentences dispense with much of the wordiness of English ones. Susan Fischer, one of the first linguists to investigate the structure of American Sign Language, noted this property in the early 1970s:

> Many of our insights into the richness and diversity of sign have come from our deaf informant, Bonnie Gough. Often we ask her to translate some sentence, which we have written down in English, into her own language. She will almost invariably point to a large number of words in the sentence and tell us, "Get rid of that, get rid of this, get rid of that," etc. This happens so frequently that we have termed this phenomenon the "get-rid-of-it" syndrome. What is it that our informant so earnestly wishes us to do without? . . .
>
> One of the sentences which we gave to several informants to translate into A.S.L. was (1):
>
> (1) It is against the law to drive on the left side of the road.
> This sentence has fourteen words. A speaker of English might say it in fewer words, for example by contracting *it* and *is* into *it's,* and perhaps even leave out the last three words, leaving us with (2), which has ten words:
>
> (2) It's against the law to drive on the left side.
>
> Of these ten words, *it's, to, on,* and *the* (twice) are what have been termed *function* words, as opposed to *content* words, such as nouns, adjectives and verbs. Sign language, like Russian, does not use the copula, nor does it use articles. The translation into sign of sentences (1) or (2) is (3):
>
> (3) ILLEGAL DRIVE LEFT-SIDE.

In just three signs, the information is preserved, but in a kind of condensed form, and all the elements which are not really essential to convey the message have been eliminated.

Because of this property, ASL is very poorly served by English transcriptions. As the psychologist Harlan Lane and his co-authors Robert Hoffmeister and Ben Bahan write in their book, *A Journey into the Deaf-World:*

> Those who assume signed language is concrete are led to assume that it is primitive. They are encouraged in this mistaken belief when they read word-for-word transcriptions of ASL (called *glosses*), as in ME MOTHER RESPONSIBLE CHILDREN ME TAKE-CARE-OF FEED CLEAN LIST. This method of transcription may well leave the reader with the impression that there are only verbs in the present tense and a few nouns in ASL. Such transcriptions record very little of the grammar of the utterance, much as Tonto left out grammar when addressing the Lone Ranger. The glosses may seem to be close to the original utterance, but in fact they can be very far from conveying its meaning. An actual *translation* of the original sentence, which takes into account not only the basic signs but also how they were modified to convey the structure of the sentence, yields: *I'm a mother, which means I have a lot of responsibilities. I must take care of the children, feed them, clean them up—there's a whole list.*

On the Gallaudet campus stands a life-size bronze statue by Daniel Chester French, the sculptor of the seated Abraham Lincoln at the Lincoln Memorial. Wendy would have passed it every day on the way to teach her class. The statue depicts a seated man, clad in a vest and long-tailed coat, the attire of a nineteenth-century gentleman. Standing beside him, nestled in the crook of his left arm, is a girl of no more than ten. She wears a long dress with a ruffled neckline; her hair tumbles in loose curls past her shoulders. The man is looking down at her, soberly, but with immense tenderness. With his right hand, the one not around the girl, he forms a loose fist, fingers curled under, thumb pressed against the side of the hand: the letter "A" of the manual alphabet. The girl, leaning into him, extends her own right hand and makes an "A" in imitation of his as her left hand presses an opened book to her breast. Her face is alight, like the face of a Renaissance angel. He has just given her language.

The girl's name was Alice Cogswell, and the man was her next-door neighbor in Hartford, Connecticut, Thomas Hopkins Gallaudet. Born in Philadelphia in 1787, Thomas Gallaudet moved with his family to Hartford when he was a boy. The eldest of twelve children, he was a brilliant student, entering Yale at fourteen and graduating at the top of his class in 1805. But for all his prowess, young Thomas lacked direction. After college, he studied law in Hartford, but quit after just a year to return to Yale, where he worked as a tutor and received a master's degree. But he soon left Yale to become an itinerant peddler of dry goods: he hoped the outdoor life would restore his always delicate health. After two years roaming Kentucky and Ohio on horseback, selling pins and needles and tinware and cloth (his health apparently did improve), he decided to enter business and took a position as a clerk. One can imagine how numbing the work must have been for a man of such questing intellect.

During this time, Gallaudet, like many New Englanders of the early nineteenth century, was intensely preoccupied with the condition of his soul. "His New Year's resolutions for 1808 included: to pray morning, noon, and night in private; to be kinder to his parents and brothers and sisters; to be less indolent, less self-indulgent with food and drink," Harlan Lane writes in *When the Mind Hears: A History of the Deaf.* In 1812, Gallaudet heeded the inevitable: he left his clerk's job and entered Andover Theological Seminary, where he would train for a career in the ministry. While he was still a student there, he met Alice Cogswell, and in Alice, Thomas Gallaudet found his life's work.

Alice was about eight when he met her; she was a playmate of one of Gallaudet's young brothers. Her father, Mason Cogswell, was a prosperous Hartford physician and a prominent member of the community. Born hearing, Alice was by all accounts a pretty and vivacious child, with blond curls and hazel eyes. When she was two, not long after she had begun to talk, Alice contracted "spotted fever"—cerebrospinal meningitis. She recovered, but the illness left her deaf. What speech she had gradually withered away, disappearing altogether by the time she was four.

Alice's father was desperate: he had helped a great many children through illness but could do nothing for his own daughter, now marooned without language. There were no schools for the deaf then, and deaf children lived isolated, marginal lives. Kept at home, dependent, often a source of shame to their families, they were barely educated and nearly always illiterate. Deaf boys could expect at best a life of manual labor, deaf girls, domestic tasks.

An erudite, cultured man (his personal library was said to be among the finest in Connecticut), Mason Cogswell was determined to see his daughter educated, a breathtakingly forward-thinking position for the time. Like many deaf children, Alice had developed on her own a repertoire of simple signs, largely imitative, which she used to communicate her basic needs to her parents and siblings. Linguists call these "homesigns." But her deafness cut her off completely from the world of real language: from communication with anyone beyond her immediate family; from the ability to learn to read and write English; and, as Mason hoped, to lipread the language and even to speak it.

For a deaf child growing up in a hearing family (and 90 percent of deaf children do), surrounded by talk she cannot hear, deafness threatens to separate her from language, and, by extension, from learning altogether. Several years ago, a hearing woman named Valerie Sutton who works closely with the deaf described the deaf child's predicament to me this way: "Imagine you were born in a glass cage. There are people on the outside mouthing Japanese at you, but you don't know Japanese. How would you ever learn to lipread the language?"

In the absence of language, in the absence of a way to communicate, receive and discuss abstract ideas, the intellectual development of even the brightest deaf child can be permanently arrested. This was the danger for Alice.

One day in 1813, on a visit home from the seminary, Thomas Gallaudet observed Alice at play with other children in his family's garden. He decided he would teach her to spell a simple English word: "hat." Gallaudet picked up a stick, and wrote the word in the dirt. He showed the girl his own hat, then placed it on the ground beside the written word. He demonstrated the connection again and again. "Alice seems to understand," Lane writes. "To test her, Thomas rubs out the letters with his shoe and scratches them again a few feet away. Alice picks up the hat and places it on its new label. Thomas runs, overjoyed, to the Cogswell home to announce his success." For modern readers, the tableau calls to mind a canonical scene: another little girl, three-quarters of a century later in Alabama, her hand held under a rushing pump as a young woman fingerspells W-A-T-E-R again and again into her outstretched palm. Both are stories of creation—the creation of being through the epiphany of language.

On visits home, Gallaudet continued to tutor Alice. Mason Cogswell was delighted. He had learned meanwhile of other deaf children in the area and conceived of establishing a school for them nearby. Cogswell convened a committee of sponsors, among them Hartford's wealthiest men. They voted to send Gallaudet to England to study the methods by which deaf people there had apparently been taught to speak and read lips. Gallaudet, who had graduated from Andover and was now a Congregationalist minister, set sail in the spring of 1815.

At the time, education of the deaf in Britain was a for-profit enterprise controlled by a single family, the Braidwoods of Edinburgh. The patriarch, Thomas Braidwood, had been a teacher of elocution to the hearing before opening the first of his family's franchise of schools for the deaf in the 1760s. The success of the schools was widely reported: Braidwood students were frequently exhibited in public, where they gave demonstrations of their skill in speaking and lipreading, a profitable venture for the Braidwood entrepreneurs. Wary of competitors, the Braidwoods kept their instructional methods a closely guarded secret; employees of the schools were under bond not to disclose them.

On his arrival in Britain, Gallaudet was turned away from one Braidwood academy after another. The fact that he was planning to open a school an ocean away did nothing to soften the family's position: Thomas Braidwood's grandson was just then attempting to start a school in America himself. Though he never did so (he instead embezzled the advance tuition paid by hopeful American parents), the family perceived Gallaudet as a threat. Gallaudet remained in Britain for several months, making repeated entreaties. Eventually, the Braidwoods agreed to teach him their methods—on the condition that Gallaudet first work for them for three years, far longer than he was prepared to remain abroad.

The impasse turned out to be a blessing, for it gave Gallaudet time to nurse profound doubts about the Braidwoods' methods. The vaunted success of the schools, as he came to see, was not all it appeared. Part of the Braidwoods' secret lay in their highly selective admission policies: rather than working with the profoundly deaf (who, lacking auditory feedback, are at a huge natural disadvantage when forced to learn to speak), the academies favored students who were merely hard of hearing, or those who had lost their hearing late enough in life to have acquired a fluent command of spoken language first. The exhibitions of "talking deaf-mutes" that dazzled loose the public's purse strings were, in the words of an early-nineteenth-century observer, the Scottish philosopher of mind Dugald Stewart, demonstrations "which should rank only a little higher than the art of training starlings and parrots."

Gallaudet soon realized that the Braidwoods' approach would be of little real help to a child born deaf—or to a child like Alice, who had become deaf very early. Gallaudet, who met Dugald Stewart on this trip and became greatly influenced by him, would come to share the philosopher's view that what was needed, for all deaf children, was a way "not to astonish the vulgar by the sudden conversion of a dumb child into a speaking *automaton;* but . . . to convert [the] pupil into a rational and moral being."

Call it providence. Purely by chance, there was another exhibition of deaf pupils taking place in London while Gallaudet was there. This one was as different from the Braidwoods' drawing room sideshow as can possibly be imagined. Presiding was a French priest, the Abbé Roch-Ambroise Sicard, director of the National Institution for Deaf-Mutes in Paris. Accompanying him on a tour of Britain were his two star graduates, Jean Massieu and Laurent Clerc. Through the Abbé, who interpreted into signed language, members of the audience posed searching philosophical questions to the two young deaf men: "What is eternity?" "Does God reason?" (and, on a somewhat worldlier plane, "What difference do you find between English women and French women?"). Massieu and Clerc, the first of generations of great deaf intellectuals produced by the school, signed their responses, or wrote them in French on a chalkboard. Eternity, Massieu replied, is "a day without yesterday or tomorrow, a line that has no end." God, he said, "is omniscient; He never doubts; therefore, He never reasons." From Clerc: "The English ladies are in general tall, handsome, well-shaped. The beauty of their complexion is particularly remarkable. But I beg their pardon for saying that, in general, they are somewhat deficient when it comes to deportment and elegance."

The audience was enthralled. The hall was packed to overflowing: the crowd included ambassadors, noblemen and members of Parliament. It also included Thomas Gallaudet. Though signed language struck Gallaudet as primitive (despite his misgivings about the Braidwoods' ethics, he remained committed to his mandate of teaching the deaf to speak), he allowed himself to flirt, intuitively, with an idea that would not be formally articulated by linguists until 150 years later: deaf people are better equipped physiologically to use a signed language than a spoken one. With sign, Gallaudet speculated, deaf people, far from being "speaking automatons," could enjoy unrestricted access to a world of language, ideas, social intercourse and, above all, contemplation of the divine presence. On a practical level, he knew the Braidwoods would offer him nothing. Gallaudet approached the Abbé Sicard. Yes, the Abbé would be delighted to have him come to Paris and learn their methods. Gallaudet joined him there in the winter of 1816.

In Paris, Gallaudet took instruction from Jean Massieu, and from Sicard himself. Little by little, his aversion to sign diminished. "I am now convinced of the utility of their language of pantomime to a *certain extent,*" he wrote to Mason Cogswell in the early spring. "Don't be alarmed at this system of signs. I shall learn and practice just as much of it as I think best."

The "system of signs" Gallaudet was learning was in large part the work of Sicard's predecessor, the great Abbé Charles-Michel de l'Épée, who had founded the school, the first institution of its kind in the world, in 1771. Épée is sometimes called the father of French Sign Language, but in the slums of Paris, where a critical mass of deaf people had long since concentrated, a spontaneous signed language had been born, and was thriving, decades before the Abbé became interested in their welfare. Montaigne, in his *Essays* of the late sixteenth century, briefly mentions a system of signed communication then in use among the deaf: "Our deaf-mutes have discussions and arguments, telling each other stories by means of signs. I have seen some who are so nimble and so practised at this that they truly lack nothing necessary for making themselves perfectly understood."

What Épée did, beginning in the late 1760s, was to make this community his vocation, working among the Paris deaf, instructing them, and—a radical step—learning their manual language. Épée realized what none before him had: that signed language furnished the best possible vehicle for giving the deaf literacy in written French and, through French, a Catholic education.

What Épée didn't realize (it would not be understood for two centuries), was that the signed language he encountered in the streets of Paris was already a robust, efficient whole, amply equipped to serve any linguistic contingency. But because it lacked visible grammatical endings, the *-ents* and *-onts* and *-esques* that are the lifeblood of French, Épée saw it as lacking grammar. As Harlan Lane writes:

> Sentences in French Sign Language have fewer words than their French translations; they can dispense with articles, many prepositions, and other words of grammar that French requires because it cannot express relations spatially the way gestures can; and the order of the words is different from that of French. All of these differences could only confirm Épée in his prejudice that sign was not a true language that he could use to instruct his pupils.

Once he had moved the language out of the streets and into the schoolroom, Épée contrived to give it rigor, in short, to make it look a lot more like French. He invented gestures, which he called "methodical signs," to stand for the "missing" prepositions and articles, and for the grammatical inflections that in French signal tense, mood, number and gender. He also retooled the word order of the language to conform to the syntax of spoken French. The result was what today would be called Manually Coded French, or Manual French. It was not a natural language—outside the classroom Épée's deaf pupils continued to use their own time-honored sign language—but for the purpose of teaching written French to deaf pupils it seemed at the time a necessary intermediate step.

It was awesomely cumbersome. In Épée's system, Lane writes:

> Even the simplest sentence took on enormous complexity. One example: a line from Racine, "To the smallest of the birds, He gives their crumbs," required forty-eight signs from Épée's pupils. "Gives" alone required five signs: those for verb, present, third person, singular, and "give." To the deaf pupil accustomed to expressing such an idea in five or six signs in a different order, the sentence in methodical signs lacked unity, was full of distractions, was far too long for a single unit of meaning, and, in the end, was unintelligible. This did not prevent Épée's pupils from signing French sentences given a text and, conversely, from writing perfect French given a sentence in manual French;

it just prevented them from understanding those sentences—they had to be explained in French Sign Language.

After Épée's death in 1789, the Abbé Sicard took the helm of the school, where he continued the system. It was this Manual French that Gallaudet learned when he came to Paris, and he eventually decided to employ a version of it, adapted to English, in the school he would found at home. Laurent Clerc told him it would take at least six months to become proficient enough in Signed French to be able to teach it. But after two months in the City of Light, Gallaudet was overwhelmed by homesickness for the clean Puritan lines of Connecticut. He was also prudent enough to realize that when it came time to teach the deaf children of America, he would be no substitute for a native signer. He persuaded the thirty-year-old Clerc, considered the most brilliant of Épée's disciples, to return with him. Clerc assented, forsaking his family, his homeland, his church and his beloved school, where he had lived and studied since he was a boy. But Clerc saw himself foremost as a deaf man and a teacher, and wherever a teacher of the deaf was needed, he would go. Gallaudet's people, the deaf of America, would be his people. It was a decision that would in large part cast the form of language known today as ASL.

The two men sailed for America in June of 1816. On board, Clerc continued Gallaudet's lessons in Manual French. Gallaudet taught Clerc written English. Ten months later, on April 15, 1817, the Connecticut Asylum for the Education and Instruction of Deaf and Dumb Persons opened its doors in Hartford to a class of seven. The first registered pupil was Alice Cogswell.

The language of the school was a version of the Manual French that Gallaudet had learned from Clerc, reconfigured to mirror as closely as possible the structure of English, with "methodical signs" for English word endings like *-es, -ed* and *-ing,* and, of course, English word order. It was a kind of Early Manual English, as contrived, rigid and unwieldly as its French parent.

It didn't stay that way for long. By the end of the first year in

Hartford, the initial group of seven local students had grown thirty-one deaf people from ten different states. (Both Clerc and Gallaudet would eventually marry older deaf pupils.) By the school's second year, enrollment had grown to more than a hundred. The students brought signs with them. Most, like Alice, possessed some rudimentary homesigns, developed to communicate with their hearing families. There were also a number of students from an insular community on Martha's Vineyard, where, as the result of a very high incidence of inherited deafness, an indigenous signed language had sprung up, used by deaf and hearing villagers alike for more than 250 years, an American Al-Sayyid.

From these diverse sources, a contact language, a kind of simple signed pidgin, arose outside the classroom among the first generation of students at the school. This is exactly what happens in spoken language when mutually unintelligible languages butt up against each other as the result of colonization, enslavement or trade. Like spoken pidgins, this signed pidgin would have been quite rudimentary, consisting of basic nouns and verbs and extremely simple sentences, all in all very short on grammar. It was the native language of no one. But later generations of students at the school, exposed to this simple linguistic stew, did what second-generation pidgin speakers have done since the dawn of cultural contact: they spontaneously upgraded the pidgin into a creole, a full-fledged language with a rich grammar, able to convey complex ideas. Thus the language that would be known as ASL was born, the product of Manual French, Early Manual English, Martha's Vineyard Sign, a diverse array of homesigns, and the inborn capacity of children to create grammar where none existed before.

After Sicard's death in 1822, his successor in Paris acknowledged the difficulty of the "methodical signs," and by the 1830s the cumbersome system had been abandoned in both France and America. The natural language of the deaf at home, at play and in the streets at last became the language of the classroom as well. By the mid-nineteenth century this authentic signed language was in full flower among the American deaf, spread across the country as Hartford-trained teachers established dozens of new residential schools elsewhere. In the schools, it was transmitted from one class of children to the next. In deaf families, it was passed down the generations, acquired by children from their parents as a native language.

This golden era was not to last. The second half of the nineteenth century witnessed the start of a public campaign to eradicate sign language, a continuing chapter in American history that in its sweeping paternalism reads a great deal like a colonial narrative. By the middle of the century, some prominent hearing educators, few of whom knew anything about sign, had begun to argue that sign language isolated and marginalized deaf people. Only through elocution and lipreading, they insisted, could the deaf be properly restored to society—the society of the hearing. This powerful faction, which came to be known as the oralists, included Horace Mann and Samuel Gridley Howe and, toward the end of the century, a man intimately associated with the mechanisms of speech, Alexander Graham Bell. One by one, the residential schools that helped transmit sign language and deaf culture from one generation to the next were supplanted by "oral" schools that taught speech and lipreading. Deaf teachers were replaced by hearing ones who could not sign; deaf pupils were forbidden to sign in the classroom. Until well into the 1970s, oralism remained the dominant model for the education of the American deaf.

ASL endured anyway. In deaf families, it continued to flourish, passed down from parent to child. In the schools, it simply went underground, a kind of manual samizdat. (There are today deaf adults, the product of oral schools of the 1950s and 1960s, who refer to ASL familiarly as "bathroom sign"—it was the one place in school where they could converse openly in their own language.)

As long as the deaf community survived, so, too, it seemed, would American Sign Language, a human language as vital as any other. But this fact, the essential *languageness* of ASL, was not recognized until 1960, nearly a century and a half after the language was born, when an English professor named William Stokoe became a laughingstock for suggesting as much. And it would take a decade more for linguists to see in sign language a living testament to how the mind, in the absence of speech and hearing, makes language anyway. For as it turns out, sign language, in all its complexity, offers a wealth of information on how all human language operates inside our heads: how it is acquired by children; how it is stored in memory; how it is handled neurologically by the brain. Today, nearly 250 years after the Abbé de l'Épée first learned to converse with the deaf of Paris, the study of signed languages has assumed a central role in the cognitive science of the twenty-first century.

CHAPTER 3

The Road to Al-Sayyid

The blue Fiat noses its way out of Haifa. Mark is driving; Irit, Shai and I occupy the back seat. Carol is in the front passenger seat, with Wendy tucked into the small center seat next to her so she can translate the English and Hebrew conversation into ASL as needed. Carol was born hard of hearing, which allowed her to acquire a good command of spoken English when she was a child. As she grew up, her hearing loss progressed; by the time she was a teenager she was almost completely deaf, daily crossing and recrossing the border between the deaf culture of her family and the world of the hearing. In the bouncing van, however, with everyone seen in profile, lipreading is all but impossible.

The Fiat, we soon discover, can either air-condition or climb a gradient but not both at once, so it is quite warm for a time as the van grumbles up and down the hills of the Carmel. Things cool off when we hit the straightaway. We drive all day, past the sea, past olive groves and fields of nodding sunflowers, pausing just long enough to check into a hotel in the small town nearest Al-Sayyid. Then we continue far beyond the town, following the highway until we reach what looks like the last outpost of Western imperialism anywhere on earth: an enormous McDonald's standing watch over the barren, dusty corner where the road turns toward Al-Sayyid.

We turn off the highway. The road from here is unpaved. It is only slightly wider than the van, deeply rutted and filled with dust and loose, rattling stones. Everyone is heaved from side to side as Mark negotiates the narrow passage; from the back of the van, the boxed sets of dishes protest noisily. Up ahead, in the distance, is Al-Sayyid.

It is more expansive than the tiny hamlet I had been imagining, a swath of houses spread over an undulating series of brown, scrub-covered hills. The houses are low structures with roofs of red tile or corrugated tin, most with sheer, smooth faces of unadorned white concrete. From this distance, the village looks like a Bauhaus mirage.

We pass wooden rail fences, broken in places, and the hollow skeleton of what appears to have been a boxcar. Beyond the fences, on either side of the road, are fields of stubble dotted with grazing sheep and a few enormous bales of hay, and beyond the fields, small groves of olive trees. The air smells pleasantly of burning charcoal. A little farther down the road, Mark inches off to the side and cuts the engine. Beyond this point, the road we are traveling branches off into a labyrinth of even narrower unmarked paths, each leading to a different cluster of houses. It is impossible to find anything in Al-Sayyid on one's own. So we sit and wait for Hassan, Wendy's liaison in the village, who will guide us to the house where the first recording session is scheduled to take place.

It seems at first as if we are the only people anywhere, but as we wait, signs of life begin to emerge. A boy strides briskly through the olive groves. Down the road, opposite us, comes a small truck, which churns up a cloud of dust as it edges past the van. Behind the truck comes a boy on a bicycle, racing ahead of a lumbering bulldozer. From the back seat of the van, Irit calls Hassan on her cell phone and, speaking Hebrew, asks for directions to the rendezvous point, which turns out to be a little farther up the road.

We pass more fields of stubble. The rail fences have given way to chain link, covered in places with green plastic tarpaulin or tin sheeting. There are more olive groves, and grazing goats. At the top of a small hill sit two abandoned cars. We pass a construction site, with pyramids of stacked cinder blocks, then more skeletal cars. Another bulldozer passes us, a boy riding gleefully in the empty scoop. Still no sign of Hassan.

In a little while we pass the first few houses, the very beginning of Al-Sayyid. Mark asks directions in Hebrew of two men squeezing by us in a car. A couple of boys on foot approach the van as well. Everyone wants to know where we're going. Then somebody spots Hassan's little white truck, and we follow him through the outskirts of the village. Here, the olive groves are punctuated by frequent construction sites. Many of the men of Al-Sayyid work in the construction trades, and it is inexpensive for them to build. Everyone seems to be erecting a large house here these days, and it has given Al-Sayyid a much altered appearance from when the team was last here and the village consisted of simple, one-story homes. "The first time I went there, I actually visited someone in a tent," Wendy told us. "You never see that anymore. It was the oldest deaf person. I think he also had rooms, but he received visitors in a tent."

We bump along in Hassan's wake until we come to the half-finished house where the linguists have been invited to hold their first session. It, too, is surrounded by cinder blocks, and an ocean of sand. The owner of the house, Hassan explains to us, wants to have the taping here because his current home is small and dark. The new house will be large and fancy, one of just a few in the village to have electricity.

We park in front of the house, scrabble up the concrete ramp, and arrange ourselves at the table in the large empty room. The owner, Omar, comes in and greets us in Hebrew. He is a beefy man in early middle age. Though Omar is hearing, he has deaf siblings and knows the village sign language. Carol immediately starts to sign to him, using gestures international enough that they can be quite readily understood. Omar replies expansively in Al-Sayyid Bedouin Sign: the seeds of a simple contact pidgin have been sown. When signers of different languages come together like this, communication is achieved partly through the use of the most transparent gestures possible, partly through a shared understanding of the particular devices that signed languages use to convey meaning. (Just such a contact language, called International Sign Pidgin, has developed over the years at places like sign-linguistics meetings, where deaf people from many countries converge.) Signing to Omar, Carol uses the fingers of one hand to count, while with the other she pats imaginary heads in a descending series: she is asking him how many children he has, and their ages. In the polygamous society of the Bedouins, it is not uncommon for a man to have a dozen or more. "I remember how Hassan's mother laughed at me for having only one child," Wendy told me, recalling an earlier visit. "You call *that* having children?" she imagined the older woman thinking.

More chairs appear, and the plates of food. Two small girls and a boy peek into the room; others join them until the doorway is crowded with children, the sons and daughters and nieces and nephews and cousins and neighbors of Omar. Wendy says that if this house were at the center of the village rather than on the edge there would be even more children in evidence. One of the boys in the doorway, who appears to be around five, is wearing a yellow T-shirt that like nearly all the male apparel in the village is emblazoned with English text. His shirt has a great deal of it. It reads: "Hi, my name is Amal. I live here in this street with my friends. We're a real street gang, and I'm the only boy." There are no actual streets in Al-Sayyid.

Hassan takes a seat at the head of the table. He is wearing a photographer's vest and dark glasses and has a shaved head; he looks like a young, lithe Telly Savalas. On the team's previous visit he has proved the ideal liaison: a teacher of English, university-educated, Hassan speaks fluent Hebrew and, because he grew up with a deaf father, the village sign language as well. He has two deaf children of his own.

The room continues to fill with people and before long is awash in signing. Because so many hearing people are also deep in signed conversation, it is not always possible to tell who can hear and who can't. In Al-Sayyid, there is no social stigma attached to being deaf.

Carol has left Omar and is signing with a small group of children; when she leans out of one of the open windows to photograph the desert, several children remain plastered to her. The boy brings in the glasses for tea. He is hearing, Hassan informs us, but he also signs. A small girl in a red T-shirt, who is deaf, shrieks with laughter as she and another girl chase each other through the room. Carol and a deaf boy look out the window, pointing together at features of the landscape. Omar, meanwhile, is busy signing to another knot of children. From outside come the sound of the wind and a rooster crowing.

The room is bathed in late-afternoon sun. All this, the eating and the drinking and the talking and the signing, will go on for a long, unhurried hour, what Irit calls "a Mediterranean minute," a characteristic prelude to the formal session that will follow. Then a man in his thirties, tall and thin and wearing a black shirt with "Adidas" printed on the front, enters the room. He sits down at the table next to a man in a University of Arizona T-shirt. The man in the Adidas shirt is Ibrahim, Omar's deaf younger brother. Carol sits down opposite Ibrahim, who has a lavish black mustache, and starts to sign to him. He responds in Al-Sayyid Bedouin Sign, telling her which of his children are hearing and which are deaf. She nods deeply. On the team's previous trip here, Carol picked up some Bedouin signs—the signs for YES and NO, for instance, quite different from their ASL counterparts—and one can see her interspersing them into her conversation along with her own simplified gestures. She will tell me afterward that she can understand most of what the Bedouin signers are saying, though not everything. As Carol and Ibrahim sign back and forth, the little girl in the red shirt peers around the doorway, eyes on their conversation.

Gradually, Hassan starts to ease everyone into the formal portion of the visit. The men and boys take their places around the table. There are no adult women anywhere in evidence, nor will there be for the entire time we are in this house. That is the custom, in Bedouin society, for gatherings at which men are present. "Hassan says we're in luck," Wendy tells us down at our end of the table. "We got more people than we bargained for. They're showing interest and he's pleased."

One surprise addition is Ibrahim himself: he hadn't been scheduled to take part but decided at the last minute that he wanted to. He is a master mechanic, famed throughout the village for his ability to fix anything. The linguists are especially excited about working with him, because Hassan has assured them that Ibrahim knows only the local sign language—"Arab Sign," the villagers call it—and no Israeli

Sign. Ibrahim confirms this, signing to Hassan that when he sees deaf Israelis talking it looks to him like gibberish. Like this, he says, thrusting his palms forward and circling them around in a huge amorphous wash. Visual static.

Hassan stands, and addresses the group around the table, a lit cigarette dangling precariously from one hand as he signs. The villagers reply in Al-Sayyid Bedouin Sign, which Hassan translates into spoken Hebrew, which Wendy translates into ASL for Carol and English for me. Hassan reminds the assembled villagers why we have come: the team is studying how their sign language is passed from one generation to the next—it's the most cogent short explanation of what they're trying to do—and I, in a corner with my notebook, am studying the team. It all seems acceptable.

More food is brought in. Omar says it's all right to throw the sunflower shells on the ground, since the floor hasn't been laid yet. Shai opens his tripod and sets up the video camera: after some discussion it is decided that Omar, as host, will take the first turn. Wendy takes a chair at the head of the table, seats Carol on her left and Omar on her right. She opens her laptop and sets it in front of him. The screen fills with the image of a large dog. Behind Wendy, six boys peer around the door frame at the screen.

They begin with the slide show. Signing, Carol instructs Omar to give the name of each object as it appears on the screen. He faces the camera, nods and smiles, and the images start to scroll by: *Dog . . . Cat . . . Chicken . . . Snake . . . Fly . . . Scorpion.* Omar makes a sign for each. For FISH, he holds his palms together, parallel to the floor, and wiggles the thumb of the top hand. It is strikingly different from the Israeli sign FISH: there, as in ASL, a single outstretched hand, palm sideways, weaves sinuously through imaginary water.

The images continue to scroll: *Donkey . . . Tomato . . . Eggs . . . Pear . . . Banana . . . Lemon . . . Steaks . . . Leaf.* There are now seven boys following the action from the doorway. *Sunflower . . . Tree . . . Pen . . . Kitchen scale . . . Knife . . . Spoon.* Omar hesitates at *fork.* "It's not something they use," Mark says. Irit tells him the name in Hebrew—*mazleg*—and he makes the sign.

Next come pictures of clothing and other household things (sandals, a child's shoes, pants, a dress, a pillow, a newspaper). Omar gets the stapler immediately—the sign is the thumb and forefinger pinching the fleshy part of the opposite hand; it looks a little like the ASL sign MEAT. Shai's glasses float by, followed by the handsome stove. Next comes the array of colors, which concludes the first of the test's two vocabulary segments.

With Omar watching the screen, Wendy launches the next part of the test, a series of short video clips designed to elicit the syntax of the language. The linguists are especially interested in how Al-Sayyid Bedouin Sign Language expresses spatial relationships, the kind that in spoken language depend on prepositions like "around," "through," "over," "in front of" and "behind." Carol tells Omar to watch each clip, then relate in sign what he has seen: *A man walks up to an empty chair and sits down. . . . A man walks past the chair without sitting.* As Omar signs, the smallest boy in the room tries to clamber into his lap. He shoos the child away. *A man and a woman face each other, and one hands the other a ball. . . . A man thrusts a coffee mug toward the camera, then yanks it back.*

The sun streaming through the windows makes it too bright for Shai to film. An older boy, one of Omar's nephews, fetches a thin mattress covered in flowered fabric, props it against the sunniest window and stands in front of it to hold it in place. The taping resumes, with the small boy again trying to climb into Omar's lap. A bigger boy ducks under the table with the Thermos and quietly pours himself a glass of tea.

Wendy starts the segment on morphology. It consists of a series of drawings, meant to show the ways in which sign-language verbs can change shape depending on the behavior of their subjects and objects. In a great many spoken languages, the relationship of subject to object—the who-did-what-to-whom of a sentence—is conveyed through verb endings, and by pronouns: "*I give* the ball to *him*"; "*He gives* the ball to *me*." In the world's signed languages, however, this information is often incorporated directly into the movement pattern of the verb—subject, verb and object bundled together in a single, meaning-laden sign. The linguists are eager to see whether the Bedouins' signed language works this way as well. There is a drawing of a woman buying food from a grocer, and one of the grocer in turn selling the food to her. Someone sends a letter, and somebody else receives it. There is a rather odd drawing of a man shouting at a camel, with little cartoon lines indicating speech bursting from his mouth.

After the drawings comes the animated cartoon of Sylvester and Tweety. The linguists are using this to see how Al-Sayyid Bedouin Sign Language employs three-dimensional space to talk about objects of specific shapes and sizes, something signed languages are singularly well equipped to do. In the cartoon, Sylvester the Cat, in his relentless pursuit of Tweety, stacks piece after piece of furniture into a tower beneath Tweety's cage, which hangs from the ceiling. Sylvester climbs the tower and reaches for the cage. As he does, the cage, which is suspended by a *very* elastic cord, springs vigorously up and down, sending Sylvester hurtling through the air, foiled again. Following instructions from Carol, Omar views the cartoon twice. As he watches, two of the boys look on over his shoulder, signing along with the action. After the second viewing, he retells it in sign, his hands describing in the air the relationship of bird, cat and cage.

The session concludes with the second set of vocabulary items: people looking happy, sad, angry and frightened, followed by a drawing, which in its stylization looks almost pre-Columbian, of a man vomiting. Then, a final slide show: *A pile of cut logs . . . An airplane . . . A long highway . . . Fire . . . Sunset . . . A mask . . . A row of books on a shelf . . . A cellular telephone.* There is a photo of one of those long-bladed metal spatulate things that masons use to tamp down mortar, the English word for which none of us, back in Haifa, could remember. Omar works in construction and produces the sign for it easily. *Hammer . . . Wrench . . . Screw . . . Truck . . . Crane . . . Tractor . . . Car . . . Binoculars . . . Flashlight.* He hesitates before the image of a large blue disc, swirled with white. It is a photograph of Earth, taken from space. He doesn't recognize it, but he knows the ones that follow: *Moon . . . Snow . . . Sea . . . Rain.*

CHAPTER 4

The Sign-Language Instinct

"We all come from the factory wired for language," my friend Pat O'Conner has evocatively written. The linguist's task is to diagram that wiring: to use the structure of human language as a way to illuminate the structure of the human mind. That, ultimately, is what has brought Wendy and her team to Al-Sayyid, and it is the defining objective of modern linguistics. But it wasn't always the case.

Until the late 1950s, linguists were merely collectors. Their discipline was then a dusty annex of anthropology, and their principal task (some would say their only task) was to compile data: list upon list of words in exotic languages. They concentrated their efforts on Native American languages, many of which were undocumented and in danger of dying. Looking back, one can almost imagine them stalking through the wild with specimen bottles and outsize nets, in determined pursuit of the Ojibwa adverb or the Cherokee pronoun. The result was a spate of published accounts, or grammars, of the world's languages, with titles like *Menomini Texts, Abnormal Types of Speech in Nootka* and *The Dialect of the Gypsies of Wales.*

But after allowing themselves to be bagged and published, the data just sat there, like so many butterflies under glass. Undeniably, the grammars had some intrinsic value: they documented endangered languages, an inherently worthwhile endeavor; they had a certain utility to anthropologists and missionaries heading into the field; and some of them went so far as to sketch the phonology and morphology of the language under study. But beyond that, the grammars didn't do very much. They didn't say anything *about* anything.

They raised no large theoretical questions, captured no generalizations that might apply to all human languages, and they certainly didn't say anything about the mind. For these linguists, the act of collection was pretty much an end in itself.

There was a deep-seated ideological reason for this, and it was known as structuralism. Structuralism had its intellectual roots in the empiricist tradition of the seventeenth century, the "blank-slate" school of philosophers like John Locke. In its most concentrated form, empiricism maintains that a newborn enters the world with his mind a vacuum. As he moves through life, information accretes in the mind little by little as the result of external experience. In an empiricist account, every facet of the human condition, including language, is learned through this outward experience alone, experience that can be observed, documented and measured.

By the early 1900s, linguists had ardently embraced this model, and for the first half of the twentieth century, structuralism held sway as the field's dominant methodology. Language, they believed, was simply another form of learned social behavior, like toolmaking, table manners or playing bridge. The goal of linguistics was to document this "behavior" and no more, drawing only on directly observable evidence. The idea that man might possess a special capacity for language that is biologically innate—in today's parlance, hardwired in—was beyond contemplation: a structural linguist had no more business speculating about the nature of the mind than he did about the nature of the moon. As a result, linguists could do little more than amass reams of data, and that is just what they did, traveling to remote villages, sitting down with native speakers and eliciting hundreds of words. In this respect, their work was not that different from the team's in Al-Sayyid, minus the laptop and video camera.

As they worked their way through language after language, the structuralists were dazzled by the ways in which each one differed from the next. That was their job: to value linguistic difference above all else. Structuralism considered every language to be a unique entity, with its own grammatical structure. The linguist's goal was to describe the structure of as many different languages as possible, with their thousands of atomized features.

It is easy to see now that this approach blinded linguists to the figure in the carpet: the larger similarities of form hiding beneath the surface of outwardly dissimilar languages. To the structuralists, this was of little concern; vast generalizations about the nature of language were neither possible nor desirable. How could they be, when, in the words of the titan Leonard Bloomfield, "Features which we think ought to be universal may be absent from the very next language that becomes accessible."

But throughout history, the mind has periodically entered the equation. In fits and starts, philosophers since antiquity have described language in what now seems like quite modern terms: the product of a uniquely human endowment, an outward manifestation of inner cognitive processes. The linguist Victoria Fromkin and her colleagues cite an Egyptian papyrus from about 1700 B.C. that "includes medical descriptions of language disorders following brain injury."

In the fourth century B.C., Aristotle, discussing the relationship of words to their meanings, a central preoccupation of classical philosophy, recognized spoken language to be a system of arbitrary symbols, whose meanings had been agreed upon by the community. "A sound is not yet a word, it only becomes a word when it is used by man as a sign," he wrote. "The articulated signs [of language] are not like the expression of emotions of children or animals. Animal noises cannot be combined to form syllables, nor can they be reduced to syllables like human speech." Pondering the origin of language, Epicurus (341–270 B.C.) concluded that it was not a God-given attribute, as his predecessors had believed, but rather an aspect of man's essential nature. "To him," the language scholar Otto Marx writes, "language was a biological function like vision and hearing."

During the Enlightenment and after, rationalist thinkers took up these ancient questions again. Among them, Wilhelm von Humboldt (1767–1835) in particular addressed the relationship between language and man's inborn capabilities. Humboldt observed that children raised in different places, and under quite different conditions, nonetheless acquire language at the same age, much as children learn to crawl and then to walk at comparable stages. As he noted, it was "characteristic for the unfolding of other biologically given attributes that a certain time is denoted for their development."

For Humboldt, "language capacity is an attribute of intellectual man's physiology," Marx writes. "Man can understand meaning attributed to sound, or the single word as a concept, only because language as a whole is innately in him." Most important, as Marx points out, Humboldt recognized that beneath the surface of seemingly disparate languages, "the similarity of . . . language structures results from the fact that *all languages are the expression of man's inborn language capacity, which should be the central point of all language studies.*" As the heirs of rationalism came increasingly to believe in the course of the nineteenth century, human language was a window on the mind.

These ideas found little favor in the structuralist era of the early twentieth century. As Marx writes:

> The study of cultures flourished with the development of anthropology. Linguists had advanced beyond the early nineteenth century philologists' preoccupation with grammars and dictionaries, and had directed their attention to spoken language as the expression of a society or culture. In this task they had the aid of anthropologists who shared their interest in languages. This development served to reinforce the tendency to consider linguistics as a social science, and concern with the psychological and biological basis of language receded into the background.

Staunch empiricists that they were, the structuralists trafficked only in observable phenomena. If you couldn't see it, hear it, smell it, touch it or measure it, it wasn't a fit subject for investigation. To them, the rationalists' conception of language was a kind of smoke-and-mirrors mentalism, nothing more than vaporous, and unverifiable, speculation. "Philosophers, to this day," Bloomfield wrote acidly, "sometimes look for truths about the universe in what are really nothing but formal features of one or another language." In such a rigidly empiricist framework, an abstraction like "the mind" had little place. At its most orthodox, structuralism didn't countenance that such a thing as the mind existed at all.

There was worse to come. By the 1930s, linguistics had become closely allied with an especially militant form of empiricism: behavioral psychology. The marriage of laboratory psychology to the study of language was meant to confer on linguistics the scientific authority it seemed to lack. Before long, linguists had appropriated the jargon of animal experiments (in which rodents were taught to work mazes, or pigeons to peck at lighted discs) to their discussions of human language. To a linguist at mid-century, language was no longer language. Now it was "verbal behavior."

In the behaviorist view, every human utterance—every statement, exclamation, demand, plea or question—exists as a response to some environmental stimulus. Here at long last was the rigor linguistics had been seeking: human speech, and the environmental conditions that provoke it, could now be isolated, observed, objectified and codified. This the structuralists set eagerly out to do. The results are comical today. Here is Bloomfield in 1933, describing ordinary speech in language so resolutely clinical it now reads like parody:

> Suppose that Jack and Jill are walking down a lane. Jill is hungry. She sees an apple in a tree. She makes a noise with her larynx, tongue, and lips. Jack vaults the fence, climbs the tree, takes the apple, brings it to Jill, and places it in her hand. Jill eats the apple. . . .
>
> Viewed in this way, the incident consists of three parts, in order of time:
>
> A. Practical events preceding the act of speech.
>
> B. Speech.
>
> C. Practical events following the act of speech. . . .
>
> The events in A concern mainly the speaker, Jill. She was hungry; that is, some of her muscles were contracting, and

> some fluids were being secreted, especially in her stomach. Perhaps she was also thirsty: her tongue and throat were dry. The light-waves reflected from the red apple struck her eyes. She saw Jack by her side. Her past dealings with Jack should now enter into the picture; let us suppose that they consisted in some ordinary relation, like that of brother and sister or that of husband and wife. All these events, which precede Jill's speech and concern her, we call the *speaker's stimulus.* . . .
>
> The speaker, Jill, moved her vocal cords (two little muscles inside the adam's-apple), her lower jaw, her tongue, and so on, in a way which forced the air into the form of sound-waves. These movements of the speaker are a reaction to the stimulus S. Instead of performing the *practical* (or *handling*) reaction R—namely, starting realistically off to get hold of the apple—she performed these vocal movements, a *speech* (or *substitute*) reaction, which we shall symbolize by a small letter r.

The behaviorist approach dominated the study of language for the next two and a half decades. It reached its most exquisite distillation in 1957, when the Harvard psychologist B. F. Skinner published the book *Verbal Behavior,* the most comprehensive attempt yet at a behaviorist account of grammar. Invoking the terminology of the laboratory, Skinner analyzed all human language in terms of stimuli, learned responses, operant conditioning and reinforcement. Young children, he argued, learned language by imitating the speech of their parents, with correct speech reinforced by parental praise. In this way the child, in ceaseless pursuit of reinforcement, learns to talk. All adult utterances, Skinner maintained, proceeded from the same model—speech in response to an environmental stimulus—with parental approval replaced later in life by social reinforcements like peer acceptance, professional advancement and material gain.

There were a few dissenters, among them the psychologists Roger Brown and Eric Lenneberg, whose work in the mid-1950s explicitly linked language to innate cognitive faculties. But in the prevailing behaviorist weather, they were largely ignored. By the time *Verbal*

Behavior was published, and with their grammar-making enterprise largely completed, many linguists felt their field had run its course and there were few problems of consequence left to be solved.

Then along came Chomsky. Born in Philadelphia in 1928, Noam Chomsky was the son of the eminent Hebrew scholar William Chomsky. (Noam helped proofread an early version of his father's best-known work, a grammatical study of thirteenth-century Hebrew, when he was about twelve.) Entering the University of Pennsylvania, Noam studied mathematics and philosophy, and eventually gravitated toward linguistics, attracted as much by the discipline itself as by the progressive politics of his mentor, the linguist Zellig Harris.

Harris was an avowed structuralist, and in his earliest work Chomsky also steered that course. His master's thesis, on the phonology and morphology of Modern Hebrew, is firmly in the structuralist tradition. But early on, Chomsky began to be troubled by aspects of language he felt the structuralist model couldn't account for. His first important publication, the monograph *Syntactic Structures,* which appeared in 1957, shows Chomsky trying to reconcile these problems with the structuralist approach and finding it inadequate to the task.

One of the problems centered on what Chomsky calls our innate "'feel' for sentence structure"—the half-conscious intuitions about language that each of us possesses. Every speaker of English is aware, for example, that the sentences *John kissed Mary* and *Mary was kissed by John* are somehow fundamentally related. A structuralist analysis, with its emphasis on difference rather than similarity, ignored this essential truth, for structuralism not only prized diversity *among* languages, it also emphasized diversity *within* a single language. To a structuralist, every sentence a speaker utters is a discrete piece of data. But to Chomsky, this approach overlooked a crucial body of linguistic evidence: ordinary speakers' intuitive knowledge about the way their language works.

There were other difficulties. If, as the structuralists believed, every sentence of a language is a separate entity; and if, as they also believed, we all learn language through imitation, then how is it possible for speakers to produce, as they do hundreds of times daily, sentences that have never before been uttered? How is it possible for listeners to understand them?

This point was brought forcibly home to me not long ago. Working in the kitchen of my New York apartment, I had occasion to say the following sentence aloud: *Don't put your head on the panini grill.* Never mind that the utterance was directed at a cat; it was a perfectly comprehensible, well-formed English sentence. Had my husband entered the room and overheard it, he might have thought it a trifle bizarre socially, but the point is, he would have understood it at once. And this despite overwhelming odds that no one in recorded history had ever uttered it before.

This same feel for language allows us to "get" the basic Englishness of nonsense verse like Lewis Carroll's "Jabberwocky." Chomsky himself famously coined the sentence *Colorless green ideas sleep furiously:* meaningless on its face, it nevertheless "feels" like good English. (Observe, too, that the same thing strung in a different sequence—*Furiously sleep ideas green colorless*—feels jarringly wrong.) A structuralist model, in which all sentences are learned individually through external experience, is hard-pressed to account for these facts.

For Chomsky, the most serious problem centered on a single large question: How is it that children acquire language spontaneously, fluently and in a very short time, without being formally taught? The psychologists of language Jenny R. Saffran, Ann Senghas and John C. Trueswell recently described the problem this way:

> Imagine that you are faced with the following challenge. You must discover the internal structure of a system that contains tens of thousands of units, all generated from a small set of materials. These units, in turn, can be assembled into an infinite number of combinations. Although only a subset of those combinations is correct, the subset itself is for all practical purposes infinite. Somehow you must converge on the structure of this system to use it to communicate. And you are a very young child.

This system is human language. The units are words, the materials are the small set of sounds from which they are constructed, and the combinations are the sentences into which they can be assembled. Given the complexity of this system, it seems improbable that mere children could discover its underlying structure and use it to communicate. Yet most do so with eagerness and ease, all within the first few years of life.

The behaviorists maintained that children did so by imitating their parents. But consider the actual adult utterances that filter down into the child's environment. As even the most cursory analysis reveals, they are almost always corrupt, bereft or in some way unrepresentative.

No one, not even the most pedantic parent, speaks perfectly. The child hears tired speech, hurried speech and drunken speech. She hears sentences marred by stammering, interruptions, hesitations, false starts, *uh*'s and *er*'s and *um*'s. And, by definition, the body of linguistic evidence to which the child is exposed can never be complete—it constitutes only a minute percentage of the possible sentences in her native language. Chomsky characterized this set of problems as "the poverty of the stimulus."

As Chomsky realized, there must be a great deal more going on than the behaviorists would allow. For one thing, children acquire a fluent command of language astonishingly quickly: though she will continue to add vocabulary through adulthood, a child of five can construct and understand sentences of virtually every type, including those she has never heard before. As the linguists Victoria Fromkin and Robert Rodman write, "Before they can add 2 + 2, children are conjoining sentences, asking questions, selecting appropriate pronouns, negating sentences, forming relative clauses, and using the syntactic, phonological, morphological, and semantic rules of the grammar."

For this to be possible, Chomsky speculated, the child must be drawing on some innate capacity for language, a biological imperative as fundamental and automatic as learning to walk. This faculty allows her to augment the impoverished signal in her environment with information drawn from a kind of inborn linguistic blueprint. Clearly, there is much more at work here than learned behavior.

The very process by which children acquire language, Chomsky argued, demonstrates this innate capacity. A child begins to produce individual words around the time of his first birthday. Over the next few years, he will pass through a series of recognizable developmental stages, as he appears to test, reject and revise unconscious hypotheses about what "feels right" in his native language and what doesn't. Among English-speaking children, one of the most graphic instances of this can be seen in the case of verbs that have irregular past tenses: "see"/"saw," "go"/"went," "fly"/"flew," and so on. Very young children appear, somewhat surprisingly, to have mastered this complex scheme, using the forms "went," "saw" and "flew" in the appropriate context: "I saw the doggy"; "Mommy went to the store"; "The bird flew away." But this mastery turns out to be an illusion. The child's "correct" past tenses are merely rote imitation of the sentences he hears around him. The behaviorists have it right at this stage of the game.

It's what happens next that is so striking. At a certain point, the child, who up till now has appeared to use irregular past-tense forms successfully, begins to make "mistakes." Now he says, "I seed the doggy"; "Mommy goed to the store"; "The bird flied away"—sentences that can't possibly have come from overhearing his parents. But beneath their sticky charm lies something psychologically profound: the work-in-progress of a skilled hypothesis tester. Without ever having been taught, the child has internalized a linguistic rule—*To form the past tense, add "-d" or "-ed"*—and is faithfully applying it to every verb he encounters. He will persist in using these "incorrect" forms until the distinction between regular and irregular verbs eventually resolves itself in his mind, and he unconsciously "reverts" to using all past-tense forms correctly. While children hit these developmental marks at slightly different ages (some are more precocious at language acquisition than others), all of them will ultimately pass through comparable stages, in roughly the same order.

No amount of parental correction or cajoling, persuasion or praise, or anything else the behaviorists might call reinforcement, will make the child swerve from this grammatical timetable: he appears to be responding to a deep-seated developmental imperative. The following dialogue between an earnest mother and a young child, recorded by the linguist David McNeill and widely reprinted in linguistics texts, makes this vividly clear:

CHILD: Nobody don't like me.

MOTHER: No, say, "Nobody likes me."

CHILD: Nobody don't like me.

[This exchange is repeated eight more times.]

MOTHER: No, now listen carefully; say, "Nobody likes me."

CHILD: Oh! Nobody don't *likes* me.

As Chomsky has written: "The young child has succeeded in carrying out what from the formal point of view, at least, seems to be a remarkable type of theory construction. Furthermore, this task is accomplished in an astonishingly short time, to a large extent independently of intelligence, and in a comparable way by all children." Structuralism was able to account for none of this.

In 1959, Chomsky, who was by this time on the faculty of the Massachusetts Institute of Technology, published a thirty-page evisceration of Skinner's *Verbal Behavior* in the journal *Language.* Nearly half a century later, the review is still considered a classic, renowned for having destroyed the behaviorist approach to the study of language in virtually a single stroke. Point by point, with occasional acerbic wit, Chomsky dismantled Skinner's program:

> A typical example of "stimulus control" for Skinner would be the response to a piece of music with the utterance *Mozart* or to a painting with the response *Dutch.* . . . Other examples of "stimulus control" merely add to the general mystification.

> Thus a proper noun is held to be a response "under the control of a specific person or thing." . . . I have often used the words *Eisenhower* and *Moscow,* which I presume are proper nouns if anything is, but have never been "stimulated" by the corresponding objects. . . . Furthermore, how can one's own name be a proper noun in this sense?

Of Skinner's belief that children learned language by imitation, Chomsky wrote: "It is simply not true that children can learn language only through 'meticulous care' on the part of adults who shape their verbal repertoire through careful differential reinforcement, though it may be that such care is often the custom in academic families."

What is it then, Chomsky asked, that allows a child to internalize and test hypotheses on her way to acquiring her native language? What allows her to acquire language fluently, unconsciously and with amazing rapidity, without being formally taught? What allows any speaker to produce sentences that have never been expressed before, and allows a listener to understand them?

The answer Chomsky proposed marked a radical break from behaviorism, and a radical development in the history of ideas. Human beings, he argued, possess an innate ability to acquire language. Unique to our species, this ability is a biological predisposition—an *instinct*—much like that of birds to migrate or of spiders to spin webs. This genetic endowment is what lets children develop language spontaneously and with rapid efficiency, without recourse to imitation or formal instruction. It is what allows them to pick up not only a first language but, if they are exposed to them, a second and a third and a fourth and on ad infinitum, without the classroom agonies adult learners typically undergo. It is what allows all of us to speak and understand an infinite number of sentences, even completely novel ones. And it is what gives us our deep, tacit "feel" for language. In essence, the script for acquiring, using and understanding human language is something each of us is "born knowing."

From now on, linguistics would be concerned not with behavior but with biology. This new paradigm for thinking about human language marked the beginning of modern linguistics and would come to be known as the Chomsky Revolution. It would be compared to Darwin's theory of evolution and Freud's theory of the unconscious in terms of its importance in the history of Western thought. Instead of languishing as a dimly lit adjunct of anthropology whose central questions had been solved years before, linguistics was now something fresh and vital.

Chomsky's work quickly became the cornerstone of the emerging discipline of cognitive science, in which ancient questions about the nature of the mind were taken up once more, this time by practitioners of psychology, linguistics, neurology and computer science. "In field after field, behavior once seen as acquired has been found to come under the guidance of neurobiological structures," the linguist Derek Bickerton would write. "Language, perhaps the most complex of human achievements, certainly the most distinguishing characteristic of our species, falls within this class of behavior." The behaviorists scuttled away; the few who remain active today are regarded by linguists with deep disdain: "Rat runners," Mark Aronoff calls them.

As radical as it was, the Chomsky Revolution harked back to older models, heralding a return to the Cartesian rationalist tradition so reviled by the structuralists. Language was once again a window on the mind, and the task of the linguist was to look through the window and map what he found there. Under Chomsky, the central question of linguistics became this: What exactly does our inborn "blueprint" for language consist of? Over the years, this blueprint, this innate "feel" for language, has been given various names. Chomsky has called it the "language faculty," the "language organ" and the "language acquisition device." More recently, it has come to be called "the language instinct" or "the bioprogram." As Bickerton writes, "The role of the bioprogram for children acquiring a . . . language . . . is to furnish elementary forms and structures from which (guided by input from the target language) they can develop other and more complex forms and structures." Since Chomsky, the aim of linguistics has been to delineate the precise set of mental instructions the bioprogram comprises—to describe what is sometimes called the child's "initial grammatical state."

It is not possible to map the bioprogram by any direct means. For one thing, you can't go mucking about in people's brains. (Even the most advanced imaging technology is years away from being able to map a neurological seat of language with the level of detail that linguists desire.) For another, "the language organ" denotes not so much a single physical structure in the brain as it does an abstract psychological entity. It *is* possible, however, to create an abstract model of this entity by means of quasi-mathematical algorithms, and that, since the Chomsky Revolution, is what linguists have endeavored to do.

Linguists were still in the business of publishing grammars, but after Chomsky, the nature of these grammars changed dramatically. The grammar of a language was no longer the stagnant word list of the Bloomfield era. Instead, it was a set of formulas: symbolic equations that represented the unconscious mental operations a speaker performs whenever he uses that language. There were rules for turning active sentences into passive, declarative sentences into questions, simple sentences into complex ones laden with dependent clauses, and many more. Ideally, Chomsky proposed, this set of formulas would be so comprehensive, and so powerful, that it could generate every *possible* sentence in a language, and no impossible ones—it would be, as he called it, a "generative grammar."

Besides writing the generative grammars of individual languages, linguists now had a larger aim. Where the structuralists had focused on the differences among languages, Chomsky and his disciples homed in on their essential similarities. To these linguists, the thousands of languages of the world are simply surface variations on a universal biological theme. They all spring from the same kind of human brain. They all are acquired, on the same developmental timetable, by children who enter the world with the same endowment for language: it is simple geographic happenstance that a particular child grows up speaking English rather than Urdu or Swahili or French. The ultimate aim of linguistics, then, should be to describe, in terms general enough to apply to all human languages, this innate faculty shared by every member of our species, to construct, as Chomsky put it, a "universal grammar."

"Particularly in the case of language," he has written, "it is natural to expect a close relation between innate properties of the mind and features of linguistic structure; for language, after all, has no existence apart from its mental representation. Whatever properties it has must be those that are given to it by the innate mental processes of the organism that has invented it and that invents it anew with each succeeding generation."

In the five decades since the Chomsky Revolution began, many competing linguistic models have sprung up. Chomsky himself has revised his own methodology drastically on several occasions. But whatever the theoretical framework looks like, the aim of linguistics remains unchanged: to describe the inborn mental "device" that lets human beings acquire, use and understand language. As Chomsky wrote in 1959: "The fact that all normal children acquire essentially comparable grammars of great complexity with remarkable rapidity suggests that human beings are somehow specially designed to do this, with data-handling or 'hypothesis-formulating' ability of unknown character and complexity." He added, in an explosive understatement: "The study of linguistic structure may ultimately lead to some significant insights into this matter."

Since the end of the 1950s, linguists have worked energetically to carry out Chomsky's mission, teasing apart hundreds of languages strand by strand in an attempt to uncover the universal features beneath the surface. The field has produced thousands of books and monographs, with titles like "A Multifactorial Approach to Adverb Placement: Assumptions, Facts, and Problems," "Lexical Representation and Morpho-Syntactic Parallelism in the Left Hemisphere," and *The Mental Representation of Grammatical Relations.*

Their task is heavy going. Some critics of the Chomskyan approach argue that if there really were a universal "bioprogram," linguists ought to have uncovered it by now. Linguists respond that it can take a lifetime to unpack even a single language, much less all the languages of the world. What's more, they point out, their job is confounded by the sheer length of time human language has been around.

No one knows for certain when human language first arose. In the most current thinking, it is believed to have emerged anywhere from about a hundred thousand years ago, with the dawn of man, to about fifty thousand years ago. It has certainly been around for tens of thousands of years. As a result, the more than five thousand languages spoken in the world today have pedigrees stretching back millennia into the past. English, for instance, can be traced back in a continuous line through the Middle English of Chaucer to the Anglo-Saxon of *Beowulf* through West Germanic and Proto-Germanic all the way to Proto-Indo-European (the progenitor of hundreds of the languages of present-day Europe, Southwest Asia and northern India), which was believed to have originated in about the fifth millennium B.C. "Languages," the linguist Calvert Watkins has written, "have perhaps the longest uninterrupted histories of all the cultural phenomena that we can study."

The longer a human language has been around—the more time elapsed from the moment it sprang from man's brain—the more grammatically complex it can get. Over time, many languages can become quite rococo, acquiring bells and whistles that younger languages don't have: nouns inflected for case and gender; verbs conjugated for person and number and tense; sentences with subordinate clauses nested like a Russian doll. Consider Hungarian, which has more than two dozen different cases for nouns, depending on their role in the grammar of a sentence. These include: Nominative (*ház,* "house"); Genitive (*háznak,* "of the house"); Instrumental (*házzal,* "with the house"); Associative (*házastul,* "with the house and its parts"); Translative-Factive (*házzá,* "change into a house," "becoming a house"); Illative (*házba,* "into the house"); Sublative (*házra,* "onto the house"); Inessive (*házban,* "in the house"); Superessive (*házon,* "on the house"); Elative (*házból,* "out of the house"); Terminative (*házig,* "as far as the house"); and Essive-Formal (*házként,* "as a house").

Then there is Dyirbal, an Australian aboriginal language, in which every noun belongs to one of four linguistic categories whose representative members include: (1) men, kangaroos, fishing line, the moon, storms, rainbows and boomerangs; (2) women, dogs, fireflies, water, fire, stars and the hairy mary grub; (3) ferns, honey, cigarettes, wine and cake; (4) meat, bees, the wind, mud, grass, stones and language itself. And there are the lavish sentences, heavy with dependent clauses, familiar to any speaker of English: *This is the farmer sowing the corn that kept the cock that crowed in the morn that waked the priest all shaven and shorn that married the man all tattered and torn that kissed the maiden all forlorn that milked the cow with the crumpled horn that tossed the dog that worried the cat that killed the rat that ate the malt that lived in the house that Jack built.*

Over the course of its lifespan, a language can take on more and more of this grammatical water. As a result, anyone trying to divine universal grammar from the languages in use today is faced with a series of near-impassable linguistic bogs stretching across the globe, one after another after another. For linguists, the ideal language would be one in its infancy, pure and streamlined, not yet staggering under the weight of its accumulated grammar. A language just moments past creation, carrying nothing but its own linguistic skeleton—the essential ingredients of human language and no more.

If you are short on conscience, you could arrange for such a language to happen: simply grab a couple of babies, lock them in a room for a few years and record the utterances they produce. This is a scenario linguists surreptitiously dream of at night. It has come to be known, quite reasonably, as the Forbidden Experiment.

It's been tried. The historian Herodotus, writing in the fifth century B.C., told the story of the Egyptian pharaoh Psammetichus, who, in an attempt to discover what the oldest civilization was, took two infants from their mothers and dispatched them to an isolated hut under the care of a mute shepherd. Eventually, one of the babies uttered the word *bekos,* which turned out to be the Phrygian word for "bread," bringing the experiment to a happy conclusion. Modern ethical sensibilities preclude a repetition.

But near the end of the twentieth century, linguists began to realize that their sought-after virgin language existed in their midst: the sign language of the deaf. Signed languages spring naturally from the same mental machinery that spoken languages do, but they are far younger—their age is measured not in millennia but in centuries. ASL has been around for barely two hundred years; its historical parent, French Sign Language, is not much more than a century or two older. The earliest written references to a signed language in Britain date from the 1600s. Sign languages are linguistic saplings. They demonstrably have grammars, but they haven't been around long enough to acquire the encumbrances that can frustrate the analysis of spoken language.

In the first decades of the Chomsky Revolution, everything that was known about the "language instinct" came from the analysis of spoken language. To linguists of the period, human language was defined as a system in which signification depended on sound. But by the 1970s, linguists had discovered that this external layer of sound, the stream of consonants and vowels that happens to be the delivery system for spoken language, could be peeled back, revealing underneath pieces of the mental apparatus that drives all human language. As the linguists Ursula Bellugi and Edward Klima wrote in 1979, "We are now beginning to see how this language in a different modality may hold remarkably deep and unexpected clues to constraints on the possible form of language."

What is a language, really? At bottom, it is nothing more than a symbolic code, whose function is to convey meaning. The code is normally realized through speech. That is the default setting for our species: no tribe of hearing people has been found in which a signed language has arisen as the primary means of communication. Endowed with a functioning auditory-vocal channel through which the linguistic signal can pass, man resorts to speech every time.

The speech signal is transmitted by sound waves, produced when air is forced from a speaker's lungs past the vocal cords and out the mouth. These vibrations travel through the air until they hit the receiver—the human ear—which converts them into a set of electrical impulses that are relayed to the speech-processing centers of the brain. That, in essence, is all spoken language is: little disturbances of air. A string of these vibrations is a word; a longer string a sentence, with users of a language agreeing on what the vibrations signify. For most people, mouth, air and ear are more than adequate to the job: the auditory-vocal channel offers a powerful medium for communication.

But what happens when this channel is unavailable? Most deaf people are able to use their vocal organs to produce sounds; the term "deaf-mute," besides being deeply pejorative, is simply inaccurate. But for someone born deaf, or who becomes deaf early, fluent speech without auditory feedback is difficult at best. It is likewise difficult to lipread the speech of others.

There is, however, another channel available through which a linguistic signal can pass: the manual-visual one. Human language will out, and where the auditory-vocal channel is not an option, it is here, by means of hand and eye, that language automatically takes hold.

Philosophers since antiquity have sometimes pondered what would happen if the *sounds* of language suddenly became transparent. Would the result, they wondered, embody the essential character of language, the very distillation of "languageness"? In a 1636 treatise on mathematical physics, the French philosopher Marin Mersenne speculated:

> If one could invent a language whose expressions had their natural signification, so that all men could understand the thought of others by pronunciation alone without having learned its signification, as they understand that one is happy when one laughs, and that one is sad when one cries, this language would be the best of all possible; for it would make the same impression on all hearers as would the thoughts of the spirit if they could be communicated immediately between men as between the angels.

This, in essence, is what happens in the signed languages of the deaf, in particular the youngest sign languages. They strip away the acoustic veneer of spoken language, leaving the essential linguistic scaffolding below. (The phenomenon calls to mind the wonderful remark attributed to Michelangelo, who, asked how he carved his exquisite David out of a lifeless block of marble, replied simply, "I chipped away everything that wasn't David.") For, as linguists have discovered, language in the manual-visual channel behaves remarkably like language in the auditory-vocal one: it employs similar grammatical structures; it is acquired in parallel developmental stages; and it is disrupted, as the result of aging or injury, in strikingly similar ways.

Between the ages of about six months and ten months, hearing infants babble, producing random strings of syllables, the *ma-ma*, *ba-ba* and *da-da* we call baby talk. The babbling has a linguistic purpose. At first, babies produce a wide range of speech sounds, including those not found in the language of the home: an American infant may include in her repertoire the trilled French *r* or the palatal German *ch*. Over time, though, as the infant gains more exposure to her mother tongue, these "foreign" sounds disappear, and her babbling falls in line with those sounds actually present in the adult language around her. Linguists regard the babbling stage as a kind of extended phonological rehearsal—quite literally, an *audition*—in which, from the set of all possible speech sounds, the infant gradually homes in on the particular subset she'll actually need.

As it turns out, exactly the same thing happens with deaf infants exposed to sign as a first language, only here the babbling is manual. Using their hands and fingers, these deaf babies rehearse a wide range of "nonsense" gestures. Over time, they unconsciously zero in on the set of meaningful gestures in the particular sign language to which they are exposed. Like the verbal babbling of hearing babies, the manual babbling of deaf babies, seemingly random at first, gradually tailors itself to the linguistic demands of the babbler's native language.

For these deaf infants, the rest of language acquisition will proceed according to a timetable very much like the one many hearing children follow: single-sign utterances at age one or before; two-sign combinations at about a year and a half; and the transitory appearance of "mistakes" that result from the overapplication of grammatical rules.

At the opposite end of the life cycle, signed and spoken languages break down similarly. Deaf native signers who have suffered strokes or other brain injuries display a range of language dysfunctions (that is, *sign-language* dysfunctions) that are directly comparable to the spoken-language pathologies of hearing patients. Like hearing patients, deaf signers can experience word-finding difficulties, have trouble assembling grammatical sentences, or have severe comprehension problems. Significantly, comparable pathologies in deaf and hearing patients were discovered to result from injuries to the same part of the brain—the left hemisphere, which has been known since the late nineteenth century to control the production and comprehension of spoken language.

As the linguists Fromkin and Rodman write, "The more we learn about the human linguistic ability, the more it is clear that language acquisition and use are not dependent on the ability to produce and hear sounds, but *on a much more abstract cognitive ability, biologically determined,* that accounts for the similarities between spoken and sign languages."

Could sign, then, be the sought-after window on the workings of a young language in the human mind? Would the structure of the youngest sign languages, decoded, reveal the nature of the bioprogram? The possibilities of language in another modality were thrilling, and beginning in the 1970s, linguists set to work analyzing signed language with the same zeal their predecessors had applied to spoken language. "As questions about the nature and fundamental properties of human languages—questions about universal grammar—are formulated," Bellugi and Klima wrote, "understanding the properties of sign languages becomes of increasing importance." This new generation of researchers, including Bellugi, Klima and their disciples, produced hundreds of books and articles on the grammatical structure of ASL and other signed languages, as well as studies of sign-language acquisition and the neurological workings of sign.

But as it turns out, sign languages offer less than pristine data. For the linguist in pursuit of the bioprogram, there are three major stumbling blocks. First, because no signed language exists in a vacuum, over time the surrounding spoken language inevitably exerts some influence. As Wendy and her colleagues have written, contemporary sign languages "exist in settings in which deaf people are bilingual, acquiring the ambient language to some degree." Many ASL signers, for instance, also read and write English; some, like Carol, speak it as well.

The second problem centers on a basic demographic fact: the overwhelming majority of deaf children—some 90 percent—are born to hearing parents. As a result, very few of these children have the chance to acquire sign language in the most natural human way, by soaking it up from the environment at home. "Most deaf children," the team has written, "are not exposed to a full-fledged language in early childhood, and so develop a linguistic system on the basis of impoverished and inconsistent input."

If they are lucky, these children will be exposed to sign early, at a program for deaf preschoolers, or through contact with a deaf babysitter hired for that purpose. But even then, what they're actually exposed to—what passes for "sign language" in a given educational setting—can vary wildly. Still other children won't encounter signing of any kind until years later, when they go to school, or, if they are raised orally, in adulthood. As the team has written:

> Deaf children born to hearing families may be exposed to no signing at all, or to a wide variety of types of signing, and at different ages. The signing to which they are exposed may range from a natural sign language (like ASL in the U.S. and ISL in Israel) to various contrived signing systems (Signed English or Signed Hebrew), to some other kind of a contact language. Both contrived sign systems and more spontaneous contact systems between deaf and hearing people differ dramatically from

> natural sign languages. In such systems, speaking and signing occur simultaneously, [and] word order follows that of the spoken language.

For most deaf children, then, the experience of acquiring language is not at all comparable to that of hearing children.

The third and most insurmountable obstacle is that many of the world's major sign languages are historically interrelated. In the early nineteenth century, ASL emerged as a direct offspring of French Sign Language after Clerc and Gallaudet established their school in Connecticut. To a lesser extent, British Sign Language also influenced ASL, by way of the deaf pupils from Martha's Vineyard who came to Hartford to study: Martha's Vineyard Sign has been traced back to a small group of intermarried families from the same region in England, who came to the New World together in the seventeenth century.

ASL in turn exerted its own influence abroad. By the end of the nineteenth century, American-educated teachers of the deaf, as well as missionaries trained to work with the deaf, had fanned out across the globe, carrying ASL to Latin America, sub-Saharan Africa and elsewhere. Even today, the signed languages of these countries—from Dominican Sign, Puerto Rican Sign and Bolivian Sign to Ghanaian Sign, Nigerian Sign and Chadian Sign—bear the stamp of ASL. Meanwhile, Épée's disciples helped French Sign Language spread throughout Europe, shaping the national signed languages of Belgium, Switzerland, Denmark, Spain, Ireland and elsewhere. Through colonization, British Sign Language also influenced the signed languages of Australia, New Zealand and South Africa.

Because of these shared bloodlines, the structural similarities among sign languages (and there are many) are automatically suspect. They could, ideally, be evidence of the bioprogram at work, with similar linguistic structures springing from similar human brains. But given the history of signed language around the world, they could merely be family resemblances among close cousins. For linguists, there has never been any way to be certain.

Faced with these difficulties, sign-language researchers began to dream a dream of their own, a signing version of the Forbidden Experiment: a bunch of babies (deaf this time), a locked room, time passing, a linguist's eye at the keyhole. . . . The result, if all went well, would be a kind of manual Shangri-la, where everyone spoke a signed language that leapt straight from the brain onto the hands, with nothing to waylay it in between. But as before, it was an experiment to be wished for but never performed.

Once in a great while, however, nature carries out just such an experiment on its own. The result is a "signing village" like Al-Sayyid, where a signed language arises unbidden, spoken by deaf and hearing alike. This natural experiment requires very particular conditions: a traditional, isolated community (these languages are often found on islands); the presence of hereditary deafness; and intermarriage, which concentrates the gene pool and raises the incidence of deafness to a level well above that of the general population. Throughout history, perhaps a dozen of these villages are known to have existed. Besides Martha's Vineyard, whose indigenous signed language is now dead, signing villages have been described in rural Mexico, in Ghana, on Bali, on Amami Island in Japan's Ryukyu chain and on Colombia's Providence Island in the Caribbean Sea.

To a scientist seeking a "virgin" sign language, arisen of its own accord, outside the influence of any other, these signing villages would seem to be the fulfillment of every clandestine dream. "A linguist never has the opportunity to see how language is born," Wendy explained. "All spoken languages are either thousands of years old or came about as a result of contact between languages that are thousands of years old. So in spoken language there is no such thing—*there can be no such thing*—as a new language born of nothing. Only in a sign-language situation can that happen. If you get a deaf community, then a language will be born, and there are no other languages in the environment that are accessible."

Unhappily, though, the linguistic evidence from these signing villages has been fragmentary at best. Although the history of the Martha's Vineyard community has been fascinatingly described by the medical anthropologist Nora Groce in her 1985 book *Everyone Here Spoke Sign Language,* there is little documentary evidence of what the language actually looked like. The island's last deaf signer died not long after World War II, and in the eighteenth and nineteenth centuries, when the language was in its heyday, it was such an accepted feature of local life that it apparently didn't occur to anyone to record or study it.

Among the indigenous signed languages alive today, several have turned out to be less evolved than linguists would hope for—more like simple pidgins, spoken only by small numbers of people. For others, the linguistic documentation has thus far been maddeningly incomplete: the first researchers to set foot in these villages were anthropologists or geneticists, and their professional interest lay elsewhere.

Then there is Al-Sayyid. Its sign language is well established, in use for three generations. It appears, at least in the form spoken by the older villagers, to be uninfluenced by other signed languages, or by any spoken language. On first inspection, it seems more complex than a crude pidgin, but is still young enough to be unburdened by heavy linguistic trappings.

Al-Sayyid Bedouin Sign Language is also noteworthy for the sheer numbers of people that speak it: fully integrated into the community, it is used by many of the village's 3,500 residents, deaf and hearing alike. The winter after our trip, Carol got a reminder of just how remarkable those numbers are. Cleaning off her desk at the end of term, she came across a loose sheet of paper. It had escaped from a scholarly article on the signing village in Mexico, a Mayan community surveyed in the 1980s by a respected sign-language linguist. One sentence in particular caught her eye: "[I]n the village of about 400 inhabitants, there were twelve (now thirteen with a recent birth) deaf people."

Though the Mayan village has a high *rate* of deafness—more than 3 percent—the *number* of deaf people (and, by extension, the number of hearing people who sign) is small in absolute terms. As Carol explained when we met for lunch in New York that winter, in a village with only a small number of deaf residents, "it's really hard to get something going as far as a sign language. If you have a hundred—" She broke off, then finished her own thought: "And how do you get a hundred deaf people in three generations? You have large families."

In other words, the conditions that create an Al-Sayyid—a place where *hundreds* of people are habitual signers—are extremely particular. First, you need a gene for a form of inherited deafness. Second, you need huge families to pass the gene along, yielding an unusually large deaf population in a short span of time. This critical mass of deaf people allows a robust form of signed communication to develop on its own. And the presence of so many deaf signers in the midst of everyday village life in turn encourages widespread signing among the hearing.

These hearing signers turn out to play a crucial role. Because they aren't packed off to schools for the deaf, where the signed language of the majority culture infiltrates and eventually chokes off the indigenous one, hearing villagers tend to preserve the signed language at its most conservative. This in turn helps keep the indigenous language alive for the village as a whole. All in all, a case as spectacular as Al-Sayyid comes along perhaps once in a lifetime. As the team has written:

> In this community, deafness is accepted in the entire community. Deaf people marry in this society, and they usually marry hearing people. . . . Deaf children are often born to hearing parents and are surrounded by hearing relatives. But other relatives—grandparents, cousins, siblings—may be deaf. . . . The social structure is polygamous, so that even if both of a child's biological parents are hearing, an additional wife in the same domestic compound may be deaf. Deafness and sign language are thus inextricably woven into the larger community. Most deaf children and many hearing children as well acquire the sign language from infancy in the same natural way that hearing children acquire spoken language. This single fact, which arises from the social structure of the community, makes the

> language close to unique in the world. . . . The [Al-Sayyid] community and its language thus provide an unprecedented opportunity to study a language that is free of the influence of other languages, signed or spoken.

It is this that makes the prospect of fieldwork here especially promising. "Seeing how hearing and deaf people interact, and the fact that so many hearing people use the sign language—that makes it so unusual," Wendy said. She contrasted the situation of Al-Sayyid with that of several other villages in Israel, of non-Bedouin Arabs and Druze, where there is also a high incidence of inherited deafness. Here, too, indigenous forms of signed communication have arisen among the deaf. But in these villages, deaf people have been traditionally stigmatized and isolated. As a result, the hearing villagers do not sign. Even among the deaf inhabitants, there are few opportunities to congregate, giving a full-blown sign language less chance to develop than it has had in Al-Sayyid.

"With the Al-Sayyid group, not only do hearing people use sign language, but there's a clear awareness that a sign language *is* a language—that's one of the things that's so striking," Wendy told me. "We know this from statements from hearing people like, 'I don't know the sign language as well as So-and-So, because he's got deaf family members and signs better.' This is unusual, very striking. This is one of the things that attracted us, because we felt that it is a really healthy natural environment for language to thrive in."

And it is in just such a natural environment, linguists believe, that human language first began, tens of thousands of years ago. "That's what's so exciting about this population," Wendy said. "It's a really normal community. And that's the situation in which language arose first, we assume, in evolution as well."

The linguists aren't claiming that Al-Sayyid Bedouin Sign Language mirrors the evolutionary development of language in Homo sapiens. Rather, as Wendy explained, "we're able to see, given the fully developed human brain, what happens when it has to make a language out of nothing."

The four of them are deeply hopeful that this indigenous signed language, sprung from the minds of deaf people in an isolated community, will provide a window onto the riches that the human grammar-making mechanism has to offer. If it does, they may find themselves remarkably well poised to answer some of the most fundamental questions cognitive science has to ask: What, if anything, does Al-Sayyid Bedouin Sign Language share with other signed languages of the world? Even more significant, what universal features, shared by signed and spoken languages alike, will turn out to lie hidden beneath the surface of this unknown sign language in the desert?

CHAPTER 5

Starry Night

His work finished, Omar rises from his seat at the head of the table and pours a round of Diet Coke for everyone. His deaf brother Ibrahim takes the vacant chair, and Wendy starts the slide show again. The boy at the window secures the mattress. Dog, cat, horse and snake appear in turn on the screen, and Ibrahim names each one in Al-Sayyid Bedouin Sign, his first and only language. . . . *Fly* . . . *Scorpion* . . . *Fish* . . . *Beetle* . . . *Steaks* . . . *Leaf* . . . *Grass* . . . *Tree* . . . *Pen* . . . *Scale* . . . *Fork* . . . *Bowl* . . . *Teapot* . . . *Cup.*

The sun begins to set over the hills. *Pants* . . . *Dress* . . . *Blanket* . . . *Pillow* . . . *Running shoes* . . . *Newspaper* . . . *A tall stack of plates* . . . *A cup of coffee.* As the camera rolls and dusk enfolds the half-built house, Wendy pronounces the name of each item softly in English as it comes into view: "Scissors . . . Stapler—How's the light, Shai?—Highlighter . . . Paper clip . . . Pencil . . . Door . . . Window with shutters." The air grows cooler.

On to the colors: "Red," Wendy murmurs. "Blue . . . Light blue . . . Black . . . Purple . . . Green . . . White." As Ibrahim signs, a small boy, crouched next to Shai at the camera, quietly signs along with him. At the head of the table, a smaller boy wedges himself between Wendy and Carol so he can follow the action on the screen. Carol takes a tiny nectarine from the tray, eats it and then hesitates, uncertain of the etiquette for getting rid of a fruit pit in an unbuilt house in a foreign culture in the middle of the desert. The boy holding the mattress leaves his post, takes the pit from her hand and flicks it out the window into the twilight.

Al-Sayyid Bedouin Sign is a language of black and white. The languages of the world, researchers have discovered, utilize color terms differently—some employ only two basic terms to describe the entire spectrum, while others, like English, use nearly a dozen. Yet despite these differences, as a landmark study found, color terms in the world's languages conform to a larger typological pattern that is astonishingly consistent across scores of unrelated tongues.

Beginning in the late 1960s, the anthropologist Brent Berlin and the linguist Paul Kay surveyed the color vocabularies of nearly a hundred spoken languages. They focused only on basic color words—the unadorned blacks and reds and blues of language—eschewing fripperies like "mauve," "sienna," and "chartreuse" that from a linguistic standpoint are expendable luxury items. Their survey took in both the languages of modern industrial societies, like English, Russian, Hebrew and Japanese, as well as those of traditional cultures, including Lower Valley Hitigima and Pyramid-Wodo, both spoken in New Guinea; Arawak, from Surinam; Hanunóo, from the Philippines; and Eskimo, Navajo and Hopi.

As Berlin and Kay sifted the data, a pattern began to emerge. They found no languages that contained just a single color word, but they did find several that have only two: these literally translate as "black" (used to describe all dark, dull and cool hues, including green and blue) and "white" (used for light, bright and warm ones: red, orange, yellow, pink and the like). This doesn't mean that speakers of these languages fail to recognize red or yellow or blue when they see them. It's simply that they rely on just two umbrella terms to *name* them. In Lower Valley Hitigima, for instance, all light or bright colors (including white, yellows and reds) are referred to as *mola*, "white"; all dark or dull ones (including black, greens and blues) are *muli*, "black."

On the basis of these color inventories, Berlin and Kay sorted the world's spoken languages into seven different groups, or "stages": (I) languages, like Lower Valley Hitigima, with only two color terms; (II) languages with three terms; (III) those with four terms; (IV) those with five terms; (V) those with six terms; (VI) those with seven terms; and (VII) those, like English, with eight or more terms. The languages of traditional societies, they found, tended to have fewer basic color terms, while those of industrialized societies have more.

But the most striking discovery was this: across the globe, the number of basic color terms a language has is intimately tied to *which* colors those are. If a language has only two color terms, they are always "black" (which includes greens and blues) and "white" (including reds, oranges and yellows). If it has three terms, they are always "black," "white," and "red" (where "red" may describe reddish, yellowish or brownish hues). Languages with four basic color terms include the preceding three—"black," "white" and "red"—plus either "yellow" or a generic term that takes in both green and blue (Berlin and Kay call this "grue"). Languages with five color terms contain "black," "white" and "red," plus "yellow" *and* "grue." In languages with six terms, "grue" has split into the differentiated words "green" and "blue." To this list, languages with seven terms always add "brown." Finally, languages with eight terms and up, a group that includes most of the languages of modern industrial countries, will add one or more words from the list "purple," "pink," "orange" and "gray." English, with eleven terms, has all of these. So do Spanish, Hebrew, Japanese, Hungarian and a number of other languages.

"Our results," Berlin and Kay wrote, "cast doubt on the commonly held belief that each language segments the . . . color continuum arbitrarily and independently of each other language. It appears now that although different languages encode in their vocabularies different *numbers* of basic color categories, a total universal inventory of exactly eleven basic color categories exists from which the eleven or fewer basic color terms of any given language are always drawn."

In the four decades since their original study, new data from many additional languages have shown Berlin and Kay's typological scheme to be essentially correct. A few minor variations on the basic typology have been discovered, and a few languages deviate from the typology in part, but none does so entirely. As the authors wrote in 1991, "Systems of color naming do not vary randomly or capriciously across languages but are constrained to a small number of possible types."

Berlin and Kay's typological scheme predicts two things: first, a language at a particular stage almost always includes the color terms of the stages that precede it. Second, the scheme serves as a timeline of linguistic evolution: the older a language gets, the more basic color terms it adds—and it adds them in the fixed order that the typology specifies. Because languages change at different rates, it is not possible to determine the age of a given language in absolute terms by counting its color words as if they were tree rings. It is possible, however, to use color terms to compare the *relative* age of two or more languages. Since languages take on color words as they age, languages at higher-numbered stages in Berlin and Kay's scheme are by definition older than those at lower ones.

At barely seventy years old, the sign language of Al-Sayyid is right where one would expect it to be: Stage I, with signs for BLACK and WHITE. For other colors, as the team discovered, pointing to an object or piece of fabric of appropriate hue generally suffices. "They have these colorful mattresses and things," Irit explained, "so it's easy to pick out the right color." By contrast, both of the major spoken languages of the region, Hebrew and Arabic, are Stage VII languages. So is Israeli Sign. The pure black-and-whiteness of Al-Sayyid Bedouin Sign, then, is a small nugget of corroborating evidence that the language has sprung up outside the influence of those surrounding it.

The linguists are getting tired: jet lag, the long drive and the intense heat of the desert afternoon are taking their toll. Outside, lights are beginning to come on in the distant hills, and on the far horizon, where the first stars are emerging, a large "M" glows pale gold. Ibrahim continues to sign: *Happy . . . Sad . . . Angry.* A boy darts into the frame to snag a pear.

Irit relieves Wendy at the computer and, as the images scroll by, intones their names in Hebrew, which gives the parade of homely objects the quality of liturgy: *tsvat* ("pliers") . . . *patish* ("hammer") . . .

manof ("crane") . . . *traktor* ("tractor") . . . *dachpor* ("bulldozer") . . . *mechonit* ("car") . . . *mishkefet* ("binoculars") . . . *panas* ("flashlight"). Outside, the muezzin's call filters through the windows as the sky fades to black. Two boys herd the cows in for the night.

Inside the house it is now very dark. "We're finished?" Carol asks.

"We're finished with this," Irit says, "but do we want him to tell a story?"

"You lose the facial expression, is the problem," Mark says, taking note of the growing blackness.

They like Ibrahim's signing so much they keep going anyway. "This guy's *very* good," Wendy says.

"He's very smart and animated," Mark agrees.

"Can we get a light?" Carol asks. She motions to the boy at the window, who leaves the room and returns carrying a long electrical cable with a bare bulb attached to one end. He hangs the bulb in a rectangular hole in the wall where a socket will someday go. Shai unpacks one of his own lights, mounts it on a tripod, and the huge shadows bloom on the walls. Hassan tells Ibrahim in sign that the linguists want him to tell a story. Omar weighs in with signed instructions of his own. Ibrahim faces the camera and launches into a signed story.

"Wait, wait!" Wendy cries. "He has to tell it to *somebody;* he's telling it to the camera in general." She beckons to the boy at the window, seats him in a chair opposite and directs Ibrahim to start again. As he signs, the boy, who is hearing, translates the signed story into spoken Hebrew.

Ibrahim finishes the story, and the exhausted team starts packing up to leave. Irit sits down next to Ibrahim and, with help from the boy, records information on a questionnaire she has brought along: Ibrahim's age, schooling, family tree and incidence of deafness among close relatives. Irit gestures to Ibrahim in kind of pidgin ISL; when there's a communication problem, she speaks to the boy in Hebrew, who translates her questions into Al-Sayyid Bedouin Sign for Ibrahim and his replies back into Hebrew for Irit.

Wendy has left her computer open and running on the table. Several of the boys have gathered around it and are signing along as the slide show flickers by. Mark spots them first. "All *right*," he says wearily. "We're doing the kids."

Shai sets up the camera again and a boy of about seven, one of Ibrahim's sons, takes the chair next to Wendy. A number of his signs are noticeably different from the ones the men used. His sign for FISH, unlike the two-handed sign the men made, is done with a single hand extended, palm sideways, weaving an undulating path. This is the sign for FISH in Israeli Sign Language: the boy goes to a school for the deaf where ISL signs are used, and FISH has insinuated itself into the traditional signing he uses at home. (The deaf children of Al-Sayyid even have a sign PURPLE, lifted straight from ISL.)

The boy finishes, and Irit starts to fill in the questionnaire.

"Don't you want the big brother?" Mark asks. He means the boy who held the mattress.

"I don't think I can take any more," Wendy says.

"But I think he'd be interesting," Mark persists. "He has no ISL interference." Mark means that because this boy is hearing, he isn't exposed to Israeli signs at school, as the deaf kids are. "Can we come back tomorrow?"

"Not to this house," Wendy says firmly. "It's too much."

As the group starts to break up, Omar motions to Carol and me to join him outside. He wants to show us the roof. He sleeps up there, in the open desert air, while his new house grows beneath him. The roof is reached via another concrete ramp, this one attached to the side of the house like a barnacle. It is even steeper than the ramp we climbed to get into the house this afternoon, rearing up from horizontal at a daunting 50-degree angle. Slats of the thinnest wood are set in at intervals for treads, but they will be of little help: the ramp, like everything else in Al-Sayyid, is coated with a layer of slithering sand.

Omar starts energetically up the ramp and beckons us to follow. That morning, stepping off an unseen curb in the Haifa parking garage, I had sprained my ankle savagely, and can walk on level ground only with difficulty, much less an inclined plane with no handrails and no traction. But how often is one invited to the summit of a half-built house in a Bedouin village on a night flush with stars? I grasp Carol's hand and together we grope our way up the ramp. It is deep, enveloping black outside; if I were to ask her to slow down she couldn't see to read my lips.

Half-walking, half-crawling, we reach the roof. There, with the night sky spread above us, the mild desert wind blowing, and the lights of faraway villages glimmering on the horizon, Omar signs expansively to Carol about the nights he passes here, under the canopy of stars. She understands much of what he is saying, which she translates into English for me, though not all of it. At one point, Omar makes a tube with one hand and moves it straight out like a telescope from the center of his forehead, a sign that to my layman's eyes conjures up a cross between a mariner and a unicorn. "I don't know what that is," Carol says. "I'll have to find out."

How is it possible for Carol and the Bedouins to understand each other as well as they do? Some of it, of course, is pure gesture. When Carol first visited Al-Sayyid, she simply began gesturing to the first person she met, the young wife of one of Hassan's uncles. "It was very easy," Carol told me over lunch in New York. "I just sort of—" (She breaks off and mimes huge gestures of exaggerated scale in the air.) "They would ask me, *'Did you fly here?'* " (She makes the ASL sign AIRPLANE, a fist with thumb, index finger and pinky extended, swooping upward.) "*'Where's your husband?'*" (She motions with one hand over her shoulder as if to reply, "*Back there.*") "Family kinds of things. I've traveled around, so I know what kind of gestures tend to work."

But besides a certain transparency of gesture, there is something else that lubricates understanding between Carol and the people of Al-Sayyid. Cognitive psychologists call it "theory of mind." Despite its name, theory of mind is not itself a scientific theory. It refers instead to a particular cognitive skill: a person's ability to ascribe abstract mental states to others, to be, in essence, "inside someone else's head." It is theory of mind, in part, that allows each of us to get jokes, to understand irony, to tell when a person is lying, and to recognize that when somebody asks us a rhetorical question, we are not actually supposed to answer it.

Theory of mind takes time to develop. Children begin to acquire it in the second year of life, and it is this, psychologists believe, that allows them to begin "pretend play." But a full-fledged theory of mind—the trick of endowing another person with a consciousness separate from one's own, and then of inhabiting that consciousness so completely as to intuit that person's intentions, desires or beliefs—is an ability that very young children do not yet have. The British psychologist Mike Eslea reports a splendid example of this in a telephone conversation he had with a three-year-old boy:

ME: What have you been doing today?

HIM: Playing with this.

ME: Oh, right. What is it?

HIM: THIS!!!

In a famous psychological experiment from the 1980s, children were presented with a scenario known as a "false-belief" task. In one version of the scenario, a boy named Maxi has a bar of chocolate, which he puts into a blue cupboard. He goes out to play and, while he is out, his mother moves the chocolate from the blue cupboard to the green cupboard. Later, Maxi comes in and wants to eat the chocolate. Where will he look for it?

Only children four years old, or very nearly, were able to ascribe to Maxi a belief they knew to be at odds with reality, responding correctly that he would look in the blue cupboard. Younger children always said that Maxi would look in the green cupboard—because that was where *they* knew the chocolate to be. Strikingly, theory of mind appears to be unrelated to general intelligence. Children with Down's syndrome consistently do well on false-belief tasks, while autistic children of normal intelligence consistently fail them.

Some researchers believe that theory of mind is a direct outgrowth of a person's linguistic ability. It certainly seems tied, at least in part, to the richness of the linguistic environment one is exposed to early on, as Carol noted when we met in New York. "To have an idea of the other person's mind with respect to your own means you can do irony," she explained. "I've met a lot of deaf people who didn't start learning sign till later: they went to an oral school. It's very hard to joke with them; it's very hard to have an interesting conversation, because they're so language-impaired in some way."

Carol's observation has been borne out experimentally. In a 1995 study, the Australian psychologists Candida C. Peterson and Michael Siegal presented a false-belief task to a group of deaf children. Most of the children had been born to hearing parents and had spent their early years in households that were, for them, linguistically impoverished. Two, however, had been born to deaf parents and were exposed to an accessible language (that is, a *signed* language) from the moment they were born. The children of deaf parents (the early-language-learners) performed significantly better on the false-belief task than those of hearing parents, who had encountered sign language only later.

It is theory of mind, in part, that allows users of different signed languages to make informed tacit assumptions about meaning. In ASL and many European sign languages, for example, there is a constellation of semantically related words having to do with mental processes: THINK, KNOW, REMEMBER, BELIEVE, UNDERSTAND, DECIDE. All are signed at or near the head. As a result, speakers of these languages can intuit, at least roughly, what someone making a sign in the vicinity of the head might be trying to convey. It is this capacity that allows the Bedouins to comprehend much of Carol's signing and, in turn, allows them to sign in a manner accessible to her. "They think, 'What do I have to do to make the other person understand this?'" she said.

These tactics aren't fail-safe, however, as Carol discovered on a trip to Japan, when she tried to communicate with deaf signers there. "It's difficult to gesture with the Japanese, because you have a different iconography in the culture," she explained. "So you're very often wrong." The Japanese sign UNDERSTAND, for instance, is made on the chest; DECIDE is made on the palm of the opposite hand.

In Al-Sayyid, however, communication has proved fairly easy. "With the Bedouins, I found that the gestures I use with Europeans tended to work well," Carol said. "You know right away whether it's working or not. . . . The Bedouins are 'with it'! You can joke with them; you can use a lot of irony." She was surprised at first to encounter this in Al-Sayyid: many scholars assume that only a complex, long-established language can promote a theory of mind. The language of Al-Sayyid, just seventy years old, is linguistically simpler than many. But the more time Carol spent observing it, the more she came to believe that its sheer ubiquity accounts for the robust theory of mind she found among the villagers. "They're cognitively like early-language-learners," she explained. "They have been immersed in this environment of communication from the time they were very young."

We make our way gingerly down from the roof. In front of the house, the team says its last round of goodbyes before climbing into the van for the rattle-banging trip down the dirt road. Mark leaves the dome light on so that Carol can see Wendy's signing. The tiny van fills with English and Hebrew and ASL as everyone, brimming with the day's events, starts to talk at once.

As they drive, the linguists talk about the difference between Omar's signing and the boy's. "The boy was naming things; the older man was describing what he saw," Carol observes. Scrutinizing one of the test pictures, a photograph of a truck carrying a load of concrete pipes, Omar, who works in the construction trades, launched into an enthusiastic signed description of exactly what kind of pipes they were. The boy, by contrast, merely signed the rote response TRUCK, as a student might do in a classroom vocabulary drill.

"That's my concern," Mark says. "Words are such an artificial task." He has a low, growly voice, and when he speaks, each stressed syllable gets a barely perceptible extra push. The effect betrays either ironic detachment or extreme shyness; after almost thirty years I am still not completely certain.

"But naming is so basic," Wendy responds.

"To you," Mark says. "But it's not part of normal language. It's a part of literate culture." There are some spoken languages, he says, that don't even have a unique word for "word."

Giving McDonald's a wide berth, we stop for dinner at an outdoor café near the hotel. During the meal, the conversation is about what it always is when linguists find themselves together. Tonight's topics range from a type of grammatical suffix appended to words of direction in Maltese to the nuanced semantic distinction between the English common nouns "thong" and "jockstrap."

The talk turns to Omar. "It was a real sign he was beginning to accept us, that he asked us to his 'new' house," Wendy says.

"The amount of money they spent on us today was astonishing," Mark adds. "All that Coca-Cola: that's serious money."

"He's not poor," Wendy says. Omar, who drives heavy equipment for a living, is able to support two wives.

Irit turns to Carol. "Remember ______ [she names a man they met on their previous visit to Al-Sayyid], who wanted to marry you?"

"I got another offer tonight," Carol says, smiling. (She declined: he has three wives already.)

After dinner, the six of us pile into the van and pull onto the highway for the drive to the hotel. Only Carol, now in the back seat, notices the small white car in the lane next to ours. She peers at it closely. "Are those people signing in that car?" she asks. In the Mediterranean, where talking with the hands is as essential as air, it can be hard to tell.

"When I want to see if people are signing, I look at the face, not the hands," Irit says. Signed languages convey grammatical information not only with the hands, but also with the body, including the face, head and eyes. In signed conversations, the addressee looks directly at the signer's face, leaving peripheral vision to attend to the hands.

We stop at a red light and the car pulls up alongside us. There are two young men inside. Carol rolls down her window, extends a hand and waves it to get the driver's attention. She points to him. "Are you deaf?" she gestures. "Yes," the young man signs back, and a gestured conversation ensues between the two cars. Carol tells the man she's deaf from America; he tells her he's deaf from a nearby Israeli town. They talk some more, and then the light changes. Carol and the young man smile at each other warmly, wave goodbye, and the little car pulls away, out of sight.

CHAPTER 6

The Atoms of Sign

In the autumn of 1955, a young scholar arrived at Gallaudet to take up a teaching position in the English Department. His name was William Stokoe, and he was thirty-six years old. Stokoe was a specialist in Old and Middle English literature, hired to teach Chaucer. Like the great majority of the Gallaudet faculty, he knew absolutely nothing about sign language.

The school he came to, today the world epicenter of deaf scholarship and culture, was then a very different place. Known as Gallaudet College, it was in many ways a provincial institution, an unaccredited college whose faculty produced almost no research and whose students received little of real intellectual rigor.

Until the end of the nineteenth century, many teachers of the deaf in America were deaf themselves. Signing was in its heyday then, and it flourished not only in the homes of deaf people but also in the classroom: it was the primary language of instruction in the network of residential schools that by this time spanned the country. Deaf children thrived in these schools (many encountering an accessible language for the first time in their lives), and the schools themselves played a crucial historical role in the formation, transmission and perpetuation of the language and culture of the American deaf.

But toward the end of the century, oralists like Alexander Graham Bell began to wield increasing influence. Bell favored the assimilation of deaf people into the majority culture through intensive drills in speech and lipreading and, needless to say, the eradication of sign language. An ardent eugenicist, he feared that if the deaf remained together as a group, united by a common language, intermarriage would lead to the inexorable spread of their condition. "It is the duty of every good man and every good woman to remember that children follow marriage, and I am sure there is no one among the deaf who desires to have his affliction handed down to his children," he said in an address at Gallaudet College in 1891.

To Bell, as grave a concern as intermarriage itself was the sheer number of deaf people who had gone into teaching. As he wrote in a cautionary monograph of 1883, *Memoir Upon the Formation of a Deaf Variety of the Human Race,* "Nearly one-third of the teachers of the deaf . . . in America are themselves deaf, and this must be considered as another element favorable to the formation of a deaf race—to be therefore avoided."

By this time, Bell and his supporters had already won a considerable victory. In 1880, even now a black date in deaf history, an international congress of educators of the deaf had convened in Milan. There, over the protests of Thomas Gallaudet's son Edward Miner Gallaudet, head of the college that bore his father's name, the assembly passed a resolution condemning sign language as an instructional method in schools for the deaf everywhere.

The oralists brought to their cause a missionary fervor, and a deep Victorian distaste for sign's expressive qualities. Harlan Lane quotes one speaker at the Milan congress:

> Oral speech is the sole power that can rekindle the light God breathed into man when, giving him a soul in a corporeal body, he gave him also a means of understanding, of conceiving, and of expressing himself. . . . While, on the one hand, mimic signs are not sufficient to express the fullness of thought, on the other they enhance and glorify fantasy and all the faculties of the sense of imagination. . . . The fantastic language of signs exalts the senses and foments the passions, whereas speech elevates the mind much more naturally, with calm, prudence and truth and avoids the danger of exaggerating the sentiment expressed and provoking harmful mental impressions.

By the early twentieth century, spoken English had almost completely supplanted signing in American classrooms. Hearing teachers who couldn't sign had replaced deaf ones. The network of residential schools, formerly the wellspring of deaf culture, increasingly called to mind the federal Indian schools of the frontier era, whose pupils, forcibly shorn of their long hair, traditional dress and native language, were, after four years, discharged into the world "civilized." By mid-century, when William Stokoe joined the Gallaudet faculty, nearly 80 percent of American secondary schools for the deaf used the oral method exclusively.

The colonial attitude that informed the education of the deaf throughout the United States was in full flower even, or perhaps especially, at Gallaudet. "The history of Gallaudet is inextricably woven into the history of the worldwide conflict between oralism and sign language," Jane Maher, the author of *Seeing Language in Sign,* a fine study of Stokoe's life and work, has written. "As oralism became the accepted mode of teaching and communication, it logically followed that the teachers and top administrators in schools for the deaf tended to be hearing advocates of oralism, depriving deaf people of the ability to represent themselves and their interests."

In the 1950s, Gallaudet viewed its student body as a population of handicapped people with limited prospects. There was no deaf political consciousness then, no deaf pride movement and no sense among the deaf that they constituted an authentic linguistic minority. Those things were a decade and more away, for they would grow directly out of the work that would make William Stokoe ridiculed, reviled and, after a great many years, revered: demonstrating that "the sign language," as it was then called, was a real language, as full, complex and emphatically human as any other.

The Gallaudet faculty was overwhelmingly hearing. Few of its members could sign at all well. Classes were conducted in an unnatural mixture of spoken and signed English, with the instructor signing along, in English word order, as he delivered his lecture. English words like "is," "was" and "the," which do not occur in ASL because its syntax does not need them, were spelled out using the manual alphabet. The net effect, reminiscent of the Abbé de l'Épée's cumbersome "methodical signs," was a contrived "English on the hands," effortful to produce and, for a native signer, nightmarish to comprehend. Students in turn were expected to use this manual English in class, or to speak aloud. Small wonder that most of them struggled mightily just to keep up, both with the bastard manual language of the classroom and with the written English of their textbooks. "No one, not even the deaf students and deaf faculty," Maher writes, "believed that their signing was a suitable medium of instruction, much less a legitimate language."

"Real" sign language—it wasn't yet called ASL—was considered a poor stepchild of English, used as a kind of slang among deaf people but unsuitable for formal settings like the classroom. Hearing people were embarrassed by it, and deaf people were made to feel ashamed of it. "None of us at the time had any notion that sign language was anything but a visual coding of English," George Detmold, the Gallaudet dean who had hired Stokoe, told Maher in 1991. "This is what we were told, by the experts, by people who had worked with the deaf all their lives. If deaf people, among themselves, used these signs in obviously different ways, which translated into some horribly garbled English order, that proved how lacking they were in 'language.'"

Signs were believed to be no more than gross holistic gestures, which stood for English words (mostly everyday nouns) in a one-to-one correspondence. They appeared to lack the complex internal structure of the words of spoken language. In addition, signed sentences were thought to have no grammar. Especially offensive to the Gallaudet administration were the facial gestures that are an indispensable part of sign-language grammar. It was bad enough that students had to talk with their hands. But the exaggerated movements of the mouth, tongue, eyes and lips, suggesting grimacing or excessive emotional display, triggered in hearing observers the same prudish horror so richly on display in Milan seventy-five years earlier. During the 1950s, the university attempted to make its students stop moving their faces when they signed, which is tantamount to asking hearing people to speak only in declarative sentences, uttered in robotic monotone.

"Signing had been seen, up to this time, as . . . something without internal structure or coherence or rules, something far below the level of language," the neurologist Oliver Sacks has written. The attitude was so unreservedly accepted that in 1958 Gallaudet awarded an honorary degree to Helmer Myklebust, the psychologist who two years later would decree, "The manual sign language must be viewed as inferior to the verbal."

But though sign language was officially taboo, in a place like Gallaudet, where so many deaf people were gathered together, it was impossible to eradicate completely. It simply went underground, surfacing in stolen moments in the hallways, the bathrooms and the dormitories, anywhere students could congregate out of the reach of the hearing. Like the *conversos,* the Spanish and Portuguese Jews who converted to Christianity but practiced their own faith in secret during the Inquisition, many mid-twentieth-century deaf people were forced, in their daily lives, to become crypto-signers.

On his arrival at Gallaudet, Stokoe was placed in the university's sign immersion course for new faculty members. There, he was taught the crude manual English and fingerspelling he would be required to use in class. Stokoe realized two things almost immediately. First, that his students, though clearly bright, were struggling with written English because the jury-rigged language of instruction offered them no way into it. As he wrote in the late 1970s, "The teacher who learns signs and puts them into English phrases and sentences to teach Deaf pupils will fail to communicate, unless pupils already have mastered the sentence-forming and the word-forming systems of English—a most unlikely chance."

Second, he observed that the signed communication his pupils used among themselves was something quite different from the lumbering manual English of the classroom. It had precision and form and rhythm. It seemed to be able to convey complex ideas, and convey them efficiently. It employed not only the hands and arms, but also the face, eyes, head and torso. It could apparently do anything English could; it simply did it by different physical means. "I had come into a community," he would later say, "where deaf people communicated with one another in a rapid and apparently quite satisfying manner without any need to speak or hear."

As Stokoe would recall for Jane Maher:

> I remember once when one of the old-line teachers complained about her students at a faculty meeting. . . . Even in class, she said, when she'd ask a question, there wouldn't be anybody volunteering an answer, so she'd ask the question again.
>
> As a member of the audience I stood up and said to the teacher, "How did you ask the question?" She said that, for instance, when she asked her students who was the author of *The Red and the Black*, she signed "who" with the finger at the mouth while she fingerspelled "was." I don't remember whether she fingerspelled "the" and "writer." . . . "Red" and "black" were signed. Then with her finger she made a little question mark at the end. That was precisely the way I had been taught . . . to ask a question in signed English.
>
> I looked at the teacher's signing and said, "You know, to a deaf student, you haven't asked a question at all. What you did is make a series of word signs and letter signs and then you dropped your hands as soon as you were finished. That is the way a declarative sentence ends in sign language. . . . If you want to ask a question, when the signing is finished, keep the gaze straight, eye to eye, and the hands up; . . . that is the sign of a question. That pose is held for a split second. Any deaf person who knows sign language perceives that a question has been asked and that an answer is expected.
>
> "On the other hand, when a teacher puts a question in English question-order and drops the hands and the gaze at the end of the performance, the student has been sent the signal 'I have just finished a sentence and am about to begin another.'

No wonder you weren't getting any answers to your question—you hadn't asked a question."

That's the kind of thing our students had to put up with.

Stokoe, who died in 2000 at the age of eighty, was an original. A farm boy from upstate New York, he attended Cornell University on a scholarship and went on to get a doctorate from Cornell in medieval literature. With his large square features, strong jaw, deep-set eyes and hair often cropped in an inverted-bowl tonsure, he looked rather medieval himself, just the way a scholar of fourteenth-century literature ought to.

He didn't behave like a dusty medievalist, though. He rode a motorcycle, flew airplanes and brewed his own beer. Fiercely proud of his heritage (his name, pronounced "Stokey," is from the Scottish border), he was partial to dressing in a kilt and tam and playing the bagpipes, which he often practiced on campus. In this pursuit, at least, he must have found a hospitable home in Gallaudet.

One of the students who worked for Stokoe in the mid-1970s was a nineteen-year-old Georgetown sophomore named Carol Padden. "Bill was absolutely unselfconscious, eccentric, kind of wild," she told me. "He didn't care about being a spectacle." Carol's parents were friends of Stokoe's. Her mother taught in the Gallaudet English Department; her father, who worked at *The Washington Post* as a printer, a traditional occupation for generations of deaf men, also taught physical education at the college. Carol had always been fascinated by language, and at the end of her freshman year, she wrote to Stokoe and asked for a job in his lab. "He didn't really have a project for me, but he gave me a job anyway," she recalled.

Although Stokoe has been called the father of sign-language linguistics, he was not a linguist himself. He was a scholar of literary texts, an authority on the translation of Old and Middle English poetry. Nor did he sign especially well. The problem wasn't mastering the language—besides Old and Middle English, he had studied Latin, Greek, French and German, and could understand ASL perfectly. For him, it was a question of manual dexterity: when it came to speaking the language he helped demystify, Stokoe simply had trouble getting his big blunt hands around it. Carol remembers that his fingerspelling was especially difficult to read. However, as she told Jane Maher, "I'd rather have novelty and intelligence with bad fingerspelling than oppression and intolerance disguised in great signing skills."

But Stokoe had other assets that equipped him well to challenge entrenched assumptions about sign. His work on medieval texts had accustomed him to examining language with the scrutiny of a microscopist. Maher recounts how in the course of his early research Stokoe once spent the better part of a year deciphering the meaning of a single Old English word.

He had another great asset as well: by the mid-twentieth century, deaf education in America had become an extensive commercial enterprise, embracing secondary and vocational schools across the country as well as a large network of doctors, audiologists, speech therapists, hearing aid manufacturers, teacher-training programs, and, of course, Gallaudet itself. To this industry, Stokoe was very much an outsider. He had few institutionalized biases and little political agenda. He possessed a basic liberal humanism that allowed him to see his deaf students as capable, intelligent people, and to sympathize with their struggles to keep up with classes taught in a language so different from their own. And, faced with an obstacle, he seldom backed down. As his obituary in *The New York Times* reported, "He earned the nickname Stubborn Stokoe in high school after convincing his physics teacher that he deserved a 100, not a 98, on an exam."

Stokoe began to study what he saw. With virtually no support from the university, he opened a small laboratory on campus, dedicated to investigating "the sign language." It was largely a rogue operation. Using a movie camera powered by a transformer cannibalized from one of his boyhood electric train sets, Stokoe, with two deaf associates, recorded the language of his deaf students. Running the finished film through a Movieola, he examined it frame by frame: Exactly how were signers' hands and arms moving? Where did they go? How were they shaped and held? Where was the signer's gaze directed? What was the face doing, and the head?

What Stokoe saw solidified his original conviction: the signs his students used among themselves were not holistic pictures in the air but complex, highly organized symbols, functioning as abstract linguistic code. In a language that was supposed to have no grammar, Stokoe found signs that corresponded to the same parts of speech that spoken language has. There were nouns, of course, but also verbs and adverbs and adjectives. There were systematic ways of describing past, present and future actions. There was a matrix of pronouns richer than that of English, including a separate sign for the second-person plural, which Modern English (with the exception of Southern "you-all" and New York "youse") does not have, as well as a "dual" pronoun, meaning "we two," used to refer to the speaker plus one other person. (Anglo-Saxon, as it happens, also has a dual pronoun.) There were, as in many European languages, separate words for male and female cousins. There were ways of stringing words into sentences very different from those of English: in signed questions, for instance, words like WHO, WHAT, WHERE, WHEN, WHY and HOW often came at the end of the sentence, as in ICE-CREAM YOU WANT WHICH?—"Which (flavor of) ice cream do you want?" It was very different from English, but it was a system all the same. In short, as Stokoe told a colleague not long after he began his investigation, "It looks to me that they've got a real language here."

A language is a symbolic code in the sense that its basic symbols—the words in its lexicon—bear only an arbitrary relationship to the things they signify. There is no Platonic canine essence bound up in the string of sounds pronounced "dog," nothing that can't be embodied just as effectively by *chien* or *canis* or *Hund* or *kelev.* It is simply that the community of English speakers agreed long ago on what this string of small acoustic signals would stand for. "The linguistic sign is arbitrary," the late-nineteenth-century Swiss linguist Ferdinand de Saussure famously said. More than fifty years later, a group of twentieth-century British philosophers made the same point spectacularly well in a 1964 radio interview:

RINGO: John thought of the name Beatles, and he'll tell you about it now.

JOHN: It's just that it means Beatles, isn't it, you know? That's just a name, you know, like "shoe." . . .

PAUL: "The Shoes." See, we could've been called "The Shoes," for all you know.

There is onomatopoeia in spoken language, of course, but in most languages, these words, like "splat" and "squish" and "tintinnabulation," constitute only a minuscule subset of the lexicon. And they are in their own way arbitrary as well, as anyone who has wondered why *cock-a-doodle-do* should reflect a rooster's cry any better than *kukuriku* has realized.

The arbitrary relationship between a word and the thing it signifies is one of the essential design properties of human language, and is part of what gives language its limitless nature: it allows us, as long as the result is agreed upon, to come up with a word for absolutely anything. As the historian of English W. F. Bolton has written:

> This ability to attach meaning to arbitrary clusters of sounds or words is like the use and understanding of symbolism in literature and art. The word *one* does not somehow represent the numeral, somehow embody its essence the way a three-sided plane figure represents the essence of triangularity. Rather, *one* merely stands for the prime numeral 1, giving a physical form to the concept, just as the word *rosebuds* gives a physical form to the concept "the pleasures of youth" in the poetic line, "Gather ye rosebuds while ye may." Thus the sound . . . spelled *one* . . . has a dual quality as a sound and as a concept. This can be seen from the fact that [the same acoustic sequence], spelled *won,* matches the identical sound to a wholly different concept. This feature of duality is both characteristic of and apparently unique in human communication, and so linguists use it as a test to distinguish language from other kinds of communication in which a sound can have only a single meaning.

The words of spoken language are not holistic symbols but are instead complex, analyzable structures. They possess an internal anatomy, and this fact is essential to the operation of the code. Any schoolchild knows that words can be subdivided into syllables, and syllables further divided into consonants and vowels. But words possess an even more microscopic level of organization that is a crucial design feature of any linguistic system. Every consonant and every vowel, it turns out, is a highly structured entity in itself.

It works this way. Each distinct sound of spoken language, every *p* and *b* and *m* and *o* and *u*, possesses discrete physical properties: each is made by a different combination of small movements of the tongue, lips and vocal cords. The result, in each case, is a unique acoustical signal streaming out of the mouth. The consonants *p*, *t* and *k*, for instance, differ only in the position of the tongue and lips when the sounds are made: *p* is made by briefly closing the lips and then opening them, releasing a small puff of air; *t* is made by quickly touching the tip of the tongue to the gum ridge behind the upper teeth; *k* by raising the back of the tongue and touching it to the soft palate. Similarly for vowels, where the position of the tongue—raised or lowered, toward the front of the mouth or the back—plus the roundness of the lips, determines the sound that comes out.

Consonants like *p*, *t*, *k* and *s* can be altered to produce further sounds. When *p*, *t*, *k* and *s* are made, the vocal cords are relaxed, and air from the lungs simply streams past them. This is what gives these consonants their soft, whispery quality. By contrast, when the vocal cords are tensed, the rushing stream of air sets them vibrating. The same lip position that produced *p* now produces *b*. Similarly, *t* becomes *d*, *k* becomes *g* and *s* becomes *z*, sounds that, because the vocal cords are engaged, have a "noisier" quality. The difference is palpable: place your fingers in your ears and say *sssssss*. Then, fingers still in place, say *zzzzzzzz*. The buzz you hear is your vocal cords, engaged and vibrating.

The ability to vary the acoustic signal in minute but perceptible ways is the engine that drives the coding operation at its most basic level, for it gives language the power to create millions of differentiated signals. Often, only a minuscule change is all that is needed to produce a completely new signal: simply by altering the position of the lips and tongue, we can move from *puff* to *tough* to *cuff*. By engaging the vocal cords, we also get *buff* and *duff* and *guff*. And that is just one small syllable. These alterations are the building blocks of spoken language: the sounds that result have no meaning, but can be combined to form larger elements that do. Strung together in various patterns, this small finite inventory of speech sounds (there are only about three dozen in English) can easily encode the entire lexicon of a language, hundreds of thousands of words.

As Charles Hockett, among the last of the great structural linguists, explained in 1958:

> Any utterance in a language consists of an arrangement of the phonemes of that language; at the same time, any utterance in a language consists of an arrangement of the morphemes of that language, each morpheme being variously represented by some small arrangement of phonemes. This is what we mean by "duality": a language has a phonological system and also a grammatical system.
>
> The duality principle is convenient in any communicative system where a fairly large number of messages must be distinguished. If Paul Revere and his colleague had needed a total repertory of several hundred messages, instead of just two, it would have been inconvenient and expensive to have on hand, in the Church tower, several hundred lanterns. But it could have been agreed that each message would take the form of a row of five lights, each of which would be either red, or yellow, or blue. Only fifteen lanterns would then be needed (one of each color for each position), but the system would allow a total of $3^5 = 243$ different messages. The meanings, we assume, would be assigned to the whole messages, just as in the system described by Longfellow: thus "red light in first position" would not have any separate meaning of its own, but would merely serve to distinguish some messages from others, as the

recurrent initial /b-/ of the English morphemes *beat, bat, but, bottle* distinguishes these from morphemes like *meat, rat, cut, mottle* without having any meaning of its own.

This system would then manifest duality: its "phonological" subsystem would involve the five positions and the three colors, while its "grammatical" subsystem would involve only the whole messages and the semantic conventions established for each.

But suppose the message can't be encoded acoustically. For deaf signers, it is encoded visually, in surprisingly similar ways. This was William Stokoe's great discovery. Signs, Stokoe found, were not holistic gestures at all, but organized linguistic symbols, as complex and arbitrary as the words of spoken language. Signs could be analyzed into "subatomic" components just as words could. The primary difference is that the symbols of sign language are encoded not by the passage of air through the vocal organs but *by the movements of the hands in space.* "None before [the Abbé de l'Épée] and all too few after him to the present day have been willing to face the fact that a symbol system by means of which persons carry on all the activities of their ordinary lives is, and ought to be treated as, a language," Stokoe wrote in 1960.

The hands turn out to be first-rate encryption devices. Hands can grasp and clench and push and tap and brush and thrust and slice and dive. Fingers can point and poke and wiggle and spread and curl and bend. These movements can be performed high in the air or low; in front of the body or off to the side; in contact with the face, chest, arm or opposite hand; rapidly or slowly; with straight or circular or repeated motions. Every one of these visual operations, meaningless in itself, can be conscripted to act as linguistic code, just as the acoustic signals of spoken language can.

From this large gestural inventory, Stokoe isolated the essential components that every sign is built on—the consonants and vowels, as it were, of sign. Each sign, he discovered, comprises three basic structural elements: first, the shape of the signer's hands; second, the location of the hands in space; and third, the manner in which the hands are moving. (Later researchers added a fourth element, orientation, which describes whether the palms are facing up, down, left or right.)

Like the sounds of spoken language, these structural elements are the recombinant DNA of sign, fastening together in thousands of different permutations to produce the lexicon of the language. As the linguist Robbin Battison explains:

> Just as we know that the two English words "skim" and "skin" are different words with different meanings, we know that they are *minimally different.* That is, the only difference between these two words is the final sound unit: "m" or "n." Of course we can find thousands of these *minimal pairs* (pairs of words that differ in only one *minimal* way). From them we can determine what types of sound units play an important role in distinguishing meanings in a spoken language. We can do the same with a signed language.

Take, for example, the ASL sign BORED. It is made with the extended index finger (the handshape) held to the side of the nose (the location) and rotated with a twisting motion (the movement). Other signs that share this index finger handshape are YOU, ME, DEAF, HEARING, DAY, WEEK, DEPEND, CANCEL, CAN'T, SIGN-LANGUAGE, GO-TO, WHERE, LONELY, BLACK, SUCCEED and BITTER. Consider next the sign SHOE, which is made by holding the closed fists side by side in front of the body and banging them together twice in quick succession. The same fist handshape also shows up in DRIVE, LOVE, WORK, COFFEE, SENATE, UMBRELLA, YEAR, BICYCLE, YES and PROPAGANDA.

Altering just a single element, as Battison indicates, can produce an entirely different sign. If you hold one hand sideways, all five fingers spread, and touch your thumb to your forehead, you have just made the ASL sign FATHER. If you alter the handshape by folding in your ring finger and pinky so that only the thumb, index and middle fingers are extended, you have now said ROOSTER. If you extend only the index finger and touch it to the forehead, that is THINK.

Like handshapes, locations and movements can also be varied to produce new signs. The sign SUMMER is made by drawing the extended index finger across the forehead, ending with the finger crooked; it suggests wiping a bead of sweat from one's brow. If the location is changed to the upper lip, it is the sign UGLY. Drawing the index finger across the chin in this way means DRY.

The signs COFFEE, WORK and YEAR are all made in front of the body with two closed fists. But the manner in which the hands move differs for each. For COFFEE, one fist sits atop the other and makes a small circular motion, as if grinding beans. For WORK, one fist taps down twice on the back of the other. For YEAR, one fist circles the other, symbolizing the earth orbiting the sun.

In all, Stokoe identified nineteen distinct handshapes (these included the flat palm, the extended index finger, the index and middle fingers splayed in a V shape, the thumb and forefinger opened in an L shape, a C-shaped hand, an O-shaped hand, and a closed fist); twelve locations (signs articulated in front of the signer or off to either side, as well as directly on the signer's head, face, chest, shoulder, arm or opposite hand); and twenty-four discrete types of movement (including linear and circular motions of the arms; touching, linking, grasping, rotating, brushing and pointing).

Formational elements like these underpin all the sign languages of the world. While some languages employ a larger number of discrete handshapes, locations or movements, others get by with fewer. Finnish Sign Language has more than thirty different handshapes, Taiwanese Sign Language more than fifty. But the indigenous sign language of Providence Island in the Caribbean seems to make do with just seven or eight.

Like spoken languages, which utilize only a small subset of the inventory of possible speech sounds, each sign language chooses differently from the store of available handshapes, locations and movements. In Taiwanese Sign Language, BROTHER is signed with the extended middle finger of one hand; this handshape, perhaps in deference to cultural propriety, is not used in ASL, though it does occur in British Sign. Other sign languages may use other unfamiliar handshapes, as Carol has written in a discussion of Chinese Sign Language (a distinct language from Taiwanese Sign): "ASL signers learning Chinese Sign Language need to learn new handshapes or movements which are not found in ASL. Thus, in the same way that an English speaker speaks heavily accented German, the ASL signer's Chinese signs will also be heavily accented."

Spoken language assembles its signals in linear order. That is the only way sounds can be articulated by the mouth, and the only way they can be processed by the ear. The word "hat" comprises three such signals, strung together in strict temporal sequence: first the *h*, then the *a*, then the *t*, one small piece of code after another. The string is short, and the time between its component sounds is minimal, but it is a linear string nonetheless. All words are.

Sign language, however, assembles its words in another mode, where the possibilities for structure go far beyond straight lines. Because the human visual system is better than the auditory system at processing simultaneous information, a language in the visual mode can exploit this potential and encode its signals *simultaneously.* That is exactly what all signed languages do. Whereas words are linear strings, signs are compact bundles of data, in which multiple units of code—handshape, location and movement—are conveyed in virtually the same moment.

Unlike spoken language, sign language possesses two articulators, the left and right hands. These can operate separately or together. While some signs (GRANDFATHER, DOG, TUESDAY, APPLE, SORRY) are made with only one hand, others (BROTHER, SISTER, LANGUAGE, MEAT, COFFEE, SURPRISE) require two. In some of these signs (LANGUAGE, SURPRISE) both hands are in motion. In others (BROTHER, SISTER, MEAT, YEAR) one hand acts on the other, which serves as a stationary base. Right-handed people use their right hand as the dominant hand when signing; left-handers use their left. From the addressee's point of view, the handedness of the signer has no effect on comprehension.

About 60 percent of the signs of ASL are made with both hands. During my time in Israel, I had a hair-raising reminder of just how high that number really is. It was a few days after our trip to Al-Sayyid. The team had gone back to Haifa to look at their data and I had followed them there. One afternoon, Wendy, Carol and I drove to a Druze village southeast of the city. I would like to be able to report that it was in the service of further research. In truth, we were going shopping: the Druze sell marvelous textiles. Wendy was at the wheel, with Carol beside her. I was in back. As Wendy's little car wound over the hairpin turns of the Carmel hills, she and Carol were deep in conversation.

The one-handed signs weren't so bad. At least Wendy got to keep her left hand on the wheel. But during long utterances, filled as they inevitably were with two-handed signs, the car would start to nose its way off the mountainside until Wendy, at the last moment, interrupted what she was saying and pulled it round again. The year before, when I was in negotiations to be allowed to make the trip, I had assured Wendy profusely that I would be the proverbial journalistic fly on the wall. I would never interpose myself in the narrative, and under no circumstances would I attempt to influence the course of events as they unfolded. That day on the mountainside, I failed. As the little red car slipped its moorings for the dozenth time, with the Mediterranean, laid out far, far below, rushing up through the windshield to meet us, a strangled voice rose up from the back seat before I could stop it: *No two-handed signing in the car! No two-handed signing in the car!* But they kept on talking anyway.

You cannot simply mold your hand into a shape, place it somewhere, wave it around and call it ASL. Of the hundreds of thousands of possible combinations of handshape, location and movement, only a particular subset actually occurs in a given sign language. "There are restrictions on what is physically possible to articulate," the linguists Edward Klima and Ursula Bellugi have written. "More importantly, there are arbitrary constraints on the form of signs."

All languages, signed and spoken, have constraints on the form the code can take. In English, a word is allowed to start with three consonants only if the first one is "s," the second is "p," "t" or "k" and the third "l" or "r": "splatter," "street," "scream," "sclerotic." Other combinations, though physically possible, do not occur in English, though they may in other languages. German and Yiddish words, for instance, are allowed to start with "shtr" (the German word for "street" is *Strasse*, pronounced SHTRAS-suh; the Yiddish term for the fur-trimmed hat worn by some Hasidic men is *shtreiml*). To most native English speakers, "shtr" at the start of a word sounds simply un-English. It violates the rules of English phonology, which they unconsciously internalized as very young children. Without constraints like these, human language would be pure anarchy. Constraints circumscribe the borders of the linguistic system, and without a linguistic system there is no way for meaning to be encoded.

In signed languages, there are similar constraints. These, as Stokoe and his disciples would discover, include rules that govern how the hands may be used in combination. One such rule, known as the "symmetry constraint," mandates that in two-handed signs where both hands are active, each hand must have the identical shape. Furthermore, the location of both hands has to be symmetrical: they need to occupy the same vertical or horizontal plane. Finally, the hands must move symmetrically, either as a unit, in mirror image or in strict alternation. In the sign SENTENCE, for instance, the hands are held in front of the body, the thumb and index finger of each hand touching, as in the colloquial gesture "OK"; the hands are then drawn apart in an undulating motion. The net visual effect is one of perfect symmetry. In SURPRISE, the fists, held at the temples, burst open into L shapes. Similarly for DECIDE, which is made with each hand extended in front of the signer in the "OK" position as the arms travel downward from head- to waist-level. JUDGE, by contrast, is made with the same handshapes, and the same extended arms, but this time the hands move alternately up and down, as if "weighing" a decision. "The tendency toward symmetry," the linguists Klima and Bellugi write, "represents another pressure toward systematizing the symbols."

Rules like this are known tacitly by every native signer. It doesn't "feel" like sign language if the moving left hand is in one configuration while the moving right hand is in another. The resulting sign, though perfectly possible physically, is untenable linguistically, "ungrammatical" according to the rules that govern the form of signs. (Linguists believe there is a cognitive reason for the symmetry constraint: though it is possible for the eye to attend to multiple stimuli at once, a sign that employs the hands in competing shapes—playing them off against each other, as it were—demands too great a processing load.) It is the graphic parallelism of the symmetry constraint, I think, that gives the language of fluent signers its characteristic crisp appearance.

Another restriction on the form of signs is known as the "dominance constraint." It affects two-handed signs like BROTHER, ACCURATE and YEAR, in which one hand serves as a base for the other. In signs like these, if the shapes of the active and the base hands differ, then the base hand must assume one of only six prescribed shapes: a flat hand, fingers together; a fist; a flat hand, fingers spread; an extended index finger; an O-shaped hand; or a C-shaped hand.

First identified by the linguist Robbin Battison in the late 1970s, these two constraints, symmetry and dominance, have been found to operate in all known signed languages of the world. The particular set of strictures they impose can differ from one language to another, however: in British Sign Language, for instance, the dominance constraint specifies just four permissible handshapes.

Because of the order these constraints impose, new words can be added to the lexicon with little difficulty: the linguistic system has already provided empty slots to plug them into. Every spoken language contains these slots, wordlike strings of consonants and vowels to which no meaning has yet attached. They *sound like* words but happen not to *be* words. Linguists call these "lexical gaps." English is full of them. Consider "blaff." It has a nice Englishy feel to it, but doesn't mean anything—at least, not yet. (Compare it to a word like "bnaff," which, because English happens to prohibit *bn-* at the start of a word, sounds pretty awful to native ears.)

The same thing occurs in signed languages. While not every permissible combination of handshape, location and movement is realized as an actual sign, to native signers, these hypothetical forms "feel" like signs in ways that proscribed combinations don't. Human language has so strong a desire for systematicity that in many cases a sign that enters the lexicon as an obvious mimetic gesture will change over time to become more arbitrary—that is, more systematic. It does so even if its imitative quality (its iconicity, as linguists call it) gets sacrificed in the bargain.

All languages change with time, and linguists have studied historical change in ASL and other signed languages. There are written descriptions of ASL as it existed in the nineteenth century; in England, there are descriptions of British Sign that date back to the mid-seventeenth century. There is also a marvelous cache of motion picture footage of master American signers, shot between 1910 and 1920 by the National Association of the Deaf in an effort to preserve a documentary record of its beloved language, then under siege from the oralists. To modern linguists, these films offer invaluable evidence of the historical development of sign.

The sign HOME, for instance, was historically a compound, derived, as Klima and Bellugi explain, "from the two highly transparent ASL signs EAT and SLEEP." In EAT, as in the colloquial gesture for eating, one hand appears to bring food to the lips; in SLEEP, which also resembles colloquial gesture, the palm is laid against the cheek, as if the head were resting on a pillow. Originally, HOME was signed by stringing these two signs one after another: EAT + SLEEP. Over time, however, HOME changed. In its modern form, it has coalesced into a single sign, made in one fell swoop: a flattened O hand (the handshape of EAT) moves in a small fluid arc from the jaw to the upper cheek. Drawing on the work of the sign-language linguist Nancy Frishberg, Klima and Bellugi write:

> The current merged sign is no longer a compound: the same handshape prevailed throughout the sign; the contact points moved closer together so that instead of one contact on the

> mouth and one on the cheek there are now two separate contacts on the cheek alone. . . . A consequence of these changes is a complete loss of the iconicity of the original two signs; the sign HOME is now one of the more opaque signs of ASL.

To sign-language linguists, historical evidence like this furnished an elegant and satisfying rebuttal to those who believed sign was merely iconic gesture. "In general," Klima and Bellugi write, "when signs change, they tend strongly to change away from their imitative origins as pantomimic or iconic gestures toward more arbitrary and conventional forms."

When brand-new signs enter the lexicon, they, too, yield to the pull of the linguistic system, even if the lexical slots they wind up filling fail to give them the most iconic representations possible. In the 1970s, Klima and Bellugi saw it happen in their own laboratory, at the Salk Institute for Biological Studies in La Jolla, California. The deaf researchers working with them needed a sign for the reel-to-reel videotape recorder used in the lab; there was no such sign in ASL. The sign they came up with, a two-handed sign made with side-by-side index fingers circling in a counterclockwise direction, perfectly mimed the movement of the reels on the recorder. At least it did at first. "Within a short period of time, however, some of the realism of the representation was lost," Klima and Bellugi write. Without consciously being aware of it, the researchers had altered the movement of the sign, so that it was now made "with the index fingers describing circles that both moved inward." It was unlike the tape recorder, but in line with the symmetry constraint on two-handed signs: now the hands were moving in mirror image.

A minute change, on the surface. But to the linguist studying sign language, it belies the claim that signs are simply holistic gestures or crude pantomime. Here was a sign coined out of necessity, in the service of pure visual mimicry. Signers were physically capable of performing it in the most realistic manner possible, and there should have been every reason to preserve its original form. But practically overnight, this "ideographic" sign was recruited into the *linguistic system* of ASL, with no motivation to change it other than the rage for order all human languages possess in abundance.

In 1960, Stokoe published his early findings as the monograph *Sign Language Structure: An Outline of the Visual Communication Systems of the American Deaf.* In it, he described the signs of ASL as complex linguistic symbols, enacted in space, formed by the rule-governed combination of a finite set of handshapes, locations and movements. It was the first scholarship published in America to treat ASL at all seriously—to recognize it as being a real human language. As Stokoe wrote:

> The work so far accomplished seems to us to substantiate the claim that the communicative activity of persons using this language is truly linguistic and susceptible of micro-linguistic analysis of the most rigorous kind. . . . Moreover, the analysis here presented seems to offer a sound basis . . . for further analysis and description of the structure of this unique, most useful, and linguistically interesting language. Perhaps it is not futile to hope that this work and what it will lead to may eventually make necessary the change of a famous definition to read: "A language is a system of arbitrary *symbols* by means of which *persons in a culture carry on the total activity of that culture.*"

Though considered groundbreaking today, *Sign Language Structure* was all but completely overlooked at the time. That, throughout the course of Stokoe's career, would be one of the kinder responses to his work. To the uninitiated, the monograph could be bewildering. Stokoe used esoteric, hard-to-remember names for the components of sign language he wanted to describe: instead of the plain English terms "handshape," "location" and "movement," which came years later, he used the labels "dez," "tab" and "sig." Where spoken-language linguistics uses the term "phoneme" to describe the sound units of words, Stokoe coined the term "chereme" (KEH-reem, from the

Greek root *cher-*, "hand") to describe the formational units of signs; the analysis of signs he called "cherology." (In recent years, sign-language linguists have reverted to the term "phonology" to describe the formative units of this soundless language and the rules for their combination.)

Stokoe also developed a system for notating signs on paper that, though important, was difficult to use. Employing a series of letters, idiosyncratic squiggles and Greek-like symbols, it recorded every physical nuance of how and where a sign was made. The result, while valuable to sign-language researchers, was almost impossibly unwieldy, requiring a string of abstract symbols to represent just a single sign.

Reaction to his work was nearly undiluted hostility. Few hearing people were disposed to reconsider the long-standing view of "the sign language" as something threadbare and marginal, unfit for human communication. "With the exception of . . . one or two colleagues, the entire Gallaudet faculty rudely attacked me, linguistics, and the study of signing as a language," Stokoe said years afterward.

What is so surprising today is that many deaf people also held this view. Some, mindful of the long paternalistic tradition of hearing people tampering with sign language, distrusted Stokoe's motives. But for others there was something deeper, which betrayed how profoundly the campaign against deaf people and their language had been internalized by the deaf themselves. Eighty years after the Milan congress, most deaf people were utterly persuaded that the language they used every day was substandard. "The worst crime the white man has committed has been to teach us to hate ourselves," Malcolm X wrote. Substitute "hearing" for "white" and you have a pretty accurate picture of what it was like to be deaf in early 1960s America. As Gil Eastman, a deaf member of the Gallaudet faculty who later became one of Stokoe's staunchest advocates, recalled: "My colleagues and I laughed at Dr. Stokoe and his crazy project. It was impossible to analyze our Sign Language."

Stokoe persevered. In 1965, he and two deaf co-authors, Dorothy Casterline and Carl Croneberg, published *A Dictionary of American*

Sign Language on Linguistic Principles. The dictionary, unlike other published lexicons of "the sign language," arranged its thousands of signs neither alphabetically nor by semantic category (lists of foods, colors, kinship terms and so on), but according to their linguistic constituents: handshape, location and movement. For the first time, the structural principles underpinning the signs of ASL were laid out for all to see.

With the publication of the dictionary, attitudes toward Stokoe's work, and toward sign language in general, began very gradually to change. "It was unique to describe 'Deaf people' as constituting a cultural group," Carol has written. "It represented a break from the long tradition of 'pathologizing' deaf people. . . . In a sense the book brought official and public recognition of a deeper aspect of Deaf people's lives: their culture." It was in the dictionary's introduction that the formal name American Sign Language was first conferred on the manual communication system of the American deaf.

Despite Stokoe's growing renown, Gallaudet did not always treat him kindly. In one of a series of indignities, the university administration, where Stokoe still had many detractors, closed his Linguistics Research Laboratory in 1984. Stokoe kept working, doing research on his own and putting out the academic journal *Sign Language Studies,* which he founded in 1972 and which is still published. But his linguistic work remained squarely structuralist, and in the late 1970s, with the Chomsky era well underway, linguists were finding it lacking in rigor. "His role," Carol said, "was more to spread the word."

That he tirelessly did, writing, publishing, traveling, lecturing and encouraging young sign-language scholars, deaf and hearing. By the late 1970s, the next generation of scholars, many of whom came out of Stokoe's lab, was vigorously unpacking the structure of ASL and other signed languages. And the deaf cultural consciousness Stokoe's work helped foster had taken on a clamorous life of its own. It reached a highly public apex in the spring of 1988, when Gallaudet students, protesting the appointment of a hearing woman as the university's new president, shut down the campus for a week to worldwide attention, the Stonewall of the emerging deaf pride movement. Stokoe, at home caring for his wife, who had Alzheimer's disease, watched the protests on television: there were his proud deaf students, making impassioned arguments before the world in the language he had demystified. The students prevailed: the president-elect stepped down, and a deaf man, I. King Jordan, was chosen to fill her place. Later that year, almost three decades after the publication of *Sign Language Structure*, the magnitude of Stokoe's achievement was at last officially recognized: in May of 1988, when William Stokoe was nearly 69 years old, Gallaudet University awarded him an honorary doctorate.

CHAPTER 7

The House of Blue Roses

The founding father of Al-Sayyid came from Egypt in the early nineteenth century. He was a businessman. He journeyed to Palestine, where he settled and bought land. After some time, there was a fight with another family, and he killed a man. In reparation, he gave all his land to the dead man's family and pulled up stakes. He gathered his sons and traveled far away, to another part of Palestine. There, he told his sons to dig a hole in the ground and then fill it back in. They did, and as the man watched, the loose earth sifted down to the bottom of the hole until it lay well below the level of the ground. "This land is no good," he said. So they traveled to another place, and once more the man had his sons dig a hole. Again the earth sank down. "This land is no good," he said. So they traveled until they reached Al-Sayyid. There, the sons dug a hole, and this time, when they filled it in, the earth mounded up into a little hillock, higher than it had been before. "This land is good," the man said, and so they stayed.

Tariq is telling us this story in Hebrew. It is the morning of the team's second day in the village, and we are seated in Tariq's living room. Tariq is a cousin of Omar, our host in the empty house last night; one of his wives is also Omar's half-sister. Tariq is a prosperous man, the owner of several businesses, mostly to do with construction. He has thirteen children, several of whom are deaf. The linguists plan to videotape them this morning.

How do you document a language you've never encountered before? A century ago, linguists in the field relied on pictures and pointing. On one level, the team's mandate today is no different: to coax out hundreds of words—terms for foods, kinship, household objects, parts of the body and more—and the best way to get them is still to show people pictures. That is what the slide show is for. In addition, the team has come armed with a set of testing materials, prepared by the Max Planck Institute for Psycholinguistics in the Netherlands, designed for use with unfamiliar spoken languages. These include the video clips of people walking, sitting and handing one another various objects. They are meant to elicit sentences with subjects, direct objects and indirect objects. To these materials the team has added the set of line drawings, which they hope will elicit particular types of constructions, found in all known signed languages, in which space is used as a grammatical device.

The Max Planck materials are supposed to be "culture-neutral," designed to work anywhere in the world. But in Al-Sayyid, they have produced a few unanticipated results. "The people in the video clips are graduate students who work at the Max Planck Institute," Wendy explained to me several months after the trip. "One was a guy who had jeans and a big shirt and a ponytail, and the other one was a girl with jeans and a big shirt and short hair. And in this traditional society, they had trouble telling who was the man and who was the woman." Eliciting a simple sentence like "The man gives the ball to the woman," the team discovered, proved more complex than expected. "We need to fix that," Wendy said. "We need to have men who look like men according to the criteria they would use."

For the team, another concern in the field is the potential influence, however subtle, of their own presence. Mark recalled the experience of a friend of his, an anthropologist who did long-term fieldwork among the Afar people of Ethiopia. It has been said that in Afar tradition, a man may not marry until he has killed another man. "All those years you lived with them—weren't you afraid?" Mark asked his friend. "Not at all," the anthropologist replied. "I didn't count."

For Mark's friend, a happy outcome. But for the team, "not counting" can mean not being privy to the local language as it is really used. "When people are aware that their speech is being investigated, their self-monitoring devices are turned up," the sociolinguist Dennis Preston has written. "The resulting performances are a combination of their unconscious, most systematic (*vernacular*) language rules and superposed models of schooling, proscription, prescription, erudition, deference, defensiveness, formality, and who knows what else. Because recordings of actual language use awaken this monitor, and because surreptitious collection is difficult, illegal, and/or immoral, sociolinguists are confronted with the *observer's paradox.*"

Mark remembered this happening on a visit he made to Tunisia. "As long as there were any foreigners present, people spoke French," he said. "Every language has its own social situation. It's the language of the home versus the language of the outside."

In Al-Sayyid, the team worries especially that younger villagers who also know some Israeli Sign will be inclined to slip into it in their presence. It happened on their last trip, when they brought along a native ISL signer, a deaf architect from Haifa who works with them as a language consultant. With him around, ISL signs seemed to blossom from these villagers' hands everywhere they turned. This time, they asked the consultant to sit the trip out.

If the samples you collect in the field are inauthentic, extrapolating about the nature of human language becomes a risky venture. "People can use suspect data to talk about really big theories," Mark says. He cites the case of a linguist he knows, born in a provincial village in France, whose family moved to small-town America, isolated from anyone else who spoke their language, when the linguist was a child. The linguist grew up fluent in English, though he continued to speak the family's highly idiosyncratic brand of French at home. At scientific meetings, this man routinely makes sweeping claims about the structure of Standard French based on his oddball family tongue, which is, Mark says, "a language only he speaks." The French linguists in the audience, Mark said, simply roll their eyes in bewilderment.

The linguists had left the hotel right after breakfast and driven straight back to the village. As the van bumped along in the dust, we passed a shepherd with his flock and, just beyond a stand of olive trees, a herd of grazing camels. Hassan had told Mark that camels have come back in fashion here only recently. Although camels, "the ships of the desert," were historically the foundation of Bedouin economic life, here in settled Al-Sayyid the original herd was sold off long ago. Lately, though, they have enjoyed a small renaissance. Their milk is considered healthy to drink, and these days it is something of a status symbol to own one. "Now they're all settled in these big new houses, everyone wants a camel," says Mark.

"Instead of getting a Jacuzzi, you get a camel," Irit observes.

We pull over to wait for Hassan, this time in front of a tin shed that appears to be the village grocery, with stacked pyramids of fruit and vegetables visible through the open doorway. Hassan pulls up and we follow, turning in the opposite direction from yesterday, onto another unpaved road. We drive deeper into the village until we come to a small cluster of whitewashed houses. Al-Sayyid is a web of these clusters, strung out over the hills and connected by a network of narrow dirt paths. Often arranged around a central courtyard or small garden, each compound typically houses members of an extended family.

We stop in front of a house with geraniums blooming beside the door. A girl emerges, wearing a red T-shirt that says "Brazil" on the front. She is Tariq's daughter, one of the deaf children the linguists have come to see. Carol starts to sign to her. "She's twelve," Carol says.

We follow the girl inside. The house is low-ceilinged, dark and cool, with concrete-floored rooms opening off a long central hallway. The rooms are almost completely bare. The balance of the furnishings, we discover, is concentrated in the living room, at the far end of the house. Though small, the room is a lavish affair, with a floor of imitation marble tile. The furniture is huge, and it all matches: three heavy, high-backed sofas and three large armchairs, all upholstered in plush, in a pattern of enormous blue roses on a turquoise ground. Underfoot is a thick Oriental rug in black, gold and cream. A television set rests on a table against one wall, and in a corner, on another table, sits a decorative sculpture: a massive oval of clear glass the size of a suitcase, with a bouquet of artificial flowers encased inside. Above the sculpture, a plastic vine with orange flowers trails up the wall. Through the living room window, a squat palm tree, an abandoned oil drum and a few chickens in a pen are visible behind the house.

We range ourselves on the furniture. One of Tariq's sons, a boy of about eleven, enters and makes a circuit of the room, shaking hands all around. His name is Ali, and he is also deaf. He is an exquisitely beautiful child, with delicate features, gray eyes and high cheekbones. Carol signs to him, "How old are you?" but Ali only looks down shyly and giggles. She asks the boy to show her his room, and they go off together. An older boy brings in a tray of black coffee in tiny glasses. More children appear, carrying cookies and Coca-Cola. Off in a corner, Hassan, again dressed in jeans and a photographer's vest, is helping Irit work out the household's elaborate family tree.

Ali returns with Carol, grinning broadly. Wendy tells Tariq that Carol also comes from a deaf family. "My parents don't speak English," Carol confirms aloud, as Wendy translates into Hebrew. "They can read and write English, but they don't speak it."

In the corner, Hassan is now telling Mark that when he meets Bedouins from other villages, he can understand only about half their spoken Arabic. It sounds distasteful to him, clipped and military, like German, whereas the Arabic of Al-Sayyid sounds lovely and mellifluous, like Italian.

He could just as well be from Alabama. For the past decade, the linguist Dennis Preston has made a specialty of studying "folk linguistics," the set of beliefs, attitudes and prejudices that ordinary people have about language. As Preston and his colleagues have found, what nonlinguists assume to be true about language reveals a great deal about the deep-seated regional, ethnic and class-based prejudices that underlie these beliefs. As Preston writes in an article wonderfully titled "They Speak Really Bad English Down South and in New York City":

> Although linguists believe that every region has its own standard variety, there is widespread belief in the US that some

> regional varieties are more standard than others and, indeed, that some regional varieties are far from the standard. . . . Please understand the intensity of this myth, for it is not a weakly expressed preference; in the US it runs deep, strong and true, and evidence for it comes from what real people (not professional linguists) believe about language variety.

Preston, who teaches at Michigan State University, assessed these entrenched beliefs experimentally. He asked a group of nearly 150 people, all of whom were white, lifelong residents of southeastern Michigan, to rate the fifty states, plus Washington, D.C., and New York City, based on the "correctness" of the English spoken there.

The South fared abysmally. On a scale of 1 to 10, with 10 being "most correct," Texas, Arkansas, Louisiana, Mississippi, Tennessee and Georgia each received a mean score in the 4 range. (Only New York City and New Jersey were rated as low.) Alabama did worst of all, earning the lowest marks in the nation, with a mean rating in the 3 range. Michigan, it so happens, came through with flying colors, ranking first in the nation for "correct" language, with a mean score in the 8 range.

Preston next asked the Michiganders to rate the states based on the "pleasantness" of their language. The results were similar: the "most pleasant" speech in the nation was to be found in Michigan (which was tied with Minnesota, Illinois, Colorado and Washington state), the least pleasant in Alabama and New York City, tied for last place. "Preston has taken this to indicate that northern speakers have made symbolic use of their variety as a vehicle for 'standardness,' 'education,' and widely accepted or 'mainstream' values," Preston and his colleague Gregory Robinson have written.

An interesting wrinkle developed when Preston repeated the study in Alabama. Based on the Michigan results, one would expect Alabamians to rate their own state highest in the country for "correctness." But that's not what happened. Using the same 1-to-10 scale, they rated Alabama toward the bottom of the pack for language "correctness," assigning it (along with more than twenty other states) a mean score in the 5 range. Only Texas, Louisiana, Mississippi and New York City scored lower. Scoring high, though not spectacularly so, was a scattering of states in the 6 range (including Washington, Oregon, Nevada, Minnesota, Illinois, much of the mid-Atlantic and all of New England). The "most correct" language in the nation was that of Maryland, ranked in the 7 range.

It was as if the Alabamians had bought into the prevailing stereotypes about Deep South speech. "Just as one might have suspected," Preston and Robinson write, "Alabamians are much less invested in language 'correctness' (and well they should not be, since they are constantly reminded in popular culture and even personal encounters that their language is lacking in this dimension)."

But as it turned out, the Alabamians *were* invested in something else: an unshakable faith in how pleasing their language sounded. Asked to rate the states for "pleasantness," they put Alabama alone at the top, weighing in with a stellar 8. Michigan and Minnesota, in comparison, though they had been quite highly rated for "correctness," both scored a dismal 4 for "pleasantness." (Only New York City, condemned to a 3, came in lower.) It was as though the Alabamians, having dutifully swallowed the stereotype of their dialect as ignorant, redneck and just plain wrong, compensated by reveling in its sheer pleasantness. Sure, their speech may be backward, they seemed to be saying, but to them it embodied comfort, a pleasing familiarity and, above all, social cohesiveness. "Like all groups who are prejudiced against," Preston writes, "Southerners (and New Yorkers) fight back by making their despised language variety a solidarity symbol."

Historically, the villagers of Al-Sayyid are of low social status. The traditional Bedouin class system comprises four levels, with Bedouins whose ancestors came from Saudi Arabia occupying the highest level. The Al-Sayyid are on the third rung down. Only the descendants of the Sudanese slaves once owned by the first-tier Bedouins are lower. "Among the Bedouins themselves, there's this hierarchy," Irit explained. "The 'real' Bedouins are considered superior to the peasants who settled in the desert," as the people of Al-Sayyid did.

In the living room, Hassan is now locked in passionate discussion with Tariq. They have expanded the debate to take in the dialects of various countries throughout the Middle East. None, they concur, can compare with the beautiful Arabic of Al-Sayyid.

It has been seven generations since the patriarch first arrived in Al-Sayyid. After he settled there, he took a local woman for a wife. They had five sons who lived to adulthood. Two of the sons happened to carry a gene for a recessive form of inherited deafness. All of the deaf people in the village today, geneticists have concluded, are directly descended from these two men. The patriarch's sons married local women as well, but from the third generation on, it became customary for the young men and women of Al-Sayyid to marry within the family, usually to a cousin. Exchange marriage is also traditional here: the daughter of one family is promised to the son of another and, in a symmetrical arrangement, the bride's brother is promised to the groom's sister. As a result of these cultural practices, the gene pool of Al-Sayyid has become tightly circumscribed over time.

In its two centuries of existence, Al-Sayyid has remained remarkably self-contained. Though there are dozens of Bedouin villages scattered throughout Israel, contact with other villages is limited. Because of the low social position of the Al-Sayyid, few other Bedouins condescend to associate with them. In spite of this, many in the village have done well, and Al-Sayyid today is in conspicuous flux. You can see it in the fancy furniture shoehorned into traditional homes like Tariq's, where a generation ago families and their guests sat on hand-loomed rugs on the floor. You can see it in the large modern houses everywhere under construction, with multiple stories, ornate balconies, electric lights and indoor plumbing.

Life has sped up here. Although few of the homes have regular telephones, many people own cell phones now, as well as TVs and VCRs. Just a few years ago, families would sit around the fire on cool evenings and regale one another with stories, in Arabic and sign language. Wendy saw it happen on one of her early visits. No one does that anymore. Carol once asked Hassan what the villagers used to do, in the days before cell phones, when they wanted to arrange to meet. "We walked," he replied. "When I want to go see someone, the young people here say, 'Why don't you just call them on the cell phone?' The older people say, 'I want the eye-to-eye contact.'"

It reminded Carol of something from her own childhood. "When I was growing up, we didn't have a telephone"—by this she means a TTY, the telephone relay device with attached keyboard that until the advent of faxes and e-mail was the primary artery of deaf long-distance communication. "People always dropped by to visit, and we would drive an hour to visit a friend. If they weren't home, we'd turn around and go home again. Or you'd send a letter by prearrangement, with the time." Even today, Carol says, many deaf people of her parents' generation prefer face-to-face contact. "If my parents have to go to the Social Security office, they'd rather do it in person than use the telephone. They don't trust the telephone—they think it's better to go in person."

Of Al-Sayyid's 3,500 residents, about one in twenty-five is deaf—4 percent of the population. For deafness, a rate of 4 percent is a staggering figure: in Israel, as in the United States, the incidence of deafness in the general population is about 0.1 percent, one in a thousand.

It is quite unremarkable to be deaf here. In Al-Sayyid there is neither deaf culture nor deaf identity politics, because there is little hegemony of the hearing. Deaf men do the same kinds of jobs as hearing ones, working in construction or as day laborers in the closest Israeli towns. A few own small herds of goats or cattle; others farm olives and wheat. Deaf villagers go on pilgrimages to Mecca, just as hearing ones do. Most of the deaf adults of the village are married, and all are wed to hearing spouses.

In Al-Sayyid, the deaf are viewed as people who happen to speak a different language, one a large number of hearing villagers also share. Many hearing villagers can sign at least to some extent. Some, like Hassan, are completely bilingual, as fluent in Al-Sayyid Bedouin Sign as they are in spoken Arabic. The hearing child of a deaf parent, or a child with older deaf siblings, often acquires sign language from the cradle, just as the deaf children do.

Tariq's children prove frustrating subjects. Wendy has placed her laptop on a stool at the front of the room, with two plastic chairs positioned nearby. To the accompaniment of a large rooster in the yard, Shai sets up the camera. Wendy seats Tariq's deaf daughter, whose name is Noura, in one of the chairs, with Ali facing her. Carol instructs Noura that she should sign to Ali.

"Should we explain to her to try and use the local signs?" Mark asks.

"Carol explained to her," Irit says.

The slide show begins, and Noura starts to sign. Mark says he's seeing a lot of ISL. "Hassan says he doesn't understand her signs, because a lot of them are Israeli Sign Language," he tells me. Noura moves on to the video clips. When she signs "A man sits down," it looks to the linguists like unreconstructed ISL. They are also concerned that her signing appears diffident; she seems uninterested in her task, and isn't really signing *to* Ali. Shai, behind the camera, is disgusted. "She's too lazy to explain to him what's happening," he mutters darkly in English. "She needs to explain with passion. She's not serious, she's shy."

They decide to have Ali repeat the girl's signing back to her. They resume taping, with the boy now repeating Noura's signs. He seems to be signing with understanding and not merely copying his sister. Carol nods to Noura in approval. "She was not fully *communicative* before," Mark says.

The girl does seem a bit more involved. Now, when Ali doesn't understand what she is trying to convey, Noura shakes her head emphatically and repeats her signing with a little more elaboration. "What do you think, Irit?" Mark asks. "Is the signing more authentic?"

"The signing is not that fluent," Irit says, watching. "It's more restrained. I'm not sure what we're getting from her." They move on to sending and receiving a letter, which Noura, despite repeated efforts, cannot make the boy understand. Tariq asks Mark if he wants to smoke the water pipe.

Wendy has the boy and girl switch places. Tariq reaches over, smiling, and straightens his son's shirt for the camera. Father and son are dressed exactly alike, in jeans and matching polo shirts. Ali starts to sign to Noura. His signs are small and tentative. Wendy gestures to him to sign *to* the girl. She has to tell him several times. They resume the vocabulary. Ali looks at the computer screen, sees Shai's eyeglasses floating there, looks up and points straight at Shai's face. Everyone laughs.

What the linguists will learn by the end of this trip is that when eliciting from Al-Sayyid's deaf children, it works best to have them sign to hearing ones. Because the hearing children don't attend special classes for the deaf, their signing is in many respects more "authentic" than that of their deaf brothers and sisters. Pairing a deaf child with a hearing one, the team will discover, forces the deaf one to revert to "traditional" Al-Sayyid Bedouin Sign, and as a result, much less ISL intrudes.

The linguists tape one more child, a girl a little older than Noura. She is hearing but also signs. Wendy gives the girl instructions in Hebrew, with Ali chiming in from the sidelines in sign language. She starts the test. When she reaches the drawing of the man yelling at the camel, she doesn't understand it. Explanations are offered in Hebrew, Arabic and Al-Sayyid Bedouin Sign, to no avail. They move on to the pictures of emotional states, "happy," "sad," "angry." These images, the linguists are discovering, turn out not to elicit much real vocabulary. The expressions they depict are so universal, that it is easiest for signers just to imitate them. As a result, the sign language of Al-Sayyid has few separate signs for these concepts, because it doesn't really need them. "Anger and sadness are universal across mammals," Mark explains.

The work in this house is finished. As the team packs up to leave, Irit sits with Tariq and, with Hassan's help, completes her questionnaire. "They're talking about deaf siblings and hearing siblings, and they have to figure out who's deaf, who's hearing, whose mother is whose," Mark tells me, listening to the three of them converse in Hebrew. Sorting the tangled skein of kinship, Hassan and Tariq are reminded of a particularly tough case: a woman they knew who was married to four men consecutively, two of them brothers. They debate whether her children by these two men ought to be called siblings or cousins.

The team says its goodbyes. On our way out of the house, we pass the open doorway of one of the children's rooms. The room is nearly empty, except for a table with a computer on it and, just above, a poster of the very blond Olsen twins, Mary-Kate and Ashley, smiling dazzlingly down from the plain whitewashed walls. We step outside. In an open-air kitchen at the front of the house, a woman in a full-length dark blue dress, her hair covered with a white kerchief, is sitting cross-legged on the floor. She is Tariq's first wife, the mother of the hearing girl. She is making the day's pita bread for the household, draping rounds of dough over the dome of a metal oven shaped like a beehive. In front of her is a growing stack of finished pitas, each nearly two feet across and soft as cloth. She takes a circle of bread from the pile and presses it on us, fragrant and still warm.

CHAPTER 8

Everyone Here Speaks Sign Language

There are two ways a new sign language can arise. One is when a group of unrelated deaf people is brought together by an outside agency, like a school or the state. That is what happened in Hartford in 1817, when Thomas Gallaudet and Laurent Clerc opened the Connecticut Asylum. The language that sprang up there, which William Stokoe would one day christen "the American Sign Language," grew out of the ferment of the dozens of homesign systems brought to Hartford by the deaf pupils who came there to study. It is also what happened in Nicaragua just a quarter-century ago.

Until the 1970s, Nicaragua had no widespread education for the deaf. For deaf children there, prospects were as grim as they were in the America of Alice Cogswell's day: they were kept at home, isolated from other deaf people, often a source of shame to their families. Conditions improved somewhat in 1977, when a small private primary school was opened in Managua with about fifty deaf pupils. Real improvement came two years later, with the Sandinista revolution of 1979. Soon after it came to power, the revolutionary government enacted sweeping public health and literacy initiatives. As part of these, the Managua school was nationalized and became much more widely accessible, admitting deaf students of all ages from the surrounding area. By 1983, the primary school, together with a vocational school for deaf adolescents in Managua, had a combined student body of more than four hundred. Suddenly, sustained contact among large numbers of deaf people was possible in Nicaragua. "For the first time," the psychologists Ann Senghas and Marie Coppola write, "a community existed, with continuity from childhood through early adulthood."

All of the students had hearing parents. None had ever been exposed to a full-fledged sign language. In the classroom, they were taught by the oral method, learning to read and write Spanish and, with predictable difficulty, to speak it. But there was something else happening at the same time, for each pupil had brought to school with him the homesigns, known in Spanish as *mímicas,* that he was accustomed to using with his family. Outside the classroom, on the playground and the school buses, students immediately began swapping *mímicas* back and forth, pooling their diverse homesigns for collective use. "As they started to communicate with each other," Senghas and her colleagues have written, "the children began to converge on a common system—an early, rudimentary sign language."

For linguists, the Nicaraguan situation was an unprecedented opportunity. Here at last was their chance to witness the creation of a language from its earliest days. Starting in the 1980s, Judy Kegl, an MIT-trained linguist who wrote her doctoral dissertation on the structure of ASL, began intensive fieldwork at the Managua vocational school. With her husband, she later established a third school for the deaf in the port city of Bluefields. (The village's name is the legacy of the European colonial adventure in Nicaragua.) Since the late 1980s, Ann Senghas, a cognitive psychologist who teaches at Barnard College, has been studying the students at the Managua primary school.

The language of the early Nicaraguan pupils was pretty barebones, not much more than a simple contact argot. It worked best for talking about concrete things: its lexicon contained little more than basic nouns and verbs. Complex sentences were rarely possible. The signs themselves were large, expansive and to a great extent resembled gesture, and the signing was done quite slowly. There was little of the grammatical use of space that is the hallmark of signed languages throughout the world, and only the barest use of the face to convey grammatical information.

During the early 1980s, this rudimentary sign language continued to jell. Each year, a new group of deaf pupils of various ages was admitted to the school, and they picked up the system from the earlier arrivals. But over the next few years, something remarkable occurred: on the hands of the new students, the crude language of the early ones had transformed itself into something fast and streamlined. It was far more complex than the original, exploiting space to construct elaborate phrases and sentences—it had grammar, in other words, where none had existed before. It was an act of linguistic creation, done spontaneously, unconsciously and without formal instruction, in the space of just a single academic "generation."

This new sign language, Kegl, Senghas and Coppola write in a joint article, "is crisper, more fluid and articulated in a small signing space. . . . The output is multifaceted and orchestrated, with a distinct rhythm and flow. The face . . . is used more systematically and in more grammatically distinctive ways."

As the researchers discovered, the year a child entered the school turned out to be decisive. Students who had arrived before 1983 (the "first cohort") never progressed beyond the simple signed argot. But those entering after 1983 (the "second cohort"), in particular the very young ones, wound up speaking full-blown Nicaraguan Sign Language. "The youngest members of the second cohort, as children, surpassed their input, taking a partially developed language and systematizing it in a specific way," Senghas and Coppola write.

How had this happened, spontaneously and without instruction, in the space of just a few years?

Children make language. In every generation, they take the nebulous linguistic wash around them and, without consciously trying, shape it into something cogent and systematic. They are uniquely well suited to the task. As Senghas and Coppola point out, "Children surpass adults at learning languages, even though adults are better at mastering most other complex bodies of knowledge." A child exposed to a second language—and a third and a fourth and a fifth—will acquire it in just the same way: effortlessly, unconsciously and with the fluency of a native speaker.

These linguistic halcyon days soon come to an end. For neurological reasons that are still not well understood, our inborn ability to suck languages out of the environment begins to wane with the onset of adolescence or even sooner. From then on, learning a second language is no longer the spontaneous product of immersion and instinct. It now requires formal instruction, is accomplished with concerted effort, and is rarely mastered with the proficiency of a native. It is as if the language organ, having done its work energetically in early childhood, is now spent. As linguists have grumbled for years, one of the enduring ironies of foreign language instruction in American public schools is that it starts so wildly, inappropriately late—usually around the seventh grade—just when most children have passed out of the period in which they could pick up another language without a second thought.

But youth and biology alone will not allow the mind to make language. There must also be experience, in the form of continued exposure to one or more native tongues. It is this welter of unsifted data, this rush of English or Gujarati or American Sign the child is exposed to, that appears to set the bioprogram in motion. And it is this formless mass of data, in turn, that the bioprogram attacks, imposing order by supplementing the impoverished areas by means of an innate linguistic "script." That, until a certain age (about ten in some estimates; as early as five or six in others), is what each of us is biologically equipped to do. Linguists call these formative years the "critical period" for language acquisition.

Failure to provide exposure to language during this time can have devastating consequences. In a vacuum, the bioprogram cannot work, and the result is profound, irreversible language impairment. In the rare documented cases of "feral children," left to grow up on their own with little or no human contact, a recurrent theme is that even once they have been rescued and vigorously tutored, these children never master more than the crudest command of language. For language acquisition, it is simply too late: the critical period has come and gone. This is the reason, too, that the deaf children of hearing parents risk being cut off from human language altogether if they are not exposed to signing early. As Kegl, Senghas and Coppola have written, "Deaf individuals left in their homesigning environment past their critical period for language development show permanent effects of language deprivation and even with subsequent intensive exposure are unable to acquire even the rudimentary aspects of human-language grammar beyond naming."

The deaf children of Nicaragua made language, and they did it in especially unusual circumstances. For them, there was no mother tongue: there were no fluent, signing parents in their midst to pass a familiar native language along. What they had instead was a group of older schoolmates. The language of the older students wasn't really a language at all, just a rudimentary argot born of assembled homesigns. But for the new arrivals, this impoverished stimulus was enough. As Senghas and Coppola write:

> Over their first several years together, the first cohort, as children, systematized these resources in certain ways, converting raw gestures and homesigns into a partially systematized system. This early work evidently provided adequate raw materials for the second-cohort children to continue to build the grammar.

Among the new pupils, Senghas and her colleagues found, it was with the children ten and younger that grammatical innovation originated. Those who had entered the community at seven or below attained particular fluency. Significantly, these young children had far less signing experience than their older peers did. By the late 1980s, the first cohort had been signing together for nearly a decade, while the new arrivals had been exposed to sign for only a year or two. But the essential difference was age: most of the new pupils were young enough to be squarely within the critical period for language acquisition. It was these children who took the impoverished input of their elders and unconsciously gave it grammar. And in so doing, they created a full-blown language where none had existed before.

Where the language of the older Nicaraguan children was slow, heavily reliant on gesture and made little use of the face, the younger children's signing was faster, more systematized and began to exploit facial expression to signal sentences of different types. In a yes-or-no question ("Are you hungry?" "Is Papa here?"), the children's signing was accompanied by raised eyebrows, a protrusion of the head and a shrug of the shoulders. WH-questions (which start with "who," "what," "where," "when," "why" or "how") were marked by a strong wrinkle of the nose. Above all, the sentences of these young pupils were far more complex. One reason for this was the grammatical deployment of three-dimensional space.

In all languages, one of the tasks of grammar is to establish the relationships among various elements of the sentence, the who-did-what-to-whom of syntax. Actors must be linked with the corresponding actions; descriptive words with the things they modify; pronouns with the nouns they refer back to. Spoken languages do this in a variety of ways. Some, like English, rely primarily on a rigid word order to convey who is the actor and who is the acted-upon: to any native speaker, the sentence "The man bites the dog" is unequivocal in terms of who is doing the biting. Similarly, in "Brutus sent the big man the book" we know it is the man that is big; by contrast, in "Brutus sent the man the big book," the change in word order tells us it is the book.

Other languages may instead alter the form of words, using devices like prefixes and suffixes to encode grammatical relationships. In Latin, "The man bites the dog" can be rendered either "Vir can*em* mordet" or, for special emphasis, "Can*em* vir mordet." In either instance, it is the inflections of the nouns—where man (*vir*) is nominative and dog (*canem*) accusative—and not the order of the words, that shows unambiguously who bites whom. In the sentence "Brutus sent the big man the book"—"Brutus vir*o* magn*o* librum misit"—it is again inflection rather than word order that tells the listener which elements of the sentence go together: here, "big" (*magno*) and "man" (*viro*) are marked by their suffixes as referring to the same entity. On the other hand, in "Brutus sent the man the big book"—"Brutus magn*um* viro libr*um* misit"—it is "big" (*magnum*) and "book" (*librum*) that share the common reference.

Sign languages can also indicate shared grammatical reference, but they do it by linking the shared elements visually, in three-dimensional space. In signed conversations, not only the hands and fingers but the arms, head and torso are in motion, and the world's mature signed languages exploit the available space in the quarter-sphere defined horizontally by the sweep of the signer's arms from extreme right to extreme left, and extending vertically from the top of the signer's head down to the waist. Within this large area signs can be made—and matched—in a kind of spatial concord. A sign for a verb ("bite") can travel through space from a particular spot, previously established in the conversation, that represents the actor (the man), to another, representing the thing acted upon (the dog). A noun can be signed in a certain location, say, off to the signer's left, and, later in the sentence, an adjective signed in the same spot is understood to refer back to it. This, as Senghas and Coppola write, is what the younger Nicaraguan signers had spontaneously begun to do:

> We believe this use of a common location can link the signs grammatically (e.g., a noun and its adjective, or a verb and its object). For example the sign "cup" in spatial location A, followed by the sign "tall," also in location A, could indicate that "tall" modifies "cup." Similarly, "see," "push" and "pay" might be produced in a common direction to indicate that different events happened to one man: He was seen, pushed, and paid. . . . This use enables long-distance grammatical relationships among words, and brings the language closer to other, older sign languages.

The first Nicaraguan cohort had relied heavily on word order to convey grammatical relationships. That is what very young languages, signed or spoken, tend to do. But the second cohort infused the language with spatial grammar. The result was longer, more complex sentences that were far less dependent on word order to convey grammatical relations. Now, the relationships between widely separated words could be conveyed without ambiguity. The young signers, in short, had taken the crude language of the older ones and *grammaticized* it. While the signing of the first cohort, Kegl and her colleagues write, "marks the beginning of the linguistic use of gesture," that of the second cohort "marks a quantum leap to a full-fledged signed language."

The birth of Nicaraguan Sign Language generated considerable media attention. It was trumpeted in the popular press as a naturally occurring Forbidden Experiment, a window on the bioprogram in action. Though few articles were able to explore the underlying theoretical issues in depth, the idea of Nicaraguan Sign captured the public imagination off and on during the closing decade of the twentieth century. For their part, the investigators in Nicaragua have been more cautious: they know better than anyone that the grammar of a language, even a very young one, can take a lifetime to dissect. Led by Judy Kegl in Bluefields and Ann Senghas in Managua, the research into Nicaraguan Sign Language continues.

As a young language, created by children from impoverished input, Nicaraguan Sign Language looked a great deal like something that linguists, on the trail of the bioprogram, had already encountered: a creole. Beginning in the 1970s, researchers came to believe that creole languages, like those of Jamaica, Haiti and many parts of Africa, had much to tell them about the workings of the human language instinct.

Most scholars believe that creoles start life as pidgins, auxiliary languages born of necessity. The British and French colonial enterprises in Africa produced a spate of pidgins, as African speakers of mutually unintelligible languages were thrust side by side onto the same plantations. The Atlantic slave trade, with its radical dislocation of populations, likewise gave rise to pidgins throughout the Americas and the Caribbean.

A pidgin is no one's first language. Rather, it serves as a lingua franca, enabling communication among speakers forced to pool their linguistic resources in a hurry. As a rule, pidgins are heavy on basic nouns and verbs—good for naming things, and for creating very simple sentences. Grammatically, they are skeletal, with little in the way of word endings or other inflections. To convey grammatical relationships within sentences, for instance, pidgins usually rely on fixed word order. "The speech of pidgin speakers," the linguist Derek Bickerton has written, is "extremely rudimentary in structure."

Pidgins look a lot like the rough signed argot of the first Managua students. And, like the early Nicaraguan system, a pidgin can change radically, in the space of just one generation. All it takes is for the pidgin to be acquired by children as a native language—to find its way into the mouths of babes. Then, without having been taught to do so, the children transform it into a creole: a richer, more complex system, in short, a "real" language. As Bickerton writes:

> It is hypothesized that creole languages are largely invented by children and show fundamental similarities, which derive from a biological program for language. . . . It is suggested that the bioprogram provides a skeletal model of language which the child can then readily convert into the target language.

These children have taken their parents' rude lingua franca and given it grammar. The result is no longer a simple contact argot but a full-blown language, boasting the complex sentences and grammatical concord that pidgins do not have. This is exactly what the youngest Nicaraguans did in creating a language from their predecessors' jumble of homesigns. For this reason, most linguists consider Nicaraguan Sign Language to be a creole itself, born in the benign "plantation" setting of the Managua school, when a new generation of pupils acquired the primitive signed pidgin of their elders as a native language.

In the early 1970s, Bickerton, who taught for many years at the University of Hawaii, made extensive field recordings of Hawaiian

Pidgin English, a contact language developed among the immigrants from the Far East and elsewhere who had come to Hawaii in the early twentieth century to work the sugar plantations. Among the pidgin sentences he collected from these immigrants, now old men and women, were the following:

> Mi kape bai, mi chaek meik. ("He bought my coffee; he made me out a check.")
>
> Bilding—hai pleis—wal pat—taim—nautaim—aen den—nau tempicha eri taim sho you. ("There was an electric sign high up on the wall of the building which showed you what time and temperature it was.")

The pidgin "sentences" are mainly strings of nouns, with few or no verbs. They have no copula, which lends them their characteristic telegraphic style. Though they may retain small fragments of the grammar of their parent languages, on the whole, as Bickerton writes, they "have no recognizable syntax." Pidgins have no consistent means of expressing past, present or future tense; nor can they express mood (indicative, imperative, subjunctive) or aspect (whether an action is completed or in progress). They have little to no grammatical inflection. With such barren grammar, the expressive capabilities of pidgins are also severely curtailed: there can be no complex assertions, no embedded sentences, no grammatical construction more complicated than a single clause.

Creoles, by contrast, show many more of the hallmarks of real language. They have copulas. They contain much more complex sentences, employing syntactic structures like relative clauses. Bickerton cites the following examples of Hawaiian Creole English, spoken by the children of the early-twentieth-century plantation workers, who had acquired Hawaiian Pidgin as their native tongue:

> Wan dei haed pleni av dis mauntin fish kam daun. ("One day there were a lot of these fish from the mountains that came down [the river].")

Samtaim dei stei kam araun, polis. ("Sometimes the police used to come around.")

To a speaker of Standard English, these sentences may look primitive at first glance, little different from pidgin. But underneath their nonstandard exteriors lies a range of grammatical devices far more sophisticated than those found in pidgins. The first sentence actually makes use of a relative clause: ". . . dis mauntin fish *kam daun*." Though the clause has no overt relative pronoun (the "that" of the English translation), clauses like this are grammatically permissible in Hawaiian Creole English, and serve the same syntactic function as their Standard English counterparts.

In the second sentence, we see a verb grammatically marked for aspect. Here, the word *stei* in front of the verb indicates the "durative" aspect: "the police *used to* come around." *Stei* is clearly a functional, and necessary, part of Hawaiian Creole grammar. Without it, as Bickerton points out, the sentence would have a logically impossible meaning: "Sometimes the police came around once."

In creoles, grammar is created where there was none before. Like the fledgling sign language of Nicaragua, creoles are created by children, without instruction, from degenerate input. And, because of the historical circumstances that gave rise to them, the creoles in use today are young languages, free of the grammatical deadweight of many established ones. Could creole languages, as linguists increasingly began to wonder, be another way to get at the bioprogram?

Bickerton has spent the last three decades comparing creoles from around the world. Historically, these creoles have sprung from hundreds of different languages, perhaps even a thousand. Between 1500 and 1900, many creoles were formed from the forced marriage of local languages with those of the great imperial powers: English, French, Spanish, Portuguese and Dutch. Others, like Hawaiian Creole (an amalgam of English, Chinese, Japanese, Korean, Portuguese, several languages of the Philippines and indigenous Hawaiian), are the product of a diverse group of immigrants working in the same place. But for all their disparate origins, Bickerton and his colleagues have found, creoles display a surprising number of structural similarities. As the linguist and social critic John McWhorter has written, "The languages traditionally identified as creoles are indeed definable linguistically as well as sociohistorically."

It is not only that creoles contain "more grammar" than the pidgins they came from. It is the *form* this grammar takes that is strikingly similar from one creole to the next. For one thing, creole languages (like pidgins) contain virtually no inflectional affixes—the prefixes and suffixes that many established languages use to convey grammatical information. This dearth of affixes, as McWhorter points out, appears to be a function of the emergency cognitive conditions that give rise to creoles:

> The paucity of inflection in creoles initially results, of course, from the fact that the rapid non-native adoption of a language as a lingua franca entails stripping down a system to its essentials, for optimal learnability and processibility. The natural result is the virtual or complete elimination of affixes. . . . Even when all of the groups in a contact situation speak highly inflected languages, a pidgin or creole resulting from this contact nevertheless usually has little or no inflection.

What is more, the grammatical constructions that *do* occur in creole languages turn up in creole after creole around the globe. One such construction, known as "verb serialization," can be seen in the following examples from Hawaiian Creole English:

Dei gon *get* naif *pok* you. ("They will stab you *with a knife.*")
Dei *wawk* fit *go* skul. ("They went to school *on foot.*")

Here, the use of two verbs in sequence (*get* and *pok* in the first sentence; *wawk* and *go* in the second) serves the same function that grammatical case does in many established languages—it signals the relationship between actors. By means of serial verbs, these Hawaiian Creole sentences are able to encode a relationship that in languages like Finnish and Hungarian is marked with the instrumental case: "*with a knife.*"

The use of serial verbs to convey various kinds of grammatical relationships is found in creoles throughout the world. Strikingly, it is also found in Nicaraguan Sign Language. The sentence meaning "A man pushes a woman" is signed MAN WOMAN PUSH FALL (or, alternatively, MAN PUSH FALL WOMAN). Here, the use of serial verbs (PUSH FALL) functions, as Senghas and her colleagues write, to indicate "how subjects and objects are linked to their respective verbs." To a speaker of Nicaraguan Sign, the sentences are unequivocal as to who is pushing (the man) and who is being pushed (the woman). The existence of these constructions both in creoles and Nicaraguan Sign Language, as Kegl, Senghas and Coppola write, "at least points to the possibility that [serial verb constructions] can be a natural concomitant of language emergence."

Researchers have found serial verbs in still another kind of emerging language: children's acquisition of their mother tongue. The linguist Robert Wilson recorded the developing utterances of a two-year-old called Seth. At the age of twenty-seven months, as Bickerton reports, Seth began to produce sentences like these:

> "Let Daddy *hold* it *hit* it" (meaning "Let Daddy hit the ball *with the bat*").
> "Let Daddy *get* a pen *write* it" (meaning "Let Daddy write it *with the pen*").

Constructions like these, which have been observed in the utterances of some young children, look strikingly like the serial-verb structures of creole languages. Here, too, they are used to signal an "instrumental" relation between actors: "*with the bat,*" "*with the pen.*" "At the time," Bickerton writes, "Seth had not acquired the preposition *with.*" When he acquired it a short time later, "serial instrumentals ceased, and prepositional phrases using instrumental *with* replaced them."

The parallels between child language and creoles are more than superficial. It's not that creoles, or the people who speak them, are in any way childlike. It is, rather, that speakers of both creoles and child language must draw on the bioprogram to supplement the impoverished linguistic data to which they are exposed. In the case of creoles, this linguistic input is especially bankrupt: a child acquiring a creole is getting nothing like the full, rich native language of her parents, but is exposed to the bare-bones linguistic anarchy of a pidgin. In the acquisition of creoles, Bickerton writes, "the normal generation-to-generation transmission of language is severely disrupted." As a result, many linguists now believe, the child must tacitly draw on the bioprogram to "fill in the gaps," allowing her to convert the impoverished input into a full-fledged linguistic system.

The more impoverished the input, Bickerton argues, the more heavily the child must rely on the bioprogram to make up the difference. As he wrote in 1984:

> The innovative aspects of creole grammar are inventions on the part of the first generation of children who have a pidgin as their linguistic input, rather than features transmitted from preexisting languages. The [Language Bioprogram Hypothesis] claims . . . that such inventions show a degree of similarity, across wide variations in linguistic background, that is too great to be attributed to chance. Finally, the LBH claims that the most cogent explanation of this similarity is that it derives from the structure of a species-specific program for language, genetically coded and expressed, in ways still largely mysterious, in the structures and modes of operation of the human brain.

Like signed languages, creoles appear to furnish linguists with a version of their long-sought Forbidden Experiment. Creoles are young languages, sprung from the minds of children in the course of a single generation, unburdened by the ornate grammar that established languages contain. Studying the structure of creoles, as many linguists came to believe, could be a way to force the contents of the bioprogram to light.

But while creoles come close to duplicating the Forbidden Experiment, from a scientific standpoint they are imperfect models. In reality, every creole "comes from" somewhere: it originates as a pidgin. This pidgin in turn originated through contact between long-established languages like English, French, Dutch, Chinese, Japanese, Swahili and others. Every creole, in other words, has identifiable antecedents, and as a result may show marks of influence from one or more of its linguistic parents.

Even Nicaraguan Sign Language, a creole born from the signed pidgin of the early deaf pupils, proves less than ideal, for it did not originate in the most conventional way possible. Instead, the team argues, the circumstances that gave rise to it were socially engineered, created with the establishment of schools for deaf children.

For creole linguists, as for their sign-language counterparts, the ideal language would be one that arose completely on its own, with no discernible parent languages, in the most organic human way possible. A language that is what linguists call "autochthonous," from the Greek *autōkhthōon,* "one sprung from the land itself." It is Mark's favorite word. That is exactly what happened on Martha's Vineyard three centuries ago, and it brings us to the second way a new sign language can arise.

In 1978, the medical anthropologist Nora Ellen Groce was driving around the Vineyard with Gale Huntington, a longtime resident then in his eighties. They drove past a house that had belonged to a neighbor, now long dead, a man named Jedidiah. As she recounts in her book *Everyone Here Spoke Sign Language:*

> "He was a good neighbor," said Gale. "He used to fish and farm some. He was one of the best dory men on the Island, and that was pretty good, considering he had only one hand."
>
> "What happened to the other one?" I asked.
>
> "Lost it in a mowing machine accident when he was a teenager." As an afterthought, he added, "He was deaf and dumb too."
>
> "Because of the accident?" I asked.
>
> "Oh, no," said Gale. "He was born that way."

A little farther on, Huntington pointed out another house, which had belonged to Jedidiah's brother Nathaniel, a prosperous dairyman:

> "He was considered a very wealthy man—at least by Chilmark standards. Come to think of it, he was deaf and dumb too."
>
> I wondered aloud why both brothers had been born deaf. Gale said no one had ever known why; perhaps the deafness was inherited. I suggested that it might have been caused by disease. But Gale didn't think so, because there were so many deaf people up-Island, and they were all related. There had been deaf Vineyarders as long as anyone could remember. . . .
>
> "How many deaf people were there?" I asked.
>
> "Oh," said Gale, "I can remember six right offhand, no, seven."
>
> "How many people lived in town here then?"
>
> "Maybe two hundred," Gale replied, "maybe two hundred fifty. Not more than that."
>
> I remarked that that seemed to be a very large number of deaf people in such a small community. Gale seemed surprised but added that he too had occasionally been struck by the fact that there were so many deaf people. . . . When he was a boy in the early 1900's, ten deaf people lived in the town of Chilmark alone.

Groce's professional interest was piqued. She decided to research the history of deafness on the island, in an attempt to determine how it came to be so widespread. On her next visit, she sat down with Huntington and recorded everything he could tell her about the deaf villagers:

> I had already spent a good part of the afternoon copying down various genealogies before I thought to ask Gale what the hearing people in town had thought of the deaf people.
>
> "Oh," he said, "they didn't think anything about them, they were just like everyone else."
>
> "But how did people communicate with them—by writing everything down?"

"No," said Gale, surprised that I should ask such an obvious question. "You see, everyone here spoke sign language."

"You mean the deaf people's families and such?" I inquired.

"Sure," Gale replied . . . "and everybody else in town too."

As Groce would learn, an indigenous signed language, spoken by deaf and hearing villagers alike, flourished on Martha's Vineyard from the early 1700s to the mid-1900s. It was localized in the two "up-Island" towns of West Tisbury and Chilmark, near the western end of the island. In these towns, a form of hereditary deafness had been passed along for decades, concentrated through settlement patterns and intermarriage until it reached unusually high proportions. The signed language that had sprung up as a result, spoken by almost the entire population of the two towns, endured for twelve generations, a good 250 years.

The language was everywhere. At the combination post office and general store, a group of men, deaf and hearing, would sit and pass the time swapping stories in sign. In church, hearing adults would sign the pastor's sermon to their deaf spouses. Deaf children signed with hearing playmates. Neighbor signed to neighbor, customer to tradesman. There was signing between courting couples, at town meetings and clambakes and socials. The language was even used by hearing villagers when no deaf people were present. A group of men telling a risqué story would, if a lady entered the room, turn their backs and finish the tale in sign. It was also extremely useful on the water, for communication between fishing boats, where distance precluded shouting. "The entire community," Groce writes, "was bilingual in English and sign language."

Even at the end of the nineteenth century, with oralism dominating the rest of the country, Vineyarders held steadfastly to their signed language, which was known on the island as "deaf and dumb." As *The Boston Sunday Herald* wrote in 1895:

> There has never been any attempt made to send any of the congenitally deaf children to oral schools. The feeling, in fact, is so

> strong in favor of the prevalence of a non-speaking race that any one who should go there and offer by the use of some magician's wand to wipe out the affliction from the place and to prevent its recurrence, would almost be regarded as a public enemy and not as a benefactor.

On the Vineyard, there was no stigma attached to being deaf. Deaf villagers owned property, married (most to hearing partners) and worked the same kinds of jobs as their neighbors. Men fished and farmed, or plied manual trades like blacksmithing and carpentry. Some deaf women took in ironing, or worked as seamstresses. As Groce writes: "Perhaps the best description of the status of deaf individuals on the Vineyard was given to me by an island woman in her eighties, when I asked about those who were handicapped by deafness when she was a girl. 'Oh,' she said emphatically, 'those people weren't handicapped. They were just deaf.'"

The first known deaf Vineyarder was a man named Jonathan Lambert. Lambert was born on Cape Cod in 1657 and moved to the Vineyard in 1694, settling in Tisbury. He had married a woman, Elizabeth Eddy, who by all accounts was hearing. Two of the couple's seven children were born deaf. Sifting the archival record, Groce began to piece together the genealogy of Vineyard deafness. She determined that the genetic mutation responsible for it could not have originated with Lambert himself, but came instead from one of his ancestors:

> The origin of a trait for deafness that will follow a classical recessive inheritance pattern presumably begins with a single genetic mutation in an individual. That is, a gene affecting one aspect of the neural or anatomic development of the hearing mechanism is altered in such a way that normal development does not occur. The result of such a mutation is not evident in that individual, as Mendel showed. The individual carrying the mutant gene, however, may pass it on to some or all of his or her children. If a descendant of these children then mates with

another descendant of the person in whom the mutation first occurred, the offspring may receive a gene for deafness from each parent, be homozygous for that trait, and thus deaf.

Groce traced the mutation back to a small group of English families who inhabited the same part of rural Kent, an isolated region known as the Weald. The Weald was a Puritan stronghold, and in 1634, several families from the area, spurred by economic motives as well as religious persecution, set sail for the Massachusetts Bay Colony. After landing in Boston, they moved to Scituate, where some earlier Kentish immigrants had settled. Five years later, after a doctrinal argument split the community, many of the Weald families followed their pastor to the town of Barnstable, on Cape Cod. "Barnstable continued to grow," Groce writes, "but the Kentish contingent remained the single largest regional group in town." In this tight-knit community, many of the children and grandchildren of the original Weald group would eventually intermarry.

In the 1660s, with the population of Barnstable swelling, several of the Weald families, desiring more land, moved across the sound to Martha's Vineyard. By the end of the seventeenth century, many Cape Codders of Kentish ancestry had resettled on the Vineyard. One of them was Jonathan Lambert. His daughter Beulah, the first known deaf person native to the Vineyard, was born in Tisbury in 1704.

Tisbury and Chilmark were quite insular. Most people born there remained in their hometowns for the rest of their lives. Villagers fraternized among themselves almost exclusively; in the days of horse travel and rough roads, it was rare to socialize with anyone who lived farther away. Young people were likely to marry someone with whom they'd grown up. Marriages between first cousins, Groce writes, were "fairly common"; those between second or third cousins even more so. "Because marriage between cousins was permitted, and because there was very little new blood to choose from on a relatively isolated island, as generations passed, lines of descent on the Vineyard became entangled," she writes.

By the late 1700s, as Groce discovered, more than 96 percent of married villagers were wed to a blood relation. By the mid-1800s, "almost 85 percent of the second cousins who married on the Island were also related as third, fourth, or fifth cousins through other lines of descent." As these marriage patterns continued, the gene pool became more tightly circumscribed, and "the chances of deaf children being born," Groce wrote, "rose with every generation." Forty-five deaf children were born on the island during the 1840s alone. On the Vineyard as a whole, the average number of deaf people was one in 155. In the village of Tisbury, it was one in forty-nine.

The rate was even higher in Chilmark. By the mid-nineteenth century, one villager in twenty-five there was deaf, the same rate as Al-Sayyid's today. In a particular Chilmark neighborhood of about sixty people, the rate was an astronomical one in four. "In all," Groce writes, "in a town whose average population was only 350 from the eighteenth to the twentieth century, 39 individuals are known to have been born deaf."

In 1895, when the *Boston Sunday Herald* reporter visited the island, its lively indigenous signed language was very much in evidence:

> You make a neighborly call—they don't have such things as afternoon teas. The spoken language and the sign language will be so mingled in the conversation that you pass from one to the other, or use both at once, almost unconsciously. Half the family speak, very probably, half do not, but the mutes are not uncomfortable in their deprivation, the community has adjusted itself to the situation so perfectly.

Regrettably, there is no documentary record of what this language looked like. Although Martha's Vineyard Sign Language would influence the shape of ASL (from the 1820s on, the island's deaf children were sent to Hartford for their education), anecdotal evidence suggests it may have been quite different. By the time Groce began her work, there were no deaf Vineyarders living, but she did interview many older hearing residents who knew how to sign. "My informants remembered signs for many specific words that were different from the ASL signs," she writes, "and Islanders who recalled the language commonly said that they found it very difficult or impossible to understand the sign language spoken by deaf off-Islanders or the occasional translations for the deaf on television."

Martha's Vineyard Sign Language appears to have resembled British Sign, suggesting it may already have been in use in England among the intermarried families of the Weald. In the late 1970s, linguists elicited samples of Martha's Vineyard Sign Language from elderly hearing islanders and showed them to a deaf British signer. He identified 40 percent of the signs as having British cognates. An American signer, by contrast, found only a 22 percent overlap with ASL.

By the early twentieth century, with an influx of new residents to the island, Vineyard deafness had come to an end. The last deaf signer died in 1952. In the 1980s, the neurologist Oliver Sacks, fired by reading Groce's book, leapt into his car and drove to the island to see if he could find traces of the language still extant:

> My first sight of this, indeed, was quite unforgettable. I drove up to the old general store in West Tisbury on a Sunday morning and saw half a dozen old people gossiping together on the porch. They could have been any old folks, old neighbors, talking together—until suddenly, very startlingly, they all dropped into Sign. They signed for a minute, laughed, then dropped back into speech. At this moment, I knew I had come to the right place.

Among the people Sacks observed in the village was one very elderly woman:

> This old lady, in her nineties, but sharp as a pin, would sometimes fall into a peaceful reverie. As she did so, she might have seemed to be knitting, her hands in constant complex motion.

> But her daughter, also a signer, told me she was not knitting but thinking to herself, thinking in Sign. And even in sleep, I was further informed, the old lady might sketch fragmentary signs on the counterpane—she was dreaming in Sign.

The first deaf children were born in Al-Sayyid seventy years ago, about ten of them in a single generation. Hassan's father was one of these children. So was Omar's. These ten children turned out to be the first link in a chain of deaf villagers that is now three generations long. By the time of our visit, only one member of the first deaf generation was still alive, an elderly woman too infirm to be interviewed. Today, the 150 or so deaf people of Al-Sayyid include the second generation, men and women in their thirties and forties; and the third generation, their children.

When they were small, the first-generation signers had developed systems of gestures to communicate with their families. "What they were doing was homesign, only there were ten of them," Wendy explained. The fact that so many homesigners had appeared in close proximity meant that a functional pidgin could develop quickly. And in just one generation, the children of these signers, like children of pidgin speakers everywhere, took their parents' signed pidgin and gave it grammar, spontaneously transforming it into a creole, the signed language of Al-Sayyid. These children, deaf and hearing, are the men and women of Hassan's generation. "They're the first generation to have a signing model, and the model was the first ten deaf people in the tribe," Wendy said. Although it is impossible to reconstruct what their parents' signed pidgin looked like, she explained, "I bet it's very different from what these forty-year-olds are doing."

In Al-Sayyid, the three ingredients necessary for an organic sign language had come together in one place: hereditary deafness, isolation and intermarriage. But there was also a fourth ingredient, and it is this, combined with the first three, that helps create a "signing village," a place where the entire community (and not merely its deaf residents) speaks sign language. Whenever a signing village arises, researchers have discovered, the gene responsible for its deafness is almost always recessive.

There are many ways to become deaf. Deafness can result from accident, aging or from a childhood illness like scarlet fever. During the mid-1960s, thousands of children were born deaf because their mothers had contracted rubella during pregnancy. Besides these acquired types of deafness, there are also inherited kinds, transmitted along generational lines. There are many forms of hereditary deafness; estimates range from seventy to one hundred different varieties. Of these, some are genetically dominant, others recessive.

When they are passed down in a community, dominant and recessive traits distribute themselves very differently. With a dominant trait, a single mutated gene is all that is required for a child to inherit the condition. In families with a dominant type of hereditary deafness, there is at least a one in four chance of producing a deaf child if just one of the parents is deaf. If both parents are deaf, the likelihood rises to at least 75 percent. The result, for dominant traits, is a kind of de facto segregation within the community: the inherited condition occurs only in certain families, and everyone in town knows exactly which families those are.

In a village where a dominant form of hereditary deafness is prevalent, a spontaneous sign language may well arise. But when it does, as Harlan Lane and his colleagues have discovered, it is almost always "walled off," used only by the deaf villagers and their immediate families. Though the deaf families may not be overtly stigmatized, they are seldom integrated into community life as fully as the deaf villagers of Martha's Vineyard were. A "dominant" village will have people in it who sign, but it probably won't be a signing village.

Recessive traits, by contrast, are much more atomized. Here, it requires two genes with the identical mutation—one from each parent—for the condition to appear. In a family with just one deaf parent, the chance of having a deaf child is fairly small: the hearing parent would need to be a carrier of the gene for it even to be possible. Recessive traits tend to "skip generations," sometimes many generations, in families. In an insular community, where marriage between cousins has concentrated the gene pool, recessive deafness may in fact crop up frequently, but it does so, as Groce writes, "seemingly at random." Anyone in the village, or so it appears, might have a deaf child, a deaf sibling, a deaf uncle or aunt or grandparent. On Martha's Vineyard, Groce writes, "deafness was viewed as something that could happen to any family."

As Groce's genealogical research strongly indicated, the hereditary deafness on Martha's Vineyard was recessive. And in such cases, as Lane and his colleagues found, a sign language that arises will be spoken by the entire community. In these "recessive" villages, the deaf are integrated into every aspect of local life, living, working, marrying and conversing side by side with their hearing brethren. The result is the Forbidden Experiment writ large, an entire signing community, where sign language is fully woven into the lives of all its inhabitants, deaf and hearing alike. It is used everywhere, to talk about anything imaginable, from abstract ideas to the immediacies of daily life.

When I met Wendy and Irit in New York the winter after the trip, Wendy described a visit she'd made to another remote Israeli village. In this village there was only a single deaf person, a man married to a hearing woman. The deaf man had developed a system of signed communication for use with his wife and family. On her visit, Wendy brought along the same elicitation materials the team used in Al-Sayyid. "The difference is just night and day," she recalled. "This man didn't have any concept of the fact that he has a language."

She showed the man some pictures, and asked him to describe them to his wife. Even the simplest vocabulary items failed to elicit much. Rather than naming an object depicted in a photograph—a chair, for instance—the man would simply locate the actual object in his house and point to it. If no such object was present, he would point to the place it might conceivably go. Presented with a picture of a small animal or a bug, he simply pointed toward the ground. "He doesn't seem to realize that he has the power to tell his wife what is in the picture without a context," Wendy said. "All his communication, it seems to me, is directly related to the here-and-now."

She compared this with the linguistic robustness of Al-Sayyid. "People can talk about things that are not in the here-and-now. They can talk about the traditional folklore of the tribe and say, 'People used to do it this way and now they don't.' They're able to transmit a lot of information—and things that are quite abstract."

"The first time we were there," Irit recalled, "they were talking about Social Security rights in sign language."

"Another signer told us about the traditional method of making babies immune to scorpion bites," Wendy said. "It takes a high degree of sophistication about their culture, and it also takes a high degree of abstraction to be able to convey it."

In Al-Sayyid, too, the deafness is recessive. And, true to prediction, the signed language that has arisen there informs every facet of village life, day in and day out. What is more, it is arisen out of nothing—nothing more than man's innate capacity to make language. "We want to distinguish this from the Nicaraguan situation in that it's 'socially normal,'" Mark told me some months after the trip. "The Nicaraguan situation was a bunch of kids that were *brought* together in a school, and whatever you say about it, it's not a normal situation. There was no organic community."

He paused, contemplating the phenomenon of Al-Sayyid. "This comes out of the ground," he said after a moment. "This is Martha's Vineyard."

CHAPTER 9

Hyssop

We bid Tariq's wife goodbye and climb into the van, following Hassan through the labyrinth of Al-Sayyid. The linguists are going to call on a deaf woman named Aminah to fix a time for a recording session later in the day.

We pass stands of prickly pear, more abandoned cars and a low fieldstone building with a caved-in roof. Dating from the 1820s, it is the oldest structure in Al-Sayyid. A little farther along is the village mosque, a low concrete building with a gently scalloped roofline. Opposite the mosque is another small dwelling compound, a few houses arranged around a garden. Aminah's house is one of these, tiny and white, with a tin roof. In the front yard are olive trees and a fig tree, and beside them a pen with chickens dozing in the dust.

We pull up in front of the house, and Aminah steps out to greet us. She is pretty and plump and quite young, probably in her mid-twenties. (Because a person's birthdate is not considered salient information in the culture of Al-Sayyid, many adults here do not know precisely how old they are.) The second wife of one of Hassan's uncles, she is also a sister of Ibrahim, the deaf man from the half-built house. Aminah is wearing a long brown skirt, a flowered blouse and a brown-and-white-patterned headscarf. Her face lights up at the sight of Carol, whom she befriended on the linguists' last visit.

We follow Aminah into the house. It is the most traditional home we have been in so far. The front door opens directly into the small main room, which has neither sofas nor chairs. The seating, which lines the perimeter of the room, consists of mattresses on the floor, thin and cloth-covered like the one used to good effect at Omar's house yesterday afternoon. The decor is rather less traditional. Above the front door hangs a framed needlepoint picture of three swans. Nearby is a large clock in a shining gilt frame, whose face is also done in needlepoint. Both are Aminah's work. In one corner, a sheaf of artificial daffodils hangs upside-down.

We remove our shoes. Aminah disappears through a doorway hung with tassels of brightly colored yarn and returns with a stack of the white plastic patio chairs that everyone in Al-Sayyid seems to own. She and Carol take two chairs facing each other and immediately plunge into conversation. Aminah smiles broadly as Carol tells her, in sign and gesture, about our groping our way to Omar's rooftop last night. The rest of us sit on the floor in the traditional manner.

Aminah ducks outside and returns with handfuls of herbs from the garden; a few minutes later, she is handing round glasses of scalding tea stuffed with the freshly cut sprigs. The herb's taste is intense but indefinable, something like a cross between thyme and mint. It is known here as *zaatar.* The linguists, after some debate, decide it is hyssop. "If we videotape her, we'll ask her exactly how she makes the tea," Wendy tells her colleagues in English. "That will be a good story." They arrange to return for a taping session late this afternoon.

The door opens, and Aminah's husband, Fareed, steps inside. He is a gaunt man, much older than she; he looks close to sixty. (Aminah will be able to take part in the taping, in mixed company, as long as he is present.) Fareed has a long face, tinted glasses, and is wearing a pale green button-down shirt open at the collar. He is hearing, but also knows the village sign language: his brother, Hassan's father, was deaf. Fareed sits down next to Irit, lights a cigarette and starts speaking to her in rapid Hebrew. He speaks and speaks and speaks. Irit nods patiently. On the floor, Mark, jet-lagged, leans back against some brightly woven cushions and falls asleep. Outside, the muezzin calls. The birds chatter in the fig tree. A Mediterranean minute passes.

Over the team's subsequent visits, Aminah became quite attached to Carol. Whenever the linguists returned to Al-Sayyid, she invited her to spend the night. The linguists are careful to maintain a professional distance from their research subjects, but after so many entreaties it would have been rude to refuse. So on one of their next trips, the year after I joined them, Carol agreed. This time, the team had invited Ann Senghas, the Barnard psychologist who works on the emerging sign language of Nicaragua, to come along with them. One afternoon, their work over, Wendy, Mark and Irit drove back to the hotel, leaving Carol and Ann to stay overnight with Aminah in the little house.

It was an eventful visit. The three women sat and talked until darkness began to fall. Sign language needs light, so Aminah asked Fareed to go outside and fire up their ancient generator. It wouldn't start, leaving the women with no way to converse. Aminah dragged a car battery into the living room and attached to it a single tiny bulb, no bigger than a Christmas light. It was just enough light to sign by.

When it was time to go to sleep, Aminah bedded Carol and Ann down on the thin foam mattresses and plied them with quilts against the chill desert night. She turned out the little light. "It was just *completely* dark," Carol told me afterward. "There were no lights anywhere outside: it was like Girl Scout camp in fourth grade. I thought, 'Oh, my God, I can't even talk to Annie!'" With nothing to do but go to sleep, Carol took out her hearing aids, put them on the floor beside her and dropped off.

When they woke the next morning, Aminah was already making breakfast. "She's got figs; she's got some sort of bulgur," Carol recalled. "Would we like an omelet? We say yes, and she says we'll have to wait till the chickens lay the eggs." Carol went outside and collected them, and Aminah made an omelet, spiced with the fragrant *zaatar.*

Before they sat down in the garden to eat, Carol went to gather her things. She looked for her hearing aids, but could find only one. "You put them on the floor?" Aminah signed to her. "We have mice."

They found the other one eventually. It had been spirited off to the far side of the room and partly eaten. "I could still wear it," Carol said, "but it was full of these little nibble marks."

At four o'clock on the day of our visit, the blue Fiat pulls up to Aminah's house once more. Aminah has changed clothes since we were there this morning and is now dressed in a long gray skirt and a slate blue blouse with matching headscarf. We remove our shoes and sit on the floor. Aminah sits on the raised doorsill that separates the living room from the tiny kitchen, her head under the curtain of bright yarn. Fareed enters and is soon locked in conversation with Irit. Outside, the rooster clamors to be heard above the muezzin.

A half-hour passes. Fareed, cigarette dangling from his lips as he talks, is far from finished. "As my father-in-law would say, he could talk a dog off a meat wagon," Mark says to Wendy in English. The team decides to videotape Fareed first.

Wendy and Aminah set two plastic chairs at the head of the room and wheel a small wooden console in front of them. Wendy sits down in one of the chairs, and places her laptop on the console. Fareed, still talking, takes the second chair. It looks like the set of an extremely low-tech game show. In the corner, Mark dozes off again, propped on cushions. "Let him sleep," Aminah signs, smiling.

Wendy starts the slide show, with Fareed signing the vocabulary to Aminah. She nods each time, signing back to show she has understood. Confronted with certain pictures (the steaks, the videocassette, the binoculars, the man vomiting) Fareed turns to Wendy and says, in Hebrew, "*Ma ze?*"—"What's that?" The rooster gets progressively louder. Mark continues to sleep. "It's hard to stay awake, it's so hot," Carol murmurs.

Watching Aminah sign, Carol turns to Irit. "I asked her if the women and the men signed differently," she tells Irit in English. "She said no, she thought they signed pretty much alike."

It's a reasonable question in Al-Sayyid. In societies where the sexes are so often separate, distinct men's and women's forms of speech can arise, in spoken language or signed. It happened in Ireland, where for more than a century, the deaf men and women of Dublin spoke radically different dialects of Irish Sign Language.

From the mid-1800s on, as the linguist Barbara C. LeMaster has reported, the education of Dublin's deaf children was centered in two residential schools in the Cabra district there, St. Mary's School for Deaf Girls and St. Joseph's School for Deaf Boys. St. Mary's began using sign language after two Dominican nuns from the school traveled to Normandy to learn the teaching methods employed there. Much as Thomas Gallaudet had done in America at the beginning of the century, they adapted the French "methodical signs" for use with English. This sign language was used at St. Mary's from 1846 on. In the mid-1850s, the nuns shared it with the Christian Brothers, who ran St. Joseph's School.

Because students from the two schools rarely mixed socially, over the next hundred years, the language of deaf girls and that of deaf boys developed dramatically different vocabularies. Although Dublin's deaf men and women were using the same repertory of handshapes, locations and movements, quite often their signs for the same concepts were unrelated in all three parameters. The male sign GREEN, for instance, was made by sliding the extended index finger once down the cheek. The female sign GREEN was made with the pinched thumb and forefinger moving in an up-and-down motion in front of the body.

After they graduated, many St. Mary's girls married St. Joseph's boys. The women learned the men's signs for use with their husbands or in mixed groups. Few men deigned to learn the women's signs; it was considered unmanly. Most women retained their own signs for use at all-female gatherings. At especially important English-language functions, like big religious meetings, two Irish Sign interpreters would be present: one for the men's dialect, one for the women's.

The two dialects endured until the mid-1950s, when oralism replaced signing in Dublin schools for the deaf and Irish Sign Language in both its forms began to die out. The differences could still be observed as late as the 1980s, however, when LeMaster began her research among Dublin's elderly deaf. Eliciting signs for the same basic concepts from men and women, she found that nearly 70 percent of the signs they produced differed. While the women could understand the men's signing quite well, the men claimed to understand the women's signing only a little. In tests administered by

LeMaster, the women proved far better than the men at producing the signs used by the opposite sex.

Sadly, as LeMaster and her colleague John P. Dwyer write, although some younger deaf people in Dublin have made a point of learning Irish Sign, what they are learning is the residue of the male form. Most are unaware that another dialect ever existed. "The issue of 'male' and 'female' language status," LeMaster and Dwyer write, "may soon become a non-issue for this community."

Fareed finishes signing and changes places with Aminah. The linguists have just fifteen minutes before Fareed has to go to the mosque to pray. They start with the video clips: the man walking past an empty chair, thrusting a mug toward the camera, kicking a ball. As he translates Aminah's signing into spoken Hebrew, Fareed observes that the man doing all these things is a "strange man."

Irit relieves Wendy at the computer as Aminah signs the drawings: buying and selling groceries, sending and receiving a letter. Fareed gets them immediately. The linguists look at one another and smile; not every signer had been able to convey the paired pictures correctly. "She understood the sequence," Carol says. "Mailing it and then getting it."

Mark stirs, sits up and motions toward Irit and Aminah. "What are they doing?" he asks.

"Drawings," Wendy tells him. "She's trying to elicit verb agreement using the drawings." In nearly all signed languages that have been studied so far, verbs display grammatical agreement—that is, agreement *using space*—with one or more nouns in the same sentence. For the team, a fundamental question about the new language of Al-Sayyid is whether it, too, has verbs that agree.

The front door opens and a young woman of about seventeen enters, dressed in a lavender blouse and a floor-length denim skirt. She leads by the hand a girl of two, clad in a white tulle dress and a pink straw hat. She takes a chair next to Carol and, in perfect, careful English, says, "How are you?" His session over, Fareed goes off to pray.

The door opens again and another young woman enters, carrying a newborn wrapped in a pink blanket. She is a year or two older than the first girl, dressed in an identical denim skirt and a beige blouse. The girls are sisters, Fareed's daughters by his first wife. The infant and the toddler are the older girl's children. The young woman hands the baby to Aminah, who coos over it. With the baby, drowsing in its blanket, nestled in the crook of her left arm, Aminah uses her right hand to talk. Fareed's daughters, both of whom are hearing, respond in sign.

Fareed returns from the mosque, and immediately resumes his talk with Irit. Shai joins them, telling Fareed that he and his wife are expecting their first child. *"Bat o ben?"* Fareed asks him in Hebrew. "Girl or boy?"

"Ben," Shai says proudly. Fareed jumps up and claps him on the back. *"Mazal Tov!"* he cries.

The door opens once more, and an older woman enters. She is Fareed's first wife, small and round, her face heavily lined. She is the most formally dressed person we've seen in the village, wearing a long peacock-green caftan with heavy white embroidery at the neck, and a large white headscarf. *"Shalom, shalom!"* she greets us in deep, Arabic-accented Hebrew, clasping each of our hands in turn.

In a little while, Hassan pulls up in his truck to take us to our next house. We say our goodbyes. Irit gives Aminah one of the boxes of china, and we step outside. No one is quite certain where we're supposed to go next. "I think we're going to see the two brothers," Wendy says, referring to a pair of deaf teenagers the team saw on its last visit. It will be some time before we can leave, though: Fareed has beaten us to Hassan's truck and is leaning in at the window.

CHAPTER 10

The Web of Words

The words of spoken language are complex creatures. We tend to think of words as indivisible entities, little lumps of language that can't be broken down further. In reality, most words are made up of smaller pieces, and it is these pieces, and the orderly architecture in which they are arranged, that allow words to encode meaning. Even a seemingly simple English word like "cats" comprises two discrete linguistic building blocks: the stem *cat* and the suffix *-s*. Though tiny, *-s* is a powerful device for encoding meaning: it tells the listener, "Take the noun to which I am attached and give it the reading, 'more than one of these.'" It is at this level of the grammar, the level of word formation, that the sounds of a language start to signify.

Every language has its own rules of word formation, and these rules are part of what every child acquiring the language must master. In most languages, it is possible to build up highly complex words from an inventory of component parts. Reading an article by Jonathan Franzen in *The New Yorker* not long ago, I came across the marvelous word "unwoodpeckerish." Although I had never seen it before, I knew instantly what it meant. The rules of English word formation told me so.

The meaningful building blocks from which words are assembled are known as morphemes, and their scientific study is called morphology. Mark made his reputation, in the 1970s, by integrating a theory of morphology into Chomskyan generative grammar.

In the early 1970s, one of the first tasks of sign-language linguists was to find out whether the manual language of the American deaf also possessed a system for assembling complex words from smaller linguistic units. For these early linguists, an empirical question was this: Were the words of signed language simply holistic lumps, or were they, like the words of spoken language, made from still smaller parts?

William Stokoe had laid the groundwork, but there was much more to be done. In identifying the three formational parameters of handshape, location and movement, Stokoe had isolated the basic means by which ASL could encode and differentiate a visual signal. He had, in effect, discovered ASL phonology—the "consonants and vowels" of the language. But Stokoe wasn't a linguist, and his findings left many questions still unanswered. His approach to ASL, while hugely important politically, was classically structuralist. Stokoe wasn't trained to pursue large questions about sign as an aspect of mind, and he wasn't especially interested in them. If Stokoe had used the same methods to describe French, for example, he would have come away with a detailed inventory of the sounds of the language, and some description of a system by which they might combine to form simple words. But he would have offered little indication of whether the language had a system on top of that for forming more complex words, and whether it had a system on top of *that* for ordering those words into structured, comprehensible sentences. If Stokoe was ASL's first anatomist, what the language now needed was a physiologist, a linguist who could bring the study of sign into the flourishing enterprise that was generative grammar, and in so doing acknowledge that it was a vital, untapped resource for investigating human language as a whole.

It found its physiologist in Ursula Bellugi. Bellugi is the director of the Laboratory for Cognitive Neuroscience at the Salk Institute, where she has worked for more than three decades. Her lab was established in 1970 to study the biological foundations of signed and spoken language. Trained as a developmental psycholinguist under Roger Brown at Harvard, Bellugi spent her early career studying the acquisition of spoken language by young children.

As Stokoe's work caught the attention of linguists, Bellugi began to ponder a basic psychological question: If sign was a real language, as Stokoe's analysis suggested, how was it organized in the minds of signers? She decided to begin her investigation by studying how the deaf children of signing parents acquired ASL. But before she could proceed, she needed to understand just what it was the children were acquiring. And so, starting in the early 1970s, she and her colleagues, working with native deaf informants, began bit by bit to unravel the word and sentence structure of ASL.

They didn't know what they had at first. Stokoe had shown that ASL looked like a real human language. But did it also act like one? Did its words and sentences belong to a structured, rule-governed system—a grammar—as those of spoken language did? "At that time," Bellugi and her husband and frequent collaborator, Edward S. Klima, wrote in their seminal 1979 book, *The Signs of Language,* "it was claimed that ASL had no grammatical structure, and, as a matter of fact, we then had no evidence to the contrary."

Bellugi set out to demonstrate scientifically what Stokoe had dared to suggest: that sign language, like all other human languages, was a structured linguistic system. She began with the word.

In spoken language, morphology is easy to spot. Complex words are usually formed from simple ones by tacking on the small strings of sound known collectively as affixes. The affixes of the world's spoken languages can perform a variety of grammatical jobs. In Latin, Finnish and Hungarian, for instance, affixes encode the relationships among the actors in a sentence—"into the house," "out of the house," "as far as the house." They are the grammatical endings, or inflections, painfully familiar to language students. In English, affixes of this kind, called inflectional affixes, happen to be rare. Besides the plural suffix, there is the *-s* ending on verbs that signals the third-person singular. There is *-ed,* which marks the past tense of regular verbs. There is the present participle ending, *-ing,* which attaches to verbs to denote an action or state in progress. There are only a few others.

But English is rich in affixes of another type, known as derivational affixes. Derivational affixes turn simple words into complex ones with related meanings. From the simple noun "beauty," derivational affixes give us the adjective "beautiful," the verb "beautify" and the complex noun "beautification." They turn "wine" into "winery" and "nun" into "nunnery." They give us "seaworthy" and "roadworthy," "youngster" and "mobster." They let us grasp the meaning of coinages like "newsworthy" and "oldster" and "unwoodpeckerish." Where inflectional affixes mark grammatical relationships, derivational affixes make new words. In English, the system of derivational affixes is a rich and productive mechanism for encoding meaning, and it is part of what every speaker "knows" when he uses the language. As the linguist Victoria Fromkin has written:

> Since the words of a language can consist of more than one meaningful element, words themselves cannot be the most elemental units of meaning. "Tolerant," "sane," "active" and "direct" are all English words; so are "intolerant," "insane," "inactive" and "indirect." The latter set includes the meanings of the former plus the meaningful unit "in-," which in these instances means "not." In learning a language we learn these basic meaningful elements called morphemes and how to combine them into words.

When Bellugi began her research, there was still little reason to see the signs of ASL as anything other than unitary wholes, with little or no internal structure. Many observers, both before Stokoe and after him, even believed that ASL lacked distinct "parts of speech"—the nouns, verbs and adjectives of spoken language. What use, after all, could a pantomime have for them? But as sign-language linguists would discover, ASL had the power to form signs as complex and meaningful as the words of spoken language are, from nouns and verbs and adjectives to signs elaborately modulated for grammatical aspect.

"While one might expect any communication system to have syntax, one might not necessarily expect sign languages to have internal structure to their words," Wendy and the linguist Diane Lillo-Martin have written. "Yet sign languages do have a great deal of morphological complexity. Such complexity is one of many sources of evidence that systematic grammatical structuring strongly dominates the presumably iconic origins of these languages."

And, as the first generation of sign-language linguists would also discover, the complex anatomy of signs was like nothing they had ever encountered before.

In spoken language, morphology is a largely horizontal affair: complex words are formed from simple ones by stringing prefix, stem and suffix one after another in a straight acoustic line. "Cat" is a small string of sound, "cats" a slightly longer string. But with sign language, linguists were confronted with a system that didn't work that way. ASL contains only a few affixes. The best-known one, probably borrowed from English, is the agentive suffix, equivalent to English *-er.* Made with two flat hands, palms inward, moving downward in space as if outlining a human torso, this suffix can be tacked onto the end of certain verbs, like TEACH, to form occupational nouns like TEACHER. But in ASL, as in all the world's signed languages, sequential affixes like this are relatively rare.

Sign languages choose instead to build their words vertically. In all known signed languages, complex signs are formed from simple ones by altering the spatial signal *while the simple sign is being made.* By manipulating aspects of a sign's movement pattern—its manner, intensity or other features—ASL can form complex nouns like CAR from simple verbs like DRIVE; expand simple words like SICK into elaborate matrixes of related meanings ("to be sick for a long time," "to get sick over and over again," "to become fully sick"); and communicate detailed relationships between an action and its recipients ("give continuously to each in turn, that action recurring over time"). In ASL, each of these concepts is expressed with a single sign that can be modified in complex ways.

Spoken language has nothing quite like this. The speech signal is by its very nature sequential: it is impossible to utter "cat" and *-s* at precisely the same time. It is possible, however, to do the equivalent in sign language. But this layered method of word formation was so different from what linguists were accustomed to, that even in the 1970s, many doubted that sign language had the ability to make complex words at all.

In spoken language, a very fruitful way of creating complex words is through compounding. English compound words are legion: from "blackboard" and "cupboard" to "greenhouse" and "charterhouse" and "porterhouse." When words coalesce into a compound, two things typically happen. First, the meaning of the compound often differs substantially from the sum of its parts. Blackboards aren't always black; many are green. "Cupboard," historically a board that held cups, today conjures up something quite different. "Greenhouse" is not a green-colored house but rather a glassed-in place for plants.

Second, the pronunciation of the compound can differ from that of its component words taken alone. For one thing, compounds almost always involve a change in stress. Take "black" plus "board." In isolation, each word is stressed equally: "bláck boárd." But as a compound, "bláckboard," only the first syllable is stressed. Pronunciation can change even more radically as it has in "breakfast," historically a compound of "break" plus "fast." "Cupboard" is even more extreme: in the compound word, the "p" of "cup" has been lost altogether, assimilated into the "b" of "board."

As the linguists of the 1970s began to discover, sign language also has an active compounding mechanism at its disposal. ASL contains dozens of compounds, signs that have coalesced into single, complex words built from smaller simpler ones. Most of these compounds are unique to the language, with no English equivalents:

MOTHER⁀FATHER	"parents"
BLUE⁀SPOT	"bruise"
THINK⁀MARRY	"believe"
FACE⁀NEW	"stranger"
JESUS⁀BOOK	"Bible"

FACE⁀STRONG “resemble”
SICK⁀SPREAD “epidemic”
SLEEP⁀SUNRISE “oversleep”
THRILL⁀INFORM “news,” “entertainment”
NAME⁀SHINY “fame”
NUDE⁀ZOOM-OFF “streaker”

As with spoken-language compounds, the meaning of ASL compounds often can’t be predicted from the meanings of their components. BLUE⁀SPOT does not refer to a spot that is blue. The sign glossed WEDDING⁀CELEBRATE denotes not the actual marriage ceremony but rather “anniversary.” The ASL compound GOOD⁀ENOUGH means something far worse than the English phrase “good enough”; it means “just barely adequate.” BED⁀SOFT doesn’t mean a soft bed; it means “pillow” or “mattress.” The sign glossed RED⁀SECRET is a regional sign meaning “strawberry.”

As in spoken language, compounding in sign language can also result in new “pronunciations.” ASL compounds are somewhat reduced in form, taking barely more time to articulate than either of their component parts does alone. As with the compounds of spoken language, ASL compounds have coalesced over time into smooth, unitary words.

Studying the structure of complex signs like compounds also allowed sign-language linguists of the 1970s and 1980s to make important revisions to Stokoe’s account of sign formation. In Stokoe’s classic model, the formative elements of a sign—handshape, location and movement—occur together in a simultaneous stack. That made sign language conspicuously different from spoken language, where the most basic elements of a word—the consonants and vowels—are strung in a linear sequence.

As a later generation of linguists, chief among them Scott Liddell of Gallaudet and Wendy Sandler, have discovered, the phonology of signed language works more sequentially than Stokoe realized. While signs do exploit the potential for simultaneity of a visuospatial language, they have an internal structure that is nonetheless linear and sequenced. Like the words of spoken language, the words of sign language, these linguists found, contain "syllables," small, repeated units of linguistic structure strung one after another.

In Wendy's analysis, research that occupied much of her career in the 1980s and 1990s, a typical sign-language syllable comprises three segments: an initial *location* (the starting point of the sign), followed by a *movement* (during which the hands travel through space) and a final *location* (the endpoint of the sign). This canonical syllable structure, abbreviated as L-M-L, can describe nearly any sign in the lexicon of any sign language in the world. Many grammatical processes in sign language, linguists have found, entail regular changes in a sign's syllable structure. Compounding is one of them. When a compound is formed, one or more segments of the original signs may be eliminated, resulting in a compound that, though derived from two separate signs, ends up looking like a single sign, with canonical L-M-L structure. Now widely accepted, first Liddell's work and, more recently, Wendy's, has helped bring the analysis of the "phonological" structure of sign language much closer to that of spoken language.

At the time they were looking at compounds, linguists also began to examine the belief that ASL had no distinct parts of speech—no signs, that is, corresponding to the nouns, verbs, adjectives and adverbs of spoken language. Well into the twentieth century, oralists invoked this belief to support their claim that sign was not a "real language." (Their reasoning calls to mind the Abbé de l'Épée, who two hundred years earlier assumed that because it lacked affixes, the language of the Paris deaf had no grammar.) Even Stokoe was partly misled. In his landmark *Dictionary of American Sign Language* of 1965, he claimed that ASL often made no distinction between nouns like CAR and their corresponding verbs, like DRIVE: a single sign, he believed, had to suffice for both.

If this were the case, it would make sign language radically different from other human languages. The vast majority of spoken languages contain both nouns and verbs, and the existence of these two distinct parts of speech has been posited as one of the defining properties of language. In many spoken languages, there are pairs of nouns and verbs, related in meaning, that are also related in form. English sometimes signals these relationships with suffixes: "beauty"; "beautify." In other cases, it encodes them by shifting the stress from one syllable to another: "cómbat"/"combát"; "réject"/"rejéct"; "dígest"/"digést."

ASL has neither abundant affixes nor stressed syllables. Yet generations of deaf people have had no problem understanding, swiftly and unequivocally, whether a signer means DRIVE or CAR, SIT or CHAIR, EAT or FOOD. Clearly, as the early sign-language linguists began to suspect, there was something more than context at work. But what was it?

In the 1970s, Ted Supalla, a deaf graduate student in psychology at the University of California, San Diego, began to study these noun-verb pairs in earnest. With his colleague Elissa Newport, he compiled a list of one hundred pairs, some familiar from English, others unique to ASL. They found the noun TYPEWRITER and the similar-looking verb TYPE; the noun STAPLER and the similar verb STAPLE; VACUUM-CLEANER and VACUUM. Also on the list were SHIP and GO-BY-SHIP; TRAIN and GO-BY-TRAIN; BED and GO-TO-BED; LIPSTICK and PUT-ON-LIPSTICK; MELON and THUMP-MELON; BROOM and SWEEP; AIRPLANE and GO-BY-AIRPLANE.

If Stokoe was right, and pairs like these were formally identical, then the tendency to distinguish nouns from verbs, found in a great many of the world's spoken languages, would not hold for ASL. Participants in a signed conversation, the implication went, would need to rely heavily on context to discern the signer's intent. But, as Supalla and Newport discovered, there *was* a distinction—not a fastened-on affix, as there might be in spoken language, but a systematic alteration in the signs' movement. It was a grammatical process so subtle that most hearing observers missed it, so automatic that most deaf signers were unaware of it. Like Épée before him, Stokoe had been looking for grammar in all the wrong places.

Spoken languages can also use a *process* to encode meaning. Some encode complex meanings by repeating all or part of the word's stem, a process known as reduplication. Reduplication can signal a variety of grammatical relationships, among them intensification (in which "big" becomes "very big"); pluralization; and verbal inflection. In Samoan, third-person singular verbs are made plural when the next-to-last syllable is repeated: *manao,* "he wishes," *mana**na**o,* "they wish"; *punou,* "he bends," *puno**nou**,* "they bend." In Tagalog, spoken in the Philippines, reduplication is used to intensify verbs: "cook" is *magluto;* its intensive form (meaning "cook thoroughly" or "cook repeatedly") is *maglu**lu**to.*

As the linguist Susan Fischer had already discovered, sign language also uses reduplication to form complex words. But instead of sound, it is *the visual signal* that gets repeated. ASL used just such a process, Supalla and Newport found, to distinguish related noun-verb pairs. Take the signs SIT and CHAIR. To a hearing observer, they look identical at first: the index and middle fingers of one hand tap down onto the corresponding fingers of the opposite hand. But the difference lies in the nature of the tapping. For SIT, the movement is fairly large and relaxed, with the hands starting out some distance apart. The fingers tap down once. For CHAIR, the movement is smaller (the hands start closer together) and the fingers tap twice in quick succession. The same is true of EAT and FOOD: in both signs, as in the conventional pantomime, the thumb and fingertips appear to bring something to the mouth. But while the verb EAT is made with a single large motion, the noun FOOD entails several small repeated ones. Similarly for the rest of the noun-verb pairs on Supalla and Newport's list, including GUN and SHOOT; SCISSORS and CUT; CIGARETTE and SMOKE; UMBRELLA and OPEN-UMBRELLA; TOOTHBRUSH and BRUSH-TEETH; and FLYING SAUCER and GO-BY-FLYING-SAUCER.

By studying the subtle variations in the manner of movement of these signs, the linguists had uncovered a grammatical process of word formation in ASL, a systematic device by which it derived one set of words from another. The nouns shared the handshape and location of the corresponding verbs, *but their movement was always restrained and repeated.* Using Wendy's model of syllable structure, we can say that the nouns were formed by repeating a syllable of the verb.

As with many derivational processes in spoken language, the process Supalla and Newport discovered could be used to form new coinages with readily accessible meanings. Klima and Bellugi saw it happen in their own lab. One of their deaf associates needed to talk about "language acquisition," but at the time, the ASL lexicon had no noun meaning "acquisition." Before long, it did: the verb GET, made with repeated, restrained movement.

Throughout the 1970s and 1980s, as linguists continued to unravel ASL, they saw that the visual signal could be systematically altered to serve a variety of grammatical functions. One of the most potent examples came, like so many discoveries of the period, from Bellugi's lab. It happened early in their research, when Bellugi and Klima, like observers before them, were still operating under the sway of spoken language. The linguists were conducting a study that examined the ways in which signers paraphrased written English stories. One story concerned a fisherman out on the water. The English version contained the sentence "His face became red in the wind." As the signers retold the story, Bellugi and Klima noticed something odd happening. In signing that sentence, many signers appeared to omit the verb "became." Instead, they produced signed sequences that the linguists glossed variously as FACE RED or RED FACE or WIND [against face] RED.

Why did so many signers leave out the word "became"? Perhaps, Klima and Bellugi speculated, they had simply chosen to disregard it. There was an alternative explanation, though the linguists, still searching for affixes, discounted it at the time: "Another remote possibility," Klima and Bellugi wrote, "was that *there might be something in the manner of signing* that expressed the change of state, 'became.'" Little by little, as they reviewed hours of footage, the linguists realized that that was exactly what was happening:

> Looking again at the videotaped stories of the fisherman whose face became red, we can now see that the sign RED was made in a variety of ways that we did not then distinguish, and it seems odd that we so steadfastly ignored these variations. For we were then on the threshold of discovering that to express many distinctions of meaning, ASL exhibits a rich system of *modulations* on the form of signs. In retrospect it is we who are red-faced. . . . The meaning "became red" was often coded in the sign itself.

How was this coding accomplished? Once again, the linguists discovered, it was done by varying the sign's movement, specifically its speed, length and tension.

Like spoken language, ASL contains many adjectives—including SICK, ANGRY, EMBARRASSED and DIRTY—that denote transitory characteristics. Each of these adjectives can be signed with different modulations of movement, and each modulation alters the meaning in characteristic ways. In one modulation, which the linguists called the predispositional, the basic form of the adjective was repeated three times, with the hand traveling in a smooth circular path. This added the meaning "prone to be" or "tends to be." Signed with this modulation, the sentence glossed JOHN SICK means "John is prone to be sick."

Another modulation, which the linguists called the incessant, was made with rapid small intense movements, like a tremolo. It carried the meaning of "apparent incessant duration": signed in this way, JOHN SICK means "John gets sick incessantly."

What the linguists had come upon was *aspect*, a grammatical device first noted in ASL by Susan Fischer. Used in many spoken languages (though not in a huge way in English), aspect gives a range of nuanced meanings to the predicates of sentences. Where English often adds extra words to convey these meanings ("John *tended to be* dirty"), many languages do it by inflecting the word itself. These inflections, as Klima and Bellugi write, encode a range of subtle distinctions in "the onset, duration, frequency, recurrence, permanence, or intensity of states or events."

Aspect differs from tense. Although both can apply to verbs, as the linguist Andrew Spencer explains, "Tense refers to anchoring in time, as with English *wrote* (past) as opposed to *writes*. . . . Aspect refers to the manner in which an event unfolds over time. A very common aspectual distinction is that between completed (perfective) and non-completed (imperfective) events." Many Slavic languages, as well as ancient Greek, make such distinctions.

ASL encodes similar distinctions. Besides the predispositional and incessant aspects, Bellugi and Klima identified a half-dozen others. These included the intensive aspect ("to be very sick"), made with a rapid single movement and the hands visibly tense. There was also the continuative aspect ("to be sick for a long time"), made with the sign reduplicated three times in a slow ellipse. And there was the resultative aspect, made by starting the sign slowly and then accelerating, denoting a change of state ("to become fully sick"). It was the resultative aspect that the signers had used to describe the fisherman's face growing redder and redder. The movement of the sign RED automatically encoded the meaning of the English word "became."

Remarkably, these grammatical modulations can sometimes override a sign's iconic properties. The ASL sign SLOW is made by sliding the fingers of one hand along the back of the other at moderate speed. Under the intensive aspect, SLOW is performed with a rapid tense movement, and the resulting sign is made much more quickly than the original. Its meaning? "Very slow." Linguists couldn't ask for a better demonstration that ASL is operating as a system of arbitrary code—that is, a *linguistic* system.

Like adjectives, verbs in ASL can also be modulated for aspect. As Klima and Bellugi found, varying a verb's movement can differentiate: "(a) whether a specific act presents itself as an indivisible whole or as several separate actions, (b) whether the actions are specified for occurrence at distinct points in time, (c) whether the actions are specified for their order of occurrence, and (d) how the actions are distributed with respect to individuals participating in the action—an action for each one, or actions for certain ones, certain groups, or just anyone."

Take the verb GIVE. Inflected for the exhaustive aspect (in which the sign is made repeatedly as the hand travels across a lateral plane), it means "to give something to each one." The ASL sentence glossed DIPLOMA, PRINCIPAL GIVE[exhaustive]; (ME) NONE, for example, actually means, "The principal gave out a diploma to each one, except for me."

Similarly, verbs can be inflected for apportionative aspect. As its name suggests, this aspect conveys the way in which an action is distributed around a group or object. Apportionative aspect can take two forms. The first, apportionative external, is made by repeating the movement of a sign in a circular path in the horizontal plane, parallel to the floor. Its meaning is "to do (the action of the verb) to members of a collected group." The second, apportionative internal, is also made by repeating the sign in a circular path, but this time in the vertical plane, parallel to the wall. It means "to do (the action of the verb) all around" or "all over a singular object."

The same sentence, inflected for each type of apportionative aspect, means two completely different things, as Klima and Bellugi show:

> HOUSE, (ME) MEASURE[apportionative external]. "I took measurements of the houses in the group."

> HOUSE, (ME) MEASURE[apportionative internal]. "I took measurements all over the house."

Another type of verbal aspect is the protractive, made by holding the sign without movement. It gives the meaning "to (do the action of the verb) uninterruptedly." Made with the protractive aspect, the ASL verb LOOK-AT means "to stare at uninterruptedly." Still another type is the durational, made with a circular repeated movement. Made with this motion, LOOK-AT now means "to gaze at." There is also the continutative aspect ("to look at for a long time"), made with slow elliptical repetitions, and the iterative aspect ("to look at again and again"), made with a series of tense movements.

In ASL, multiple aspects can be layered on top of a single verb, resulting in sentences with exceedingly baroque predicates. GIVE, for example, might be inflected first for exhaustive distributional aspect ("give to each"), then for iterative aspect ("give again and again"). The resulting complex sign, made with repeated tense movements as the hand travels smoothly along a horizontal path, means "give to each, that act of giving occurring again and again." But if the inflections were reversed—first iterative, then exhaustive—in the resulting sign, GIVE would be made at several discrete points along a horizontal plane. The meaning would be "give again and again to each in turn" or "for each in turn, there is repeated giving."

By manipulating a sign's movement in a variety of ways, ASL is able to derive complex words of seemingly infinite range and nuance, from compounds to noun-verb derivations to constellations of aspectual inflections. Its ability to do this makes it one of the most morphologically rich languages now known, something early observers believed was far beyond the capacity of a language of hands in space. As Klima and Bellugi wrote in 1979, "The existence of such elaborate formal inflectional devices clearly establishes ASL as one of the inflecting languages of the world, like Latin, Russian, and Navajo."

CHAPTER 11

The House Built from the Second Story Down

We climb into the van and follow Hassan along another narrow road of dust and stones. We pass more simple houses like Aminah's, as well as several larger, fancier ones in various stages of construction. At the far end of the village, Hassan pulls off to one side, near a large fenced garden full of blooms, and we pull in behind him. Behind the garden stand two low houses very different from the whitewashed ones we've grown accustomed to. One of the houses is painted a deep, warm yellow, the other ocher, the colors flaked by the sun. Along one edge of the garden, clusters of fat grapes dangle from an arbor made of lashed-together pipes. Along another side, a small pen holds chickens and sheep. A large yellow dog, whose job it is to guard the livestock, is curled up asleep in the sun, and in the field beyond, a boy prods two reluctant goats with a stick. If it weren't for the encroaching desert, we might think we had landed in rural Italy.

Opposite the houses, on the near side of the garden, a third house, much larger than the others and painted apricot, is being built. It seems, curiously, to be under construction from the top down, like an impossible building in an M. C. Escher lithograph. The lower story, which has no walls, consists of only a concrete floor and some support pillars and stands open to the air like a pavilion. The upper story, however, is largely complete, with leaded glass windows and a veranda overlooking the fields. We are expected up there.

We climb a staircase that, like the one at Omar's, clings to the outside of the house. Here, too, there are no balustrades, and the stairs slither with sand. We ascend gingerly to the second floor, joining the man of the house, Samir, and several of his children, who are already crowded onto the veranda. Samir, who is hearing, has ten sons and three daughters. Two of the sons are deaf. On their first visit, the linguists recorded the two boys along with one of their hearing brothers, who also signs.

The deaf brothers look to be in their late teens. One of them is wearing a shirt with a huge Chinese character printed on it; the other is dressed in what looks like a homemade soccer jersey, made from a plain white T-shirt with maroon letters spelling "No. 7" cut from felt and sewn on by hand with enormous stitches. The hearing brother, who is about the same age, is wearing a blue shirt that says "Golf Studio 54" on the front. With the four linguists, Shai and me, plus assorted family friends, there are well over a dozen people on the little balcony. We have a fine view of Al-Sayyid spread below us: small compounds of houses, each widely spaced from the next, connected by a web of narrow roads threading through the olive groves.

Irit seats herself in a tiny wooden chair, like a schoolroom chair, and sets the laptop on a bigger chair. The rest of us pile onto cushions on the floor of the balcony. Malik, the deaf boy in the soccer jersey, takes the chair next to Irit and begins to sign the vocabulary on the computer screen. The hearing boy, Hakim, goes into the house, what there is of it so far, and returns with sunflower seeds, a tray of mint-filled glasses and a pot of tea.

Irit moves on to Sylvester and Tweety. Malik signs the story to one of his hearing brothers, seated opposite; the hearing boy repeats it aloud in Hebrew. The linguists don't look happy: Malik's signing is restrained and spare. Carol turns to him, signing that he should tell "all of it." The boy's signing grows more detailed.

"There we go," says Carol.

"He has more 'face' than anybody else," Mark comments approvingly.

As Malik signs the cartoon, his hearing brother translates his signing into Hebrew. "*Haya tsippor,*" he says—"There was a little bird"—which invests Tweety with a biblical grandeur.

Carol resumes her conversation with the other deaf brother, Kamal, who sits on the balcony railing, signing animatedly and eating sunflower seeds. At one point, she turns to Wendy inquiringly and holds up two hands, palms out, each middle finger touching the thumb. "Does this mean 'ten'?" she asks in English.

"I don't know," Wendy says. "It's not ISL."

It does turn out to be the Al-Sayyid sign TEN. Kamal was telling Carol that there are ten brothers in the family.

The afternoon sun floods the balcony and Shai worries once more about glare. From his seat on the floor, Mark jumps up to block the light and as he does so knocks over a tea glass. It shatters, and one of the shards flies up and strikes his sandaled foot, giving him a small cut. Irit, seeing this, thinks immediately of the grant application the team has just submitted to the National Institutes of Health. She thinks: *We told the NIH that there was absolutely no danger in our research.* There are no Band-Aids in the half-built house, but Carol rummages through her purse and comes up with a small tube of Vaseline, which she dabs on Mark's foot. She insists it will stanch the blood.

Irit turns back to the test, and the hearing brother, Hakim, replaces Malik in the chair. Watching him sign, Mark looks pleased. "He's showing exactly what's happening," he says. "Both of the brothers have *faces.*"

In the face lies grammar. Hearing people who watch deaf signers often remark, not without condescension, on how *expressive* they seem, for in the course of a conversation a signer may puff out her cheeks, furrow her brow, wrinkle her nose, open her eyes wide and purse her lips in what can look like an exaggerated grimace. Hearing people use these expressions, too, of course. But in the signed languages of the world, these facial gestures have nothing to do with emotion. Instead, they have taken on a grammatical role, encoding extra linguistic information while the hands are "busy talking."

One thing the face can do splendidly is distinguish among sentences of different types—a declarative sentence, for instance, and the corresponding question. Spoken languages do this in a variety of ways. One is to shuffle the order of the words in the sentence. In English, a declarative sentence like "Father is home" has a fixed word order: subject first, verb after. If, however, the verb is moved to the beginning and the sentence uttered with rising intonation—"Is Father home?"—the sentence becomes a question.

Another way English can express questions is by keeping the word order intact and manipulating intonation alone. As every English speaker knows, a sentence like "You're leaving," uttered with falling intonation, is a declarative statement. The same sentence, uttered with rising intonation—"You're leaving?"—is instantly understood as a question. Sign language can make exactly the same distinctions. Through systematic movements of the face, head and eyes, signed languages can ask questions, make negative and conditional statements, modify verbs and perform a range of other grammatical tasks.

In ASL, facial expression can be used to signal several different types of questions. These include yes-or-no questions, rhetorical questions and the WH-questions, which in English start with a word like "who," "what," "where," "when," "why" or "how." Suppose I sign FATHER HOME. If I sign the sentence with a neutral facial expression, it is declarative: "Father is home." But if, while signing the same sequence, I also widen my eyes, raise my eyebrows and incline my head forward, the sentence immediately becomes a yes-or-no question: "Is Father home?" The order of the signs is the same: the face transmits the grammar.

To ask a WH-question, by contrast, the signer squints her eyes and furrows her brows. Signed with this expression, the phrase MARY WHERE means "Where is Mary?" (In the world's signed languages, for reasons that scholars do not yet agree upon, question words often come at the ends of sentences.) Rhetorical questions are signaled with still another expression. If a signer signs the following sequence, I TIRED WHY, STUDY ALL-NIGHT ("Why am I tired? Because I studied all night"), and, as she signs WHY, raises her eyebrows and shakes her head slightly, the addressee knows that no answer is actually expected.

The face can do far more than ask questions. It can negate an entire sentence, as, with a headshake and a frown, FATHER HOME becomes "Father isn't home." It can also alter the relationship between clauses in a sentence. If someone signs the sequence SNOW, CLASS CANCEL with a neutral facial expression, it is understood as two conjoined declarative sentences: "It's snowing, and class is canceled." But if he raises his eyebrows and tilts his head a little to the side while signing the word SNOW, the sentence becomes conditional: "If it snows, class will be canceled."

Certain adverbs are also made with the face. They modify the predicate of the sentence as the hands are signing it. In one such adverb, which linguists gloss as *mm,* the lips are pressed together and protruded. It indicates an action performed effortlessly or with enjoyment. In another, glossed *th,* the tongue protrudes between the teeth. It denotes something done awkwardly or with effort. "When these two facial expressions accompany the same verb (e.g., DRIVE)," the sign-language linguist Karen Emmorey has written, "two quite different meanings are conveyed, that is, 'drive effortlessly' or 'drive carelessly.'"

Other facial adverbs in ASL include an intensifier, made with the lips drawn back and the teeth clenched, which means "surprisingly large," "unusually great" or "extremely far"; and one glossed *puff,* in which both cheeks are filled with air, which means "too much," or "a large amount."

Naturally, signers also use their faces to convey emotion, just as hearing people do. But grammatical facial expressions are different. "Linguistic and emotional facial expressions differ in their scope and timing and in the facial muscles that are used," Emmorey writes. "Facial expressions that function linguistically have a clear onset and offset, and they are coordinated with specific parts of the signed sentence. . . . In contrast, emotional expressions have more global and inconsistent onset and offset patterns, and their timing is not linked to specific signs or sentential structures."

It was all this that Gallaudet had asked its students to suppress in the 1950s, when it told them not to move their faces as they signed. As the linguist Susan Fischer observed in 1972, when sign-language linguistics was in its infancy, "A signer who does make use of facial and bodily expression looks like a zombie." Gallaudet, in short, had demanded that its students do something unhuman: it asked them to relinquish grammar.

All known signed languages make grammatical use of the face. The same facial expression can mean completely different things in different languages, and different sign languages conscript the face for different grammatical purposes. In the emerging sign language of Nicaragua, a strong nose wrinkle is used to indicate certain types of questions. In Chinese Sign Language, a nose wrinkle can negate a sentence. In Japanese Sign Language, a mouth gesture glossed *po* can turn the present tense into the past.

The sign-language linguist Sherman Wilcox tells a story about attending a convention of the National Association of the Deaf and watching two men hold an animated conversation in sign. One of the men was a double amputee, with a hook where each hand should have been. His conversation partner, Wilcox said, seemed to have absolutely no trouble understanding him. The signer's face was almost certainly working overtime.

As the linguists gather their data in the desert, back in Haifa, a young woman named Svetlana Dachkovsky is waiting for them. A black-haired, porcelain-skinned émigré from the former Soviet Union, Sveta is a graduate student in Wendy's lab. Sveta studies the face. She wrote her master's thesis on a particular kind of squint in Israeli Sign Language, which is used, she found, to signal information that the signer and the addressee are presumed to share. When the linguists return, she will review their tapes frame by frame, scrutinizing the facial expressions of the Bedouins as they sign. For each expression that flickers across their faces, she will ask herself: Is this simply an expression of emotion, or does it have a linguistic function? If so, what does it mean? Each squint or widening of the eyes, every movement of the lips and tongue and brows and head, will be dissected and coded. It takes Sveta an entire day to code six seconds of tape. On the basis of what she finds, Wendy and her colleagues hope to discover what role facial expression plays in the emerging sign language of Al-Sayyid, and whether it has had sufficient time to coalesce into a formalized system like those of other signed languages.

Hakim finishes the test and a fourth brother, also hearing, takes his place. Carol stands up. "I'll ask if they have a bathroom here," she says.

"I doubt it," Wendy says from the floor, "but you can look around." She rises to join Carol but stumbles as she does.

"Don't you break another cup," Mark admonishes her, laughing. The team was fast running out of presents.

From his perch on the balustrade, Kamal spots someone passing on foot in front of the house. He throws a handful of sunflower seeds onto the passerby to catch his attention. Then he leans over the railing, extends his hands and strikes up a conversation with his friend below.

The hearing boy in the chair moves on to the film clips: someone gives a cup to the camera; a man hands a woman a tennis ball. From these simple actions, the linguists hope to answer one of the most fundamental questions about the sign language of Al-Sayyid: Has its grammar developed enough to display verb agreement, as the grammars of a great many human languages do? Established sign languages like ASL make abundant use of verb agreement, with the hands tracing different paths in space depending on whether John is doing something to Mary, or Mary something to John. As the linguists watch the young men sign, it is not yet clear, from their moving hands, whether the verbs of their language actually agree, or whether the signers are simply imitating what they see on the screen. What the linguists will eventually find, as they sift their data back in Haifa, will provide the foundation for their first published discoveries about the language of Al-Sayyid.

Kamal leaves his post at the railing and takes his turn in the signer's chair. He gets to the unusual drawing of the man yelling at the camel, which is also designed to elicit verb agreement. He signs something, and in response, Carol starts to sign elaborately to him. She is asking him to sign the picture again, this time with the actors reversed; she wants to see if he will also reverse the movement of the verb. He seems bewildered by her suggestion.

Carol persists. "What if *you* were the camel," she signs to him, "and the man were yelling at *you*?"

Kamal looks at her for a moment before replying, in sign, "Then I'd run away."

The sun starts to go down. From below, the sound of children's laughter mingles with the bleating of goats. The muezzin calls. Looking out over the village below and the hills beyond, I find myself thinking, "I could stay here forever."

It's a preposterous sentiment, of course, the flip side of "What am I doing here?" and every bit as self-dramatizing and unreal. And yet. . . . At that moment, with the fields washed in gold, the chain link receding into the shadows, and the muezzin's voice wafting in on the desert wind, Al-Sayyid was the loveliest unlovely place on earth.

CHAPTER 12

Grammar in Midair

"It seems very pretty," she said when she had finished it, "but it's rather *hard to understand!" (You see she didn't like to confess, even to herself, that she couldn't make it out at all.) "Somehow it seems to fill my head with ideas—only I don't exactly know what they are! However,* somebody *killed* something*: that's clear, at any rate—"*

—ALICE, ON HEARING "JABBERWOCKY,"
LEWIS CARROLL, *THROUGH THE LOOKING-GLASS*

In human language, the task of showing who did what to whom is one of the principal functions of grammar. Spoken languages accomplish this in a variety of ways. One of these is verb agreement. Verb agreement links a verb grammatically to a noun in the same sentence, usually the subject. It is an efficient way of encoding the relationship between the doer and the deed, and many spoken languages make use of it.

The English verb-agreement system is today a threadbare remnant of its Anglo-Saxon splendor. Only a single verb inflection remains: the final *-s* that gets tacked onto present-tense verbs to encode the third-person singular. *I write*; *he writes.* Because English has so little in the way of inflection, it must find other means of encoding the grammatical relations between actors in a sentence, other ways of showing who did what to whom. It does so through rigid, invariant word order. In the English sentence "The boy sees the girl," we know who does the seeing, and who is seen, entirely by means of word order. When the order of the actors is reversed—"The girl sees the boy"—the meaning of the sentence is reversed as well.

Languages with richer systems of grammatical inflection can exploit freer word orders. In Latin, the sentence *Puer puellam videt* ("The boy sees the girl") retains its meaning even when the words are shuffled in a half-dozen different configurations. It can do this because both of the nouns, and the verb, carry grammatical inflections that encode their grammatical roles unambiguously. The noun *puer* ("boy") is in the nominative case and, as a result, is always understood to be the subject of the sentence. The verb *videt* ("sees") is third-person singular, present tense. The noun *puellam* ("girl") is in the accusative case and is always understood to be the direct object. As a result, the who-did-what-to-whom of the sentence is completely clear, regardless of the order of individual words. While the following sentences may differ slightly in style and emphasis, each one means "The boy sees the girl":

Puer videt puellam.

Puellam videt puer.

Videt puellam puer.

Puer puellam videt.

Puellam puer videt.

Videt puer puellam.

In spoken language, fixed word order and grammatical inflection tend to vary in inverse proportion. As the linguist Charles Osgood has written, "Inflection seems to compensate with word-order as an alternative means of keeping the syntactical house in order." Either way, the world's spoken languages do a masterful job of encoding distinctions between the actor and the acted-upon. The ability to do this is one of the defining properties of human language.

What about sign languages? In American Sign Language, word order is a little freer than it is in English. The ASL sentences GIRL

LOOK-AT BOY; BOY GIRL LOOK-AT; and GIRL BOY LOOK-AT are all perfectly acceptable ways of saying "The girl looks at the boy." Yet signers have no difficulty distinguishing fundamental differences in the meanings of sentences—no trouble, in other words, telling "The girl looks at the boy" from "The boy looks at the girl." If this is true, then ASL must possess a very rich system of grammatical inflection, as languages like Latin, Finnish and Hungarian do. But since sign language has little in the way of traditional grammatical affixes, what does that leave?

Once again, signed language encodes grammar by manipulating space. One of the most spectacular displays of the grammatical use of space can be found in their systems of verb agreement. And while verb agreement can look extremely pantomimic, in recent years linguists have discovered that it bears the hallmarks of a fully functioning linguistic system.

ASL encodes verb agreement by manipulating the direction in which a verb travels through space. Take the verb HELP. If I want to sign the sentence "I help you," the sign HELP, a two-handed sign in which the closed fist of one hand rests on the upturned palm of the other, moves through space from me to you. My hands start at my chest and travel forward until they are near your chest. With this simple directional movement, the verb HELP has been encoded for agreement, traveling from a first-person singular starting point ("I") to a second-person singular endpoint ("you"). If, however, I want to sign "You help me," the direction of the movement is reversed. HELP is made with the same handshape, but this time the sign starts with the hands held outward (near you) and travels through the air toward me. In each sentence, two discrete locations in space—the starting and endpoints of the verb's movement—serve as visual "inflections" for person and number.

In spoken languages that use inflection, conjugating the verb often allows the speaker to leave out the corresponding pronoun. In Spanish, it is perfectly acceptable to say either *Yo vengo a la casa* ("I am going home") or, simply, *Vengo a la casa.* Because the verb (*vengo*) does the work of encoding the concept "first-person singular," it is not necessary to express the pronoun *yo* ("I") overtly, though a speaker may choose to do so for emphasis.

The same is true in sign language. Because an ASL sentence like "I help you" already encodes information about person and number through its movement, it is unnecessary to sign the pronouns "I" and "you" separately. As it travels through the air from me to you, HELP encodes these meanings all by itself: an entire sentence, collapsed into a single sign. And in its flight through space, this single sign encodes more information than verbs in many spoken languages do. In English, verb agreement encodes information about the subject only: in the sentence *He walk**s***, the verb encodes a third-person singular subject. The same is true for most Western languages: Latin *Am**o*** ("I love," encoding a first-person singular subject); German ***Wir*** *spiel**en*** ("We play," encoding a first-person plural subject).

Sign-language verbs encode even more information. As the verb HELP travels through the air in the sentence "I help you," it encodes not only the subject of the sentence ("I") but also the direct object ("you"). Through the path of its movement, HELP is inflected for *both* a first-person-singular subject *and* a second-person-singular direct object. Though verbs that inflect for both subject and object may seem peculiar to speakers of English, they are found in the grammars of some spoken languages, including the Algonquian languages of North America.

Though many ASL verbs inflect for both subject and object, these "inflections" don't tack extra linguistic material onto the verb, as they would in most spoken languages. In ASL, grammatical inflection involves not so much a process of affixation as it does simply a *process*—in this case, the process of altering a sign's trajectory through space.

Spoken languages can also encode grammatical information by means of a process. It happens routinely in many European languages, where a grammatical process known as ablaut can convey linguistic information simply by changing a vowel in the word, without adding an affix. Ablaut even occurs in a small way in English, encoding the past and perfect tenses of a small set of verbs, among them "s*i*ng"/"s*a*ng"/"s*u*ng" and "r*i*ng"/"r*a*ng"/"r*u*ng." Another process that English uses is the shift in stress between certain English verbs and their corresponding nouns: "convíct"/"cónvict"; "subjéct"/"súbject"; "rebél"/"rébel."

Semitic languages, among them Hebrew, Arabic and Maltese, depend centrally on ablaut to encode grammar. In these languages, families of related words share the same phonological "root," usually a group of three consonants. Changes in meaning are encoded by plugging different vowels into this consonantal template. In many Semitic languages, the root *k-t-b* is shared by a family of words having to do with writing. Notice what happens in these examples from Arabic when different vowels are inserted into the template:

***k**a**t**a**b**a*	"he wrote"
***k**aa**t**a**b**a*	"he corresponded"
k**u**t**i**b	"was written"
***k**a**tt**a**b**a*	"he caused to write"

In signed language, verb agreement is encoded through a process of alteration—alteration in a sign's movement. But is this really grammar? In ASL, verb agreement can look an awful lot like mime. In the sentence "I give to you," the movement of the verb GIVE—an open palm that arcs through space from me to you—looks exactly like the mimetic gesture hearing people use. Similarly for "You give to me," where the hand moves in the opposite direction. For the last two decades, sign-language linguists have made a deep study of verb agreement, and most of them now conclude that the movement of a verb between the participants in a signed conversation is far more than pantomime. While some verbs may look mimetic on the surface, linguists have found compelling evidence of a true system of grammatical agreement at work underneath.

For one thing, not all verbs in sign language can be made to agree. While it is possible, in ASL, to sign a sentence like "I help you" using only the moving verb, there are many other verbs for which it isn't. For these verbs, among them LIKE, LOVE, WANT and TEMPT, moving the hands through space while signing them is considered ungrammatical. These verbs, in other words, are not allowed to agree with anything. If I want to sign "I tempt you," I must first sign the pronoun "I" (by pointing to myself), then sign the verb TEMPT (the curved index finger of one hand taps the elbow of the other) without moving it anywhere, and, finally, sign the pronoun "you" (by pointing to you). If ASL sentences were truly mimetic, then *every* verb would be allowed to travel through space as HELP does. One of the puzzles facing early sign-language linguists was to figure out which verbs agree, which verbs don't and what accounts for the difference.

Another reason ASL verb agreement is *linguistic* is that the verbs of the language can "agree" with people and things that aren't physically present. It's easy to mistake "I help you" as pantomime when both you and I are in the room. But what about a sentence in which neither of the actors is there? One of the hallmarks of spoken language is its ability to refer to nonpresent entities—like truth, justice or a car I owned twenty years ago. Sign language can do the same thing.

If I want to say, "The teacher helps the student," and both teacher and student happen to be in the room, nothing is easier: I start the verb HELP near the teacher and move it through space until it gets to the student. But what if they aren't? Signed languages have an extremely efficient way of getting around the problem, and, once again, it involves manipulating space.

To sign "The teacher helps the student" where neither is physically present, I do the following: First, I sign TEACHER. Then, I point to a spot somewhere in space, say, off to my right. For the rest of the conversation, that spot will stand in for the noun TEACHER. Next, I do the same thing with STUDENT, first making the sign, then pointing to another spot, say, off to my left. TEACHER and STUDENT now hang invisibly, yet palpably, in space at the points I've designated. A verb traveling between these two points is understood to involve these two actors. If I place TEACHER to my right and STUDENT to my left, and then sign the verb HELP so that it travels from my right to my left, I have just said, "The teacher helps the student." If the verb travels from left to right, I've said, "The student helps the teacher." Participants in a signed conversation, linguists have found, can keep track of dozens of these invisible points. Each one functions as a kind of pronoun, embodying the actor to which it's been assigned and hanging in space until someone needs to refer to that actor again. By the end of a long conversation, the air around the signers fairly bristles with these invisible pronouns.

When linguists began studying ASL in earnest in the 1970s, they didn't recognize verb agreement for what it was. They were English speakers, wedded to affixes. But once they recognized that in this language of space, agreement could be encoded by a *process*—and that the process involved a change in a sign's directional movement—they came to see verb agreement as the centerpiece of the great array of morphological riches that signed languages display.

One of the first linguists to study verb agreement seriously was Carol Padden, in work begun for her doctoral dissertation in the early 1980s. Carol discovered that ASL verbs can be divided into groups based on the ways in which they inflect. Many spoken languages group their words based on their inflectional patterns. In English, most verbs, like "walk," form the past tense by adding *-d* or *-ed*. However, a small class, including "weep" and "sleep," also employs ablaut. We call these "irregular" verbs. Latin assigns its nouns to one of five declensions, and its verbs to one of four conjugations, based on the endings that can attach to them.

ASL verbs, as Carol discovered, can be divided into three classes. The first, which she called agreeing verbs, are those, like HELP, that move through space from subject to object. Other verbs in this class are ASK, BAWL-OUT, GIVE, COMMAND, CONVINCE, FLATTER, HATE, IGNORE, INFORM, KISS, LOCK-HORNS, LOSE-CONTACT, MOCK, PERSUADE, PICK-ON, REJECT, SCOLD, SELL, SEND, SHOW, TEACH, TEASE, TELL, THROW-TO, TELEGRAPH and WARN.

The second class, which Carol called spatial verbs, includes BRING, CARRY-BY-HAND, EXAMINE, GO-AWAY, INSERT, MOVE, POINT-

TO, SCRUB, TRACE and WRITE. These verbs, like agreeing verbs, also move through space. Unlike agreeing verbs, they encode neither subject nor object. Instead, they encode physical locations, as in the sentence "I moved the book from here to there," in which the movement of the verb—from the signer's right, say, to his left—is analogous to the movement of an object in the physical world.

The third class, which Carol called plain verbs, includes verbs like TEMPT that do not inflect at all. Other plain verbs are ACCEPT, ACQUIESCE, BATHE, BE-CAREFUL, BRUSH-TEETH, DON'T-CARE, EAT, ENJOY, FORGET, GUESS, JUDGE, LAUGH, LIKE, LIPREAD, MEMORIZE, SET-UP, SUSPECT, THANK, THINK, THROW-AWAY, VOTE, WALK, YAWN and YELL.

Within the class of agreeing verbs, Carol identified a special subset. These verbs also agree, but in a curious way. One of these verbs is INVITE. For normal agreeing verbs, the starting point denotes the subject, and the endpoint the object, as in the sentence "I bawl you out," where BAWL-OUT moves from me to you. INVITE is different. If I want to say "I invite you," the verb starts out in space (near *you*) and travels *inward* (toward *me*). It moves, in other words, from object to subject, the diametric opposite of pantomime. Other agreeing verbs that behave this way include BORROW, COPY, EXTRACT, MOOCH, STEAL, TAKE and TAKE-ADVANTAGE-OF. Carol called this curious subclass of verbs "backwards verbs."

Nearly every sign language that has been studied so far handles verb agreement by altering a sign's movement in similar fashion. What is more, the set of three verb classes that Carol discovered in ASL—agreeing, spatial and plain verbs—as well as the strange subset of backwards verbs, are also found in all known signed languages. Even the emerging sign language of Nicaragua appears to have these classes. In one sign language after another, the same verbs tend to fall into the same classes: EAT is almost always plain, MOVE is almost always spatial, GIVE is almost always agreeing, and INVITE is almost always backwards. Even unrelated sign languages, like ASL and British Sign, organize their verbs into similar groups.

What makes sign-language verbs behave this way? And why is their behavior so similar across dozens of signed languages? Are these shared patterns merely an effect of the modality in which sign language is transmitted, or do they reveal something deeper? These were the questions confronting sign-language linguists of the 1980s and after. As they would gradually discover, the way in which signed languages divide up their verbs *does* stem from the modality in which they're transmitted, *and* it reflects something deeper. The behavior of sign-language verbs, it turns out, is rooted in the intersection of visuospatial cognition with visuospatial language.

One of the linguists to look deeply at these questions has been, coincidentally, Irit Meir. In work begun in the late 1990s, she examined the structure of agreeing verbs in Israeli Sign Language, a class that, like the one in ASL, includes ASK, HATE, HELP, GIVE, INFORM, SHOW, TELL and SEND. All of these verbs, Irit found, denote some type of *transfer.* They might entail the transfer of a concrete object, as with GIVE, SEND or FEED. They can also entail transfer of a more metaphorical kind, as with HELP (in which assistance is transferred), TEACH (knowledge), ASK (information), HATE (animus) and many others. When these verbs move between points in space, they denote transfer between the grammatical subjects and objects those points represent.

By contrast, the endpoints of spatial verbs like BRING denote not subjects and objects, but points in real space, as in the sentence "I brought the book from *here* to *there.*" Plain verbs, finally, involve neither transfer nor movement. They don't agree with anything, and, as a result, they don't move through space at all. This tripartite classification—verbs of transfer, which encode grammatical subjects and objects; verbs of movement, which encode locative information; and plain verbs, which encode neither—has been found in every signed language that has verb agreement.

Irit noticed something else about agreeing verbs that was strikingly systematic. It had to do with the direction in which the signer's hands were pointing when the verbs were being made, a phenomenon she called "facing." Facing is somewhat like orientation: it describes the direction in which the palm or the fingertips point. For agreeing verbs, Irit discovered, the direction in which the signer's hands face depends crucially on who is doing what to whom. The ISL verb HATE is an agreeing verb. A one-handed sign, it is made with the open palm, fingers spread. If I sign "I hate you," my hand travels from near my chest to yours, with the palm facing you, as if I were pushing you away in disgust. But if I sign "You hate me," the sign not only travels from your chest to mine, but my arm is also rotated 180 degrees at the elbow so that the palm now faces me. There is no physiological reason for this: it is perfectly possible for the hand to travel from you to me without the arm rotation. But that small physical change, Irit discovered, is a potent grammatical signal. For agreeing verbs, the facing of the hand is always toward the *object* of the verb. The same holds true for other agreeing verbs, like GIVE, which in ISL also involves the palm arcing from subject to object. When the signer completes the movement, her fingertips always point toward the object, whether the sentence is "I give you" or "You give me."

Without realizing it, speakers of the world's signed languages were moving their hands in a way that encoded an essential piece of linguistic information: the "whom" of who-does-what-to-whom. In all known sign languages, the facing of the hands in agreeing verbs has been found to encode the grammatical notion "object." It does so as simply and efficiently as Latin or German words encode the same information with suffixes.

Irit also examined the curious case of backwards verbs. Like ordinary agreeing verbs, these verbs move between endpoints in space representing the grammatical subject and object. But, in one sign language after another, they do it "backwards," starting at the object and ending at the subject. The result is a set of verbs that, like INVITE, move in oddly counterintuitive ways. In language after language, a similar set of verbs—INVITE, COPY, TAKE-ADVANTAGE-OF—behaves in this way.

There is a remarkably elegant explanation for this, as Irit discovered. It lies in the *semantic* roles that the actors in signed sentences play. In human language, a sentence always contains a verb, plus at least one noun or pronoun. (Even imperative sentences, like "Stop!" contain the implied pronoun "you.") In the grammars of most languages, these nouns play fairly straightforward parts. Nouns name things, and that is all they do. Nouns pretty much just sit there, and in terms of the demands they make on the grammar, they are largely straightforward.

Verbs are another story. They carry much more linguistic baggage. Because verbs denote actions or events or states of being, the presence of a verb also requires the presence of one or more actors to carry out, experience or feel whatever it is the verb is describing. These actors can be nouns, pronouns or a combination of the two.

In the world's spoken languages, different types of verbs demand different types of actors. It is this fact, as the linguist and philosopher of language George Lakoff points out, that makes the first sentence below acceptable and the ones that follow increasingly bizarre:

(1) *My uncle* realizes that I'm a lousy cook.

(2) *My cat* realizes that I'm a lousy cook.

(3) *My goldfish* realizes that I'm a lousy cook.

(4) *My pet amoeba* realizes that I'm a lousy cook.

(5) *My frying pan* realizes that I'm a lousy cook.

Syntactically, these five sentences are beautifully made. But in Sentences 2 through 5, the level of semantic weirdness mounts. That is because the actors in these sentences fail increasingly to meet the semantic demands of the verb "realize," which requires a subject that is both animate and sentient. Other verbs of cognition, like "imagine," "suppose" and "reckon," take similar subjects.

Other verbs require other actors. "Kill" demands an animate direct object: "I killed *my guppy*" is a fine sentence; "I killed *my frying pan*" is not. "Murder" requires a direct object that is not only animate but also human. Compare "I murdered *my boss*" with "I murdered *my pet amoeba.*" "Assassinate" takes a direct object that is not only animate and human but is also a person of great distinction, usually a political figure. "I assassinated *the president of Fredonia*" is semantically fine, "I assassinated *the milkman,*" less so. Codifying which kinds of actors can be paired with which kinds of verbs falls to semanticists, linguists who specialize in the study of meaning.

Semanticists classify noun "actors" according to the kinds of roles, called thematic roles, that they play in sentences. Thematic roles reflect basic cognitive concepts—doing or being done to, giving or receiving—that are found in all human cultures. A wide range of possible semantic roles exists, but across the world's spoken languages, a half-dozen or so recur again and again. These roles include "agent" (the "doer" of the action of the verb, almost always the subject: *John* in "John killed Mary"); "patient" (the recipient of the action of the verb: *Mary* in "John killed Mary"); "source" (the point of origin of a verb of motion or transfer: *I* in "I gave you the book"); and "goal" (the destination, or recipient, of a verb of motion or transfer: *you* in "I gave you the book").

Since deaf signers have the same kinds of mental systems as hearing speakers do, these cognitive concepts are available to them, too. Not surprisingly, sign language is spectacularly good at finding ways of encoding them in three-dimensional space. As Irit discovered, agreeing verbs in signed languages automatically encode information about the thematic *source* and *goal* of the sentences in which they appear. Once again, they do it by the way in which they move. In signed languages, the starting point of agreeing verbs always indicates the thematic source of the verb; the endpoint always indicates the goal. If a signer wants to say "John helps Mary," her hands begin at the thematic source ("John," from whom the help emanates) and move through space until they reach the thematic goal ("Mary," to whom the help goes). If agreeing verbs look mimetic, perhaps it is more accurate to describe them as looking *semantic,* encoding through their movement a crucial thematic relationship between actors in the sentence. Many spoken languages encode the same information with inflections.

The notions of source and goal, Irit found, also explain the odd behavior of backwards verbs. Backwards verbs like INVITE look grammatically "backwards" because they move from object to subject instead of the other way around. But if you look at the *semantics* of these verbs, they become suddenly, stunningly normal. As Irit discovered, not only do regular agreeing verbs travel from thematic source to thematic goal, backwards verbs do, too. Take a sentence like "I invite you," which in ASL travels from object ("you") to subject ("I"). If you think about what the sentence is actually "doing" semantically, you realize that the verb INVITE implies a kind of movement, or transfer. If I invite you, then *you* (the starting point, or source) will ultimately come to *me* (the destination, or goal). The same is true for verbs like COPY, which is also "backwards" in many of the world's signed languages. In the sentence "I copy you," the verb's movement originates at a point near the grammatical object ("you") and ends near the subject ("I"). But if COPY is teased apart semantically, what is actually taking place? Some sort of transfer (of information, probably), starting at *you* (the source) and ending at *me* (the goal).

With her analysis, Irit demonstrated that the class of backwards verbs behaves just like the much larger class of regular agreeing verbs: in both cases, the verb moves from thematic source to thematic goal. In the case of regular agreeing verbs, the thematic source and goal are the same as the grammatical subject and object—"John" and "Mary," respectively, in "John kicked Mary." For backwards verbs, the reverse is true: the thematic source of the sentence is the grammatical *object,* the thematic goal the grammatical *subject.* The distribution of agreeing, spatial, plain and backwards verbs is so similar across signed languages because the cognitive concepts these verbs encode are so completely universal.

Like their regular counterparts, backwards verbs also encode the notion "grammatical object" through facing, as Irit found. In ASL, the backwards verb TAKE is made by extending one hand, palm out, and drawing it back toward the signer while closing it into a fist, as if grabbing a small object. If I want to sign "I take from you," my hand starts at "you" (the source of what's being taken) and travels toward "me" (the recipient). My palm, first open, then closed, remains facing you throughout the sentence. This marks "you" as the grammatical object. If I want to sign "You take from me," the reverse happens: my open palm, facing me this time, closes into a fist as it travels toward you. My hand continues to face "me," the grammatical object, the whole time.

For agreeing verbs, both regular and backwards, what looks mimetic in the signed languages of the world is in reality a great deal more than that: the movement of these verbs is part of an ordered, formalized symbolic system. As Irit has written, "By unraveling the factors that determine this classification, it is shown that the agreement system of ISL verbs is a linguistic system determined by general linguistic principles." The same has been found for other sign languages. Verb agreement is one of the most dramatic ways in which the world's signed languages use the rich spatial morphology at their disposal to encode highly complex words. And a set of unusual signs, known as classifiers, which divide the sign-language world into essential cognitive categories, is another.

In his essay "The Analytical Language of John Wilkins," Jorge Luis Borges writes tantalizingly of "a certain Chinese encyclopedia" entitled *Celestial Emporium of Benevolent Knowledge*:

> On those remote pages it is written that animals are divided into (a) those that belong to the Emperor, (b) embalmed ones, (c) those that are trained, (d) suckling pigs, (e) mermaids, (f) fabulous ones, (g) stray dogs, (h) those that are included in this classification, (i) those that tremble as if they were mad, (j) innumerable ones, (k) those drawn with a very fine camel's hair brush, (l) others, (m) those that have just broken a flower vase, (n) those that resemble flies from a distance.

Language cuts the universe up into categories, or, more precisely, the nouns of language do. "One of the basic questions in the study of language is how the perceived world is expressed and represented in, and through, language, how language refers to the perceived world, to its objects, things, and living beings," the linguist Gunter Senft has written. "We do not only perceive the world, but we also develop concepts about what we perceive and create linguistic expressions that refer to and represent those concepts. These expressions refer—among other things—to actions, temporary states, things and objects, persons and other living beings."

Many languages divide up the world by means of special terms called classifiers. Classifiers sort the nouns of the language (and, by extension, the things in the world of the speakers of that language) along all kinds of generic lines. These lines typically include: animate beings versus inanimate objects, animals versus vegetables, wide things versus narrow ones, large things versus small ones. In Yidiny, an aboriginal language of Australia, a speaker would utter a bare-bones sentence like "The girl dug up the yam" only rarely. Instead, as the Australian linguist R. M. W. Dixon writes, "It is more felicitous to include generics and say, 'the person girl dug up the vegetable yam.'"

English, like most Indo-European languages, is largely bereft of classifiers. It does have a few, chiefly the set of generic terms known as mensural classifiers. Mensural classifiers are found in all known spoken languages; they typically accompany nouns for which units of measure have to be further specified. In English, we say "a *piece* of paper," "a *cup* of coffee," "a *head* of lettuce," "a *loaf* of bread." It is certainly possible for a speaker of English to walk into a bakery and say, "Give me a bread," but it sounds extremely odd. To talk about physical quantities of nouns like *bread,* English grammar requires speakers to use a mensural classifier like *loaf, slice, piece, crust* or *crumb,* along with the noun.

In other languages of the world, classifier systems are far more elaborate. Classifiers are common in the languages of Asia and Africa, as well as in many indigenous languages of Australia and the Americas. These languages use classifiers to define a wide range of semantic properties. Some, like Japanese, have classifiers that define the dimensional properties of objects: large or small, wide or narrow, tall or short. Some, also like Japanese, classify nouns in terms of larger existential properties: animate or inanimate; human, animal or vegetable; earth or fire; wood or water. By means of its classifiers, every language slices up the world a little differently, and for this reason, classifiers have enticed scholars in a range of disciplines, from linguistics and anthropology to philosophy and psychology. Classifiers illuminate the place in the mental landscape where culture and cognition meet. As the linguist and philosopher of language George Lakoff has written:

> It is common for the grammars of languages to mark certain conceptual categories. Inasmuch as language is a part of cognition in general—and a major part at that—conceptual categories marked by the grammars of languages are important in understanding the nature of cognitive categories in general. Classifier languages—languages where nouns are marked as being members of certain categories—are among the richest sources of data that we have concerning the structure of conceptual categories as they are revealed through language.

Different languages use widely different systems of classifiers, and sorting out these various systems, itself a job of classification, has kept linguists busy for centuries. Many Asian languages, for instance, employ a set of "numeral" classifiers, which describe the physical properties of nouns that are being counted. Where English would say "five oranges" and "twelve pine trees," these languages would say, in effect, "five round-things of oranges" and "twelve long-things of pine trees."

To convey the notion "I bought three pencils," a Japanese speaker attends to very different things—to the essential properties, as it were, of pencilhood—than an English speaker is apt to do. The sentence in Japanese, *Enpitsu o sanbon katta,* contains the classifier *hon,* used when one is counting long thin rigid objects. Here, the classifier is attached to *san,* "three." (*Hon* is pronounced *bon* in certain instances, as in this and the following examples):

enpitsu	*o*	*san**bon***	*katta*
pencils	[marks direct objects]	three-**long-thin-rigid**	bought

"[I] bought three pencils."

Similarly:

toomorokoshi	*o*	*san**bon***	*katta*
corn	[object marker]	three-**long-thin-rigid**	bought

"[I] bought three ears of corn."

But compare the following sentences, which contain the classifier *mai,* used to count thin flat flexible (or foldable) things:

kami	*o*	*san**mai***	*katta*
paper	[object marker]	three-**thin-flat-flexible**	bought

"[I] bought three sheets of paper."

kimono	*o*	*san**mai***	*katta*
kimono	[object marker]	three-**thin-flat-flexible**	bought

"[I] bought three kimonos." (Kimonos are often stored folded.)

In some languages, classifiers describe even more elemental properties of the nouns they classify. Linguists call these "entity" classifiers. Entity classifiers play a vigorous role in the grammar of Dyirbal, another Australian aboriginal language studied extensively by R. M. W. Dixon. In Dyirbal, every noun in the language must be preceded by one of four classifier terms—*bayi, balan, balam* or *bala*—which marks its membership in one of the four categories into which the Dyirbal world is divided. As Dixon's work showed, the members of each category include a bewildering array of seemingly unrelated nouns. The four classes, with examples of the nouns they include, were reproduced by George Lakoff in his popular book about mental categories, *Women, Fire, and Dangerous Things*:

I. *Bayi*: men, kangaroos, possums, bats, most snakes, most fishes, some birds, most insects, the moon, storms, rainbows, boomerangs, some spears, etc.

II. *Balan*: women, bandicoots, dogs, platypus, echidna, some snakes, some fishes, most birds, fireflies, scorpions, crickets, the hairy mary grub, anything connected with water or fire, sun and stars, shields, some spears, some trees, etc.

III. *Balam*: all edible fruit and the plants that bear them, tubers, ferns, honey, cigarettes, wine, cake.

IV. *Bala*: parts of the body, meat, bees, wind, yamsticks, some spears, most trees, grass, mud, stones, noises and language, etc.

A classifier's function is to identify, describe and keep track of the noun to which it refers, and in this regard it acts as a sort of pronoun. Classifiers help keep conversations smooth and sorted. They are yet another tool human language has at its disposal for distinguishing among actors in a sentence, another way of showing who does what to whom, what is located where and how big or small or round or solid or human it is.

In most classifier languages, as in Dyirbal, the classifier closely accompanies the noun it classifies, either preceding it, following it or affixing to it directly. But there are also classifiers of another sort. These are called verbal classifiers. Like all classifiers, they describe nouns, but these classifiers attach directly to the main *verb* of a sentence. They classify properties of the verb's chief actor. Verbal classifiers are rare in the world's spoken languages, but they do occur. In Diegueño, an indigenous language of Mexico, verbal classifiers denote the physical characteristics, like the size or shape, of the object of the verb:

a'*mi* . . .	"to hang (**a long object**)"
tu*mi* . . .	"to hang (**a small round object**)"
a*xi* . . .	"to drag (**a long object**)"
c'*xi* . . .	"to drag (**a bunch of objects**)"

In Cayuga, if one needs to talk about a vehicle, one affixes the "vehicle" classifier, *treht*, before the verb:

Skitú ake'-**treht**-*áe'*

Ski-doo I-(**vehicle**)-have

"I have a Ski-doo."

Sign languages teem with verbal classifiers. Folded directly into verbs of motion or location, they describe basic properties of the verbs' subjects. Like classifiers in many of the world's spoken languages, sign-language classifiers describe a set of familiar traits among them size, shape and animacy.

In ASL, the following are perfectly grammatical sentences, in fact, quite ordinary ones:

(a) MONEY **SMALL-ROUND-SHAPE**-BE-LOCATED
"A coin is lying there."

(b) MONEY **FLAT-WIDE-SHAPE**-BE LOCATED
"A bill is lying there."

(c) MONEY **DOME-SHAPE**-BE-LOCATED
"A pile of change is lying there."

Sign-language classifiers are represented by distinctive handshapes, which are incorporated directly into the verbs. In ASL, the classifier denoting small round objects, like coins, buttons, peas or small cookies, is made with the thumb and index finger joined in a small circle, like the conventional sign for "OK." For medium-sized round objects, like cups, drinking glasses or larger cookies, the classifier is a more open, C-shaped hand. The classifier for large round objects, like dinner plates or motion picture reels, is made with two C-shaped hands, held some distance apart to describe the circumference of a circle. A flat palm, fingers together, classifies flat objects, like tabletops, rulers, dollar bills and sheets of paper. All of these are what linguists call "size-and-shape" classifiers. With respect to the physical properties they describe, they are strikingly similar to classifiers in many spoken languages.

By means of its classifiers, ASL has another potent mechanism at its disposal for forming complex words. In the three ASL sentences above, each complex verb (SMALL-ROUND-SHAPE-BE-LOCATED, FLAT-WIDE-SHAPE-BE-LOCATED, DOME-SHAPE-BE-LOCATED) is made with a single sign. The addressee already knows that the classifier describes some type of money (a coin, a bill or a pile of change) because MONEY has been signed earlier in the discourse.

Thomas Hopkins Gallaudet (1787–1851) and Laurent Clerc (1785–1869), seminal figures in the education of deaf people in America. (BOTH IMAGES: GALLAUDET UNIVERSITY ARCHIVES)

William C. Stokoe (1919–2000), the father of the linguistic study of sign language. He appears to be signing the ASL verb LOOK-AT. (GALLAUDET UNIVERSITY ARCHIVES

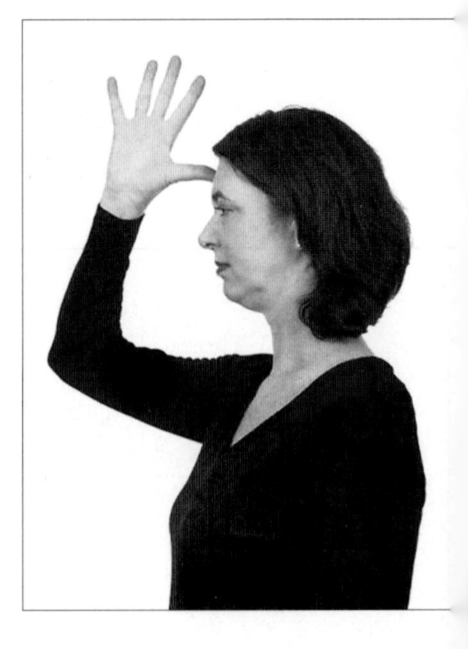

Three elements—the shape of the hands, their location in space, and the manner in which they move—combine to create all the words of a sign language. The ASL signs FATHER, ROOSTER and THINK, shown from left to right, share a location (the forehead) and movement (the signer's hand comes to rest on the forehead). The difference lies in the handshape: for FATHER, an open palm; for ROOSTER, the extended thumb, index and middle fingers; for THINK, the extended index finger. (ASL IMAGES PHOTOGRAPHED AND DIGITALLY PRODUCED BY IVAN FARKAS. THE MODEL IS JODY GILL.)

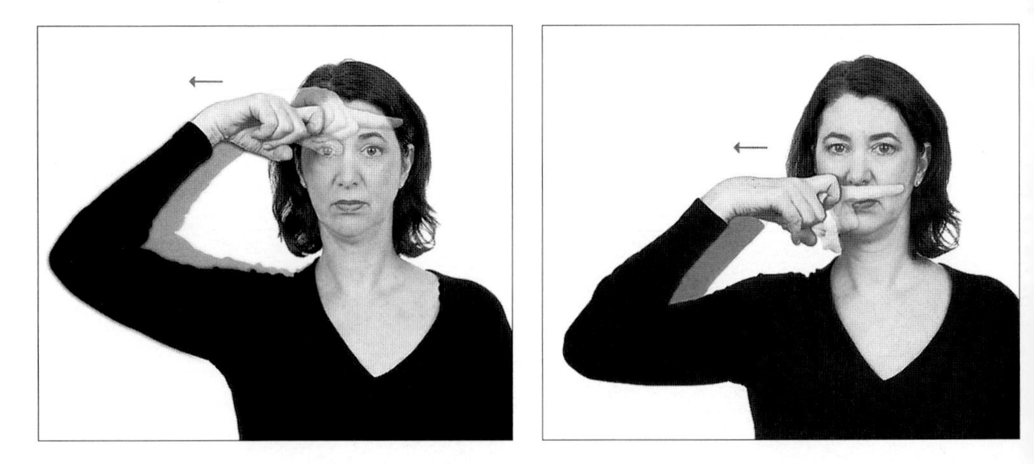

Left to right, the ASL signs SUMMER, UGLY and DRY share handshape and movement but differ in location. In these and the following illustrations, the "ghost" image represents the starting point of the hands, the full image their endpoint.

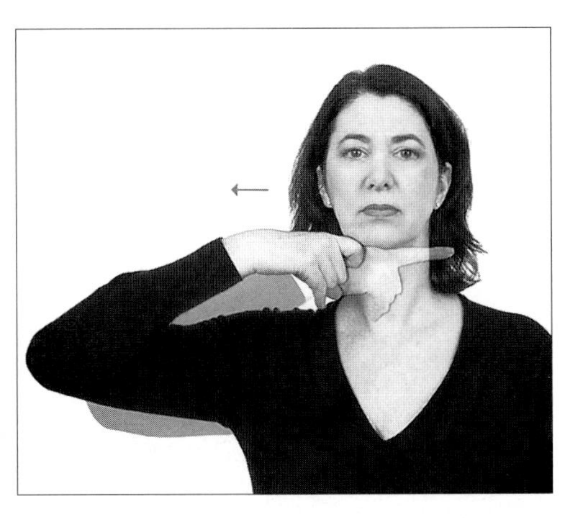

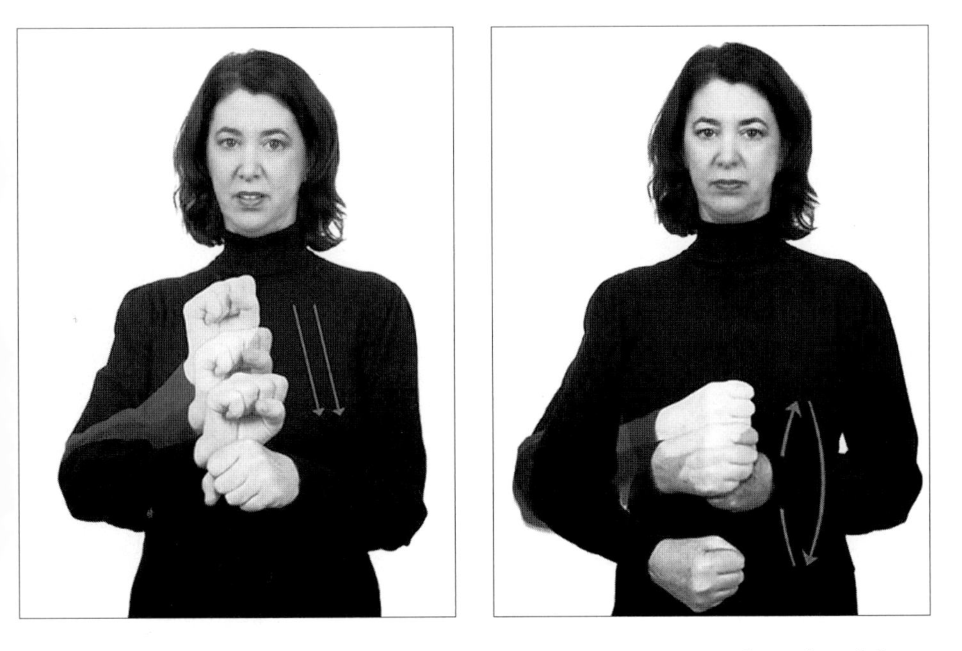

Left to right, the ASL signs COFFEE, WORK and YEAR share handshape and location but differ in movement.

Left to right, the ASL verb SMOKE and the related noun CIGARETTE. Where SMOKE is made with a large single movement, the movement of CIGARETTE is restrained and repeated. This alteration in movement is a regular grammatical process in ASL.

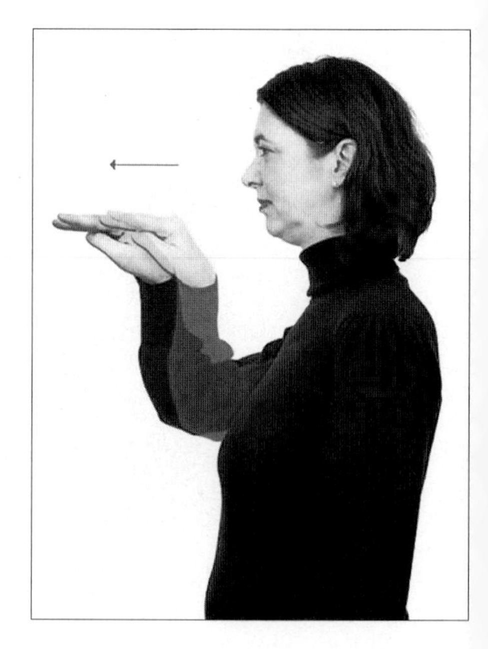

Changing a sign's movement pattern can produce a constellation of signs with related meanings. Far left, the simple ASL verb LOOK-AT, made with a single horizontal movement. Below left, the same sign, made with the hand sweeping down, then up, means "size up" or "give the once-over." (Made with only the downward movement, it means "condescend"—literally, "look down on.") Below right, LOOK-AT, made in a slow circle, means "look at intently" or "observe."

In the face lies grammar. Above, the ASL sentence "Father is home" (FATHER HOME) is signed with a neutral expression. Below, the same sequence of signs, made with raised eyebrows and a head tilt, becomes a yes-or-no question: "Is Father home?"

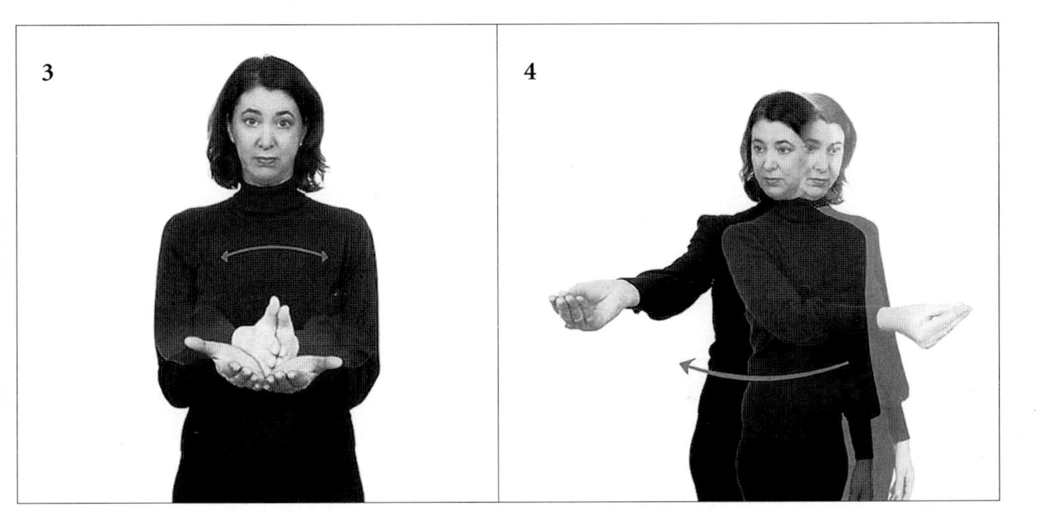

Signing an ASL sentence—"Mother gives the book to Father"—by "hanging" actors in the air for later use. In Frame 1, the signer signs MOTHER, then points to a spot on her left. For the rest of the discourse, this invisible spot will refer to MOTHER. In Frame 2, she does the same thing with FATHER, assigning it to a spot on her right. In Frame 3, she signs BOOK. In Frame 4, the verb GIVE travels through space from the spot denoting MOTHER to the one denoting FATHER. Thus, the sentence unequivocally means "Mother gives the book to Father."

In sign languages, special handshapes called classifiers can represent entire entities, as in the ASL sentences at left. Top, in the sentence "The man meandered up the hill," the verb MEANDER is signed using an extended index finger, the classifier for people. Center, in "The dog meandered up the hill," the verb is made with a bent V-shaped hand, the classifier for small animals. Bottom, in "The car meandered up the hill," it is made with the extended thumb, index and middle fingers, the classifier for vehicles.

The team loads the van for the trip to the desert. Left to right: Carol Padden, Mark Aronoff, Wendy Sandler, Irit Meir. (THIS AND PHOTOS THAT FOLLOW COURTESY CAROL PADDEN AND SHAI DAVIDI.)

Al-Sayyid.

On the floor of a Bedouin home, Wendy administers a series of tests.

The camera rolls as the videographer, Shai Davidi (front row, right), looks on. Out of consideration for local traditions, the faces of Al-Sayyid women are masked in all images produced by the team.

A Bedouin man signing.

Irit and Wendy work with a village woman.

Carol and a young informant.

Irit learns to weave a Bedouin rug.

A village man and his daughter, who is attired in traditional Bedouin dress.

Each of these complex verbs comprises several discrete linguistic units, or morphemes, each of which contributes independent meaning. Wendy and her colleague Diane Lillo-Martin provide a nice illustration of the way in which verbal classifiers work by comparing the architecture of two very similar-looking ASL signs: the simple verb DECIDE and the complex verb A-COIN-IS-LYING-THERE. Both are made, coincidentally, with the thumb and forefinger in the "OK" position, palm facing inward. For DECIDE, the two hands, each in this shape, move downward in front of the signer, from chest level to waist level. The sign A-COIN-IS-LYING-THERE is identical, except that it is made with only one hand.

But when the internal structure of the two signs—their morphology—is compared, a world of linguistic difference emerges. The first sign consists of just a single morpheme, DECIDE, just as the English word "decide" does. Here, the formational parameters of handshape, location and movement are arbitrary devices for linguistic encoding and nothing more: in this combination, they happen to mean "decide." None of these parameters signals anything by itself, just as the lone "d" of the English word "decide" means nothing.

By contrast, in the complex sign A-COIN-IS-LYING-THERE, each parameter carries independent meaning—each is a morpheme all its own. That is exactly what distinguishes classifier constructions in signed languages from simple signs. In A-COIN-IS-LYING-THERE, the *handshape* encodes the semantic class of the noun (a small round object); the *location* signals a specific location in the real world ("there"); and the *movement,* a downward drop of the hand, is the verb stem (BE-LOCATED). Assuming the signer has already established MONEY in the discourse, the entire sentence, "A coin is lying there," can be expressed with a single morphologically complex sign, glossed literally as SMALL-ROUND-SHAPE-BE-LOCATED-(THERE).

All sign languages investigated so far use classifiers. As in ASL, they are woven into verbs of motion and location; as in ASL, they classify the nouns that are the prime actors in these sentences. The result, in one signed language after another, is the capacity to form highly encoded linguistic symbols, complex signs in which handshape, location and movement each contribute independent meaning. Like agreeing and spatial verbs, classifiers are another way in which sign language uses elaborate spatial devices to form morphologically complex words.

Linguists were wary of classifiers at first. Of all the grammatical devices in signed language, classifiers look the most like pantomime. Small, tight handshapes denote small objects like peas; large, loose handshapes denote big ones like plates. A flat hand stands in for a flat piece of paper, a curved hand for cup or glass or pipe. Acknowledging the existence of these constructions, linguists of the 1970s believed, threatened to negate all the hard-won advances, begun with Stokoe, in recognizing ASL as a real language. The linguists were partly right: there is no doubt that the classifier systems of signed languages have their roots in highly mimetic gestures. However, as researchers gradually realized, classifiers provide a marvelous opportunity to watch what happens when these iconic gestures get corraled into a living linguistic system.

The first researcher to study ASL classifiers in detail was Ted Supalla. Now an associate professor of brain and cognitive sciences, linguistics and American Sign Language at the University of Rochester, Supalla is deaf, a native ASL signer. In his doctoral dissertation, written in 1982, Supalla analyzed the structure of these complex verbs of motion and location and looked at the ways in which young deaf children acquire them.

Though classifiers may look mimetic, Supalla discovered that signers were nonetheless using them as abstract linguistic symbols. For one thing, young deaf children acquiring ASL treated classifier constructions not as holistic gestures, but as abstract elements composed of separate morphemes. Supalla discovered that deaf children who had not yet mastered the complex, simultaneous form of a classifier verb often teased out its individual components—handshape, location and movement—and signed them strung one after another in a line. They did this even though the resulting construction was far less mimetic than the real one would have been.

Even the size-and-shape classifiers, easily the most mimetic of the bunch, were functioning as abstract units, Supalla found. In an earlier experiment, from the late 1970s, the psychology graduate student Carol Schwartz, assisted by Supalla and Elissa Newport, attempted to determine whether signers used size-and-shape classifiers as exact analogues of objects in the real world—that is, mimetically—or whether they used them more abstractly, as discrete, linguistic symbols.

The experimenters prepared a set of pictures showing dots of graduated sizes, from very small to very large. Interspersing these with distracter pictures, they showed them to a group of deaf signers. The subjects were asked to make a sign corresponding to each picture they saw, and their responses were videotaped. The responses were then shown to a different group of deaf subjects. Presented with the original set of pictures, these subjects were asked to choose the one that most closely matched each videotaped sign.

As Supalla explained in 1982:

> If indeed the producing subjects are varying their forms in a continuous, analogue fashion, and if the judging subjects are able to perceive these forms accurately, there should be a significant . . . correlation between the stimulus seen by the producer and the stimulus chosen by the judge. If, on the other hand . . . there are only a small number of size morphemes in ASL which are discretely different from one another, there should be a correlation between producers and judges only across boundaries of two distinct size morphemes; within a category of size, producers and judges should have only a chance relationship with one another.

The second scenario is just what happened. The judges were able to match pictures only in terms of larger categories of size, roughly "small," "medium," "large" and "enormous." Within a category—within the whole range of sizes classed as "medium," say—they selected the correct picture with a frequency no better than chance. In other words, signers were using the size-and-shape classifiers for round objects as discrete, linguistic rubrics, not as analogic pantomimes mirroring the vast continuum of sizes possible in the real world. Even here, in this most "mimetic" part of ASL grammar, formerly iconic representations had been commandeered as abstract symbols.

Besides "size-and-shape" classifiers, ASL has several other kinds. These include "tracing" classifiers, which outline the perimeter of an object like a window or a picture frame. There are also "instrumental," or "handling," classifiers, in which the handshape denotes the configuration of the hands as they manipulate an object like a toothbrush, hammer or pistol. And there is another, still more general set, which calls to mind the entity classifiers of Dyirbal. These signed classifiers, like the entity classifiers of many spoken languages, designate broad inherent characteristics of the nouns to which they refer: animate or inanimate; person, animal or vehicle.

ASL has several entity classifiers. One, made with the extended index finger, stands for people. Another, made with the bent index and middle fingers, denotes small animals like cats, dogs, birds and squirrels. A third, made with the thumb, index and middle fingers extended, palm sideways, is used for vehicles, including cars, motorcycles and motorized wheelchairs; buses and trains; boats, submarines and flying saucers. A fourth, made with the thumb, index finger and pinky extended, palm downward, is used exclusively to talk about airplanes. A fifth, made with a closed fist, thumb side up, denotes upright solid objects like houses, or knickknacks on a shelf.

Like other ASL classifiers, entity classifiers are also incorporated into verbs of motion and location. To sign the sentence "The man meandered up the hill," a signer would use the classifier handshape for people—an upright index finger—and move it through space in a haphazard, meandering way. (This, of course, is assuming that the sign MAN was previously established in the conversation.) To sign "The car meandered up the hill," the signer, with CAR previously established, uses the same movement, but this time the handshape is the extended thumb, index and middle fingers, the classifier for vehicles.

All known sign languages have entity classifiers of some kind.

While the same handshape can denote different things in different languages (a flat hand classifies flat objects in ASL; in British Sign Language, it classifies vehicles like cars and bicycles), the world's signed languages cut up the world into strikingly similar categories. What accounts for the similarity? To put the question in Lakoff's terms, what light can sign-language classifiers shed on how signed languages segment the physical world? To begin to answer this question, we need to return to Dyirbal and its four marvelous classifiers, *bayi, balan, balam* and *bala.*

As wild and variegated as the Dyirbal noun classes first appear, membership in each class, as Dixon demonstrated, turns out to be far from random. Instead, it depends on a network of associative links, a chain of metaphor that unites the members of each class under a single semantic rubric. "In the course of his fieldwork," Lakoff has written, "Dixon observed that speakers do not learn category members one by one, but operate in terms of some general principles." The principles included these:

For Class I, *bayi,* Dixon assumed men and animals to be the prototypical members of the class. It then followed that fish, being animals, are also in this class. So, by extension, are things connected with fishing, including spears and fishing line, even though they are inanimate and would seem at first glance to belong elsewhere.

In Dyirbal culture, most birds are believed to be the spirits of dead women. As a result, they appear in Class II, *balan,* with other predominantly female things. And so on, until the thickets of nouns are illuminated by the cultural and cognitive links they share.

What about the entity classifiers of ASL? Why does the language choose to highlight the categories it does? Why does it have a voraciously comprehensive category for vehicles but a completely separate category containing only airplanes? These questions await further research, but in the meantime, it is possible to sketch a preliminary taxonomy of ASL entity classifiers based on their semantic properties.

To start the taxonomy at the top, the five ASL classifiers can be split into two very general groups:

I. Stationary Things: upright solid objects, like knickknacks and houses (encoded by the closed-fist classifier, which has no fingers extended).

II. Movable Things: everything else (encoded by the other four entity classifiers, which denote people, small animals, vehicles and airplanes and are made with one, two or three fingers extended). The category of movable things can be further divided into:

   A. Animates (made with one or two fingers extended), which subdivides into:
      a. People
      b. Animals; and
   B. Inanimates (made with three fingers extended), which subdivides into:
      a. Vehicles other than airplanes
      b. Airplanes.

Why these classes? If a language deploys its classifiers, as sign language does, by plugging them into verbs of motion or location, then dividing up the world into things that move (people, animals, vehicles, planes) and things that sit in place (knickknacks, houses) is probably the most essential distinction it can make. And within the large class of mobile objects, the further division between animates and inanimates is one found in the classifier systems of a great many of the world's spoken languages. The same is true for the people-versus-animals distinction in the class of moving things.

The question remains: Why a separate category for airplanes? Why doesn't the language simply lump them under the generic "vehicle" classifier, which, thanks to associative links, includes even flying saucers?

The answer, I suspect, lies in the history of ASL. In the nineteenth century, before the advent of the airplane, it is possible that the most basic distinction of the classifier system—between things that move and things that don't—had already solidified. That was exactly the distinction a language in the visuospatial mode would be most likely to make. The class of movable things could be further subdivided into animates and inanimates, but in those days, the taxonomy probably stopped after that.

In other words, it seems probable that the classifier system of pre-twentieth-century ASL had a single class of movable inanimate objects. This class included all the vehicles of the day: boats, trains, bicycles and eventually even automobiles. But when the airplane came along in 1903, its advent was so remarkable—and its movement so different from that of familiar vehicles—that ASL placed it, quite literally, in a class by itself, capturing both its cultural uniqueness and its singular physical ability to soar through space. Like the complex signs that are the product of verb agreement, classifier constructions in signed language are rooted both in the drive of language toward symbolic abstraction and in the everyday realities of visuospatial cognition. Strikingly, the ASL classifier for airplanes (a hand with thumb, index finger and pinky extended) is much more obviously mimetic than the generic vehicle classifier (the extended thumb, index and middle fingers, palm sideways), which looks nothing like a car or a bicycle or a flying saucer or, in fact, like much of anything except a hand with three fingers extended.

In spoken languages, classifier systems can change with time. Terms drop out, or are added; categories that were once distinct can be lumped together under more general rubrics. Something similar may be happening in the world's signed languages. As a recent study by Mark, Irit, Carol and Wendy has shown, as a sign language ages, it may begin to carve the world up somewhat differently from the way it did when it was young.

The four linguists compared the classifier systems of ASL, which is about two hundred years old, and ISL, which is much younger, about sixty years old. Israeli Sign Language arose in Palestine in the 1930s and 1940s, influenced in part by deaf German Jewish immigrants and later by immigrants from North Africa. (Though it is about the same age as the emerging sign language of Al-Sayyid, Israeli Sign is descended from established sign languages and as a result is more fully developed linguistically.) The linguists recognized, of course, that the classifier systems of ASL and ISL are not identical. But the classifier systems of all sign languages are similar enough that holding a snapshot of such a system in a two-hundred-year-old language alongside one in a sixty-year-old language can give a general picture of how classifiers might evolve over time within a single language.

In ASL, entity classifiers usually cast a wide semantic net. The vehicle classifier is famously comprehensive, taking in every inanimate thing that moves and isn't an airplane. ISL also has entity classifiers, but they tend to be more specific. In ASL, the generic "vehicle" classifier is used for land vehicles like cars, trucks, bicycles and trains, as well as for marine vehicles like boats and submarines. In ISL, vehicle classifiers classify a much narrower range of objects. There is one classifier (a flat hand, palm down) used only for cars and trucks. Trains and bicycles require their own classifier, in which the palm faces sideways. Boats require an altogether different classifier, the two hands pressed together as if in imitation of a hull. In ISL, boats cannot be lumped under the general "vehicle" rubric.

Other entity classifiers in ISL are similarly specific. "Although we have found entity classifiers like LEGGED-ANIMAL in ISL," the linguists write, "we have so far found none that are as abstract in meaning and form as the two ASL entity classifiers [those for vehicles and upright solid objects] just described."

Even classifiers, the most iconic elements of sign language, seem to grow more general—and, as a result, more arbitrary—over time. There is even some evidence for this from within ASL itself. In his dissertation on ASL classifiers, completed in 1982, Ted Supalla listed, along with the familiar entity classifiers, one he called the "hull" classifier. Used for boats, it was also made with two hands pressed together in the shape of a hull. In the quarter-century since Supalla's dissertation was written, the ASL "hull" classifier seems to have disappeared. Contemporary discussions of classifiers in American Sign Language never mention it. What seems to have happened was that the "hull" classifier was folded under the more general "vehicle" rubric. And while two hands pressed together look a lot like the hull of a ship, the classifier now used to talk about boats—the extended thumb, index and middle fingers—is much less obviously related in form. As in other areas of the language, the ASL classifier system seems to be moving increasingly from iconicity to arbitrariness, from mimicry to regularity, despite the obviously imitative origin of many of its signs.

What about the sign language of the Bedouins? Does it have classifiers? That is one of the many things the linguists' computerized tests have been designed to elicit. The Tweety cartoon, with its towering pile of furniture and its rounded birdcage suspended from a long thin cord, offers especially rich possibilities. If Al-Sayyid Bedouin Sign Language has classifiers, what do they classify and how do they function in the grammar? If it doesn't, is it because the language is simply too young for a classifier system to have coalesced? As the linguists will discover, the concept of language age—what linguistic baggage a very young language can carry and what it cannot yet accommodate—will figure crucially as they begin to write the grammar of the signed language of Al-Sayyid.

CHAPTER 13

Hassan's House

It is the morning of our last day in the village. Hassan has come to the hotel and is sitting with the team in the lobby, helping Irit with her genealogy. With Wendy translating their Hebrew into ASL for Carol, Irit asks him to demonstrate the local signs for "first wife," "second wife" and "third wife." The photographer's vest is gone; Hassan is dressed today in jeans, sandals and an impossibly crisp shirt of pale yellow-green. He has made it here this morning despite car trouble: the little white truck has a blown fuse. A friend managed to jury-rig a new one for him out of cigarette paper.

Irit finishes her work, and we step outside to the van. Today, we are going to Hassan's house, but our first stop is the local grammar school, where Hassan's two deaf daughters attend a special education program. There, on the school grounds, we squeeze into the packed audience of parents who are watching a performance in honor of the last day of school. On a raised outdoor stage, a ring of boys and, at the opposite end of the stage, a ring of girls, are dancing to traditional music.

We watch the dancers awhile, then slip back to the van. Hassan's truck won't start again. Mark goes off to help him, and they make a temporary repair to the temporary repair. Mark returns, beaming. "I learned the Hebrew word for 'fuse,'" he says happily. "*Fyooz.*"

Following the little white truck, we enter Al-Sayyid for the last time. Hassan leads us through the maze until we reach a group of small buildings ranged around a lavish central garden profuse with pink and yellow roses. In the center of the garden stands a rosemary bush the size of a man. Freshly laundered clothing has been laid out to dry over the chain link fence around the perimeter of the garden. On the far side are a little house, one of several in the family compound, and a small storehouse.

Hassan's house is on the near side of the garden. It is small and low, like most of the older houses in the village. The front door opens straight into the living room, and inside, the white tile floor is so bright it looks like an extension of the desert sand. The room holds a suite of armchairs and matching sofa in wine-colored plush, piled with cushions covered in handwoven fabric of orange and red. There is a television, a glass breakfront with several vases of artificial flowers inside, and, in a corner of the room, a plastic peach tree in a large pot.

Fatima, Hassan's second wife, comes into the room and greets us in Arabic. Petite and sharp-featured, she appears to be in her thirties. She is dressed in a long brown skirt, a matching headscarf and a black blouse with silver trim that flashes brilliantly when she steps outside to cut some mint.

A girl of about twelve enters, carrying a tray of glasses filled with *zaatar* and mint. A daughter of Hassan and his first wife, she is hard of hearing, one of the children who performed in the assembly this morning. Carol starts signing to her. They are soon joined by the girl's deaf younger sister, about eight and dressed from head to toe in pink, who enters the room carefully bearing the teapot. Behind her comes their young half-sister, an elfin hearing girl of no more than three, clad in a pair of tiny blue jeans. She climbs into a plastic patio chair, tucks up her legs and sits there solemnly.

Irit takes a stack of drawing paper and a box of pastels from her bag, stretches out on the floor, and begins to draw bright pictures. The three girls quickly follow suit. There, with the sands of the Middle East rushing in through the open front door, the girls draw the universal child's landscape: a huge stylized flower and, beside it, exactly the same size, a green, scallop-edged tree, dotted with apples.

Hassan pours the tea, and into each herb-filled glass places a last bit of green, a feathery frond that none of us has ever seen before. He says it is good for shortness of breath. Fatima leaves the room and returns carrying the youngest member of the family, a baby boy less than a year old. He has enormous eyes that case the living room with an expression of unwavering seriousness. The door to the desert is left open, and the room is filled with light and air. From outside come the voices of doves cooing in the garden.

After a pleasant hour, Wendy sets the computer on a small table, with two white patio chairs in front. Irit takes one of the chairs, and the oldest girl, Zahra, takes the other as her sisters color at her feet. Irit starts the slide show, and Hassan takes a chair opposite Zahra, who will sign to him. As everyone gets into position, Carol waltzes lightly around the room with the baby, who looks faintly alarmed. A small procession of chickens parades past the front door, and in the room, children of various sizes come and go.

"I keep seeing a new baby every sixty minutes," Carol remarks.

Shai turns on the camera, and Zahra begins to sign. As the linguists immediately notice, she mouths the corresponding Hebrew word along with each sign, something she has evidently been taught to do in school.

"She has a lot of speech," Mark says to Wendy.

Wendy motions toward the girl as she makes a sign. "That's ISL," she says.

Zahra's deaf sister, eight-year-old Maryam, replaces her in the chair. She is exquisitely shy at first, looking everywhere but at the screen. Little by little, as the images scroll by, she relaxes, and before long she is signing animatedly, smiling hugely. Mark turns to Wendy.

"What kind of signs is she using?" he asks.

"The nouns are Israeli," Wendy says. "Then you get these classifiers that could be anything."

"So we're getting . . . ?" Mark lets the thought trail off. Wendy discreetly stops the test midway through, because Maryam is using so many ISL signs.

We are invited to stay for lunch. Down the length of the sofa, the bright cushions have been positioned at regular intervals, like armrests along a bank of airline seats. Across each cushion, someone has draped mounds of freshly baked pita, which hang in thick rumpled folds. The bread is made from Hassan's own wheat, grown here in the village and sent out to be milled. He pours a generous round of Coca-Cola as the children line the coffee table with plates of kebabs, fragrant with charcoal; fat green olives; and french fries, known in the local dialect as *cheeps*, a legacy of the British mandate in Palestine.

When the meal is done, and the coffee after it, Wendy reopens the computer, and Shai takes his place behind the camera. The team has been anticipating the next informant eagerly: Hassan himself. Hassan's father was a member of Al-Sayyid's first deaf generation, and Hassan grew up as fluent in the village sign language as in Arabic.

"Hassan is a native signer," Mark observes. "He says he feels it's *his* language."

Hassan takes the chair beside Wendy, and as the familiar images scroll by, the village language leaps from the hands of a master signer: *Dog . . . Cat . . . Camel. Chicken . . . Horse . . . Snake. Fly . . . Scorpion . . . Fish. Beetle . . . Bird. . . .*

The first deaf generation of Al-Sayyid is gone now, and no one knows exactly what their signing looked like. The linguists have a single videotape, just a minute or two long, showing one of the last elderly signers, a slender record. But because of pioneering work begun thirty years ago by the psychologist Susan Goldin-Meadow, it is possible to form a general picture of what the language of Al-Sayyid's first generation might have been like.

By the early 1970s, linguists had begun to study in earnest how deaf children of deaf parents acquired ASL. Around the same time, Goldin-Meadow began to study something quite different: the spontaneous homesigning of deaf children who had never seen sign language at all. When she began her work, oralism was still thriving in the United States. Hearing parents were encouraged to educate their deaf children by oral methods exclusively, without exposing them to signing of any kind. The result was a cohort of deaf children to whom no language was accessible. At home, they couldn't hear the spoken language of their parents; at school, they weren't allowed to see ASL, or any form of Signed English. Yet the children managed to communicate effectively with their hearing parents and siblings. They did so through homesign, repertoires of gestures they invented themselves.

Because homesign is made by children who inhabit a world with no available language, it offers researchers a glimpse of a natural Forbidden Experiment, as Goldin-Meadow and her colleagues realized. "The deaf children we study are clearly developing their communication systems under severely degraded input conditions," Goldin-Meadow writes in her recent book *The Resilience of Language.* "As a result, the children provide us with an opportunity to identify those properties of language so over-determined and buffered in humans that they will arise even under strikingly atypical acquisition conditions." She called these properties the "resilient" properties of human language.

That the homesigners gestured was in itself not surprising. Man is a gesturing animal. Hearing adults accompany their speech with gestures all the time, even when they are on the telephone and no one can see them. Young hearing children, acquiring spoken language, gesture along with their nascent words and sentences. Hearing people's gestures are generally holistic: broad general movements collectively understood to mean broad general things like "Huh?" and "Dunno" and "Come here!" At the start of her work, Goldin-Meadow had little reason to believe that the homesigners' gestures were especially different. But they were, in conspicuous ways.

Goldin-Meadow, who teaches at the University of Chicago, began her study in the early 1970s. Her sample was small—ten deaf children of hearing parents—but her findings were suggestive nonetheless. The children, who at the start of her work ranged from a little over a year to just over four years old, attended oral schools. None had been exposed to ASL, or to any of the systems of Manual English then popular in the education of the deaf. Nor were the children encouraged by their families to cultivate their gestures: their parents wanted them to speak and lipread. In spite of this, all ten children gestured spontaneously to communicate with their families. While each child's gestures were different, Goldin-Meadow found that the gestures of all ten children shared striking properties of structure, function and form. This was the surprising thing.

"The gestures the deaf children use to communicate are structured in language-like ways," Goldin-Meadow writes. "The children are inventing their own, simple language."

When young hearing children gesture, they often point. They point to things they want, to things that catch their attention, to things that frighten them. Their pointing gestures, like those of hearing adults, have a narrow function: they tend to be concrete, highly specific and entirely dependent on context. If a hearing child points to a dog, the gesture is universally understood to mean "This dog right here in front of me." It can hardly mean anything else. Similarly for other objects in the environment.

The deaf children in Goldin-Meadow's study also pointed. But as she and her colleagues discovered, their pointing gestures went beyond those of hearing children. For the deaf children, pointing gestures were often much more *linguistic*—they could function as nouns and pronouns in the simple grammars of homesign. In fact, as the researchers would learn, the homesigning of all ten children had clearly differentiated "parts of speech"—nouns and pronouns, adjectives, and verbs—just as conventional signed languages do. The gestures of hearing people, of course, make no such distinctions.

At least one child in the study used pointing gestures even more abstractly. This child, whom the researchers called David, sometimes "set up" objects for later reference by assigning them arbitrary locations in space. "For example," Goldin-Meadow writes, "David is telling us about a sledding incident. He 'hangs' an imaginary sled over a spot in front of him above eye level, then points at that spot and finally 'hammers' in the spot. The point at essentially nothing only makes sense because the spot has been established as the place where the hanging-nail for the sled sits."

Hearing people's gestures are typically mimetic. They represent, in analogue fashion, objects or actions in the real world, much as the hand-waving in a game of charades does. As a result, these gestures are mutable—they can be made quite differently from one person to another, and from one occasion to another. Homesigns are also mimetic—they have to be, in order to be understood by the children's hearing families. Yet they differ crucially from hearing people's gestures in being much more structured. Where hearing people's gestures tend to be unitary wholes, the homesigns of the deaf children, Goldin-Meadow found, comprised smaller structural units.

Like the words of conventional signed languages, the gestures of homesign, the researchers found, comprise discrete spatial building blocks: handshapes, locations and movements. For each child, the researchers identified a finite set of handshapes, around a dozen, that the child used again and again. For each child, these handshapes further combined with eight or more locations. The handshapes and locations differed from one child to the next, but they functioned similarly for all ten children. Over time, for each child, every handshape and every location came to have a particular meaning attached to it. Their combination resulted in new gestures with predictable meanings.

David, for instance, used the same fistlike handshape to describe holding a variety of objects, from hammers and balloon strings to umbrellas and flagpoles, newspapers and hat brims. For him, the fist handshape had become a linguistic morpheme: an abstract, meaningful gesture used to denote an entire class of things. In the grammar of David's homesign, this handshape could combine with different types of movement ("linear path," "long arc," "circle," "no motion") to denote what the object was doing.

The experimenters even saw children "deconstruct" gestures into their component parts, stringing the parts out sequentially rather than articulating them all at once. The homesigners did this even when it diminished the gesture's iconic properties, much as the young deaf children did with ASL in Ted Supalla's classifier study. Goldin-Meadow saw David do it with the gesture he typically used to describe snow falling:

> David makes a flutter gesture, wiggling his fingers with his hand held in place over his head. He then moves his palm straight

> down, his fingers no longer wiggling, to indicate the direction in which the snow falls. . . . A more accurate depiction of snow falling would have combined the wiggling motion and directional path into a single gesture since the fluttering and falling, in fact, take place at the same time.

The most prolific gesturer in the study, David also used a regular morphological process—varying a gesture's manner of movement—to signal the difference between nouns and their corresponding verbs. In his personal system, nouns tended to be made with single movements; the related verbs were made with repeated movements. "For example, if using a twist gesture as a noun to mean 'jar,' David produces the gesture with only one rotation rather than several," Goldin-Meadow writes. "In contrast, if using the gesture as a verb to mean 'twist,' he produces the gesture with several rotations."

The children's gestures not only had a simple morphology—structure within words—they also had a simple syntax, structure across words. The homesigners did far more than make individual gestures: they also combined these gestures into simple "sentences." By contrast, young hearing children seldom use gestures in combination. Neither do hearing adults. But the homesigners frequently used strings of two gestures or more; the resulting "sentences" typically involved an action, and the thing acted upon.

As the homesigners got older, their gesture strings grew longer and more complex, often involving multiple actors and actions. This meant they needed a consistent means of showing who did what to whom. The children did this in several interesting ways.

One way involved displacing a gesture in space from one location to another, for example, gesturing "beat" in the direction of a drum. In moving the gesture between the two locations, the children were creating a simple system of inflection that worked much as verb agreement in established sign languages does. "Importantly," Goldin-Meadow writes, "the children do not displace their gestures toward just any objects—they displace them toward objects playing particular thematic roles. In transitive sentences, gestures are oriented toward objects playing patient roles." When one child, Karen, wanted someone to open a jar, she made a "twist" motion, displacing her hand in the direction of the jar. The jar was the patient, or recipient, of the intended action. Many of the children's sentences displayed a similar syntactic pattern.

Besides moving their verbs through space, the children had another important way of showing who did what to whom. They did so by maintaining a consistent word order within their gesture sentences. No child strung gestures together in random order: each seemed to be adhering to a personal syntactic plan. Even more striking, nine of the ten children independently used *the same* word order, consistently placing patients before acts, as in this gesture sentence, in which David tells Goldin-Meadow to eat the snack his mother had brought in:

> *Snack* [David makes a pointing gesture]—*eat* [he makes a mimetic gesture]—*Susan* [a pointing gesture]

The order of the thematic elements in David's sentence is patient, act, actor: *snack, eat, Susan.* Most of the homesigners ordered their sentences the same way, with patients coming before acts. Though this word order may feel odd to speakers of English, the point is that the children were using a consistent order—they had created a small, structured syntax.

How universal was the deaf children's drive to create a structured communication system? Goldin-Meadow and her colleagues repeated their study in Taiwan with a group of young homesigners there. Like their American counterparts, the Taiwanese children were born into hearing families, were being educated orally, and had not been exposed to any signed language. For both the Taiwanese and the American homesigners, the researchers found, "the deaf children's gestures form a *linguistic system* in a way that hearing children's gestures do not."

Like those of the American homesigners, the Taiwanese children's gestures functioned as words, and were in turn made up of smaller morphemic building blocks. The Taiwanese children also combined strings of gestures into sentences, distinguishing who did what to whom through inflection, or with consistent word order. Interestingly, the gesture order the Taiwanese children preferred was exactly the same as for the Americans: patients first, acts second.

But where were all these homesigners getting their gestures from in the first place? Young hearing children can pull spoken language out of the environment. But the deaf children Goldin-Meadow studied had no language available. Nor were they copying the gestures of their hearing parents. Their parents' gestures were the kind that hearing people typically use with speech. They lacked the internal morphological structure the children's gestures had. Nor did the parents typically combine gestures to form sentences as their children did. When they occasionally did so, the combinations showed none of the regularities of word order that the children's gestures displayed.

"Neither the way the parents respond to the children's gestures, nor the gestures that the parents produce when talking to the children can explain the structure found in the deaf children's gestures," Goldin-Meadow concludes. "Although the children may be using hearing people's gestures as a communication starting point, they go well beyond that point, transforming the gestures they see into a structured system that looks very much like language."

But how did the homesigners do this? While young hearing children learn over time to parse the wash of speech around them, the deaf children could only parse *their own gestures.* And that, Goldin-Meadow discovered, is just what they were doing. As children attempt to sort out the tangle of language that surrounds them, all of them, deaf and hearing, begin by treating words as unanalyzable wholes. That is the reason young hearing children seem to "master" irregular verbs at first: to them, "go" and "went" are simply holistic lumps of sound, and they learn each lump by rote. Only later do they tumble to the fact that words consist of smaller units, and that each unit lends the word part of its meaning. At this stage, applying their newfound rule overzealously, they conclude that the past tense of "go" is "goed." They're wrong, but they have discovered a system.

As Goldin-Meadow found, the young homesigners went through a very similar process. Early on, they treated their own "words" as solid gestural lumps. At this stage, as far as they were concerned, words lacked component parts. Only later did they begin to "reverse engineer" their gestures—discovering that each gesture comprises smaller units, which could be used to form new words with predictable meanings. "What I am suggesting," Goldin-Meadow writes, "is that the deaf children induce their morphological systems from the earliest gestures they themselves create. Indeed, the first holistic gestures that the children used seemed to set the stage for the system each child eventually generated."

For the young homesigners, both in America and in Taiwan, these spontaneous gesture systems offered what Goldin-Meadow called "important empirical data on children's initial grammatical state." What was especially remarkable, as she observed, was that "the deaf children's gestures are structured more like the spoken language they can't hear than like the gestures they can see."

After years of study, Goldin-Meadow was able to compile a list of linguistic properties that are apparently so robust in Homo sapiens that they burst forth from the homesigners even without benefit of linguistic input. These are the "resilient" properties of language. Chief among them is the use of words as the fundamental currency of linguistic expression, even in a communication system that could easily have relied on pantomime. The words of language are sorted into grammatical categories: nouns, verbs and adjectives. Among the other resilient properties Goldin-Meadow identified was the reliance on consistent word order.

Some properties of language, however, were noticeably absent from the children's homesigning. These, which Goldin-Meadow called "fragile" properties, do not seem to develop in the absence of linguistic exposure. Fragile properties of language include the development of grammatical tense, which she did not find in any of the children's gestures.

It is impossible to tell, of course, exactly which properties of language would take hold if a lone child's homesigning somehow had the chance to develop into a full-fledged language. As Goldin-Meadow notes, the homesigners' parents, intent on educating them to speak and lipread, did not especially encourage their children's gesture lives. Nor was any of the children she studied in contact with other homesigners, with whom they might have pooled their gestures. "I have often wondered how far a deaf child could move toward arbitrariness and a more complex system without a conventional language as a model but *with* a willing communication partner who could enter into and share an arbitrary system with the child," Goldin-Meadow writes. "But the circumstance that would allow me to address this question—two deaf children inventing a gestural system with no input from a conventional sign language—has not presented itself."

Such a situation has presented itself in Al-Sayyid, where seventy years ago ten deaf homesigners—Hassan's father and nine other children—invented a gestural system. Within a generation, it had become a full-fledged language. And, as Wendy and her team will discover, more than one of the resilient properties identified by Goldin-Meadow turn out to play a crucial role in the new language of Al-Sayyid.

As the afternoon light floods the house, Hassan continues to sign the language he learned from his father's hands. *Plates . . . Coffee . . . Pencils . . . Scissors . . . Stapler . . . Wristwatch . . . Eyeglasses . . . Bed . . . Table with three chairs on each side . . . Stove . . . Table with three chairs on one side . . . String with two paper clips . . . Lamp.* He moves on to buying and selling; to anger, joy and fear; and to more homey objects, murmuring the name of each thing softly to himself in Arabic as he signs.

Hassan concludes the test, and the team packs up to leave. As the linguists walk out into the garden amid many goodbyes, Mark hands Hassan a box of china, and one of the silver trays. "*Toda raba,*" Hassan says gruffly in Hebrew, turning his head away—Thank you very much. Then he climbs into his truck to lead us to our last house.

CHAPTER 14

A Sign in Mind

By the 1970s, linguists had established beyond doubt what William Stokoe had suspected a decade earlier: that ASL was no mere pantomime. It was a natural human language, passed down the generations in deaf families. It had structure both at the level of the word and the level of the sentence, just as spoken language did. Like spoken language, it was an arbitrary symbolic code, used to convey meaning from one human mind to another. And, like spoken language, it was discrete, finite and combinatorial: its words and sentences were assembled from a limited inventory of linguistic elements that could be combined in limitless permutations.

For researchers, the very "languageness" of ASL raised a tantalizing question: How might a language of hand and eye be represented in the minds of its users? Since the Chomsky Revolution, the essential focus of linguistics had been on the mental organization of language—spoken language. Psycholinguistics, the subdiscipline that studies the production and comprehension of human language, had already learned a good deal about how spoken language is processed, stored and remembered. Now, for the first time, linguists had a language of a completely different kind with which to turn to these questions anew.

Like so much else in sign linguistics, work on the psycholinguistics of sign began with Ursula Bellugi. In the early 1970s, when she embarked on her studies of how signs are processed, stored and recalled, the mental representation of ASL was an open question. There was no reason to think that a language of hands in space might be organized in the mind in even remotely the same way as spoken language was. No one had the slightest idea how signed language was represented in the mind at all.

Stokoe had done the essential early work of classification, breaking signs down into handshapes, locations and movements. But were these parameters merely a set of convenient labels that described the surface appearance of signs? Or, as Bellugi and her Salk Institute colleagues wondered, did they reflect something deeper? Did Stokoe's parameters have actual bearing on the way signs were organized in the minds of signers? In short, did they have what linguists call psychological reality? It turned out that they did, as revealed by everything from memory experiments to the spontaneous sign errors known as "slips of the hand."

Researchers had already studied the ways in which spoken language is encoded in short-term memory. As Bellugi and her husband Edward Klima write:

> Our capacity for immediate memory plays a special role in language processing. When we hear spoken language, we must process and store a stream of ongoing speech until we have taken in enough to understand structure and meaning—we must remember, for instance, from the beginning to the end of a sentence or proposition in order to grasp a communication. The form in which linguistic signals are stored in immediate memory has been of much interest to psychologists and linguists and has been the focus for a large number of experiments.

They continue: "The form in which words are encoded has turned out to provide evidence of the psychological reality of some levels of language structure—in particular, of sublexical structure," that is, structure below the level of the word.

In a typical memory experiment for spoken language, a subject is read a list of unrelated words and, a short time later, asked to recite it back. The mistakes are of crucial interest here. "The comparison of the errors with the items originally presented shows which characteristics of the items are retained and which are distorted," Klima and Bellugi explain. "The nature of the characteristics retained and distorted in the errors suggests the basis of encoding for temporary storage."

If a long time elapses between the initial presentation of the list and its recall, the errors tend to be semantic in nature. For the target word "father," a speaker may recall "mother"; for "boat," he may recall "ship." Psychologists have learned from this that *long-term* memory for words is most likely organized along semantic lines. But if only a short time elapses, the errors are very different. Asked to recall "father," a speaker may say "bother." For "boat," he says "vote."

"For hearing people," Klima and Bellugi write, "short-term memory for words has a phonological basis. . . . This is consistent with our everyday experience of memory for language as a memory of sounds: a hearing person is accustomed to the 'inner voice' he uses when he rehearses a phrase, recalls a sentence, or remembers a list or a line."

What about deaf signers? How might they remember a language *without* sounds? Klima and Bellugi already had anecdotal evidence to suggest that the means might be visual:

> Deaf parents tell us that their children sign to themselves in their sleep; we have observed deaf toddlers signing to themselves and their toy animals before bedtime when they thought they were alone. We have seen hands "muttering" to themselves; we have seen deaf people rehearsing *a mano* before a videotape session, repeating a grocery list in sign, and signing to make clear to themselves something read in English. Deaf people tell us they dream in signs, plan conversation in signs, imagine the perfect retort in signs. Is this inner "voice" in the hands related to the way deaf people initially process the linguistic symbols of their own language?

It was impossible to know at the outset whether signers actually encoded signs visually. Most ASL signers have at least some knowledge of English; some also speak and lipread the language fluently.

Perhaps ASL signs were encoded in short-term memory in terms of their English translations. Perhaps they were encoded with mental pictures of the things the signs represented.

To resolve these questions, Bellugi and her colleagues prepared lists of simple random signs and their English equivalents. A group of deaf subjects was presented with the signed list on videotape; a group of hearing subjects heard the English list on audiotape. Immediately afterward, subjects were asked to recall the items in order. Both groups gave their answers in written English so that the responses could be compared. Again, the interest lay in the errors. "The nature of the . . . errors in each group," Klima and Bellugi write, "should be revealing of the form in which the items are stored in short-term memory."

Predictably, the hearing subjects made many sound-based errors. For "vote," someone recalled "boat." For "week," someone recalled "work." Other errors from the hearing group included these:

For "noon," a subject recalled "noun."

For "cheese," a subject recalled "keys."

For "frog," a subject recalled "fraud."

For "horse," a subject recalled "house."

For "cat," a subject recalled "hurt."

For "peas," a subject recalled "knees."

Asked to recall the same words in ASL, the deaf subjects did something altogether different. For the sign VOTE, a subject wrote down "tea." For the sign WEEK, a subject wrote down "nice." So it went, curiously, for other signs on the list:

For NOON, a subject recalled "tree."

For CHEESE, a subject recalled "new."

For FROG, a subject recalled "gum."

For HORSE, a subject recalled "uncle."

For CAT, a subject recalled "Indian."

For PEAS, a subject recalled "then."

"There was no overlap whatsoever in the . . . errors made by the two groups of subjects," Klima and Bellugi write. "Whereas hearing subjects encode linguistic material in short-term memory in phonological form . . . deaf native signers encode their language in a quite different way."

But in what way? Why did the deaf subjects write down the words they did? Their errors certainly didn't resemble the target English words phonologically. "If this were the nature of the errors of deaf subjects," Klima and Bellugi write, "there would be some support for the notion that signs are merely symbols for words—that in terms of its lexical items American Sign Language is not an independent language. But in fact the repeated . . . errors made by the deaf can not be attributed to resemblance to . . . phonological . . . forms of the corresponding English words."

Nor did the errors suggest that the deaf were coding their signs in pictures. No one misremembered CAT as "tail" or "fur" or "whiskers." The deaf subjects' errors looked completely capricious. But were they really? Was there something deeper that might cause an intelligent deaf adult to recall FROG as "gum" or CAT as "Indian"?

As Bellugi and her colleagues discovered, the errors in recall made by deaf subjects *did* resemble the target signs, but they resembled them in *form*—that is, in the visual properties of handshape, location and movement from which the signs of the language are constituted. In ASL, the sign VOTE is made by inserting the tips of the pinched thumb and index finger of one hand into the top of the other, which is held in front of the chest in a cylinder shape. The sign is made with a quick repeated movement; it recalls putting a ballot into a ballot box. The sign TEA, as it happens, is nearly identical. Like VOTE, TEA is a two-handed sign, and the shapes of the hands are the same: in the active hand, the thumb is pinched against the forefinger, while the passive hand forms a cylinder. Like VOTE, the sign is also made in front of the chest.

There is just a single thing that distinguishes TEA from VOTE, and that is movement. In TEA, the tips of the thumb and forefinger of the active hand are inserted into the passive hand and moved in a little circle: the action suggests swirling a tea bag in hot water. VOTE and TEA differ in only one formational element, just as, in English, "vote" and "boat" differ in only one sound.

Other errors differed from the target signs in notably similar ways. In the sign WEEK, the passive hand is held in front of the signer's chest, palm up, as the extended index finger of the active hand is stroked across it, from heel to fingertips. In NICE, the passive hand is also held in front of the chest, palm up. The active hand, all five fingers extended, is stroked across it from heel to fingertips. The only difference is the shape of the active hand: an extended index finger in WEEK, a flat hand in NICE. Like VOTE and TEA, WEEK and NICE differ in just a single formational parameter.

Some errors differed from the target only in location. CAT is made by moving the pinched thumb and forefinger outward from the cheek with a double motion. INDIAN (that is, "American Indian") is also made on the cheek, with the same handshape. But here the thumb and forefinger touch the cheek twice, moving from lower cheek to upper cheek in a small arc. Other sign-and-error pairs were also visually linked. FROG and GUM have similar handshapes and movements but different locations. HORSE and UNCLE have similar handshapes and locations but differ in movement. PEAS and THEN have similar locations and movements, but different handshapes.

Seen in this way, responses that looked weird and random became regular and classifiable. "The majority of the . . . errors," Klima and Bellugi write, "preserve all but one of the values of the major formational parameters of the original sign." In this and later experiments, the linguists found that 70 percent of the errors recorded by multiple subjects differed from the target sign by just one formal parameter.

As Bellugi's experiments showed, where hearing speakers of English were using the phonetic properties of their language to encode words in short-term memory, deaf signers of ASL were using the corresponding formal properties of *their* language—the visual parameters of handshape, location and movement—to do the same. As Klima and Bellugi write:

> For these subjects . . . errors do not at all reflect, as they do for hearing subjects, the phonological structure of the words; nor, rather surprisingly, do they reflect the visual form of those words in terms of the letters, their shape or number. Nor do the errors seem to reflect, as might be expected, the iconic (or representational) character of some signs. Nor do the errors reflect an essentially semantic organization in the processing and remembering of signs in the short-term memory paradigm. Rather, the multiple sign-and-error pairs reflect special organizational principles of the signs of American Sign Language, as they are described in terms of a specific, limited set of simultaneously occurring formational parameters that combine to constitute individual ASL signs. . . . The encoding and rehearsing processes for deaf native signers evidently are in terms of the visual-manual properties of the signs themselves.

Entirely by chance, sign-language linguists discovered another window onto the mental representation of signs. It came from an unlikely place: the mistakes signers make when they mean to say one thing but accidentally say another, much as speakers do when they make slips of the tongue.

As long as there has been spoken language, there have been speech errors. For a variety of reasons—fatigue, hurry or some unconscious motivation best left to Freudians—the speech signal can get garbled. Sometimes, the mistakes are semantic, with a related word or phrase uttered in place of the intended one, as in the following real-life examples:

"She's marked with a big scarlet R—uh—A."

"Are my legs, I mean tires, touching the curb?"

"You can pull off the sheets and I'll stick them in the refrigerator—(laughs)—washing machine."

Other times, however, the error is phonological. In these cases, the sounds of language are misordered, misarticulated or otherwise come out wrong:

"*T*addle *t*ennis" (for "paddle tennis").

"John dropped his cu*ff* of co*ff*ee" (for "cup of coffee").

"John *g*ave the *g*oy" (for "gave the boy").

"Shown in the p*l*easant—I mean present s*l*ide."

The best-known phonological error is the spoonerism. Named for the Reverend William A. Spooner (1844–1930), an Oxford don famed for these mistakes, spoonerisms involve the wholesale reversal of two speech sounds, often to hilarious effect. Among the utterances with which Spooner is credited are "the *q*ueer old *d*ean," "noble *t*ons of *s*oil," and this reprimand to a student: "You have *h*issed all my *m*ystery lectures. I saw you *f*ight a *l*iar in the back quad; in fact, you have *t*asted the whole *w*orm."

Although scholars now believe that most of the slips ascribed to Spooner are apocryphal, the existence of spoonerisms in everyday speech is real enough. Linguists have collected many contemporary examples:

"Don't throw your cigarette down, there's a *h*ire *f*azard."

"Who am I to sneeze at a *fl*ee *r*unch?"

"We're having *r*ot *p*ost for dinner."

"F*a*sh and t*i*ckle."

"W*i*ng's b*a*bliography."

Attested in languages around the world, speech errors are delicious. But they are more than that. In the nineteenth century, linguists began to study slips of the tongue for what they might reveal about language—language structure, language acquisition and historical language change. The most diligent of these chroniclers was the Viennese scholar Rudolf Meringer. Working at the end of the century, he amassed and analyzed the slips of his German-speaking friends and colleagues; his collection, first published in 1895, contained more than eight thousand errors. Meringer was said to have gone about his job with such zeal (for every error, he also recorded the speaker's name, date of birth and educational background, as well as the time of day, the speaker's state of health and tiredness, rate of speaking and other information) that he became, in the words of one modern linguist, "the most unpopular man at the University of Vienna."

Even Freud, who was much more concerned with the unconscious motivations of oral mistakes than with their phonetic form, recognized their potential value to the study of human language. Writing about speech errors in *The Psychopathology of Everyday Life*, he asked "whether the mechanisms of this . . . disturbance cannot also suggest the probable laws of the formation of speech."

The first linguist of the Chomsky era to study speech errors seriously was Victoria Fromkin of UCLA. Starting in the late 1960s, she began recording the errors she heard around her in a little notebook she carried for that purpose; by the time of her death in 2000, she had amassed more than ten thousand. In the interest of preserving her social reputation, Fromkin did not record quite as much supplementary information as Meringer did.

In the course of three decades, Fromkin recorded errors of every type, from semantic mistakes to reversals of whole words or phrases ("I wouldn't buy *kids* for the *macadamia nuts*"). Among the many sounds-based slips she collected were errors of phonetic anticipation ("*t*addle *t*ennis"), in which a sound uttered later in a phrase pops up too early; perseveration ("John *g*ave the *g*oy"), in which a sound is mistakenly carried over to a later word; and, of course, spoonerisms.

This linguistic flotsam, Fromkin realized, had great value for a scientist studying the mental representation of grammar. For speech errors, as she discovered, turn out to betray the speaker's tacit knowledge of his linguistic system. "A grammar," she writes, "must represent in some way a speaker-hearer's cognitive knowledge. Slips of the tongue . . . occur when we make use of this grammar."

One thing phonological errors reveal is speakers' unconscious awareness of the rules for stringing sounds together in their native language. Slips of the tongue are noteworthy for how consistently they conform to these rules. Some of the phonetic errors in Fromkin's collection, for instance, resulted in actual English words. These included "When do you heave the louse?" and "odd hack" (for "ad hoc"). Even more interesting, most of the errors Fromkin recorded were plausible but nonconcurring words, as in "my hetter baff," "the Folden Gleece Award" and "ponkutation" (for "computation"). These are all "lexical gaps" à la "blaff": they are allowed by the rules of English sound structure but don't happen to occur in the English lexicon.

However outlandish they might be, slips of the tongue never violate these rules. "Although 'slips of the tongue' can be incorrectly uttered as 'stips of the lung,'" Fromkin writes, "it cannot be uttered as 'tlip of the sung' because the sound 'tl' is not allowed as the beginning of an English word." It isn't that English speakers are incapable of saying "tl": they can easily pronounce "Tlingit" (an Alaskan native people and their language), and the *tlot, tlot* refrain of "The Highwayman," by Alfred Noyes. It is simply that the English phonological system arbitrarily bans "tl" at the start of a word.

Sound-based errors are as constrained by these rules as if they had been real words, and it is through these slips that speakers reveal their unconscious knowledge of linguistic structure below the level of the word. A speaker draws on this knowledge each time she uses language. It is what allows her to decode the uninterrupted stream of consonants and vowels that is the acoustic reality of speech.

What about errors in signed language? When Bellugi and Klima began their work, there was no reason to assume that anything like speech errors could happen in a visual language. If signs were holistic gestures, as many observers in the 1970s still believed, then what possible form, beyond the wholesale transposition of two signs, could a signed spoonerism take?

As Klima and Bellugi and their Salk Institute colleagues Don Newkirk and Carlene Canady Pedersen wrote in 1980: "Until quite recently . . . the pervasive iconicity of signs led to their being regarded as holistically distinct symbols without any formal internal structure. The question of recurring formational components—indeed, of a unified sublexical structure—was almost completely ignored. . . . This focus on the image and the icon apparently prevailed over any consideration of the internal structure of signs."

Then one day, a surprising thing happened in Bellugi's lab: "As two deaf people were conversing, one offered to get the other a cup of coffee," the four authors recount. "Asked what he would like in it, the other responded in signs, CREAM AND BUTTER. Astonished, the first asked if he really intended to put butter in his coffee. His friend, somewhat embarrassed, signed that he meant SUGAR, and had made a mistake."

But why *this* mistake? Significantly, the intended sign, SUGAR, and the error, BUTTER, were similar in form. SUGAR is made with the extended index and middle fingers of one hand brushing repeatedly downward on the chin, curling the fingers back into the palm each time. BUTTER is made with the extended index and middle fingers of one hand brushing repeatedly across the palm of the other hand, curling the fingers back into the palm each time. The linguists had witnessed a "slip of the hand." SUGAR and BUTTER shared handshape and movement; the only significant difference between the two signs was in their place of articulation. In making the error, the signer used the handshape and movement of the intended sign, SUGAR, but, accidentally, the location of BUTTER.

What might cause a signer to make SUGAR on the palm instead of the chin? The answer lay in the sign that came just before it: CREAM. Though it uses a different handshape and movement, CREAM happens to be made on the palm. In attempting to say CREAM and SUGAR, the signer inadvertently retained the location of CREAM—the palm—and carried it over to SUGAR. The result, CREAM and BUTTER, was a classic perseveration error, the signed equivalent of "John *gave* the *goy*." But instead of a sound, what persevered was one of the sublexical components of an ASL sign, in this case location.

By the time of this incident, Victoria Fromkin's work on speech errors was widely known, and the Salk linguists were intrigued by a new possibility. Was CREAM AND BUTTER simply a freak occurrence, or did signers routinely make "speech errors" that were rooted not in the sounds of words but in the visual properties of signs? Members of the lab began to watch their deaf friends and colleagues vigilantly for similar slips.

They were not disappointed. Over time, the linguists observed sign-language errors of every kind, including anticipations, perseverations and spoonerisms. The errors could affect any of a sign's formational parameters: handshape, location or movement. Attempting to sign ONE THOUSAND CLOWN ("a thousand clowns"), for instance, a signer accidentally made the sign THOUSAND (which properly involves an open palm, the four fingers bent forward at the lowest joint) with the clawed handshape of CLOWN, a handshape anticipation error. Trying to sign (HE) PLEASE HELP ("He will be glad to help"), a signer mistakenly carried over the circular movement of PLEASE, made by brushing the palm in a circle on the chest, into the sign HELP, a movement perseveration error.

The most intriguing sign errors were the spoonerisms. Here, one parameter—handshape, location or movement—switched places altogether with its counterpart in another sign. In one spoonerism, the linguists observed a signer who was attempting to sign SICK, BORED (an ASL idiom that roughly translates as "I'm sick and tired of it"). SICK is normally made with the bent middle finger of one hand touching the forehead. BORED is made with the extended index finger touching the side of the nose with a twisting movement. But in the error, the signer switched the two handshapes and left everything else intact, signing SICK with an extended index finger and BORED with a bent middle finger.

To the linguists, slips of the hand like these showed beyond doubt that the signs of ASL possessed sublexical structure. Such a structure, a level of organization below that of the word, is one of the essential design properties of human language. In addition, far from being mere descriptive labels, Stokoe's parameters of handshape, location and movement turned out to be *the very principles by which signs were organized in the minds of deaf signers.* As the four Salk researchers write:

> If signs were, as some previous investigators have thought, only holistic gestures without internal structure, we might expect signs to be organized . . . at a single primary level: that of the entire sign as a unitary object. If signs were so coded, involuntary deviations in performance from the intentions of a signer . . . should result in only whole signs being reordered. In fact, our corpus does include some exchanges of this type (9 out of 131 slips). . . . Far more frequently (and more significantly, for the nature of signs and of constraints on their formational properties), a parameter value of one sign is erroneously realized in another sign.

There was something even more significant. While some slips of the hand, like CREAM AND BUTTER, resulted in actual ASL signs, a great many others were permissible but nonoccurring signs: the lexical gaps of ASL. Slips like these resulted in combinations of handshapes, locations and movements that, though they didn't mean anything, were, in the judgment of native signers, visually "grammatical." They were the sign-language equivalents of "hetter" and "baff" and "gleece." In a language whose words were thought to have no internal structure, these errors were forcing signers' intuitive knowledge of that structure to light. "Such slips," the four authors write, "provide evidence of rules for combining abstract formational elements into lexical units in the language."

As different as signed language looks from spoken, the fact that signed and spoken errors take much the same form is exceptionally noteworthy. As Victoria Fromkin wrote in her 1980 book, *Errors in Linguistic Performance,* "If we find that the same kinds of errors occur in the sign languages of the deaf, we can conclude that we are dealing with language universals, with characteristics of this complex human cognitive system, aspects that go beyond the particular modality utilized. . . . The research team at the Salk Institute has found that ' "slips of the hand" . . . provide equally valuable clues to the organization of sign language for deaf signers' as do slips of the tongue for spoken language."

Where spoken language is a largely linear enterprise, a horizontal stream of consonants and vowels encoding the linguistic signal, sign language is a more vertical affair. As the field of sign linguistics grew and linguists turned their attention to sign languages other than ASL, this verticality appeared again and again. In all studied sign languages of the world, individual signs are made, as in ASL, through systematic combinations of handshapes, locations and movements. And while their particular appearance may differ from one language to another, complex signs are also made in much the same manner: by simultaneously altering the movement of the uninflected sign. In language after language, at every level of their makeup, signs tend to be "stacked" rather than linear.

Signers, it seemed, *require* a vertical language. This was perhaps nowhere more graphically demonstrated than in the work of the linguist Samuel Supalla. (It was he who as a boy had marveled at "how curious" hearing people were; the linguist and cognitive scientist Ted Supalla is his brother.) In work begun in the 1980s, Sam Supalla, who teaches at the University of Arizona, studied deaf children's acquisition of the artificial sign systems known collectively as Manually Coded English, or MCE.

MCE systems graft the grammar of English onto the vocabulary of ASL. Where ASL uses various spatial devices to encode its grammar, MCE tacks on invented signs that stand for the word endings of spoken English: *-ing* and *-ed* and *-ment* and so on. In its form, MCE recalls the methodical signs of the Abbé de l'Épée, and is, by most accounts, about as successful. Nevertheless, many educators consider

MCE a viable bridge to English, and even today, many deaf children are expected to acquire it as a native language.

More often than not, they fail, but, as Supalla discovered, the way in which they fail is revealing. Instead of mastering MCE's sequential structure, deaf children spontaneously change it so that it becomes much more vertical—much more, in other words, like a natural sign language. The remarkable thing is that the children do this even when they have never been exposed to ASL or to any other conventional signed language.

To derive a noun from its corresponding verb, ASL uses a spatial process: the verb is signed with repeated, restrained movement. MCE does the same thing very differently, as Supalla explains:

> For MCE, although the sign IMPROVE is borrowed from ASL, it is considered an unanalyzable unit. That is, the sign's spatial components do not serve any grammatical purpose. To derive a noun, MCE relies instead on suffixing onto the sign IMPROVE a devised sign that represents the noun marker *-ment* of English. . . . The result would be two signs strung in sequence, in contrast to ASL's compacting the same information into a single sign.

Supalla studied children who were being taught a particular variety of Manual English known as SEE 2. ("SEE" stands for Signing Exact English.) He was careful to exclude from his study children who had received even minimal exposure to ASL. In the classroom, the SEE 2 children dutifully plonked out this Manual English in all its unwieldy linearity. But whenever they signed among themselves, something quite different sprang from their hands. As Supalla observed, "SEE 2's nonspatial grammatical devices were replaced with essentially spatial ones."

Many of the children modified the verbs of SEE 2 to make them work spatially. In SEE 2, a sentence like "I give the book to you" is signed one word after another, much as it is articulated in English: I—GIVE—THE—BOOK—TO—YOU. But in private, the children took the verb GIVE and moved it efficiently through the air, creating spatial inflection in a system where none had existed before. Some children moved GIVE from a location representing the subject of the sentence to one representing the object; others began the verb near their own bodies and moved it toward the object. Whatever the method, it was utterly consistent for each child. "These spatial modifications," Supalla writes, "form grammatical systems for the children and are not merely trial-by-trial ad hoc usages."

As Supalla concludes, "Instead of acquiring and mastering MCE, deaf children exposed only to MCE change it into a spatially based structure more similar to American Sign Language . . . and other natural signed languages."

Where does this preference for vertical structure come from? Why can't the building blocks of sign language be organized in straight lines, as they are in spoken language? Why did the American children in Supalla's study resist stringing together stems and affixes, just as the Abbé de l'Épée's pupils had two hundred years earlier? As Ursula Bellugi and her colleague Susan Fischer discovered, there are cognitive reasons that the sign-language signal has to be encoded in such a strongly vertical manner.

People can speak much faster than they can sign. Compared with the lips and tongue, the arms are large and unwieldy, and a signed sentence takes about twice as long to articulate as its spoken counterpart. ASL signers produce about two signs per second, Bellugi and Fischer found, compared with about four words per second for English speakers. But through its vertical organization, sign language makes up for lost time.

The key, the linguists found, lies in the superior ability of the visual system to process simultaneous signals, something at which the auditory system does not excel. (Think of how hard it is to attend to two different spoken conversations at once. Compare this with the relative ease of taking in two different images at a time, as on a split screen on television.)

By exploiting this property of the human visual system, sign language makes back time on the processing end, as Bellugi and Fischer discovered. Because each sign of ASL is packed with simultaneous linguistic code, sign language and spoken language can transmit equal amounts of *information* in a comparable amount of time.

Bellugi and Fischer compared the rate of signed versus spoken language by comparing the number of logical propositions each can express in a given unit of time. A proposition is essentially a simple underlying sentence, often equivalent to a clause. The sentence "Mary is a liar" contains a single proposition. The more complex sentence "John thinks that Mary is a liar" contains two: "John thinks" and "(That) Mary is a liar." As the linguists discovered, when the *propositional content* of spoken and signed passages is compared, the time difference evaporates: both spoken English and ASL take the same amount of time—between one and two seconds—to express one proposition. "The subjects were producing underlying sentences at a comparable rate in the two languages," the linguists wrote in a 1972 paper, "but filling them with nearly twice as many words as signs."

The relative economy of sign language makes this possible. Signs compress a wealth of grammatical code into a single meaning-laden gesture. One complex sign, as Fischer has written, can incorporate as many as five meaningful elements all at once. Facial expression, eye gaze and head movement contribute additional layers of meaning. This can allow entire sentences to be expressed with single signs:

> If we wanted to say "may I ask you a question?" in ASL, the information that requires six words in English requires only one sign in ASL—but that sign is highly complex, and the sign utterance even more so. There is a specific sign which means "to ask a question." Further, that sign inflects for person and number of both subject and object. At the same time, raised eyebrows show the fact that the signer is asking a question of the viewer, and a slight head nodding softens the question to a request for permission. No information is gained or lost in this case, nor is any time lost.

Bellugi and Fischer speculate that "there may be a common underlying temporal process governing the rate of 'propositionalizing.'" This is one reason that Épée's "methodical signs" failed, as did later systems like SEE 2. All of these systems used grafted-on signs to stand for the grammatical endings of spoken language. But a language made by the hands in space, and received by the eye, demands a signal that is arranged largely simultaneously, not sequentially. As Fischer has written: "The structure of a language is shaped by the way it is produced and perceived. This is so much the case for spoken language that we are often blinded to the possibilities for linguistic expression outside of speech."

Sign language has another elegant mechanism for compressing information. It is called the pronoun. In spoken languages, pronouns consolidate information. As Susan Fischer points out, think how odd it would sound for a speaker of English to say the following: "John likes Mary, so John goes and visits Mary a lot, and John often takes Mary out to dinner, though sometimes John cooks dinner for Mary."

Pronouns come to the rescue, yielding the much more natural-sounding sentence "John likes Mary, so he goes and visits her a lot, and he often takes her out to dinner, though sometimes he cooks dinner for her." In every language of the world, pronouns or something like them help compress discourse and keep track of the actors in it.

Most sign languages have far richer systems of pronouns than English does. Like English, ASL has the pronouns I (a point to the signer's chest) and YOU (a point toward the addressee), as well as a genderless third-person pronoun (also a point) that, depending on what is being pointed to, can mean "he," "she" or "it." It has plural pronouns, including WE (the palm arcs from one side of the signer's chest to the other) and THEY (a sweep of the pointing finger, as if to take in multiple people). It has possessive pronouns, including MINE (the flat palm is pressed against the signer's chest), YOUR (the palm pushed out, toward the addressee), and the genderless HIS, HER OR ITS (the palm pushes toward the appropriate person or thing). Besides these, ASL has a second-person plural pronoun, YOU-ALL (the index and middle fingers, palm up, move repeatedly from side to side) and a dual pronoun, WE-TWO, signed with the hand moving back and forth between the signer and one other person.

That these pronouns look pantomimic is beyond dispute. What could be more mimetic than pointing to one's own chest to mean "I," and to the addressee's chest to mean "you"? But as the psycholinguist Laura Petitto discovered, signers use even these highly pantomimic gestures as abstract symbols. Her evidence came from studying deaf children's acquisition of ASL pronouns.

In spoken language, "you" and "I" behave oddly. Like other words, they function as linguistic symbols. But they are unlike other words in that the thing they symbolize isn't fixed. If I say "I," it means Margalit Fox. If you say the same word—"I"—it means . . . whoever *you* are. Similarly with "you," which denotes whoever happens to be the addressee at that moment. As a result of their utter dependence on context, "you" and "I" are difficult for young children to master. In the course of acquiring English, some children go through a stage where they use "you" to refer to themselves. The reason? Because the child has repeatedly heard his parents refer to him by saying "you." As far as he is concerned, "you" is exactly the right word in this context.

Remarkably, as Petitto found, the same thing happens with young deaf children acquiring ASL from signing parents, at about the same stage of development. When they are about two, many deaf children go through a period where they refer to themselves by pointing *outward*—in other words, by making the ASL sign YOU. This reflects what they have seen their parents do: point outward, toward the child, to indicate the child. After a few weeks or months, YOU and I get sorted out, just as they do for hearing children. As Petitto's work elegantly showed, even something as mimetic as pointing can backfire when it moves out of the realm of gesture and into the role of linguistic symbol.

The work of these scholars on the psycholinguistics of sign allows us to imagine what must have happened a few hundred years ago in

France, when a community of deaf signers formed in the streets and its shared pool of homesigns blossomed into an indigenous language. It allows us to see what must have happened when the Abbé de l'Épée, in his attempt to Frenchify this language, made something that in its clumsy linearity was unworkable—and how that language, rejected by his students, developed into French Sign Language and in turn into ASL. It also allows us to envision the rich linguistic future in store for Al-Sayyid—provided, that is, that the sign language of the village is allowed to survive.

CHAPTER 15

The House of Twenty Children

Hassan's truck won't start. With some difficulty, he squeezes into the back seat of the van with Irit, Shai and me. The van now holds seven people, the camera and lighting equipment, two tripods, an assortment of backpacks and briefcases, and the last remaining box of china. But without Hassan, it would be impossible to find our last house, buried deep in Al-Sayyid. With Mark at the wheel, we bang over the roughest roads yet, past fields containing huge bales of hay and a solitary black-and-white cow.

We pull up in front of a small house, removing our shoes on entering. This house is even more traditional than Aminah's. It appears to consist of just a few bare rooms, floored in slate, with a minimum of decoration. We pass through the front room, dark and cool, and into a sun-filled room at the back, where a lush olive tree is visible just outside the window. Around the perimeter of the room are mattresses and handwoven rugs; there are no patio chairs in evidence here. We take our places on the floor, Mark and Hassan on the rug along one wall, Carol, Wendy, Irit, Shai and I on cushions facing them.

Children begin to materialize from thin air. Within seconds, the doorway has filled with boys, who gaze intently down at us. There are more children in this house than in all our previous houses combined. Anwar, the head of the household, has twenty, each of whom appears to have brought along a neighbor, friend or cousin to watch the proceedings. Anwar threads his way through the crowd to greet us. He is a gregarious deaf man in his late thirties or early forties, dressed in a white T-shirt and blue sweatpants cut off at the knees. He has a warm smile and an iron handshake.

The children in the doorway start to spill into the room. A boy of about eleven enters, wearing a remarkable T-shirt. At the top of the shirt, the headline "Piece It Together" is printed in English. Beneath the headline is a large photograph of Pope John Paul II that has been divided into four fragments like a crude jigsaw puzzle. In the empty space between each fragment runs more text: "Sexist Patriarchy." "Theologians Silenced." "Contraception Ban." "Deal with CIA." The boy strikes up a signed conversation with Carol as another boy carries in a stack of bed pillows in embroidered cases. Around them, a throng of boys, a barely toddling baby and an older girl mill about. In the doorway, another girl holding a very small baby joins the onlookers. Someone brings in more mattresses.

Anwar, who has changed clothes for the taping, reemerges in a maroon-and-white polo shirt and blue trousers. It is decided that he will sign to his nephew Karim, the deaf boy in the papal T-shirt. Anwar seats himself cross-legged on a mattress at the head of the room. Irit takes her place on his right, and a tiny boy, intent on being part of the unfolding drama, sits on his left. Shai can't use a tripod—the action is happening too low down—so he props the camera atop its case on the floor. Irit opens the computer as several more small boys work their way into the room.

Anwar is a fine signer. On the linguists' previous visit, they recorded him telling a story, nearly half an hour long, of how he was lost in Egypt for several years as a child. When Anwar was about eight, he somehow found his way onto a bus bound for Egypt. Because he couldn't communicate with anyone, he had no idea where he was supposed to be going, or where to get off. He left the bus somewhere in Egypt, where he knew no one. He was taken in by a local family and lived with them for three years. One day, someone from Al-Sayyid passed through and heard the story of the mysterious deaf boy. He recognized Anwar and brought him home. Anwar recounted this for the linguists entirely in the village sign language.

Irit starts with the vocabulary. For FISH, Anwar uses the local sign, two stacked hands, thumbs wiggling. As he signs, a series of boys darts in and out of the frame, and Shai says they're blocking the image. Irit conveys the problem to Anwar in gesture, and Anwar waves the wall of boys magisterially away. Someone wedges pillows on either side of him to act as a blockade, and another tiny boy immediately clambers onto them. A small girl climbs onto the TV table for a better view. There are now twenty-five people in the little room.

Anwar's signing is lavish, almost balletic. As Irit intones the English words—"Grass" . . . "Flower" . . . "Tree"—his hands seem to describe entire landscapes in the air. Anwar's wife, Muna, who is wearing a lavender headscarf, sits in the doorway, holding an infant, surveying the scene with interest, offering a passing comment in Arabic, occasionally yelling at the hearing kids to sit down. The children become increasingly noisy and an older boy evicts them from the room. They return at once.

From his place on the floor, Anwar, sitting serenely, continues to sign. On a cushion opposite him, Karim is taking his job as receiver very seriously, shooing away a stream of boys who come anywhere near camera range. A very small boy howls. Another jangles a set of keys loudly throughout the proceedings.

Carol stands up. "I'll go entertain the children," she says, and they follow her in a body from the room. Anwar finishes a spirited rendition of the Tweety cartoon, and he and Karim switch places.

"He's doing a lot of ISL," Mark says, watching the boy sign.

"No, this is local," Wendy says. "He's signing to *him*"—she indicates Anwar—"so he's using the local signs." She watches the boy sign awhile longer. "He uses most of these same signs at home with his father," she says. "It's good; it's good."

With Irit at the computer, Karim works his way through the vocabulary.

"I like this kid," Mark says. "Lots of syntax."

"He's a third-generation signer," Irit observes from her place on the floor.

Carol reappears in the doorway. "Should I keep on entertaining the kids?" she asks.

"If you can," Wendy tells her.

"Give me my hat," Carol says. "They want to show me the camels."

Hassan leaves with them, to meet with his auto mechanic. Muna brings in the tea. It is the most delicious yet, sweet and mint-laced, with extraordinary depth.

As we drink, a boy of thirteen or fourteen steps shyly forward and signs something to Irit. Wendy, catching it from across the room, points straight at him.

"Ah!" she cries with delight. "He's signing that he knows the Arab sign language!" "Arab Sign" is what the villagers call their indigenous language. Karim signs to Wendy that of all the hearing boys in the village, this one, Mahir, signs the best. The team decides to have him do part of the test.

Mahir, who is dressed in jeans and a blue T-shirt and has the ghost of a mustache, takes a seat next to Irit and starts to sign.

"One-handed," Mark observes, impressed.

"I think he was just being cool," Wendy says.

Mahir is indeed a marvelous signer. His rendering of the vocabulary, like Anwar's, is panoramic, almost topographic.

Carol comes back and sits down on the floor. She looks at Wendy inquiringly. "Third generation in the same family," Wendy signs to her.

The room fills with children again. From the next room, where there are evidently more children, a polyphonic chorus of wails arises. Muna, who is hearing, sits calmly in the doorway, sipping a large mug of tea. In our room, children are now all around us, running, shrieking, laughing, signing. In the crowd, three teenage boys stand conversing side by side. The one in the middle says something excitedly in Arabic to the boy on his left, then turns, taps the shoulder of the boy on his right and without missing a beat, tells him something in sign.

You make a neighborly call. . . . The spoken language and the sign language will be so mingled in the conversation that you pass from one to the other, or use both at once, almost unconsciously. Half the family speak, very probably, half do not, but . . . the community has adjusted itself to the situation so perfectly.

From their place on the floor, the linguists take it all in, drunk with pleasure. "Let's stay another week," Wendy says to Mark dreamily. "We'll have enough data for a lifetime."

As long as the grant money holds out, and as long as the people of Al-Sayyid will have them, the linguists will come back to the village at least twice a year, every year for the foreseeable future. They will concentrate their efforts on Al-Sayyid's second generation, Hassan and Anwar and Aminah and their contemporaries. It is too soon to tell whether the village sign language, at least in the pure, isolated form used by these signers, will endure much beyond this generation. As the linguists saw repeatedly on this trip, the signing of the deaf children, Al-Sayyid's third generation, is already permeated with ISL, or, more accurately, with signs lifted from ISL, as rendered by hearing teachers. Most parents in Al-Sayyid believe that for their deaf children to make their way in Israeli society, they will need to know the national signed language, and no one disputes their point. But it may mean that the indigenous signed language of the village, sprung from the hands of ten deaf children seventy years ago, will, with the passing of Hassan's generation, be increasingly overrun with ISL signs.

"We don't know how the language will change, and for us, that's where the drama is," Wendy wrote me in an e-mail message a few years after our trip. "And that's why we have to keep studying it very carefully across the generations."

The deaf community itself may also change. For the first time in Al-Sayyid's history, genetic counseling is available to the people of the village. Some of the geneticists who work there have been trying to discourage the traditional practice of cousin marriage, with mixed success. On a visit to New York several months after our trip, Carol described meeting one of them. The geneticist told her, "If they don't start marrying outside the village, they'll all be deaf," Carol recalled when we met that winter.

This did not sit too well with Carol. "How do you respond to people who say that?" she asked. She had been reading a lot about genetic testing for a new book she was writing, and was convinced that the geneticists were forcing Western advice on a place where it was not especially relevant. "The way we think about genetic testing is avoiding the burden of a disabled child," she told me. "So they do things like, 'Maybe you shouldn't marry your cousins.'" But in traditional societies like Al-Sayyid, as the linguists have learned, cousin marriage has an economic function: it consolidates land, which for less-well-off villagers is otherwise impossible to get.

"If you can't hold on to land, you can't provide for your family," Carol explained. "You have to marry strategically to get it. So the exchange marriages are ways of preserving connections. Why do they have these big families? Why do they have so many wives? It's power. They want to consolidate power. It helps to establish their claim to the land."

Carol didn't say anything to the geneticist at the time, but for the team, the issue of testing is lingering and thorny. "The Bedouins are under pressure," she told me. "I don't think people are asking enough questions about what it means to bring the ideas of genetic testing to a traditional culture. They're treating deafness as an entry point to the village, when the village doesn't treat it that way."

Forsaking traditional marriage patterns can risk impoverishing the village women in particular, because it can deprive them of the opportunity to "marry land," Carol explained. For the people of Al-Sayyid, she said, deafness is simply "an epiphenomenon of marriage."

"For them, preserving ties is more important than deafness," she said. "And they all already know how to sign. The sign language is well underway; they're not traumatized. The fact that there are so many signers means that the deaf can participate in everything. I have yet to walk into a room that's made up of only deaf people."

In the café where we sat, Carol checked the messages on her electronic pager and reached for her coat. "There's something very powerful about the village and ties in the community," she said. "And when people leave, they feel alienated and come back." She rose to go, then paused a moment, remembering one of the teenagers we had met at the top-down house. By the team's next visit, the young man had graduated from high school. He told the linguists he planned to stay in the village. "My father will build a house for me right here," he said.

In Anwar's already overflowing living room, Malik, one of the boys from yesterday afternoon, drops by for a visit. He is dressed again in his homemade soccer jersey. Malik strikes up an elaborate signed conversation with another young man, both of them talking in huge two-handed signs. "Did you see the *question*?" Mark asks, watching them. Wendy doesn't reply, but on her face is a look of complete happiness.

The afternoon sun, filtered through the branches of the olive tree, casts dappled light on the floor. As Irit gives directions in Hebrew, Mahir continues his work, signing the tale of Sylvester and Tweety. Still signing, he turns to converse with a girl his age who is watching the action from the doorway. Off to one side, Anwar and Carol are deep in conversation. There is signing everywhere, and much waving to catch people's attention.

Mahir finishes the test, and slowly, reluctantly, the linguists pack up to leave. We are driving straight back to Haifa; the luggage was loaded into the van this morning. We say many goodbyes, and pass through the cool front room to the courtyard outside, where Muna is sitting cross-legged, kneading a bowl of dough. The entire family joins us outside, assembling behind the Fiat to watch us pack the last of our things. The last set of dishes is presented. We pull away from the house, past Anwar's lambs and goats and onto the rutted road, as the family watches us go. No one says anything for a while.

"He insisted that next time we eat at his house," Irit says finally.

"He says that to us every time," Wendy observes. Then she calls Hassan on her cell phone. *"Fan-tas-TEEK!"* she cries. They speak some more in Hebrew. "Hassan says he considers himself to be part of the team now," Wendy tells us after they have said goodbye. She adds softly, almost to herself, "Our team."

We stop at McDonald's for Cokes and, sipping them, turn onto the highway. The linguists marvel again at the sheer number of hearing people in Al-Sayyid who are fluent signers. "In the American deaf community, hearing native signers—how are they regarded?" Mark asks Carol.

"There's two types," she says. "There's some that only understand their parents and don't understand anybody else, because their parents didn't include them in their lives. They think of signs in terms of the family, not the community. You can tell from their signing: they look like adults signing like children. They were never expected to interact with other deaf people as adults. And then you have very skilled hearing signers who are very involved with the community."

The discussion turns to the best way of creating a searchable database from the video footage. They decide to have Shai burn a DVD on which informants can be sorted by age and gender. In just three days, the team has shot dozens of hours of video. We have visited six different houses: two traditional, two modern and two half-finished. But as the highway unfurls beneath us and we retrace our steps to Haifa, past fields of nodding sunflowers, past olive groves and the sea, it is impossible not to find oneself back at Anwar's. There, as the light dapples the floor and we sip the last of our tea, twenty people and more are crowded into the little room. There are a dozen lively conversations going on at once, but for the moment anyhow, everything is quiet.

CHAPTER 16

The Signing Brain

Even in antiquity, some observers suspected a connection between our brains and our ability to use language. "As early as the time of Hippocrates in the fourth century B.C. in Greece, it was reported that injury to the brain could result in impairment of language capacities," the researchers Howard Poizner, Edward Klima and Ursula Bellugi write. "In fact, even the ancient Egyptians knew that certain head injuries could result in loss of speech."

Pliny (A.D. 23–79) wrote of a man who was hit in the head by a stone and "fell presently to forget his letters only, and could read no more; otherwise his memory served him well enough." In the Hebrew Bible, the poet of Psalm 137 declares fervently, *"If I forget thee, O Jerusalem, let my right hand forget her cunning. / If I do not remember thee, let my tongue cleave to the roof of my mouth."* Both passages are describing the effects of a stroke or other injury to the left side of the brain, the side we now know to be specialized for language.

The link between the left brain and language wasn't conclusively demonstrated until the 1860s. Between 1861 and 1865, the French neurologist Paul Broca made a series of detailed investigations of patients who, as the result of stroke, infection or head injury, had lost the ability to use language normally. Long before today's sophisticated imaging techniques, researchers studied the pathologies of brain-injured patients as a way of investigating the workings of the healthy brain. By Broca's time, it was already generally accepted, if not yet universally believed, that in most people, the right half of the brain controls the left half of the body, and vice versa. If, after a stroke, a patient showed paralysis or weakness on one side of the body, he could reasonably be assumed to have suffered an injury to the other side of the brain.

Broca's first patient was a man named Leborgne. He was familiarly known as Tan, because, since falling ill years before, he was able to utter only a single monosyllable, *tan.* When Broca encountered Tan, he had already been hospitalized for more than twenty years. As the neurolinguist David Caplan writes:

> Despite this severe handicap, Leborgne functioned independently at Bicêtre hospital. He apparently understood what was said to him, and was able to respond appropriately and make his needs known. . . . After about ten years, Leborgne's condition worsened: he lost the use of his right arm. Shortly before his death, this paralysis extended to the right leg as well.

After Tan died, an autopsy was performed, and Broca was able to examine his brain. Tan had a large lesion in the frontal lobe of his left hemisphere. Though it would be several more years before Broca pinpointed the *left* half of the brain as the neurological seat of language—like most scientists of the day, he was focused on the lesion's anterior quality—his 1861 paper on Tan, Caplan writes, is "the first truly scientific paper on language-brain relationships." Broca named Tan's language disorder "aphemia." Today, such acquired disorders of language are known as aphasia.

Not long afterward, Broca examined another patient with impaired language. This man, Lelong, seemed to understand what was said to him, but, like Tan, could barely produce any speech. Lelong, who had suffered a stroke when he was in his eighties, was left with just four words, "yes" and "no," which he used appropriately; "three," which he used for anything to do with numbers; and "always" which he seemed to use indiscriminately. These, plus a simplified form of his name—Lelo—were all the language that remained to him. He died a year and a half later. Lelong's brain, Broca found, showed an obvious lesion in the left frontal lobe, just as Tan's had.

Over the next four years, Broca studied other aphasic patients. By 1864, as the psychologist Malcolm Macmillan writes, "he said he knew of more than twenty-five cases with the same left frontal involvement and only one in which there was not a left-sided lesion."

Frequently, as in Tan's case, aphasia occurred together with right hemiplegia, a paralysis of the right side of the body. In 1865, Macmillan writes, "Broca publicly announced his view that in most people the left hemisphere was specialized for language, a dominance that explained the common association of aphasia with right hemiplegia. The exceptional cases were left-handed people whose right hemispheres carried the language function." As Broca himself would famously declare, "*Nous parlons avec l'hemisphere gauche*"—"We speak with the left hemisphere."

Broca's 1865 paper, David Caplan writes, was "the first to call the attention of the neurological community to the fact that aphasia followed lesions of the left hemisphere and not the right." The site of these lesions, a particular region of the left frontal lobe, is today known as Broca's area.

A decade later, in 1874, a young German physician named Carl Wernicke identified a second type of aphasia, associated with damage to a different part of the left hemisphere. Broca's patients, who had lesions in their left frontal lobes, displayed halting, effortful speech. Their ability to understand language, however, was largely spared. Wernicke, in contrast, identified a language disorder that was in many ways the opposite: in these cases, patients' speech was almost excessively fluent, though what they said made little sense. What was more, their ability to comprehend language was severely impaired. Autopsies revealed that these patients also had left-hemisphere lesions—but in a different place from Broca's patients. Where in Broca's cases the lesions were toward the front of the left hemisphere, in Wernicke's they were toward the back, a part of the brain now known as Wernicke's area. Two distinct cerebral regions, two distinct types of aphasia.

In most people, damage to Broca's area results in impairments, often quite severe, in producing language. Such patients typically have great difficulty in "getting the words out," displaying halting, effortful speech. Often, like Tan and Lelong, they are left with just a small handful of words at their disposal, usually simple nouns and verbs, largely stripped of grammatical inflection. Their ability to understand the speech of others, however, is generally intact. This type of aphasia is called Broca's, or nonfluent, aphasia. The following exchange between an examiner and a patient with Broca's aphasia is typical:

EXAMINER: Can you tell me about why you came back to the hospital?

PATIENT: Yeah . . . eh . . . Monday . . . eh . . . dad . . . Peter Hogan and dad . . . hospital.
Er . . . two . . . er . . . doctors . . . and . . . er . . . thirty minutes . . . and . . . er . . . yes . . . hospital. And . . . er . . . Wednesday . . . Wednesday. Nine o'clock. And . . . er . . . Thursday, ten o'clock . . . doctors . . . two . . . two . . . doctors . . . and . . . er . . . teeth . . . fine.

EXAMINER: Not exactly your teeth . . . your g——

PATIENT: Gum . . . gum . . .

EXAMINER: What did they do to them?

PATIENT: And er . . . doctor and girl . . . and er . . . and er gum.

In contrast to Broca's aphasia is Wernicke's, or fluent, aphasia. The speech of these patients appears effortless, so much so that it can seem almost hyperfluent. But though the speech of a Wernicke's aphasic is full of sound and fury, it signifies nothing, or at least very little. The speech of such patients is typically larded with weird substitutions—one word for another, or one sound for another. At its most severe, Wernicke's aphasia sounds like gibberish, and for this reason it is sometimes called "jargon aphasia" or "word salad aphasia." Where a Broca's patient seems, quite literally, at a loss for words, a Wernicke's patient—here, responding to the question "How are you today?"—sounds like this:

> I feel very well. My hearing, writing been doing well. Things that I couldn't hear from. In other words, I used to be able work cigarettes I didn't know how. . . . Chesterfeela, for 20 years I can write it.

Identifying these dysfunctions of language, acquired after damage to the left side of the brain, also helped illuminate the right hemisphere's function. In contrast to left-hemisphere damage, injury to the right side of the brain causes little or no disruption of language. Right-hemisphere-damaged patients can almost always converse as well as they did before. They do, however, have other problems, particularly with tasks involving spatial orientation. They get hopelessly lost in familiar surroundings, have trouble copying simple drawings, and give very confused accounts of the layouts of places they know well, even their own homes. Where the left hemisphere is specialized for producing and comprehending speech, the right is specialized for the host of visuospatial tasks we perform every day, from finding our way around the neighborhood to recognizing familiar faces. If the left hemisphere speaks, then the right hemisphere turns and rotates and navigates in space.

The recognition of ASL as a natural language raised an enticing question, never before asked: Where in the brain was the neurological seat of sign language? Was it in the right hemisphere, on account of sign's visuospatial nature? Or was it in the left, where spoken language was? Compelling arguments could be made on both sides, and there was little to choose between them.

Like so much seminal work in sign-language linguistics, research on this question began with Bellugi, Klima and their colleagues, notably Howard Poizner. They speculated that of the thousands of Americans who suffer strokes each year, a small number must surely be native deaf signers. These patients, the researchers realized, provided a singular means of exploring the neurological underpinnings of a language in the visuospatial mode.

The researchers scoured the country for native deaf signers who had suffered strokes. Their earliest studies, begun in the 1980s, focused on six of them, three with damage to the right hemisphere, three with damage to the left. All were right-handed, and all had been considered skilled signers before their strokes. Each was given a battery of diagnostic tests for aphasia, specially adapted for use with ASL. Their spontaneous signing was also recorded.

At the outset, the investigators had little idea what to expect. Was sign language processed in the brain in remotely the same way spoken language was? Would an injury to the brain cause aphasia for sign language, as it did for speech? If so, to which half of the brain? If there *was* such a thing as sign-language aphasia, what would it look like? As Poizner, Klima and Bellugi write in their 1987 book, *What the Hands Reveal About the Brain*:

> Until recently, nearly everything learned about the human capacity for language came from the study of spoken languages. It has been assumed that the organizational properties of language are inseparably connected with the sounds of speech. . . . Language, however, is not limited to the vocal tract and ears. . . . These visual-gestural languages of the deaf, with deep roots in the visual modality, provide a testing ground for competing explanations of how the brain is organized for language, how the brain came to be so organized, and how modifiable that organization is.

Because ASL is transmitted visually, and because so much of its grammar—from verb agreement to classifier constructions to pronouns that hang in the air—depends on making patterns in space, it was intuitive that damage to the right hemisphere would disrupt signing severely. But to the researchers' amazement, that wasn't the case at all.

One patient, whom they called Sarah M., had been an artist before her stroke. Deaf from birth, she was seventy-one when the researchers met her. The year before, Sarah had suffered a stroke, which, as a CAT scan showed, left a large lesion in the right hemisphere of her brain. Because her left arm and leg were paralyzed, the researchers tailored the tests so that she could sign using just her right hand. Sarah did well on the tests. Her signing was virtually unaffected, as fluent as it had been before and still readily understandable, despite the fact that she could use only one hand. Her written English, which had been good before her stroke, was just as good afterward.

"Sarah M. clearly is not aphasic," Poizner, Klima and Bellugi write. "Indeed, in the language samples we analyzed, her signing is without error at any of the structural levels of ASL. Her signing has complex sentences, correct verb agreement, appropriate use of classifiers, correct morphology and syntax, and no sublexical errors."

The two other patients with right-hemisphere damage performed similarly well on tests of language skills. One, seventy-five-year-old Brenda I., had suffered a stroke three years earlier. Deaf from birth, she had paralysis in her left arm and, like Sarah, now signed with her right hand only. She had had a fair command of written English, which the stroke left unchanged. Except for some minor errors, her signing remained fluent and grammatical.

The third patient, eighty-one-year-old Gilbert G., had had a stroke three and a half years before the researchers saw him. Deaf from the age of five, he had been a skilled airplane technician and repairman. His written English, excellent before his stroke, was unimpaired. So was his signing. By the time the researchers saw him, Gilbert had recovered much of the use of his left side, and could sign with both hands. As they write:

> Gilbert G.'s poststroke signing is completely unimpaired, exhibiting full grammatical marking of morphology and excellent spatially organized syntax. Even immediately after his stroke, his wife reported that his signing was as before the stroke. . . . Gilbert G.'s signing is impeccable, perfectly full and grammatical, and without error at any level of structure. Moreover, analysis of his free conversation, his storytelling, and

> elicited language samples show that after his stroke Gilbert G. had no deficits in signing whatsoever.

Damage to the right hemisphere, it seems, does little to impair ASL, despite the overwhelmingly visuospatial nature of the language. But for the three signers with left-hemisphere strokes, the results were altogether different. In these patients, all lifelong signers, ASL was severely disrupted, a fact that was readily apparent both on diagnostic tests and in ordinary conversation. As the investigators were careful to establish, those difficulties were not the result of paralysis or other motor problems caused by the strokes. What had happened to these three patients was a disorder of language—that is, a disorder of *signed language*—after injury to the left side of the brain. And, as the researchers would discover, the nature of the disruptions was far from random, but was instead rooted in the organization of ASL itself.

The researchers examined one signer they called Gail D. Thirty-eight years old, she had suffered a stroke eight months before. Gail was deaf from birth, and by all accounts had been an accomplished signer. Her stroke resulted in a lesion that affected much of the left frontal lobe, including Broca's area. When the researchers first met Gail, she was talking with her three deaf children—or, rather, she was watching them talk:

> The difference between the mother and her children would have impressed even an uninformed outsider. The three bright-faced children were engaged in high-spirited, effortless interchange; their hands moved rapidly, smoothly, rhythmically. The commentary "changed hands" as each vied to take the conversational lead. Sitting between them, their mother looked from one to another as they took their turns. She, however, made almost no signs. She appeared to follow the conversation with eager attention, but even though she was its subject, she did not join in. An occasional nod, even an isolated sign came from her, but it was effortful, halting, and out of synchrony with the

cadence of her children's free-flowing interchanges and completed after a false start or two.

In diagnostic tests, Gail's signing was similarly labored, halting and spare. Though she seemed to have no trouble understanding the signing of others, she needed heavy prompting, and much guesswork on the examiner's part, in order to sign anything herself.

One of the tasks the researchers gave her involved describing a drawing known as the Cookie Theft picture. The picture is a standard test, long used to assess aphasia in spoken language. On the left side of the drawing, a boy, who has clambered onto a tall stool, is in the act of sneaking cookies from a jar in a high kitchen cupboard. As he does so, the stool tips out from under him and he starts to fall. A girl stands next to him, her hand outstretched for a cookie. At the right of the image, a woman stands at the kitchen sink, dreamily drying dishes. She has left the tap on and the sink is overflowing, but she seems oblivious of the cascade of water pouring onto the floor. Above the sink is a window, through which part of the yard can be seen.

The Cookie Theft picture is designed to elicit speech from aphasic patients. It also tests for hemispatial neglect, the inability to perceive information in the visual field on the opposite side from the stroke, which some aphasics also have. Here is a transcription of Gail's account of the picture; both she and the examiner were signing ASL:

EXAMINER: What's happening there? [Pointing to the water spilling on the floor.]

GAIL D.: WHAT? [Points, gestures, mouths "oh."]

EXAMINER: What is that? [Pointing to the water again.]

GAIL D.: F- . . . E- . . . F- . . . A- . . . L- . . . L. [Fingerspells "fall" laboriously.]

EXAMINER: What is the woman doing there?

GAIL D.: [Fumbles and gestures, then signs] PLATE T- . . . E- . . . O- . . . W- . . . L. [Attempts to fingerspell "towel."]

EXAMINER: What is the woman doing?

GAIL D.: TURN-OFF. TURN-OFF.

EXAMINER: What does the girl want?

GAIL D.: [Mouths "cookie" but puts finger to lips as does girl in picture.]

EXAMINER: What does the boy want?

GAIL D.: C- . . . A- . . . O- . . . O- . . . K- . . . E. [Attempts to fingerspell "cookie."]

EXAMINER: The boy wants what?

GAIL D.: [Points to boy, then to girl, then fingerspells] G- . . . A- . . . V- . . . E.

EXAMINER: The boy gave her a cookie?

GAIL D.: YES.

Gail D. showed graphic symptoms of Broca's, or nonfluent, aphasia. As with hearing Broca's aphasics, she could produce language only with great effort. Like them, she had been left largely "without words," usually speaking—or, in her case, signing—one laborious word at a time. As they are for hearing patients, Gail D.'s utterances were limited mostly to basic nouns and verbs, with a conspicuous lack of grammatical inflection. Her verbs did not agree; she did not establish pronouns in space; she did not derive morphologically complex signs from simpler ones. Her signing remarkably paralleled the speech of hearing Broca's aphasics, one of whom described the Cookie Theft picture this way:

> Cookie . . . Okay, . . . the cookie jar . . . and the kid is a . . . uh . . . Stool . . . bump . . . the skool . . . skool . . . uh . . . hurt . . . and girl . . . I don't know.

As with hearing Broca's aphasics, Gail's ability to understand the language of others, both in free conversation and on diagnostic tests, was unimpaired. In short, Gail had a classic case of Broca's aphasia—only she had it for ASL. "Although the modality is different," Poizner, Klima and Bellugi write, "Gail D.'s signing fits the description of a Broca's aphasic remarkably well."

The second patient with left-hemisphere damage was sixty-seven-year-old Karen L., who had been deafened by scarlet fever at the age of six months. A year and eight months before the examiners met her, she had suffered a left-hemisphere stroke. As the examiners found, her signing was affected, but in a manner very different from Gail's. At first glance, Karen's signing still seemed fluent. Unlike Gail's halting ASL, hers was free, rapid and voluble. Unlike Gail, she made full and accurate use of many of the spatial grammatical devices the language has at its disposal.

But though Karen's signing was for the most part intelligible, there was something odd about it. Although she used the spatial morphology and syntax of the language well, Karen made repeated errors at the sublexical level of signs, substituting the wrong handshape, location or movement in what should have been familiar signs. Her errors were very much like the involuntary substitution errors of certain hearing aphasics, who might say "skool" when they mean "stool." "Virtually all her sublexical errors, which were numerous, produced well-formed nonsense signs in ASL," Poizner, Klima and Bellugi write, adding, "The rule-governed nature of Karen L.'s errors and their occurrence in the context of fluent signing clearly confirm an aphasic disturbance." What was more, Karen, unlike Gail, had great difficulty understanding the signing of others.

The third left-damaged signer, Paul D., displayed still another pattern of disruption. Eighty-one years old, Paul had been deaf since the age of five. He became a teacher of the deaf and had been considered a master signer. Ten years before the examiners saw him, Paul had suffered a left-hemisphere stroke so severe that for a time he was unable to communicate at all. Gradually, he regained much of his ability to sign, and to write in English.

Before his stroke, Paul's command of written English had been first-rate. The examiners obtained several samples of his pre-stroke writing. In one letter, Paul wrote:

> I have never liked splinter groups. They weaken rather than strengthen an important cause, especially when the good of ALL people is concerned. You hit the nail on the head when you stated with truth that Judaism is synonymous with humanitarianism. Humanitarianism can best be served when everyone is pulling together to enhance the cause rather than to maintain "a house divided against itself." This is especially applicable to our deaf world where the need is acute for the people of all faiths and ideals to work hand in hand to better their welfare.

Three years after his stroke, Paul wrote this account of a trip to Washington, D.C.:

> I walked toward the Capitol and entered the way up the stairs. I noticed the rooms were for the wayfarers and entered the deliberation room. The senators were in a huddle of a question.
>
> I spoke to the axiom in the window. I sprintered the Green aside the window. Many times as I looked at the Capitol I wonder the many times were engaged at the same time by the representatives as they behaved the problems. The 48 states wherein the problems threshed by the senators finally thunbured [or *thundured,* not clear] to the impression. And the gathering of the warrior.

In the wake of his stroke, Paul's written English, though superficially fluent, has taken on a bizarre, Dada quality. It is often hard to guess his intended meaning, but whatever it may have been, it is clear that his English is now larded with inappropriate, even nonsensical, words: *wayfarers, sprintered, the Green, threshed.* Furthermore, Paul now violates English syntax and semantics left and right: a noun like *axiom* can never be the object of a verb like *speak,* which requires an indirect object that is ideally human but at the very least must be concrete. Similarly, the intransitive verb *behave* can't take a direct object of any sort, much less one like *problems.* Paul's writing is also marked by meaningless repetitions ("Many times . . . I wonder the many times . . . at the same time") and by phrases that in their collisions of syntax and semantics read like e.e. cummings: "in a huddle of a question."

Paul's written English was reminiscent of the "word salad" of hearing Broca's aphasics. Was his signing similarly affected?

By the time of the researchers' visit, Paul had regained the ability to sign with both hands. He signed smoothly, in long, complex sentences. But, as they quickly discovered, his signed sentences were so overelaborate that they verged on nonsense. What made Paul's signing especially hard to follow was that he frequently used a morphologically complex form of a sign—the habitual aspect, say, or the predispositional—where only the simple form was indicated. In this transcription, Paul is describing the layout of his apartment, in particular a glassed-in patio adjoining his living room (the translation that follows supplies English equivalents for Paul's morphologically baroque signs. Asterisks indicate ungrammatical or inappropriate signs):

> PAUL D.: AND HAVE ONE *WAY-DOWN-THERE [unintelligible]. MAN WALK, MAN SEE THAT *DISCONNECT E-X-T-E-N-S-I-O-N O-F *EARTH ROOM. HAVE FOR MAN CAN *LIVE ROOF, LIGHT, SHADE[Seriated Plural] *PULL-DOWN[[+ Dual] + Habitual] AND HAVE GLASS WALL. . . . FOUR DIFFERENT. . . . TO-HAMMER[Habitual] MAN MAKE *HAND *MAKE M-O-B-I-L-E-S. ROUND-OBJECT-WALL[Allocative]. WONDERFUL *BRILLIANT[Predispositional] MAN.

> And there's one (way down at the end) [unintelligible]. The man walked over to see the (disconnected), an extension of the (earth) room. It's there for the man (can live) a roof and light with shades to (keep pulling down). And there's a glass wall with four different. . . . He hammered. The man (makes hands), makes mobiles, many on the wall. A wonderful (always brillianting) man.

As Paul's signing vividly demonstrates, there are distinct types of sign-language aphasia, which closely parallel Broca's and Wernicke's aphasia for spoken language. Where Gail D.'s aphasia is nonfluent, Paul D.'s is fluent—so fluent that it gives the impression of meaningless jargon, much as the spoken "word salad" of hearing Wernicke's patients does. Karen L.'s aphasia, because of the location of her lesion, roughly in the center of the left hemisphere, has elements of both types.

As the researchers were careful to rule out, the signing difficulties of these three patients did not stem from underlying motor disorders. The problem, it seemed, came with movement conscripted in the service of language—movement, in other words, that had been made to take on a specifically linguistic function. As Poizner, Klima and Bellugi write, "This *separation between linguistic and nonlinguistic functioning* is all the more striking because for sign language, gesture and linguistic symbol are transmitted in the same modality."

Even more remarkable was the fact that these three patients, whose ability to use the spatial mechanisms of ASL had been damaged, performed well on tests of general spatial cognition. The researchers administered a standard battery of tests designed to assess spatial abilities in hearing patients after strokes. The tests involved copying simple drawings and more complex figures, matching faces, determining the orientation of lines, and arranging blocks into geometric configurations. All three left-hemisphere-damaged patients—Gail D., Karen L. and Paul D.—did well on these tests, copying drawings accurately, matching faces in a photo array with a target face, and assembling blocks into the designated patterns. They did so despite their obvious problems with the highly spatial grammar of ASL. Even Gail, whose signing was so terribly impaired, performed extremely well on every test of nonlanguage spatial cognition.

The results were the opposite for the three right-hemisphere-damaged patients, Sarah M., Brenda I. and Gilbert G. Although their signing was almost completely unimpaired, and they made excellent use of the spatial grammar of ASL, they did extremely poorly on the nonlanguage spatial tests. Asked to copy simple line drawings—a house, a flower, a cube, a cross and an elephant—they often drew figures that were grossly distorted, sometimes almost beyond recognition.

Both Sarah and Brenda omitted the entire left side of many of their drawings, a phenomenon called hemispatial neglect that is especially common after right-hemisphere strokes. Even a familiar object like a house would, in their copies, be missing its entire left-hand wall. Copying a daisy, both women gave it petals on the right side only; drawing an elephant facing leftward, both omitted part of its head or trunk. As a result of their right-side strokes, objects in the left visual field simply did not register. Sarah, who before her stroke was a painter and decorative artist, was unable to continue her work afterward. Brenda had such a disoriented sense of spatial topography that she had trouble finding her way around the nursing home in which she had lived for years.

The third right-lesioned signer, Gilbert, did much better at copying drawings, perhaps, the researchers conjectured, because he had spent years working with blueprints in his job as an airplane mechanic. He scored poorly, however, on the block configuration tests and on tests of line orientation, as Brenda and Sarah also did.

The conclusion was inescapable. For the deaf signers, *nonlanguage* spatial abilities were localized in the right hemisphere, just as they are for hearing people. Space in the service of language, however, was localized on the left. For Gail, Karen and Paul, a left-hemisphere stroke caused their visuospatial language to break down but spared nonlanguage spatial cognition. For the right-lesioned signers, Sarah, Brenda and Gilbert, the reverse was true.

The intricate combinations of handshapes, locations and movements that signers use to communicate are *language,* and, at a basic neurological level, the brain of a signer knows it. "The congenitally deaf patients are exactly the ones whose performance most clearly mirrors the classic differences in visuospatial functioning that have been found between hearing left-lesioned and right-lesioned patients," Poizner, Klima and Bellugi write. "It seems clear that auditory experience is not necessary for the development of hemispheric specialization."

In recent years, some studies of the signing brain have ascribed a greater role to the right hemisphere than previously thought. The right hemisphere appears to be involved in sign-language comprehension; this is also the case, in hearing people, for the comprehension of spoken language. And, for signers, the right hemisphere is also involved in a very particular use of space.

There are two main ways in which signed language uses space. The first is for grammar: verb agreement, placing pronouns in the air, and so on. The second is to talk about space itself. As a visuospatial language, sign is especially well suited to represent topographic information like the passage of a car across terrain or the layout of furniture in a room. If a signer uses space as grammar—moving an agreeing verb from one point in space to another, for instance—the actual points she chooses are understood to be pure abstractions. But if she uses the space in front of her to describe, say, the contents of a room, suddenly each point takes on an analogue function. She is signing, in effect. "The table goes here; the couch goes here; and the door is here." Where a spoken language uses prepositions like "on," "beside," "in front of" and "under," a signed language can use three-dimensional space to map these concepts directly.

Bellugi, Klima and their colleagues studied the effects of right- and left-hemisphere strokes on these two distinct uses of space. In a test of space-as-grammar, signers with left-hemisphere damage did poorly, while those with right-hemisphere damage were unimpaired. But in a test of space-as-space, the results were reversed, with the right-lesioned signers doing badly and the left-lesioned signers doing well. The ability to use space *as grammar* was localized in the left hemisphere, with other language functions, while the *topographic* use of space was localized on the right, with other visuospatial skills.

As Bellugi and Klima write in an article with the cognitive scientist Gregory Hickok: "These data suggest that the neural organization for language and spatial cognition are driven by the type of representation that is ultimately constructed from the signal (grammatical versus spatial), rather than by the physical properties of the signal itself."

Though most researchers now concede a place for the right hemisphere in the processing and use of signed language, the crucial role of the left hemisphere in the use of this visual language remains beyond doubt. As Hickok, Bellugi and Klima write, "Research investigating the neural organization of signed language and spatial cognition in deaf individuals has demonstrated the same hemispheric asymmetries found in hearing, speaking individuals. This suggests that the hemispheric organization of grammatical aspects of language is independent of modality and, more specifically, unaffected by the fact that signed language involves a significant degree of visuospatial processing."

The studies of deaf stroke patients did even more than advance the study of sign language. They also illuminated the long-standing discussion of the relationship between language and thought. At its center is an issue that the prominent philosopher Jerry A. Fodor calls the modularity of mind.

For centuries, philosophers have debated whether the human capacity for language is a self-contained mental faculty all its own or merely a by-product of more general cognitive powers. To put the question in modern physiological terms, Why is it, exactly, that the left hemisphere is specialized for language? Is it because that side is wired for language per se? Or is it simply that it is specialized for symbolic cognition, of which language happens to be one type?

In his influential book of 1983, *The Modularity of Mind,* Fodor, who teaches at Rutgers University, argues for a model of human cognition that comprises a number of separate modules: one for visual processing, one for auditory processing, one for memory and, importantly, one for language. If his model were diagrammed on paper, it would have something of the quality of a nineteenth-century phrenologist's chart, endowed with the respectability of late-twentieth-century cognitive science. Human language, Fodor argues, occupies a mental module of its own and, as such, is separate from other cognitive processes. The "output" of a module can in turn feed general cognition, but the modules themselves are largely insulated from general cognition, just as they are insulated from one another. In short, Fodor maintains, the human language faculty is truly a faculty *for language* and only that, and not an artifact of cognition in general. His model is not unlike Chomsky's proposal for the existence of a dedicated "language organ."

Modules, for Fodor, have several distinguishing characteristics. First, they must be what he calls "domain specific," operating only on material of a certain type, like language or visual information. Second, the operation of modules is mandatory. (It is for this reason, as the linguist Diane Lillo-Martin writes, that "we can't help but hear linguistic input as language.") Third, they operate fast, unlike many general cognitive operations: compare the immediacy of understanding language with the relative slowness of, say, solving a math problem. Fourth, modules are associated with fixed neural regions in the brain, and their operation breaks down in characteristic ways (think of aphasia) when these areas are damaged. Finally, the development of modules in individuals exhibits what Lillo-Martin calls "a characteristic pace and sequencing, such as the well-known milestones children go through in acquiring (spoken or signed) language."

The findings from sign-language aphasia studies seem to support Fodor's theory of language as modular. Data from these studies, many researchers now believe, reveal the human language faculty to be separate from more general mental capabilities, among them symbolic cognition. One of the most persuasive pieces of evidence for this comes from two recent studies of deaf signers who, as the result of strokes, lost much of their ability to sign—*but who could nonetheless use and understand pantomime perfectly.*

Because sign language and pantomime are both transmitted in the visual-gestural mode, studying their respective breakdown after brain injury lets investigators tease apart man's capacity for linguistic and nonlinguistic symbolic cognition. In 1992, the psychologist David Corina and his colleagues reported the remarkable case of a man they called W.L., a seventy-six-year-old congenitally deaf right-handed signer. W.L. had suffered a left-hemisphere stroke seven months before the researchers saw him. The stroke damaged the portion of his brain that included Broca's area, as well as other parts of the left hemisphere. The researchers had been lucky enough to obtain a videotape of W.L., made two years before his stroke, which showed him to be a fluent signer. As it also showed, he never used pantomime to communicate, something that would change dramatically after his stroke.

On meeting with W.L., Corina and his colleagues administered the standard battery of sign-language aphasia tests. The tests showed W.L. to be severely language-impaired, both in producing ASL and in comprehending it. His signing was effortful, reduced mostly to bare, uninflected verbs and a few nouns. He also had trouble understanding all but the simplest signed commands.

Curiously, after his stroke, W.L. began interspersing his signing with a great deal of pantomime, something his wife, who was also deaf, confirmed he had never done before. Unlike his halting ASL, his pantomimes were elaborate, effortless and fluent. He seemed to have little difficulty understanding the testers' instructions when they were mimed rather than signed. Here were two forms of symbolic communication, both gestural, both using the hands and arms in similar ways. In most deaf signers, the capacity to sign and the ability to use pantomime exist side by side. Yet in W.L., one of these had been severely disrupted while the other was left completely intact.

Compared with signed language, mime can be lawless. Its gestures are global, variable and analogue, without internal structure, coherence or rules. Pantomimes can vary wildly from one person to the next. They don't comprise smaller meaningful parts. There is little that is abstract or arbitrary—little that is language-like—about them. Like signed language, however, pantomime is transmitted by hand and received by eye. Like signed language, it relies on man's ability to deploy and process symbols. Sign and mime are both forms of symbolic gesture. One is linguistic, the other nonlinguistic. As Corina and his colleagues write:

> There are major differences between sign languages and communicative pantomimic gesture . . . *even when both share a common theme.* . . . Typically in pantomime, movements are continuous, there are no well-defined transitions between particular action sequences. . . . There is great variability in the particular actions that will be depicted and further variability in specific configurations of body "articulations" that are used. . . . In an ASL sign, movement of the hands is organized into a linguistic system; there are clear temporal boundaries to sign movement during which a set of discrete articulatory configurations are enacted and then relaxed.

Although W.L. could sign comfortably with both hands after his stroke, his ability to use language was badly damaged. He had great trouble retrieving even familiar words, and his signing contained many nonsense forms, typically made with inappropriate handshapes. In one standard test, W.L. was asked to sign the names of as many animals as he could in one minute. Non-brain-damaged signers produce an average of twenty-five names. W.L. produced just three correct signs. Here is his signed description of the Cookie Theft picture, which consists of a few signs and a great deal of pantomime:

> CHAIR (W.L. teeters his body to indicate the chair was teetering) STAND (tips his body rightward as if he is falling, hand outward as if to brace for a fall) WATER FLOW-DOWN (moves body to the right, following the flow of the water).

As the researchers write, "This mixture of signs and mimes is very unusual, but characteristic of W.L.'s output."

Like many signers with left-hemisphere damage, W.L. performed extremely well on tests of nonlinguistic spatial ability, including face recognition, line orientation, block arrangement and drawing. In the tests and in free conversation, he often used mime to stand in for the signs to which he no longer had access. What was striking was that in many cases, the mimes he came up with were more complicated physically than the corresponding sign would have been. In miming "flower," as the researchers write,

> W.L. produced a sequence of mime descriptors for the stem, the petals, and the blossom of a flower. In contrast, the ASL sign FLOWER appears quite simple. It consists of a hand closed at the finger tips which touches [on either side of] the nose. . . . The components of this sign are drawn from a limited set of ASL phonological components which reoccur in other ASL signs.

Even more striking was the fact that in substituting mime for sign, W.L. sometimes sacrificed iconicity: some of his pantomimes were visibly *less* iconic than the corresponding sign in ASL. "In response to a picture of a pair of scissors," the researchers write, "W.L. opened and closed his fist while miming the act of 'cutting' along an imaginary line, instead of making the ASL sign SCISSORS. This pantomimic substitution is surprising since the ASL sign for scissors uses the index and middle finger to represent the opening and closing blades of the scissors."

For W.L., though sign was damaged, mime remained intact. "This case provides a powerful indication of the left hemisphere's specialization for language-specific functions," Corina and his colleagues write, adding, "The separation in brain systems for signs and for gestures is revealing, since both of these functions involve symbolic gesturing of the hands in space."

A similar separation was observed a decade later in a speaker of British Sign Language. In 2004, a group of researchers in London reported the case of a man they called Charles. Charles was a fifty-six-year-old right-handed man who had suffered a left-hemisphere stroke two years earlier. Deaf from birth, he acquired British Sign Language in school at the age of five. He had apparently been a fluent signer. After his stroke, he had great difficulty in coming up with the names of things, a disorder called anomia that can also befall hearing speakers. Even his production of very iconic signs, the researchers write, was severely impaired.

Despite his considerable sign-language dysfunction, Charles's ability to use mime was unimpaired. Like W.L., he sometimes used pantomimes that were far more elaborate than the corresponding sign. "In the face of his linguistic difficulties Charles often turned to the nonlinguistic medium of gesture," the British researchers write. "Such gestures often involved whole body actions or narrative sequences. For example, when Charles gestured washing, he demonstrated turning on the taps, splashing water on his face, and rubbing his face with his hand."

The cases of W.L. and Charles provide a powerful argument for the modularity of human language. In these two signers, language function, deeply disrupted after left-hemisphere damage, is demonstrably separate from more general symbolic cognition, which in both men remained intact. It wasn't that these signers had been robbed of the *concepts* of "flower" or "scissors" or "wash"—it was that they could no longer gain access to *their linguistic representations.* Sign aphasia, in other words, is a genuine pathology of *language,* and not a more general inability to understand and use symbols. Sign is language and mime isn't, and the brains of signers seem very clear on the difference.

What is it that signers' brains "know"? What is it, in short, that the human left hemisphere is so astonishingly good at? It isn't speech or sign, but something more abstract that is a common denominator of both. It may have to do with what David Corina and his colleagues call "compositionality." In a compositional system, a finite number of building blocks, meaningless in themselves, combine by rule to yield units packed with meaning. The building blocks can be consonants and vowels or, as scholars now know, handshapes, locations and movements. These elements recombine according to a set of rules to create the words of human language. These words in turn are ordered by still more rules to make phrases and sentences. So few ingredients, so many possibilities.

"There is now overwhelming evidence that signed languages, as well as spoken languages, exhibit dense *compositionality* at all levels of linguistic structure," Corina and his colleagues write. It is the presence or absence of compositionality, they argue, that causes sign and pantomime to be served by different neural systems in the brain, one on the left where language is, the other on the right with spatial tasks:

> The differential disruption of linguistic and nonlinguistic gestures is not attributable to *surface* level complexity (indeed pantomimic forms are often composed of more complex action sequences than corresponding sign forms) but the *internal* organization underlying these movement systems. The critical difference between nonlinguistic and linguistic gestures is the degree of *compositionality* which underlies these movement systems. . . . Compositionality permits a systematic distinction between true linguistic gestural systems (e.g., ASL) and communicative pantomimes, which as demonstrated in the present case may be differentially disrupted.

The ability to make and use a compositional system is unique to Homo sapiens. In several highly publicized experiments of the 1960s and 1970s, psychologists attempted to teach signed language to nonhuman primates, in particular chimpanzees. Previous attempts to teach chimps to speak had failed, at least in part because they lack the necessary vocal equipment. But once linguists recognized that ASL was also language, it seemed like the ideal way past this problem: chimps certainly had no trouble waving their hands around. (Signs were modified to compensate for the chimps' lack of an opposable thumb.) But despite extravagant claims by some investigators, as Susan Fischer points out in a review of these studies, there was ultimately little indication that the chimps were actually using signs *as language.*

The chimps were able to use signs to name things, but that seems to be all they could reliably do. They never mastered the limitless possibilities of language that young children grasp effortlessly—the capacity to ask questions, to make and understand novel sentences, to "rise above" impoverished input and give it grammar. For one thing, the chimps seemed to be completely lacking in syntax: utterances of more than one sign appeared to be strung together in random order. For another, they weren't able to acquire language by pulling it out of the environment, as human children, deaf and hearing, do. The signs the chimps did master, mostly the names of things, were learned only as the result of intensive tutoring.

In any case, the significance of the chimps' signing can't be interpreted definitively. Since it is impossible to divine a chimpanzee's intentions, one can never really know whether, in making a particular sign, the chimp "means" the same thing as a human making that sign would. As a result, questions of interpretation were inescapably overlaid with the experimenters' preconceptions and, in all likelihood, wishful thinking.

"If moulding and active teaching is the only way to teach language to a chimpanzee, then there is something profoundly different between chimpanzees and human children," Fischer writes. "Just because someone, either child or chimpanzee, learns something that adults gloss as 'funny' or 'apple' does not necessarily mean that is what it means for the child or chimpanzee." As she points out later in the same article, "If non-human primates are capable of language, one might well ask why they have not developed language before now."

Today, the signing human brain is more visible than ever. In recent years, investigators have deployed the latest neuroimaging technologies to peer into signers' heads. These technologies include positron emission tomography (PET), which measures brain activity in terms of cerebral blood flow; and functional magnetic resonance imaging (fMRI), which measures activity in terms of minute changes in the brain's metabolic state. The techniques let investigators gather data from the brains of healthy signers as well as brain-injured ones. One of the most elegant studies to make use of these technologies is an experiment led by the linguist Karen Emmorey and published in 2004.

Emmorey and her colleagues investigated the mental representation of some of the most iconic signs of ASL: verbs involving tool use, and their associated nouns. Verbs like these—BRUSH-HAIR, BOUNCE-BALL, ERASE-BOARD, SCRUB-BY-HAND—typically involve the set of "handling" classifiers, whose handshape mirrors the configuration of the human hand as it holds or manipulates the implement in question. The sign BRUSH-HAIR, as Emmorey and her colleagues write, "is made with a grasping handshape and a 'brushing' motion at the head." The associated noun, HAIRBRUSH, is made with the same handshape and restrained, repeated movement. Because these signs depict "canonical tool use," as the researchers write, they are, not surprisingly, among the most obviously mimetic in the language. Many "handling" signs, in fact, are completely indistinguishable from the corresponding conventional pantomime.

Are such utterly iconic signs processed as pantomimic gesture, or as abstract linguistic code? To investigate, the researchers administered PET scans to a group of healthy right-handed deaf signers. During the scan, each signer was shown a set of pictures and asked to make the appropriate sign for each one. The images depicted tools (cup, scissors, screwdriver); actions performed with tools (brushing hair, bouncing a ball, erasing a blackboard); and actions, like yelling and sleeping, that did not involve tools. For each sign, the scan illuminated the particular areas of the brain engaged.

As the scans clearly showed, when signers used even these highly mimetic "handling" signs, the traditional language areas of the left brain were activated. "The sensory-motor iconicity of ASL signs denoting tools (e.g., SCREWDRIVER) and of handling classifier verbs denoting actions performed with a tool (e.g., STIR)," the researchers write, "does not appear to alter the neural systems that underlie lexical retrieval or sign production."

In other words, signers' brains processed even these signs as pieces of linguistic code—discrete, arbitrary and compositional—

exactly the same way they processed noniconic signs. Remarkably, as the researchers write, "*Even when the form of a sign is indistinguishable from a pantomimic gesture,* the neural systems underlying its production mirror those engaged when hearing speakers produce (non-iconic) words referring to the same types of entities, i.e., tools or tool-based actions."

Other recent imaging work has examined memory for signs, the impact of signed language on visuospatial cognition, and, of course, aphasia. The results confirm the earlier clinical studies. While a few sign-language functions appear to be the province of the right hemisphere, the production and use of signed language, like spoken, is localized overwhelmingly on the left. In the brightly colored images of signing brains that appear with these new studies, it is plain to see: the language that began life on the streets of Paris, crossed an ocean to the New World, was shaped by the signing children of Martha's Vineyard, weathered a century of suppression, and has only lately come into its own again. There it is—abstract, symbolic, infinitely combinatorial, unequivocally human—lighting up the left side of the brain.

CHAPTER 17

In a Wet Place

The linguists went back to Haifa to argue. Shai burned the DVD, and the team members spent the next week in a huddle in Wendy's lab, with its distant view of the sea, pointing, conjecturing and rewinding as the language of the village unfolded before their eyes once more. They peered at the footage again and again. How were signers' hands and arms moving? Where did they go? How were they shaped and held? Where was the signer's gaze directed? What was the face doing, and the head? The linguists had in front of them the staggering job of decoding a communication system that no outsider had ever really seen before.

The vocabulary was relatively easy. In most cases, a single sign—DOG, CAT, CHICKEN, STAPLER—corresponded to a single image in the slide show. More difficult were the signed responses to the video clips—*A man walks up to an empty chair and sits down. . . . A man walks past the chair without sitting*—for which individual descriptions could vary. Harder still were the signed stories the team had elicited on its previous trip. When they first screened the stories after that trip, the linguists had absolutely no idea what they meant. Neither did any of their Israeli consultants, native ISL signers brought in to watch them. In the end, Hassan had to make periodic trips to Haifa to translate the footage into Hebrew.

Even with Hassan's help, the work was slow and painstaking. Before the linguists could do anything else, they had to figure out where one sign ended and the next one began and, harder still, where entire sentences began and ended. For them, it was the visual equivalent of being set down in a foreign country, amid an undifferentiated linguistic wash, without so much as a phrasebook or a dictionary. Over the next few years, whenever they had the chance to convene, there was a great deal of what Ann Senghas, describing her own work in Nicaragua, calls "sitting around for two hours and arguing about where the noun is."

Besides scrutinizing the signs themselves, the linguists also had to attend to subtle cues from the signers' faces and bodies, and to the larger conversational context. All these things would eventually help them fix the boundaries between the words and sentences of the language. When I met Carol in New York the next winter, she illustrated the problem with a hypothetical scenario. Suppose, on your videotape, you see an informant sign the following string: HE—EAT—FROGS. Are you looking at a three-word sentence, "He eats frogs"? Or is it a two-word sentence, "He eats," followed by a separate sentence beginning with the word "Frogs"? If you know the larger conversational context—whether the topic under discussion happens to be frogs as a menu item, for instance—you have a better chance of working out what is actually being said.

The team encountered similar challenges in its real-life data. "One signer, for example, describing his personal history, produced the following string: MONEY COLLECT BUILD WALLS DOORS," the linguists write in a recent journal article. How to tell which words go with which? The first two signs, MONEY COLLECT, were easy. They constituted a simple sentence in the language, which translated as "I saved money." The puzzle was the relationship among the next three signs, BUILD WALLS DOORS. As the linguists write:

> The [nouns] could either be objects of the verb in the same sentence, i.e., "I built walls, doors . . ." or, alternatively, they could be in a separate fragment, conveying a list: "I built. Walls, doors . . ." on par with "I began to eat. Chicken, pickles, corn."

Only by minute study of the signer's unconscious cues, including body, head and eye movements, together with subtle pauses of the hands, could the team choose the correct interpretation. As it turned out, the signer (it was a brother of Anwar, the deaf patriarch from our last house) intended the second reading: "I saved some money. I started to build a house. Walls, doors. . . ."

And so it went, sign by sign and sentence by sentence, whenever the linguists stole time from teaching to meet at one end of the world or the other. Ever cautious, they didn't present much beyond the most preliminary findings until more than a year after our trip to the desert. "We have to go in there naively," Wendy told me when I met her and Irit in New York the winter after our trip. "We don't know what's there. We can have all kinds of assessments that the human mind is going to make a language, to make a system. But we don't know what that system's going to be."

For the next two years after our trip, I chased the linguists around the world, catching up with them in Boston and Barcelona and New Mexico and the south of France as they began, little by little, to present papers at scientific meetings on the language of Al-Sayyid. They were a bit absentminded and often forgot to tell me beforehand where they would be appearing.

But by the time we came back from the desert, one thing was beyond doubt: the indigenous communication system of the village was very much a language. A young language, perhaps, but a language all the same. It would be known officially ever after as Al-Sayyid Bedouin Sign Language, or ABSL. "If you just look at the way they communicate with each other and compare it to a homesigner, there's no question they have a full-fledged communication system going, because they have this ease of communication," Wendy told me. "At the end of the project, maybe we'll be able to say what we mean when we talk about a 'full-fledged language.'"

The linguists tried to approach their data naively, but they did, quite reasonably, have certain expectations at the outset. Chief among these was that ABSL would display the abundant spatial morphology common to all signed languages. Sign languages teem with this morphology, boasting especially rich systems of verb agreement, with the hands traveling through space to indicate the role of the actors in sentences. Furthermore, they share the three-part verb classification that Carol first identified for ASL: agreeing verbs, which denote types of transfer (often symbolic); spatial verbs, which represent real-world movement; and plain verbs, which don't agree with anything. Nearly all studied signed languages have these classes, and the verbs in each class are nearly identical across languages. No spoken language, by contrast, has this tripartite system. It seems to be an inherent consequence of visuospatial cognition finding a happy outlet in the visuospatial modality.

It is because of this intersection of cognition and modality that signed languages, even unrelated ones, share such similar verb-agreement systems. On the basis of these affinities, the team had proposed that the world's signed languages be classed together as a single "language family," much as Indo-European languages, for instance, are considered part of a common family because of their shared structural properties.

"Sign-language-universal properties are complex and rule-governed," Wendy explained when we met in New York. "But those things that are universal also all use space. That's the"—she breaks off, searching for precisely the right word—"the *privilege* of sign language, is to be able to organize its grammar in space."

That is the reason, too, that signed languages, despite their youth, have such rich morphological systems. Even emerging sign systems, like the signed language of Nicaragua, the homesigning of the children studied by Susan Goldin-Meadow, and the invented signs of children exposed only to Manually Coded English, display at least the rudiments of verb agreement. (In contrast, young spoken languages, like creoles, are morphologically quite stripped down.) Spatial morphology is such a ubiquitous presence in signed languages that when the team first attacked its data, the logical question was this: In a new signed language, is verb-agreement morphology an instantaneous development? Based on the available evidence, the linguists had every reason to think so. But to their considerable surprise, that's not what they found at all.

After hundreds of hours of scrutinizing footage, the team reached an inescapable conclusion: there was no verb agreement whatsoever in Al-Sayyid Bedouin Sign Language. There was no shortage of *verbs* in the language—words like WORK, BUILD, COLLECT, THROW, CATCH, WALK, GIVE and TAKE—and signers used them freely. But they were spare and uninflected, almost completely devoid of the spatial modulations that characterize verbs in other signed languages. In this respect, ABSL looked a bit like a creole, whose pared-down verbs make very little use of inflection.

It was the video clips in particular that told the linguists this. The clips, which showed people throwing and catching, giving and taking, were designed to elicit verb agreement in signed languages. If a language had agreement, the clips would bring it out, forcing signers to move verbs through space between their throwing and catching actors. But that's not what the Al-Sayyid signers did. It wasn't that they failed to use space. Many signers set up the *nouns* in space: a man on the right, say, and a woman on the left. It's what happened next that was completely unexpected: instead of moving the verb between these two points, as a user of an established sign language would, the Bedouins moved it straight out from the center of their own bodies, toward the camera. They did this even with verbs like GIVE, which in other signed languages *always* agrees with its subject and object. A father might give a book to his son, but in the signed language of Al-Sayyid, the verb will not travel through the air from father to son.

Of the team's fourteen video clips, eight involved obvious verbs of transfer like GIVE and TAKE. In one clip, a man gives a tennis ball to a woman. Aminah signed it this way:

> MAN *[Aminah makes the ABSL sign* MAN*, which suggests twirling a mustache]*—point *[she sets her hand at a location in space, off to the right, to stand for the man];* WOMAN *[she makes the sign* WOMAN*, in which the index and middle fingers brush downward along the bridge of the nose]*—point *[she sets her hand on the left, to stand for the woman];* GIVE *[she makes the sign* GIVE*, which*

resembles the conventional gesture of giving; the sign travels straight out from beneath her chin toward the camera].

Despite its essential visuospatial nature, Al-Sayyid Bedouin Sign Language did not appear to exploit spatial morphology. The linguists believe that the language is simply too new: morphology, even the spatial kind, takes time to develop. That is certainly the case for morphology in spoken language, as Mark, Irit and Wendy explained in a recent article:

> As a well-documented case of the emergence of an inflectional category, consider the French future tense, exemplified by *chanterai* "I will sing," descended from the Latin *cantare habeo* "I have (something) to sing" and attested in documents from 40 B.C. By about the fourth century, the string was apparently interpreted not as two clauses but as a single verb phrase with a main verb followed by an auxiliary, translated "I have to sing" or "I will sing." . . . Later, the two independent lexical items are found written in documents as a single word. . . . The auxiliary was eventually reduced from *habeo* to *ai,* and the infinitive marker *r* was interpreted as part of the tense-mood inflection. Thus, the once-phrasal *cantare habeo* became the single word *chanterai.* The first documentation of *chanterai* is found in the ninth century, indicating that the processes leading to this grammaticization may have taken up to eight hundred years. Though the new form might have been in colloquial use well before it was first documented . . . it could not have arisen before the fourth or fifth centuries. . . . Hence even under careful estimates, the processes required several hundreds of years.

In its bare morphology, the sign language of Al-Sayyid resembled new spoken languages like young creoles. Yet it was without a doubt a fully functioning language, in which signers could communicate complex states of affairs completely, efficiently and unambiguously. How, then, could they do this? How could the people of Al-Sayyid, whose language lacks verb agreement, convey who did what to whom in the thousands of sentences they signed every day? They clearly did so, and identifying the way in which they did was the team's first important discovery.

In most spoken languages, there is a tradeoff between verb agreement and rigid word order when it comes to expressing who did what to whom. And rigid word order the sign language of Al-Sayyid had with a vengeance. The second-generation signers of ABSL, the team discovered, routinely rely on word order to encode the who-did-what-to-whom of discourse. As the linguists wrote in their first major paper on the village, "In the space of one generation from its inception, systematic grammatical structure has emerged in the language."

As the team analyzed sentence after sentence of ABSL, both from the elicitation materials and the free storytelling, they saw signers use the same word order again and again: subject—object—verb, or SOV. In some sentences, subject or object might be absent (as in MONEY COLLECT, "I saved money," which has no overt subject). But in almost all of them, the verb appeared at the very end of the sentence or clause. Placing the verb at the end of the sentence, and the actors before it, happens to be what some young Nicaraguan signers did, as in MAN WOMAN PUSH FALL, "A man pushes a woman." It is also what Susan Goldin-Meadow's young deaf homesigners overwhelmingly did.

"We have found that one of the most important organizing principles in language, the grammatical relation between subject (S), object (O), and verb (V) in an utterance, has been fixed at a very early stage in the development of the language," the linguists write. "Word order is significant because it provides a conventionalized means of expressing the relation between elements in a sentence without relying on extralinguistic context."

Of 158 ABSL sentences containing two or more signs, 136, the linguists found, were made with the verb at the end. These included:

> SHEEP SLAUGHTER. ("They killed a sheep.")
>
> WOMAN APPLE GIVE; MAN GIVE. (A description of one of the

clips: "The woman gave an apple to the man," literally, "The woman gave an apple; she gave it to the man.")

WOMAN BOY SIT; SCARF GIVE; TAKE BACK. (Another clip: "The boy gives the woman a scarf, then takes it back," literally, "The woman sits here, the boy there; he hands over a scarf, then takes it back.")

There was also this marvelous utterance from Anwar, from a signed narrative in which he described the preparations for his wedding: MAN GATHER; TALK; FINISH-BUSINESS; SHAKE-HAND; TIE-UP. ("People gathered. There was talking. They reached an agreement and shook hands.")

While subject-object-verb word order may seem strange to speakers of English, it is in fact the most commonly used word order in the spoken languages of the world. Japanese, for instance, uses SOV word order. Significantly though, none of the languages that surround Al-Sayyid, signed or spoken, does. The local Arabic dialect is, like English, subject-verb-object, or SVO. (Standard Arabic is VSO.) Modern Hebrew is also SVO. In Israeli Sign Language, word order is relatively free, but the most common orders are SVO and OSV. "The robust word-order pattern exhibited by the data [is] all the more striking, because it cannot be attributed to the influence of other languages," the linguists write. "Rather, this pattern should be regarded as an independent development within the language."

To the team, even more noteworthy than the *particular* word order of ABSL was the fact that this very young language already had word order of any kind. "The fact that it *is* systematic: it's a grammar, it's a language," Mark told me the winter after our trip. "That's the big deal. They don't just have a list of signs and are giving you the signs for things. It's a language—they're signing sentences. That's one of the reasons the word-order stuff is so important: it's not just people 'making pictures.'"

Without word order, relationships among the actors in a discourse remain a puzzle, as Mark and Wendy explained when I caught up with the team at a conference in Barcelona. "One of the things you have to establish right away is who did what to whom," Wendy said. "And languages have various ways of doing that. And if you don't have one of those ways, then you have to rely entirely on context, and you don't have a linguistic system yet. Having a linguistic structure frees you from relying on the immediate context. If you didn't, you would have to rely on a very long story or pantomime."

"Did John hit Mary, or did Mary hit John?" Mark chimed in. Without word order, he explained, it would be as if someone said, with absolutely no clarification, *John. Mary. Hitting going on.* "You get who was involved," he said. "But you don't find out what they're actually doing."

Perhaps the most noteworthy thing of all about the rapid emergence of word order in ABSL, is that the language, like any signed language, could just as easily do without it. Because of the modality in which they are transmitted, signed languages have abundant *spatial* means at their disposal with which to encode the relations among actors in a sentence. That is why they nearly all have verb agreement, and why the agreement systems look so similar. For the team, this was the truly astonishing thing: the emerging language of Al-Sayyid makes vigorous use of word order *even though it doesn't have to.* In a linguistic vacuum, it appears that syntax will emerge above all else, trumping even the strong spatial imperatives of the visual modality.

"What we expected going into this village was that the language would be modality-driven," Mark said in a talk he gave at Harvard in 2005. "What we found instead is that the language was quite dramatically driven by syntax." As he had told me earlier that day: "That, to me, is what's most amazing about the word-order facts with the Bedouins. It's not driven by communicative need as far as I can tell. People just have a drive for structure in their behavior."

Besides sentences with subjects, verbs and objects, other constructions in the language were found to have fixed word order as well. In ABSL, modifiers, like numbers and adjectives, always follow the noun with which they are associated, as in the signed phrases BOY TWO and WOMAN NICE. In WH-questions, those that in English start with "who," "what," "where," "when," "why" or "how," the question word often comes at the end of the sentence in ABSL. (This is often the case for WH-questions in the world's signed languages.)

ABSL might lack agreement, but it had an abundance of word order. And word order is a feature that Susan Goldin-Meadow, based on her work with young homesigners, identifies as one of the "resilient" properties of language, "so over-determined and buffered in humans that they will arise even under strikingly atypical acquisition conditions." So is the existence of distinct grammatical categories, like "noun" and "verb," a distinction ABSL also makes.

At the start of 2005, the team published its findings about ABSL word order in the *Proceedings of the National Academy of Sciences.* The paper generated a flurry of media attention, with articles on the new sign language in *The New York Times* and elsewhere. As the four linguists wrote:

> Of greater significance to us than any particular word order is the discovery that, very early in the life history of a language, a conventionalized pattern emerges for relating actions and events to the entities that perform and are affected by them, a pattern rooted in the basic syntactic notions of subject, object, and verb or predicate. Such conventionalization has the effect of liberating the language from its context. . . . If a language does not have a conventionalized word order, a sentence such as "Kim Jan kiss" is ambiguous; it can mean either that Kim kissed Jan or that Jan kissed Kim. Once languages have had time to accrue such mechanisms as verb agreement, marking properties of subject or object, or case marking on noun[s] to indicate their relation to the verb, the roles of participants can be made clear, even without consistent word order. In the absence of such mechanisms, word order is the only way to disambiguate a message linguistically. The appearance of this conventionalization at such an early stage in the emergence of a language is rare empirical verification of the unique proclivity of the human mind for structuring a communication system along grammatical lines.

So the signed language of Al-Sayyid had syntax, and it had words. But what did these words actually look like? After spending more than a year decoding the syntax of the language, the team began to examine ABSL under even greater magnification, in order to discern the internal structure of its words. They expected to find what Stokoe had found: that each word was an abstract, compositional symbol, formed from a unique combination of handshape, location and movement. But once again, what the linguists expected is not what they found at all.

There were assuredly words in the language, mostly nouns and verbs, plus a smattering of adjectives. (This state of affairs is not surprising. In the world's spoken languages, adjectives are comparatively rare commodities. Some American Indian languages, and some of the Dravidian languages of south India, for instance, have very few of them.) But instead of being built from smaller structural units, as the words of established sign languages are, the words of ABSL appeared to be unanalyzed wholes, little lumps of language that can't be broken down further.

Of course, the villagers were using handshapes, locations and movements whenever they signed. Those units necessarily figure in every gesture made by hand. But the language of the village didn't deploy these units in a structured, systematic way. Just as ABSL lacked morphology, the language seemed to lack phonology as well.

The words of ABSL were clearly not pantomime. Many were completely arbitrary in form, and they could be used to talk about anything, from abstract concepts like Social Security to long-ago events like getting lost on a bus in Egypt. But the internal structure of these signs hadn't stabilized: a given word, the linguists discovered, could vary greatly in form from one signer to the next. Take the ABSL sign BANANA. It is one of the more obviously mimetic signs in the language, made with the active hand "peeling" the base hand. The active hand looks largely the same from one signer to the next. The base hand, however, can assume a variety of shapes: an extended index finger; a hand with the thumb and index finger touching, as in the conventional American gesture "OK"; or a hand with the thumb and index finger pinched more tightly together. Each of these signs is understood by the community to mean BANANA, but in the young language of the village, their component parts have not yet coalesced into a unique, definitive combination.

"There is a conventionalized vocabulary, but there's a great deal of individual variation in form across this vocabulary," Wendy said during a presentation the team gave in 2005 at a meeting in France. As she spoke, a series of Bedouin villagers appeared on a large screen behind her. There was Omar, from the half-built house; there was Anwar, flanked by pillows; there was Kamal, one of the teenagers from the top-down house. Each of them was making the sign BANANA, but each made it noticeably differently. "Pay attention to things like the shape of the hand, and the movement of each hand," Wendy instructed the audience.

Besides being phonologically unsettled, a number of signs the team recorded also violate the constraints on form that are found in the world's mature signed languages. On the screen, a Bedouin signer makes the sign KNIFE by moving a flat open palm in a sawing motion across the extended index finger of the other hand, while the index finger moves back and forth in the opposite direction. In an established sign language, these unbalanced handshapes, moving in tandem, would violate the symmetry constraint. "Basically we find a conventionalized lexicon, but on the whole, I would say that the phonological structure is still indeterminate," Wendy told her audience. "There is no phonology as we know it."

For all this, what's happening in Al-Sayyid is no less linguistic. "We don't know whether all of the properties that have been attributed to universal grammar exist in this communication system," Wendy told me the year after our trip. "We don't know, but if it looks like a language and walks like a language and quacks like a language, then it's a language."

It seems that phonology, too, takes time to develop, as a language moves toward an increasingly arbitrary system of representation. But in a brand-new language, where communication has to get up and running in a hurry, unanalyzable words seem to work just fine. In Al-Sayyid, holistic words serve the communicative needs of their users admirably, just as the early holistic gestures of Goldin-Meadow's homesigners did. The whole comes first, it appears. Structure follows.

The presence of words in the language of Al-Sayyid is no small thing. After all, the signers could just as easily have communicated in mime and left it at that. But they didn't. Spontaneously, naturally, and with no outside influence, the deaf villagers created a new human language, its lexicon bursting with words, each word functioning as a piece of abstract linguistic code. To judge from the natural Forbidden Experiment that is Al-Sayyid, what a language has at birth is words, and syntactic slots to put them in. And that, for the purposes of conveying meaning from one human mind to another, seems to be enough. After years of careful scrutiny, the linguists can truly say of this new language in the desert, *In the beginning was the word.*

As they sifted their data again and again, the linguists occasionally glimpsed the kernels of verb agreement. For spatial verbs, like BRING and MOVE, some signers actually moved their hands between two opposing points in space, which stood for opposing locations in the real world. As the team also noted, traditional "backwards" verbs, like TAKE, are also backwards in ABSL—the hands move inward, toward the signer's body, rather than outward, toward the camera. But the movement of verbs in a more arbitrary, more strictly *grammatical* way, is still to come. ABSL may yet develop such a system, which would bring it closer to the world's established sign languages. It may also develop a consistent system of classifiers, which are now visible in rudimentary, idiosyncratic form. It may yet develop a full-blown facial grammar. All this the language may one day have, if given time.

A year after our trip, I caught up with the linguists in Barcelona. They were delivering a paper on ABSL at an international convocation of sign-language researchers there. For three days, the meeting hall, a cavernous gilded room at the University of Barcelona, was crowded with hundreds of signers from all over the world. At every break in the proceedings, the hall filled with moving hands. As each paper was delivered, a dozen interpreters stood stationed throughout the audience, translating the proceedings into ASL and French Sign and Czech Sign and German Sign and Hong Kong Sign and Catalan Sign and many others, and into several spoken languages. At the end of especially good papers, hundreds of audience members thrust their hands high in the air, fingers spread, and shook them rapidly back and forth at the wrists, the visual applause of the deaf. At those moments, the air in the room seemed to shimmer, as if a thousand hummingbirds were beating their wings.

When it came time for the team to give its paper, each member presented part of it in turn, as is their custom. Wendy, Irit and Mark gave their portions in English; Carol delivered hers in ASL. They ended the talk as they always do, with a slide of Al-Sayyid projected onto a screen behind them. It was one of Carol's photographs. There was the village, with its undulating brown hills. There were the houses, with their sheer white faces and roofs of tile and tin. Al-Sayyid hung for a moment in the shimmering air, and then it disappeared.

Afterword: It Takes a Village

On a bright spring day in 2006, I found myself at a conference table in a glassed-in room in the middle of the woods in the eastern part of the Netherlands. Around the table sat nearly every scholar in the world who is actively engaged in studying a "signing village." There were about a dozen of them, mostly linguists and anthropologists, plus a psychologist or two. Irit was there, representing the team. The meeting, which was held at the Max Planck Institute for Psycholinguistics, in Nijmegen, marked the first time in history that the world's village-sign-language researchers had come together in one place.

They came from everywhere. Besides the Netherlands, there were researchers from the United States, Indonesia, Jamaica and, of course, Israel. The languages they were studying had sprung up, unbidden, in every corner of the globe, from Bali to Thailand to Surinam to Mexico to Ghana.

The meeting was led by Ulrike Zeshan, the linguist who is comparing the grammars of dozens of established sign languages. A native of Germany currently working at Max Planck, she has helped document the national signed languages—the so-called urban sign languages—of India and Pakistan, Turkey and Lebanon. Now she is turning her attention to village sign languages, the least documented languages of all. "I've seen lots of urban non-Western sign languages by now," Zeshan tells the assembled scholars. "But if you ask me what are village sign languages, I just don't know, because I haven't seen them. What I can't know is what type of linguistic structures these sign languages have. And that I very much want to know."

For Zeshan and her colleagues, the existence of these languages—young, isolated, spoken by deaf and hearing alike—presents a tantalizing prospect: a dozen Forbidden Experiments going on at once in a dozen corners of the globe. With the exception of the work in Al-Sayyid, the linguistic description of these village sign languages is just barely beginning.

Over that day and the next, the scholars shared what is known so far. One, a linguist from Indonesia, described his work on Kata Kolok, an indigenous sign language found on Bali. Kata Kolok is at least eight generations old, and it teems with classifiers. There are distinct classifiers for people; for small walking animals like mice and rabbits; for larger walking animals like chickens, dogs and cows; for small sliding animals like eels and little snakes; and for large sliding animals like seals and big snakes. It has classifiers for two-wheeled vehicles, four-wheeled vehicles and water vehicles. It has three different classifiers to describe flying objects: one for birds, another for planes and helicopters, a third for kites. In addition, researchers have found, the language has a robust syntax: to convey who did what to whom in Kata Kolok, signers rely on strict word order every time.

Another scholar reported on Bhan Khor Sign Language, used in a remote rural community in Thailand. The community of two thousand contains about four hundred signers, only seventeen of whom are deaf. About seventy years old, Bhan Khor Sign Language contains signs for BLACK, WHITE and RED; for other colors, signers simply point. There were also presentations on Country Sign, the indigenous sign language of a Jamaican farming village; on Kajana Sign Language, found in Surinam; and on Adamorobe Sign Language, from a community in Ghana where, a local legend has it, deafness was visited on the village by a benevolent deaf god. Also discussed were the sign language of a Mayan community in Mexico, and one on Russell Island in Papua New Guinea. There, hearing villagers will sometimes use the language among themselves, between boats on the water, where distance precludes shouting.

As scholar after scholar spoke, the bright day took on an elegiac tone, for, as almost all of them made clear, the survival of a village sign language is rarely assured. These languages usually arise suddenly, spread rapidly and just as quickly die, often within a generation or two. "Sign languages are the forgotten endangered languages," said Angela Nonaka of UCLA, who reported on Bhan Khor Sign Language. "Among the most endangered of all are indigenous sign languages."

The numbers bear her out. Jamaican Country Sign, for instance, had about two hundred speakers in the late 1980s. Today, there are twenty. Like other village sign languages, it is being choked out of existence by the majority sign language of the country.

For the scholars in the room, the precariousness of village sign languages raised urgent questions: Should the documenters of these languages also be their saviors? Are the investigators obliged to remain detached observers, or should they become activists as well, fighting to preserve the languages they study? What should their relationship be with any geneticists working in the villages? (In one deaf village, a scholar recounted, geneticists held out the promise of gifts—soap, a raincoat and a cutlass—to each resident who reported for testing.) In the two days the scholars spent together, the questions could not be answered with any finality. Perhaps they can never be.

But at the same time, another, more hopeful theme emerged: researchers believe there are even more signing villages than we know of, waiting to be discovered in distant pockets of the world. There have been reports of several undocumented village sign languages in the Middle East, and of others in Africa. In recent years, the Canadian press has carried preliminary accounts of Inuit Sign Language, an indigenous language spoken by deaf and hearing people in several Arctic communities. As John Lucy, one of the scholars around the table, said, "I'm guessing there are many more of these languages than we imagine."

If researchers can catch and hold them, these isolated sign languages, sprung from the brain onto the hands with nothing to waylay them in between, will help answer one of the most fundamental questions that can be asked about our species: *What is a human language, and how is it made in the mind?*

A Note on Sources

Among the welter of technical books and articles cited in the notes, I am especially indebted to a number of canonical books about sign language, linguistics and cognition. Most of these are accessible to a general readership:

For more on the linguistics of American Sign Language, the most companionable book for the lay reader is *The Signs of Language* (Harvard University Press, 1979), by Edward S. Klima and Ursula Bellugi. Also highly readable is *Seeing Voices: A Journey into the World of the Deaf*, by Oliver Sacks (University of California, 1989). In addition, there are several fine introductory textbooks for students learning ASL as a foreign language, among them *A Basic Course in American Sign Language* (T. J. Publishers, 1981), by Carol Padden, Tom Humphries and Terrence J. O'Rourke.

Among the most worthwhile entries on the growing shelf of books about deaf culture are two by Padden and Humphries, *Deaf in America: Voices from a Culture* (Harvard University Press, 1988), and *Inside Deaf Culture* (Harvard University Press, 2005), as well as *A Journey into the Deaf-World* (DawnSign Press, 1996), by Harlan Lane, Robert Hoffmeister and Ben Bahan; *Train Go Sorry: Inside a Deaf World* (Houghton Mifflin, 1994), by Leah Hager Cohen; and *Winning Sounds like This: A Season with the Women's Basketball Team at Gallaudet, the World's Only University for the Deaf* (Crown, 2002), by Wayne Coffey. *The Gallaudet Encyclopedia of Deaf People and Deafness* (McGraw-Hill, 3 vols., 1987), edited by John V. Van Cleve, is a useful general resource.

Several fine studies chronicle the history of ASL, including *Forbidden Signs: American Culture and the Campaign Against Sign Language* (University of Chicago Press, 1996), by Douglas C. Baynton;

and *Seeing Language in Sign: The Work of William C. Stokoe* (Gallaudet University Press, 1996), by Jane Maher. *Everyone Here Spoke Sign Language: Hereditary Deafness on Martha's Vineyard* (Harvard University Press, 1985), by Nora Ellen Groce, documents an American "signing village." One of the most accessible books on a sign language other than ASL is *The Linguistics of British Sign Language: An Introduction* (Cambridge University Press, 1999), by Rachel Sutton-Spence and Bencie Woll.

There are numerous published collections of technical articles on the psycholinguistics of sign language. Among the most approachable are *Understanding Language Through Sign Language Research* (Academic Press, 1978), edited by Patricia A. Siple; and *Theoretical Issues in Sign Language Research,* a two-volume collection edited by Siple in collaboration with Susan D. Fischer (University of Chicago Press); *Vol. 1: Linguistics* (1990), is edited by Fischer and Siple; *Vol. 2: Psychology* (1991), by Siple and Fischer. Susan Goldin-Meadow's research on homesigning is collected in her book *The Resilience of Language: What Gesture Creation in Deaf Children Can Tell Us About How All Children Learn Language* (Psychology Press, 2003). The seminal psycholinguistic work on errors in spoken language, which includes a chapter on sign-language errors, is *Errors in Linguistic Performance: Slips of the Tongue, Ear, Pen, and Hand* (Academic Press, 1980), edited by Victoria A. Fromkin. Extended discussion of classifiers in spoken language can be found in George Lakoff's *Women, Fire and Dangerous Things: What Categories Reveal About the Mind* (University of Chicago Press, 1987).

A good general text on the neurology of language and language disorders is *Neurolinguistics and Linguistic Aphasiology: An Introduction* (Cambridge University Press, 1987), by David Caplan, a neurologist who also has a Ph.D. in linguistics. *What the Hands Reveal About the Brain* (MIT Press, 1987), by Howard Poizner, Edward S. Klima and Ursula Bellugi, presents the authors' research on aphasia for sign language. More recent work on the neurobiology of sign language may be found in *Language, Cognition, and the Brain: Insights from Sign Language Research* (Lawrence Erlbaum, 2002), by Karen Emmorey.

For visual depictions of ASL signs, I have found *The Random House American Sign Language Dictionary* (Random House, 1994), edited by Elaine Costello, especially helpful. The Web site ASL University (www.asluniversity.com) includes a large photographic dictionary of ASL signs, many of them animated. The Web site Ethnologue (www.ethnologue.com), contains descriptions of thousands of the world's languages, signed and spoken.

References

Adams, Karen L., and Nancy Faires Conklin. "Toward a Theory of Natural Classification," in Corum et al. (1973), 1–10.

Aikhenvald, Alexandra Y. "Classifiers in Spoken and in Signed Languages: How to Know More," in Emmorey (2003), 87–90.

Aronoff, Mark. "In the Beginning Was the Word," presidential address, Linguistic Society of America, Albuquerque, N.M., January 2006.

———. *Word Formation in Generative Grammar* (Cambridge: MIT Press, 1976).

Aronoff, Mark, Irit Meir, Carol Padden and Wendy Sandler. "Classifier Constructions and Morphology in Two Sign Languages," in Emmorey (2003), 53–84.

———. "Morphological Universals and the Sign Language Type," in Booij and van Marle (2004), 19–39.

Aronoff, Mark, Irit Meir and Wendy Sandler. "The Paradox of Sign Language Morphology," *Language* 81:2 (2005), 301–44.

Aronoff, Mark, and Janie Rees-Miller, eds. *The Handbook of Linguistics* (Malden, Mass.: Blackwell, 2001).

Baker, Charlotte. "Sentences in American Sign Language," in Baker and Battison (1980), 79.

Baker, Charlotte, and Robbin Battison, eds. *Sign Language and the Deaf Community: Essays in Honor of William C. Stokoe* (Silver Spring, Md.: National Association of the Deaf, 1980).

Bahan, Ben, and J. Poole-Nash. "The Signing Community on Martha's Vineyard," unpublished address to the Conference on Deaf Studies 4, Haverhill, Mass., April 1995.

Ball, Martin J., ed. *Clinical Sociolinguistics* (Malden, Mass.: Blackwell, 2005).

Baron-Cohen, Simon, Alan M. Leslie and Uta Frith, "Does the Autistic Child Have a 'Theory of Mind'?," *Cognition* 21 (1985), 37–46.

Barsky, Robert F. *Noam Chomsky: A Life of Dissent* (Cambridge: MIT Press, 1997).

Battison, Robbin. *Lexical Borrowing in American Sign Language* (Silver Spring, Md.: Linstock, 1978).

———. "Signs Have Parts: A Simple Idea," in Baker and Battison (1980), 35–51.

Battison, Robbin, and I. King Jordan. "Cross-Cultural Communication with Foreign Signers: Fact and Fancy," *Sign Language Studies* 5:10 (1976), 53–68.

Bauer, Laurie, and Peter Trudgill, eds. *Language Myths* (New York: Penguin, 1998).

Baynton, Douglas C. *Forbidden Signs: American Culture and the Campaign Against Sign Language* (Chicago: University of Chicago Press, 1996).

Beatles Tapes II: Early Beatlemania, 1963–64 (Seattle: Jerden Records, 1993).

Bell, Alexander Graham. *Memoir Upon the Formation of a Deaf Variety of the Human Race* (New Haven: National Academy of Sciences, 1883; reprinted, Washington: Government Printing Office, 1884).

Bellugi, Ursula, and Susan Fischer. "A Comparison of Sign Language and Spoken Language," *Cognition* 1:2–3 (1972), 173–200.

Berlin, Brent, and Paul Kay. *Basic Color Terms: Their Universality and Evolution* (Stanford: CSLI Publications, 1999; reprint of 1969 and 1991 editions).

Berthier, Ferdinand. *Observation sur la Mimique Considérée dans Ses Rapports avec l'Enseignement des Sourds-Muets* (Paris: L. Martinet, 1854).

Bickerton, Derek. "A Bare-Bones Account of Human Evolution" (review of *The Dawn of Human Culture,* by Richard G. Klein with Blake Edgar), *American Scientist* 90:5 (Sept.–Oct. 2002).

———. "The Language Bioprogram Hypothesis," *Behavioral and Brain Sciences* 7:2 (1984), 173–221.

Bloch, Bernard, and George L. Trager. *Outline of Linguistic Analysis* (Baltimore: Linguistic Society of America, 1942).

Bloomfield, Leonard. *Language* (New York: Henry Holt, 1933).

———. *Menomini Texts* (New York: G. E. Stechert, 1928).

Bolton, W. F. "Language: An Introduction," in Clark et al. (1981), 5–17.

Booij, Geert, and Jaap van Marle, eds. *Yearbook of Morphology* (Dordrecht: Springer, 2004).

Borges, Jorge Luis. "The Analytical Language of John Wilkins," in Borges (1966), 100–110.

———. *Other Inquisitions, 1937–1952,* translated by Ruth L. C. Simms (New York: Washington Square Press, 1966).

Branson, Jan, Don Miller and I Gede Marsaja with I Wayan Negara. "Everyone Here Speaks Sign Language, Too: A Deaf Village in Bali, Indonesia," in Lucas (1996), 39–57.

Bresnan, Joan, ed. *The Mental Representation of Grammatical Relations* (Cambridge: MIT Press, 1982).

Brill, A. A. ed. *Basic Writings of Sigmund Freud* (New York: Modern Library, 1938).

Brown, Roger W., and Eric H. Lenneberg. "A Study in Language and Cognition," *Journal of Abnormal and Social Psychology* 49:3 (1954), 454–62.

Burgess, C., and J. Skodis. "Lexican Representation and Morpho-Syntactic Parallelism in the Left Hemisphere," *Brain and Language* 44:2 (1993), 129–38.

Caplan, David. *Neurolinguistics and Linguistic Aphasiology: An Introduction* (Cambridge: Cambridge University Press, 1987).

Carroll, Lewis. *Alice's Adventures in Wonderland* and *Through the Looking-Glass* (Cleveland: World, 1946).

Casson, Ronald W., ed. *Language, Culture, and Cognition: Anthropological Perspectives* (New York: Macmillan, 1981).

Chomsky, Noam. *Language and Mind* (New York: Harcourt, Brace & World, 1968).

———. Review of *Verbal Behavior* by B. F. Skinner, *Language,* 35:1 (1959), 26–58.

———. *Rules and Representations* (New York: Columbia University Press, 1980).

———. *Syntactic Structures* (The Hague: Mouton, 1957).

Christianson, Kiel Tobias. "Sentence Processing in a 'Nonconfigurational' Language," (Ph.D. diss., Michigan State University, 2002).

Clark, Virginia P., Paul A. Eschholz and Alfred F. Rosa, eds. *Language: Introductory Readings,* 3rd ed. (New York: St. Martin's, 1981).

Cokely, Dennis. "Sign Language: Teaching, Interpreting, and Educational Policy," in Baker and Battison (1980), 137–58.

Corina, David P., Howard Poizner, Ursula Bellugi, Todd Feinberg, Dorothy Dowd and Lucinda O'Grady-Batch. "Dissociation Between Linguistic and Nonlinguistic Gestural Systems: A Case for Compositionality," *Brain and Language* 43:3 (1992), 414–47.

Corum, Claudia, T. Cedric Smith-Stark and Ann Weiser, eds. *Papers from the Ninth Regional Meeting of the Chicago Linguistic Society* (Chicago: University of Chicago, 1973).

Costa, João. "A Multifactorial Approach to Adverb Placement: Assumptions, Facts, and Problems," *Lingua* 114:6 (2004), 711–53.

Craig, Colette. (See also Colette Grinevald.)

Craig, Colette, ed. *Noun Classes and Categorization: Proceedings of a Symposium on Categorization and Noun Classification, Eugene, Oregon, October 1983* (Amsterdam: John Benjamins, 1986).

Cumberbatch, Keren. "Country Sign: The Dying Indigenous Sign Language of Jamaica," paper presented at the workshop "Sign Language in Village Communities," Nijmegen, the Netherlands, April 4–6, 2006.

Curtiss, Susan. *Genie: A Psycholinguistic Study of a Modern-Day "Wild Child"* (New York: Academic Press, 1977).

DeGraff, Michel, ed. *Language Creation and Language Change: Creolization, Diachrony, and Development* (Cambridge: MIT Press, 1999).

Dively, Valerie, Melanie Metzger, Sarah Taub and Anne Marie Baer, eds. *Signed Languages: Discoveries from International Research* (Washington: Gallaudet University Press, 2001).

Dixon, R. M. W. *Where Have All the Adjectives Gone? And Other Essays in Semantics and Syntax* (Berlin: Mouton, 1982).

Eastman, Gilbert C. "From Student to Professional: A Personal Chronicle of Sign Language," in Baker and Battison (1980), 9–32.

Emmorey, Karen. *Language, Cognition, and the Brain: Insights from Sign Language Research* (Mahwah, N.J.: Lawrence Erlbaum, 2002).

Emmorey, Karen, ed. *Perspectives on Classifier Constructions in Sign Languages* (Mahwah, N.J.: Lawrence Erlbaum, 2003).

Emmorey, Karen, Thomas Grabowski, Stephen McCullough, Hanna Damasio, Laurie Ponto, Richard Hichwa and Ursula Bellugi. "Motor-Iconicity of Sign Language Does Not Alter the Neural Systems Underlying Tool and Action Naming," *Brain and Language* 89:1 (2004), 27–37.

Emmorey, Karen, and Melissa Herzig. "Categorical Versus Gradient Properties of Classifier Constructions in ASL," in Emmorey (2003), 221–46.

Emmorey, Karen, and Harlan Lane, eds. *The Signs of Language Revisited: An Anthology to Honor Ursula Bellugi and Edward Klima* (Mahwah, N.J.: Lawrence Erlbaum, 2000).

Erting, Carol J., Robert C. Johnson, Dorothy L. Smith and Bruce D. Snider, eds. *The Deaf Way: Perspectives from the International Conference on Deaf Culture* (Washington: Gallaudet University Press, 1994).

Fischer, Susan. "Appendix: Some Properties of ASL," in Bellugi and Fischer (1972).

Fischer, Susan D. "More than Just Handwaving: The Mutual Contributions of Sign Language and Linguistics," in Emmorey and Lane (2000), 195–213.

———. (1982a) "An Orientation to Language," in Sims et al. (1982), 9–22.

———. "Sign Language and Creoles," in Siple (1978), 309–31.

———. "Sign Language and Linguistic Universals," in Rohrer and Ruwet (1974), 187–204.

———. (1982b) "Sign Language and Manual Communication," in Sims et al. (1982), 90–106.

———. "The Study of Sign Languages and Linguistic Theory," in Otero (1994), vol. 4, 582–99.

———. "Two Processes of Reduplication in the American Sign Language," in *Foundations of Language* 9 (1973), 469–80.

Fischer, Susan D., and Harry van der Hulst. "Sign Language Structures," in Marschark and Spencer (2003), 319–31.

Fischer, Susan D., and Patricia Siple, eds. *Theoretical Issues in Sign Language Research* (Chicago: University of Chicago Press), *Vol. 1: Linguistics* (1990); see also Siple and Fischer.

Fodor, Jerry A. *The Modularity of Mind: An Essay on Faculty Psychology* (Cambridge: MIT Press, 1983).

Franzen, Jonathan. "My Bird Problem," *The New Yorker,* Aug. 8, 2005, 59.

Freud, Sigmund. *Zur Psychopathologie des Alltagslebens,* 10th ed. (Leipzig: Internationaler Psychoanalytischer Verlag); English version in Brill (1938).

Frishberg, Nancy. "Arbitrariness and Iconicity: Historical Change in ASL," *Language* 51:3 (1975), 696–719.

Fromkin, Victoria A., ed. *Errors in Linguistic Performance: Slips of the Tongue, Ear, Pen, and Hand* (San Francisco: Academic Press, 1980).

Fromkin, Victoria A. "The Non-Anomalous Nature of Anomalous Utterances," *Language* 47:1 (1971), 110–17.

———. "Slips of the Tongue," *Scientific American* 229 (1973), 110–17.

Fromkin, Victoria A. et al. *Linguistics: An Introduction to Linguistic Theory* (Malden, Mass.: Blackwell, 2000).

Fromkin, Victoria, and Robert Rodman, *An Introduction to Language,* 6th ed. (Fort Worth: Harcourt Brace College Publishers, 1998).

Goldin-Meadow, Susan. *The Resilience of Language: What Gesture Creation in Deaf Children Can Tell Us About How All Children Learn Language* (New York: Psychology Press, 2003).

Goodglass, Harold. *Understanding Aphasia* (San Diego: Academic Press, 1993).

Greenberg, Joseph H., ed. *Universals of Language: Report of a Conference Held at Dobbs Ferry, New York, April 13–15, 1961* (Cambridge: MIT Press, 1963).

Grinevald, Colette. (See also Colette Craig.)

Grinevald, Colette. "A Morphosyntactic Typology of Classifiers," in Senft (2000), 50–92.

Groce, Nora Ellen. *Everyone Here Spoke Sign Language: Hereditary Deafness on Martha's Vineyard* (Cambridge: Harvard University Press, 1985).

Hickok, Gregory, Ursula Bellugi and Edward S. Klima. "The Neural Organization of Language: Evidence from Sign Language Aphasia," *Trends in Cognitive Sciences* 2:4 (1998), 129–36.

Hockett, Charles F. *A Course in Modern Linguistics* (New York: Macmillan, 1958).

———. "The Problem of Universals in Language," in Greenberg (1963), 1–22.

Hughes, Elizabeth, Mary Hughes and Annabel Greenhill, eds. *Proceedings of the 21st Annual Boston University Conference on Language Development* (Somerville, Mass.: Cascadilla, 1997), 2 vols.

Humphries, Tom, Carol Padden and Terrence J. O'Rourke. *A Basic Course in American Sign Language,* 2nd ed. (Silver Spring, Md.: T. J. Publishers, 1994).

Johnson, J. S., and E. L. Newport. "Critical Period Effects in Second Language Learning: The Influence of Maturational State on the Acquisition of English as a Second Language," *Cognitive Psychology* 21:1 (1989), 60–99.

Johnson, Robert E. "Sign Language and the Concept of Deafness in a Traditional Yucatec Mayan Village," in Erting et al. (1994), 102–109.

Kay, Paul. "Synchronic Variability and Diachronic Change in Basic Color Terms," *Language in Society,* 4 (1975), 257–70; in Casson (1981).

Kegl, Judy. (See also Judy Anne Shepard-Kegl.)

Kegl, Judy, Ann Senghas and Marie Coppola. "Creation through Contact: Sign Language Emergence and Sign Language Change in Nicaragua," in DeGraff (1999), 179–237.

Kisch, Shifra. "Negotiating (Genetic) Deafness in a Bedouin Community," in Van Cleve (2004), 148–73.

Klima, Edward S., and Ursula Bellugi. *The Signs of Language* (Cambridge: Harvard University Press, 1979).

Kyle, J. G., and Bencie Woll. *Sign Language: The Study of Deaf People and Their Language* (Cambridge: Cambridge University Press, 1985).

Labov, William. *Language in the Inner City: Studies in the Black English Vernacular* (Philadelphia: University of Pennsylvania Press, 1972).

Lakoff, George. "Presupposition and Relative Well-Formedness," in Steinberg and Jakobovits (1971), 329–40.

———. *Women, Fire, and Dangerous Things: What Categories Reveal About the Mind* (Chicago: University of Chicago Press, 1987).

Lane, Harlan. "History of ASL," in Van Cleve (1987), vol. 3, 53.

———. *The Mask of Benevolence: Disabling the Deaf Community* (New York: Alfred A. Knopf, 1992).

———. *When the Mind Hears: A History of the Deaf* (New York: Random House, 1984).

———. *The Wild Boy of Aveyron* (Cambridge: Harvard University Press, 1976).

Lane, Harlan, Robert Hoffmeister and Ben Bahan. *A Journey into the Deaf-World* (San Diego: DawnSignPress, 1996).

Lane, Harlan, Richard C. Pillard and Mary French. "Origins of the American Deaf-World: Assimilating and Differentiating Societies and Their Relation to Genetic Patterning," in Emmorey and Lane (2000), 77–100.

Langdon, Margaret. *A Grammar of Diegueño: The Mesa Grande Dialect* (Berkeley: University of California Press, 1970).

LeMaster, Barbara C., and John P. Dwyer. "Knowing and Using Female and Male Signs in Dublin," *Sign Language Studies* 20:73 (1991), 361–96.

Lenneberg, Eric H. *Biological Foundations of Language* (New York: John Wiley & Sons, 1967).

———. "Cognition in Ethnolinguistics," *Language* 29:4 (1953), 463–71.

Lepore, Jill. *A Is for American: Letters and Other Characters in the Newly United States* (New York: Alfred A. Knopf, 2002).

Liddell, Scott K. "THINK and BELIEVE: Sequentiality in American Sign Language," *Language* 60:2 (1984), 372–99.

Lillo-Martin, Diane. "The Modular Effects of Sign Language Acquisition," in Marschark et al. (1997), 62–109.

Lucas, Ceil, ed. *The Sociolinguistics in Deaf Communities Series* (Washington: Gallaudet University Press), 2 vols. *Vol. 1: Sociolinguistics in Deaf Communities* (1995); *Vol. 2: Multicultural Aspects of Sociolinguistics in Deaf Communities,* (1996).

Lucy, John A. "Sign Language in a Yucatec Maya Community in Mexico," paper presented at the workshop "Sign Language in Village Communities," Nijmegen, the Netherlands, 2006. April 4–6, 2006.

Lunde, Anders S. "The Sociology of the Deaf," paper presented at the meeting of the American Sociological Society (1956). Reproduced in large part in Stokoe (1960).

Lyons, John. *Chomsky* (London: Fontana, 1970).

MacDougall, J. C. "Access to Justice for Deaf Inuit in Nunavuk: The Role of 'Inuit Sign Language,'" *Canadian Psychology* 42:1 (2001), 61–73.

Macmillan, Malcolm. *An Odd Kind of Fame: Stories of Phineas Gage* (Cambridge: MIT Press, 2002).

Maher, Jane. *Seeing Language in Sign: The Work of William C. Stokoe* (Washington: Gallaudet University Press, 1996).

Maher, John, and Judy Groves. *Introducing Chomsky* (New York: Totem, 1996).

"Mark of Chilmark, Deaf and Dumb in the Village of Squibnocket," *Boston Sunday Herald,* Jan. 20, 1895.

Marsaja, I Gede. "Kata Kolok 'Deaf Talk': A Village Sign Language from North Bali," paper presented at the workshop "Sign Language in Village Communities," Nijmegen, the Netherlands, April 4–6, 2006.

Marschark, Marc, Patricia Siple, Diane Lillo-Martin, Ruth Campbell and Victoria S. Everhart, eds. *Relations of Language and Thought: The View from Sign Language and Deaf Children* (New York: Oxford University Press, 1997).

Marschark, Marc, and Patricia Elizabeth Spencer, eds. *Oxford Handbook of Deaf Studies, Language, and Education* (Oxford: Oxford University Press, 2003).

Marshall, Jane, Jo Atkinson, Elaine Smulovitch, Alice Thacker and Bencie

Woll. "Aphasia in a User of British Sign Language: Dissociation Between Sign and Gesture," *Cognitive Neuropsychology* 21:5 (2004), 537–54.

Marx, Otto. "The History of the Biological Basis of Language," in Lenneberg (1967), 443–69.

McKee, Rachel Locker, and Jemina Napier. "Interpreting into International Sign Pidgin: An Analysis," *Sign Language & Linguistics* 5:1 (2002), 27–54.

McNeill, David. "Developmental Psycholinguistics," in Smith and Miller (1966), 15–84.

McWhorter, John H. "Identifying the Creole Prototype: Vindicating a Typological Class," *Language* 74:4 (1998), 788–818.

Meir, Irit. "The Development of Argument Structure in Al-Sayyid Bedouin Sign Language," paper presented at the workshop "Sign Language in Village Communities," Nijmegen, the Netherlands, April 4–6, 2006.

———. "Motion and Transfer: The Analysis of Two Verb Classes in Israeli Sign Language," in Dively et al. (2001), 74–87.

Meringer, Rudolf, and Carl Mayer. *Versprechen und Verlesen: Eine Psychologisch-Linguistiche Studie* (Stuttgart: Göschense Verlagsbuchhandlung, 1895). Reissued in the original German, with an introductory article and appendix in English by Anne Cutler and David Fay (Amsterdam: John Benjamins, 1978).

Mersenne, Marin. *L'Harmonie Universelle* (1636). Available in English as "Harmonie Universelle: The Books on Instruments," translated by Roger E. Chapman (The Hague: M. Nijhoff, 1957).

Mithun, Marianne. "The Convergence of Noun Classification Systems," in Craig (1986), 379–97.

Montaigne, Michel de. *Michel de Montaigne: The Complete Essays,* translated by M. A. Screech (London: Penguin, 1991), Book II:12, 507.

Morris, William, ed. *The American Heritage Dictionary of the English Language,* New College Edition (Boston: Houghton Mifflin Company, 1975).

Myklebust, Helmer. *The Psychology of Deafness: Sensory Deprivation, Learning, and Adjustment* (New York: Grune & Stratton, 1960).

Nagourney, Eric. "William Stokoe Jr., Sign Language Advocate, Dies at 80," *New York Times,* April 11, 2000, B10.

Newkirk, Don, Edward S. Klima, Carlene Canady Pedersen and Ursula Bellugi. "Linguistic Evidence from Slips of the Hand," in Fromkin (1980), 165–66.

Newport, Elissa L. "Maturational Constraints on Language Learning," *Cognitive Science* 14:1 (1990), 11–28.

Nonaka, Angela. "Establishing Speech Community Size and Membership of Undocumented Village Sign Languages: An Anthropological Heuristic from the Ban Khor Case Study," paper presented at the workshop "Sign

Language in Village Communities," Nijmegen, the Netherlands, April 4–6, 2006.

Nyst, Victoria. "Adamorobe Sign Language," paper presented at the workshop "Sign Language in Village Communities," Nijmegen, the Netherlands, April 4–6, 2006.

O'Conner, Patricia T. *Woe Is I: The Grammarphobe's Guide to Better English in Plain English* (New York: Putnam, 1996).

Osgood, Charles. "Language Universals and Psycholinguistics," in Greenberg (1963), 236–54.

Osugi, Yutaka, Ted Supalla and Rebecca Webb. "The Use of Word Elicitation to Identify Distinctive Gestural Systems on Amami Island," *Sign Language & Linguistics* 2:1 (1999), 87–112.

Otero, Carlos P., ed. *Noam Chomsky: Critical Assessments* (London: Routledge, 1994), 4 vols.

Padden, Carol A. "American Sign Language," in Van Cleve (1987), vol. 3, 47.

———. *Interaction of Morphology and Syntax in American Sign Language* (New York: Garland, 1988).

Padden, Carol, and Tom Humphries. *Deaf in America: Voices from a Culture* (Cambridge: Harvard University Press, 1988).

Peterson, Candida C., and Michael Siegal. "Deafness, Conversation and Theory of Mind," *Journal of Child Psychology and Psychiatry* 36:3 (1995), 459–74.

Petitto, Laura Ann. "From Gesture to Symbol: The Relationship Between Form and Meaning in the Acquisition of Personal Pronouns in American Sign Language" (Ph.D. diss., Harvard University, 1983).

Petitto, Laura Ann and Paula F. Marentette. "Babbling in the Manual Mode: Evidence for the Ontogeny of Language," *Science* 251 (1991), 1493–96.

Peyton, Joy Kreeft, Peg Griffin, Walt Wolfram and Ralph Fasold, eds. *Language in Action: New Studies of Language in Society. Essays in Honor of Roger W. Shuy* (Cresskill, N.J.: Hampton, 2000).

Pinker, Steven. *The Language Instinct* (New York: William Morrow, 1994).

Plinius Secundus, C. *The Historie of the World: Commonly Called the Natural Historie of C. Plinius Secundus, Translated into English by Philemon Holland, Doctor in Physicke* (London: Adam Islip, 1601).

Poizner, Howard, Edward S. Klima and Ursula Bellugi. *What the Hands Reveal About the Brain* (Cambridge: MIT Press, 1987).

Polich, L. G. *Social Agency and Deaf Communities: A Nicaraguan Case Study* (Ph.D. diss., University of Texas, 1998).

Potter, John M. "What Was the Matter With Dr. Spooner?," in Fromkin (1980), 13–34.

Preston, Dennis R. "A Renewed Proposal for the Study of Folk Linguistics," in Peyton et al. (2000), 113–38.

———. "They Speak Really Bad English Down South and in New York City," in Bauer and Trudgill (1998), 139–49.

Preston, Dennis R., and Gregory C. Robinson. "Dialect Perception and Attitudes to Variation," in Ball (2005), 133–49.

Radford, Andrew. *Syntax: A Minimalist Introduction* (Cambridge: Cambridge University Press, 1997).

Rohrer, Christian, and Nicolas Ruwet, eds. *Actes du Colloque Franco-Allemand de Grammaire Transformationnelle* (Tübingen: Max Niemeyer Verlag, 1974).

Sacks, Oliver. *The Island of the Colorblind: And, Cycad Island* (New York: Alfred A. Knopf, 1997).

———. *Seeing Voices: A Journey into the World of the Deaf* (Berkeley: University of California Press, 1989).

Saffran, Jenny R., Ann Senghas and John C. Trueswell. "The Acquisition of Language by Children," *Proceedings of the National Academy of Sciences* 98:23 (Nov. 6, 2001), 12, 874–75.

Sampson, John. *The Dialect of the Gypsies of Wales* (Oxford: Clarendon Press, 1926).

Sandler, Wendy. *Phonological Representation of the Sign: Linearity and Nonlinearity in American Sign Language* (Dordrecht: Foris Publications, 1989).

———. "Sign Language and Modularity," *Lingua*, 89:4 (1993), 315–51.

———. "Temporal Aspects and ASL Phonology," in Fischer and Siple (1990), 11.

Sandler, Wendy, Mark Aronoff, Carol Padden, Irit Meir. "A Sign Language in the Desert," unpublished manuscript (2003).

Sandler, Wendy, and Diane Lillo-Martin. "Natural Sign Languages," in Aronoff and Rees-Miller (2001), 533–62.

Sandler, Wendy, Irit Meir, Carol Padden and Mark Aronoff. "The Emergence of Grammar: Systematic Structure in a New Language" *Proceedings of the National Academy of Sciences* 102:7 (Feb. 15, 2005), 2661–65.

Sapir, Edward. *Abnormal Types of Speech in Nootka* (Ottawa: Government Printing Bureau, 1915).

Saussure, Ferdinand de. *Course in General Linguistics* (1916), Roy Harris, trans., Charles Bally and Albert Sechehaye, eds. (Chicago: Open Court, 1986).

Schein, Jerome D., and Marcus T. Delk, Jr. *The Deaf Population of the United States* (Silver Spring, Md.: National Association of the Deaf, 1974).

Schwartz, Carol. "Discrete Versus Continuous Encoding in American Sign

Language and Nonlinguistic Gestures" (Unpublished manuscript, University of California, San Diego, 1979).

Senft, Gunter, ed. *Systems of Nominal Classification* (Cambridge: Cambridge University Press, 2000).

———. "What Do We Really Know About Nominal Classification Systems?," in Senft (2000), 11–49.

Senghas, Ann, and Marie Coppola. "Children Creating Language: How Nicaraguan Sign Language Acquired a Spatial Grammar," *Psychological Science* 12:4 (2001), 323–28.

Senghas, Ann, Marie Coppola, Elissa L. Newport and Ted Supalla. "Argument Structure in Nicaraguan Sign Language: The Emergence of Grammatical Devices," in Hughes et al. (1997), vol. 2, 550–61.

Shattuck, Roger. *The Forbidden Experiment: The Story of the Wild Boy of Aveyron* (New York: Farrar, Straus & Giroux, 1980).

Shepard-Kegl, Judy Anne. (See also Judy Kegl.)

Shepard-Kegl, Judy Anne. *Locative Relations in American Sign Language: Word Formation, Syntax and Discourse.* (Ph.D. diss., Massachusetts Institute of Technology, 1985).

Silberman, Charles E. *Crisis in Black and White* (New York: Random House, 1964).

"Silent Research Is Her Sign," English-language interview with Wendy Sandler, *University of Haifa Focus* (Winter 1997); no byline.

Sims, Donald G., Gerard G. Walter and Robert L. Whitehead, eds. *Deafness and Communication: Assessment and Training* (Baltimore: Williams & Wilkins, 1982).

Siple, Patricia, ed. *Understanding Language Through Sign Language Research* (New York: Academic Press, 1978).

Siple, Patricia, and Susan D. Fischer, eds. *Theoretical Issues in Sign Language Research* (Chicago: University of Chicago Press), *Vol. 2: Psychology* (1991); see also Fischer and Siple.

Skinner, B. F. *Verbal Behavior* (New York: Appleton-Century-Crofts, 1957).

Smith, Frank, and George A. Miller, eds. *The Genesis of Language: A Psycholinguistic Approach* (Cambridge: MIT Press, 1966).

Spencer, Andrew. "Morphology," in Aronoff and Rees-Miller (2001), 213–37.

Steinberg, Danny D., and Leon A. Jakobovits, eds. *Semantics: An Interdisciplinary Reader in Philosophy, Linguistics and Psychology* (Cambridge: Cambridge University Press, 1971).

Stokoe, William C. "Sign Languages," in Van Cleve (1987), vol. 3, 31–35.

Stokoe, William C., Jr. *Sign Language Structure: An Outline of the Visual Communication Systems of the American Deaf* (Buffalo: Studies in Linguistics Occasional Papers 8, 1960).

Stokoe, William C., Jr., Dorothy C. Casterline and Carl G. Croneberg. *A Dictionary of American Sign Language on Linguistic Principles* (Washington: Gallaudet College Press, 1965).

Supalla, Samuel J. "Manually Coded English: The Modality Question in Signed Language Development," in Siple and Fischer (1991), 85–109.

Supalla, Ted. "Structure and Acquisition of Verbs of Motion and Location in American Sign Language" (Ph.D. diss., University of California, San Diego, 1982).

Supalla, Ted, and Elissa L. Newport. "How Many Seats in a Chair? The Derivation of Nouns and Verbs in American Sign Language," in Siple (1978), 91–132.

Sutton-Spence, Rachel, and Bencie Woll. *The Linguistics of British Sign Language: An Introduction* (Cambridge: Cambridge University Press, 1999).

Thesiger, Wilfred. "The Awash River and the Aussa Sultanate," *The Geographical Journal* 85:1 (1935), 1–19.

Valli, Clayton, and Ceil Lucas. *Linguistics of American Sign Language: An Introduction,* 2nd ed. (Washington: Gallaudet University Press, 1995).

Van Cleve, John V., ed. *The Gallaudet Encyclopedia of Deaf People and Deafness* (New York: McGraw-Hill, 1987), 3 vols.

Van Cleve, John Vickery, ed. *Genetics, Disability, and Deafness* (Washington: Gallaudet University Press, 2004).

van den Bogaerde, Beppie. "Kajana Signs," paper presented at the workshop "Sign Language in Village Communities," Nijmegen, the Netherlands, April 4–6, 2006.

Wade, Nicholas. "A New Language Arises, and Scientists Watch It Evolve," *New York Times,* Feb. 1, 2005, Section F3.

Watkins, Calvert. "The Indo-European Origin of English," in Morris (1975).

Wilbur, Ronnie B. "Why Syllables? What the Notion Means for ASL Research," in Fischer and Siple (1990), 81–108.

Wimmer, Heinz, and Josef Perner. "Beliefs About Beliefs: Representation and Constraining Function of Wrong Beliefs in Young Children's Understanding of Deception," *Cognition* 13:1 (1983), 103–28.

Woodward, James. "Historical Bases of American Sign Language," in Siple (1978), 333–48.

Yang, Jun Hui, and Susan D. Fischer. "Expressing Negation in Chinese Sign Language," *Sign Language & Linguistics* 5:2 (2002), 167–202.

Zeshan, Ulrike. "Interrogative Constructions in Signed Languages: Crosslinguistic Perspectives," *Language* 80:1 (2004), 7–39.

Notes

INTRODUCTION

Page

4 *Nora Groce's lovely book:* Nora Ellen Groce, *Everybody Here Spoke Sign Language: Hereditary Deafness on Martha's Vineyard* (Cambridge: Harvard University Press, 1985).

CHAPTER ONE: IN THE VILLAGE OF THE DEAF

Page

7 *an incidence forty times that of the general population:* Wendy Sandler, Irit Meir, Carol Padden and Mark Aronoff, "The Emergence of Grammar: Systematic Structure in a New Language" *Proceedings of the National Academy of Sciences* 102:7 (Feb. 15, 2005), 2661. The incidence of deafness in the general population of Israel, as in the United States, is approximately 0.1 percent, or one in a thousand. See, e.g., John V. Van Cleve, ed., *The Gallaudet Encyclopedia of Deaf People and Deafness* (New York: McGraw-Hill, 1987), Vol. 1, 251ff.; Vol. 2, 102.

7 *a veritable island of the deaf:* Cf. Oliver Sacks, *The Island of the Colorblind: And, Cycad Island* (New York: Alfred A. Knopf, 1997).

8 *the "language instinct":* Steven Pinker, *The Language Instinct* (New York: William Morrow, 1994).

CHAPTER TWO: "WHAT IS THIS WONDERFUL LANGUAGE?"

Page

16 *"I thought to myself, 'They are talking exactly as we do'"* English-language interview with Wendy Sandler, "Silent Research Is Her Sign," *University of Haifa Focus* (Winter 1997); no byline.

17 *"'The manual sign language used by the deaf'":* Helmer Myklebust, *The Psychology of Deafness: Sensory Deprivation, Learning, and Adjustment* (New York: Grune & Stratton, 1960), quoted in Carol Padden and Tom Humphries, *Deaf in America: Voices from a Culture* (Cambridge: Harvard University Press, 1988), 59.

17 *"Some communities have a* gesture language"*:* Leonard Bloomfield, *Language* (New York: Henry Holt, 1933), 39, italics in original. Also quoted in Padden and Humphries (1988), 58.

18 *The linguist Ulrike Zeshan:* Dr. Zeshan, who has been working most recently at the Max Planck Institute for Psycholinguists in Nijmegen, the Netherlands, began her project by comparing negative and interrogative constructions in thirty-seven different sign languages. She has moved on to investigate possessive and existential constructions. Her work is summarized on her Web site: http://www.mpi.nl/word/SignLang/WEB-FINAL/Zeshan.htm.

18 *"When a gesture becomes a sign, its properties change":* Ulrike Zeshan, "Interrogative Constructions in Signed Languages: Crosslinguistic Perspectives," *Language* 80:1 (2004), 11.

20 *"Sign languages are gestural systems":* William C. Stokoe, "Sign Languages," in Van Cleve (1987), Vol. 3, 31.

20 *ASL, used by a quarter- to a half-million deaf people:* This and similar figures have wide currency in the literature. See, e.g., Van Cleve (1987), Vol. 3, 44; Tom Humphries, Carol Padden and Terrence J. O'Rourke, "A Basic Course in American Sign Language," 2nd ed. (Silver Spring, Md.: T. J. Publishers, 1994), 6.

21 *I HUNGRY, WANT EAT YOU:* Adapted from Charlotte Baker, "Sentences in American Sign Language," in Charlotte Baker and Robbin Battison, eds., *Sign Language and the Deaf Community: Essays in Honor of William C. Stokoe* (Silver Spring, Md.: National Association of the Deaf, 1980), 79.

21 *the verb* GIVE*, for example:* Edward S. Klima and Ursula Bellugi, *The Signs of Language* (Cambridge: Harvard University Press, 1979), 274ff.

21 SICK *stands at the center of a linguistic paradigm:* Ibid., 267.

21 *"The . . . grammatical processes that have developed in American Sign Language":* Ibid., 69.

22 *As Sam's story went:* Padden and Humphries (1988), 15–16.

23 *"The clear implication":* J. G. Kyle and Bencie Woll, *Sign Language: The Study of Deaf People and Their Language* (Cambridge: Cambridge University Press, 1985), 162.

23 *"For centuries scholars from every country":* Ferdinand Berthier, *Observation sur la Mimique Considérée dans Ses Rapports avec l'Enseignement des Sourds-Muets* (Paris: L. Martinet, 1854), quoted in Robbin Battison and I. King Jordan, "Cross-Cultural Communication with Foreign Signers: Fact and Fancy," *Sign Language Studies* 10 (1976), 53–68.

23 *"Virtually any time Deaf people form a community":* Susan D. Fischer, "More than Just Handwaving: The Mutual Contributions of Sign Language and Linguistics," in Karen Emmorey and Harlan Lane, eds., *The*

Signs of Language Revisited: An Anthology to Honor Ursula Bellugi and Edward Klima (Mahwah, N.J.: Lawrence Erlbaum, 2000), 196.

23 *Scholars have documented more than a hundred signed languages:* See, e.g., Van Cleve (1987), Vol. 3, 31ff; and www.ethnologue.com, an online typological directory of thousands of the world's languages, signed and spoken.

24 *Its antecedents still show:* Harlan Lane, Robert Hoffmeister and Ben Bahan, *A Journey into the Deaf-World* (San Diego: DawnSignPress, 1996), 57.

24 bolna*:* Victoria Fromkin and Robert Rodman, eds., *An Introduction to Language,* 6th ed. (Orlando, Harcourt Brace College Publishers, 1998), 6.

24 *But in Danish Sign Language, the same sequence:* Elisabeth Engberg-Pedersen, personal communication.

24 *without the armpit you cannot, for instance, say* WEDNESDAY*:* Susan D. Fischer, "Sign Language and Manual Communication," in Donald G. Sims, Gerard G. Walter and Robert L. Whitehead, eds., *Deafness and Communication: Assessment and Training* (Baltimore: Williams & Wilkins, 1982), 93, cited in Lane, Hoffmeister and Bahan (1996), 79. In a recent personal communication, Fischer points out that in the last thirty years, the Hong Kong sign WEDNESDAY has migrated to a location next to, rather than in, the armpit.

25 *Many of our insights into the richness and diversity of sign:* Susan Fischer, "Appendix: Some Properties of A.S.L." in Ursula Bellugi and Susan Fischer, "A Comparison of Sign Language and Spoken Language," *Cognition* 1 (1972), 186, italics in original.

26 *Those who assume signed language is concrete:* Lane, Hoffmeister and Bahan (1996), 44, italics in original.

27 *"His New Year's resolutions for 1808":* Harlan Lane, *When the Mind Hears: A History of the Deaf* (New York: Random House, 1984), 177.

28 *For a deaf child growing up in a hearing family:* Ninety percent of children born deaf have hearing parents. This figure has wide currency in the literature. See, e.g., Jerome D. Schein and Marcus T. Delk, Jr., *The Deaf Population of the United States* (Silver Spring, Md.: National Association of the Deaf, 1974) and the Web site of the Laurent Clerc National Deaf Education Center at Gallaudet University, http://clerccenter.gallaudet.edu/about/faq.html. Kyle and Woll (1985), 58, cite a similar figure for deaf British children.

28 *"Imagine you were born in a glass cage":* Valerie Sutton, personal communication. A former dancer and choreographer, Sutton has developed a writing system for signed languages, based on dance notation. It can be seen at her organization's Web site, www.signwriting.org. The historian

Douglas C. Baynton uses a similar analogy in his book *Forbidden Signs: American Culture and the Campaign Against Sign Language* (Chicago: University of Chicago Press, 1996).

29 *"Alice seems to understand":* Lane (1984), 177–78.

30 *On his arrival in Britain, Gallaudet was turned away:* Lane, Hoffmeister and Bahan (1996), 54.

30 *Eventually, the Braidwoods agreed to teach him:* Lane (1984), 188.

30 *"which should rank only a little higher":* Quoted in ibid., 191.

30 *"not to astonish the vulgar":* Quoted in Jill Lepore, "A Is for American: Letters and Other Characters in the Newly United States" (New York: Alfred A. Knopf, 2002), 99.

31 *members of the audience posed searching philosophical questions:* Lane (1984), 159.

32 *"I am now convinced of the utility":* Quoted in Lepore (2002), 99, italics in original.

32 *"Our deaf-mutes have discussions and arguments":* Michel de Montaigne, "An Apology for Raymond Sebond," in *Michel de Montaigne: the Complete Essays,* translated by M. A. Screech (London: Penguin, 1991), Book II:12, 507.

32 *What Épée did:* For Épée's work with the deaf in the 1760s, see, e.g., Harlan Lane, "History of ASL," in Van Cleve (1987), Vol. 3, 53.

33 *Sentences in French Sign Language have fewer words:* Lane (1984), 61.

33 *Even the simplest sentence:* Ibid., 62.

34 *the Connecticut Asylum for the Education and Instruction of Deaf and Dumb Persons:* Van Cleve (1987), Vol. 1, 25.

34 *By the end of the first year in Hartford:* Lane, Hoffmeister and Bahan (1996), 56; Lane (1984), 229.

35 *an insular community on Martha's Vineyard:* Groce (1985).

36 *a continuing chapter in American history:* Harlan Lane, throughout much of his work, notably *The Mask of Benevolence: Disabling the Deaf Community* (New York: Alfred A. Knopf, 1992), also likens oralism to colonialism.

36 *This powerful faction:* For a fine history of the battle between the oralists and the manualists, see Baynton (1996).

36 *"bathroom sign":* Valerie Sutton, personal communication.

CHAPTER THREE: THE ROAD TO AL-SAYYID

Page

40 *International Sign Pidgin:* See, e.g., Rachel Locker McKee and Jemina Napier, "Interpreting into International Sign Pidgin: An Analysis," *Sign Language & Linguistics* 5:1 (2002), 27–54.

CHAPTER FOUR: THE SIGN-LANGUAGE INSTINCT

Page

46 *"We all come from the factory":* Patricia T. O'Conner, *Woe Is I: The Grammarphobe's Guide to Better English in Plain English* (New York: Putnam, 1996), ix.

46 Menomini Texts: Leonard Bloomfield, *Menomini Texts* (New York: G. E. Stechert, 1928); Edward Sapir, *Abnormal Types of Speech in Nootka* (Ottawa: Government Printing Bureau, 1915); John Sampson, *The Dialect of the Gypsies of Wales* (Oxford: Clarendon Press, 1926).

48 *"Features which we think ought to be universal":* Bloomfield (1933), 20–21. Also quoted in John Lyons, *Chomsky* (London: Fontana, 1970), 98.

48 *an Egyptian papyrus from about 1700 B.C.:* Victoria A. Fromkin et al., *Linguistics: An Introduction to Linguistic Theory* (Oxford: Blackwell, 2000), 5.

48 *"A sound is not yet a word":* Quoted in Otto Marx, "The History of the Biological Basis of Language," in Eric H. Lenneberg, *Biological Foundations of Language* (New York: John Wiley & Sons, 1967), 446.

48 *"language was a biological function like vision and hearing":* Marx (1967), 446.

49 *"characteristic for the unfolding of other biologically given attributes":* Quoted in Marx (1967), 458.

49 *"language capacity is an attribute of intellectual man's physiology":* Marx (1967), 458.

49 *"the similarity of . . . language structures":* Ibid., 458–59, italics added.

49 *The study of cultures flourished:* Ibid., 464.

49 *"Philosophers, to this day":* Bloomfield (1933), 6.

50 *Suppose that Jack and Jill are walking down a lane:* Ibid., 22ff., italics added.

51 *the Harvard psychologist B. F. Skinner published the book* Verbal Behavior: B. F. Skinner, *Verbal Behavior* (New York: Appleton-Century-Crofts), 1957.

51 *There were a few dissenters:* See, e.g., Eric H. Lenneberg, "Cognition in Ethnolinguistics," *Language* 29 (1953), 463–71; and Roger W. Brown and Eric H. Lenneberg, "A Study in Language and Cognition," *Journal of Abnormal and Social Psychology* 49 (1954), 454–62.

52 *Noam helped proofread:* Robert F. Barsky, *Noam Chomsky: A Life of Dissent* (Cambridge: MIT Press, 1997), 10.

52 *our innate "'feel' for sentence structure":* Noam Chomsky, Review of *Verbal Behavior,* by B. F. Skinner, *Language* 35:1 (1959), 42.

53 Colorless green ideas sleep furiously*:* Noam Chomsky, *Syntactic Structures* (The Hague: Mouton, 1957), 15.

53 *Imagine that you are faced with the following challenge:* Jenny R. Saffran,

Ann Senghas and John C. Trueswell, "The Acquisition of Language by Children," *Proceedings of the National Academy of Sciences* 98:23 (Nov. 6, 2001), 12,874.

54 *"the poverty of the stimulus":* see, e.g., Noam Chomsky, *Rules and Representations* (New York: Columbia University Press, 1980).

54 *"Before they can add 2 + 2":* Fromkin and Rodman (1998), 318.

55 *in the case of verbs that have irregular past tenses:* This example has been cited by Pinker (1994) and a great many others.

56 *CHILD: Nobody don't like me:* Adapted from David McNeill, "Developmental Psycholinguistics," in Frank Smith and George A. Miller, eds., *The Genesis of Language: A Psycholinguistic Approach* (Cambridge: MIT Press, 1966), 69.

56 *"The young child has succeeded in carrying out":* Chomsky (1959), 57.

56 *A typical example of "stimulus control" for Skinner:* Ibid., 31–33, italics in original.

57 *"It is simply not true that children can learn language":* Ibid., 42.

58 *"In field after field":* Derek Bickerton, "The Language Bioprogram Hypothesis," *Behavioral and Brain Sciences* 7:2 (1984), 188.

58 *"The role of the bioprogram for children":* Ibid., 185.

60 *"Particularly in the case of language":* Noam Chomsky, *Language and Mind* (New York: Harcourt, Brace & World, 1968), 81. This quotation appears as the epigraph to Judy Kegl, Ann Senghas and Marie Coppola, "Creation through Contact: Sign Language Emergence and Sign Language Change in Nicaragua," in Michel DeGraff, ed., *Language Creation and Language Change: Creolization, Diachrony, and Development* (Cambridge: MIT Press, 1999), 179.

60 *"The fact that all normal children":* Chomsky (1959), 57–58.

60 *"A Multifactorial Approach":* João Costa, "A Multifactorial Approach to Adverb Placement: Assumptions, Facts, and Problems," *Lingua* 114 (2004), 711–53; C. Burgess and J. Skodis, "Lexical Representation and Morpho-Syntactic Parallelism in the Left Hemisphere," *Brain and Language* 44:2 (1993), 129–38; Joan Bresnan, ed., *The Mental Representation of Grammatical Relations* (Cambridge: MIT Press, 1982).

61 *In the most current thinking, it is believed to have emerged:* See, e.g., Derek Bickerton, "A Bare-Bones Account of Human Evolution" (review of *The Dawn of Human Culture,* by Richard G. Klein with Blake Edgar), *American Scientist* 90:5 (Sept.–Oct. 2002).

61 *"Languages," the linguist Calvert Watkins has written:* Calvert Watkins, "The Indo-European Origin of English," in William Morris, ed., *The American Heritage Dictionary of the English Language,* New College Edition (Boston: Houghton Mifflin, 1975), xx.

61 *Consider Hungarian, which has more than two dozen different cases:* The Hungarian data are courtesy of Robert Vago.

62 *Then there is Dyirbal:* George Lakoff, *Women, Fire, and Dangerous Things: What Categories Reveal About the Mind* (Chicago: University of Chicago Press, 1987), 92–93.

62 *And there are the lavish sentences:* "The House That Jack Built" is also cited as an example of a potentially infinite nest of subordinate clauses by Wendy Sandler and Diane Lillo-Martin in their article "Natural Sign Languages," in Mark Aronoff and Janie Rees-Miller, eds., *The Handbook of Linguistics* (Oxford: Blackwell, 2001). As the authors nicely illustrate, even a long string of clauses like this can be enlarged further: "*This is the banker, his honor forsworn / That foreclosed on the farmer sowing the corn. . . .*"

62 *It has come to be known, quite reasonably:* Roger Shattuck, *The Forbidden Experiment: The Story of the Wild Boy of Aveyron* (New York: Farrar, Straus & Giroux, 1980).

62 *the Egyptian pharaoh Psammetichus:* Bloomfield (1933), 4; Shattuck (1980), 44.

63 *The earliest written references to a signed language in Britain:* Kyle and Woll (1985), 37; Van Cleve (1987), Vol. 3, 62.

63 *"We are now beginning to see":* Klima and Bellugi (1979), v.

64 *little disturbances of air:* A similar point is made in John Maher and Judy Groves, *Introducing Chomsky* (New York: Totem, 1996), 5.

64 *If one could invent a language:* Marin Mersenne, *L'Harmonie Universelle* (1636), quoted in Mark Aronoff, Irit Meir and Wendy Sandler, "The Paradox of Sign Language Morphology," *Language* 81:2 (2005), 301.

65 *Using their hands and fingers, these deaf babies:* See, e.g., Laura Ann Petitto and Paul F. Marentette, "Babbling in the Manual Mode. Evidence for the Ontogeny of Language," *Science* 251 (1991), 1,493–96.

65 *For these deaf infants, the rest of language acquisition:* Kyle and Woll (1985), 67ff. Children's over-application of grammatical rules in sign language: Klima and Bellugi (1979), 77.

66 *Deaf native signers who have suffered strokes:* Howard Poizner, Edward S. Klima and Ursula Bellugi, *What the Hands Reveal About the Brain* (Cambridge: MIT Press, 1987).

66 *"The more we learn about the human linguistic ability":* Fromkin and Rodman (1998), 20, italics added.

66 *"As questions about the nature and fundamental properties":* Klima and Bellugi (1979), 35.

67 *contemporary sign languages "exist in settings":* Wendy Sandler, Mark Aronoff, Carol Padden, Irit Meir, "A Sign Language in the Desert," unpublished manuscript (2003), unpaginated.

67 *"Most deaf children," the team has written:* Aronoff, Meir and Sandler (2005), 307.

67 *Deaf children born to hearing families may be exposed:* Ibid., 307.

68 *many of the world's major sign languages are historically interrelated:* See, e.g., www.ethnologue.com, under "Deaf Sign Languages"; Van Cleve (1987), Vol. 3, 56–118.

68 *British Sign Language also influenced ASL:* Groce (1985). For the relationship of British Sign Language to Martha's Vineyard Sign, see Harlan Lane, Richard C. Pillard and Mary French, "Origins of the American Deaf-World: Assimilating and Differentiating Societies and Their Relation to Genetic Patterning," in Emmorey and Lane (2000), 86.

69 *Throughout history, perhaps a dozen of these villages:* Mexico: Robert E. Johnson, "Sign Language and the Concept of Deafness in a Traditional Yucatec Mayan Village," in Carol J. Erting, Robert C. Johnson, Dorothy L. Smith and Bruce D. Snider, eds., *The Deaf Way: Perspectives from the International Conference on Deaf Culture* (Washington: Gallaudet University Press, 1994), 102–9; Bali: Jan Branson, Don Miller and I Gede Marsaja with I Wayan Negara, "Everyone Here Speaks Sign Language, Too: A Deaf Village in Bali, Indonesia," in Ceil Lucas, ed., *Multicultural Aspects of Sociolinguistics in Deaf Communities* (Washington: Gallaudet University Press, 1966), 39–57; Ghana: Victoria Nyst, "Adamorobe Sign Language," paper presented at "Sign Language in Village Communities" workshop, Nijmegen, the Netherlands, April 4, 2006; Amami Island: Yutaka Osugi, Ted Supalla and Rebecca Webb, "The Use of Word Elicitation to Identify Distinctive Gestural Systems on Amami Island," *Sign Language & Linguistics* 2:1 (1999), 87ff.; Providence Island: James Woodward, "Historical Bases of American Sign Language," in Patricia Siple, ed., *Understanding Language Through Sign Language Research* (New York: Academic Press, 1978), 333–48.

70 *The island's last deaf signer:* Groce (1985), vii.

70 *"[I]n the village of about 400 inhabitants":* Johnson (1994), 104.

71 *In this community, deafness is accepted:* Sandler, Aronoff, Padden, and Meir (2003).

CHAPTER FIVE: STARRY NIGHT

Page

75 *The languages of the world, researchers have discovered, utilize color terms differently:* Brent Berlin and Paul Kay, *Basic Color Terms: Their Universality and Evolution* (Stanford: CSLI Publications, 1999; reprint of 1991 and 1969 editions).

75 *Lower Valley Hitigima and Pyramid-Wodo:* Ibid., 45ff. Today, Lower Valley Hitigima is more commonly known as Lower Grand Valley Hitigima.

76 *Berlin and Kay call this "grue":* See, e.g., Paul Kay, "Synchronic Variability and Diachronic Change in Basic Color Terms," *Language in Society* 4 (1975), 257–70, in Ronald W. Casson, ed., *Language, Culture, and Cognition: Anthropological Perspectives* (New York: Macmillan, 1981), 291ff.

76 *"Our results," Berlin and Kay wrote:* Berlin and Kay (1999), 2, italics in original.

76 *"Systems of color naming do not vary randomly":* Berlin and Kay, v.

81 *it is this, psychologists believe, that allows them to begin "pretend play":* Simon Baron-Cohen, Alan M. Leslie and Uta Frith, "Does the Autistic Child Have a 'Theory of Mind'?," *Cognition* 21 (1985), 38.

81 *ME: What have you been doing today?:* Web site of Mike Eslea, University of Central Lancashire, http://www.uclan.ac.uk/psychology/bully/tom.htm.

81 *In one version of the scenario, a boy named Maxi:* Heinz Wimmer and Josef Perner, "Beliefs About Beliefs: Representation and Constraining Function of Wrong Beliefs in Young Children's Understanding of Deception," *Cognition* 13 (1983), 103–28.

81 *Children with Down's syndrome consistently do well:* Baron-Cohen et al. (1985), 37–46.

82 *In a 1995 study:* Candida C. Peterson and Michael Siegal, "Deafness, Conversation and Theory of Mind," *Journal of Child Psychology and Psychiatry* 36:3 (1995), 459–74.

83 *The Japanese sign* UNDERSTAND, *for instance:* Susan Fischer, personal communication.

84 *There are some spoken languages, he says:* Piaroa, for instance, an indigenous language of Venezuela, appears to lack a unique word for "word." Laurence Krute, personal communication.

CHAPTER SIX: THE ATOMS OF SIGN

Page

87 *"It is the duty of every good man":* Quoted in Lane (1984), 361. Bell's assertion in 1891 that deaf intermarriage would lead to "the formation of a deaf variety of the human race" was based on the still widespread ignorance, or faulty understanding, of the principles of genetic heredity outlined in the 1860s by Gregor Mendel (1822–1884).

87 *"Nearly one-third of the teachers of the deaf":* Alexander Graham Bell, *Memoir Upon the Formation of a Deaf Variety of the Human Race* (New Haven: National Academy of Sciences, 1883; reprinted, Washington: Government Printing Office, 1884), 48 of 1884 edition, quoted in Jane

Maher, *Seeing Language in Sign: The Work of William C. Stokoe* (Washington: Gallaudet University Press, 1996), 17. See also Lane (1984), 341ff.

87 *Oral speech is the sole power:* Quoted in Lane (1984), 393–94.

88 *By the early twentieth century:* Anders S. Lunde, "The Sociology of the Deaf," paper presented at the meeting of the American Sociological Society, 1956, quoted in William C. Stokoe, Jr., *Sign Language Structure: An Outline of the Visual Communications Systems of the American Deaf* (Buffalo: Studies in Linguistics Occasional Papers 8, 1960), 26.

88 *"The history of Gallaudet is inextricably woven":* Maher (1996), 25.

89 *"No one, not even the deaf students":* Ibid., 66.

89 *"None of us at the time":* Ibid., 55–56.

89 *During the 1950s, the university attempted:* Ibid., 28.

90 *"Signing had been seen, up to this time":* Oliver Sacks, Foreword to ibid., xi–xii.

90 *in 1958 Gallaudet awarded an honorary degree:* Maher (1996), 27–28.

90 *"The teacher who learns signs":* Quoted in Dennis Cokely, "Sign Language: Teaching, Interpreting, and Educational Policy," in Baker and Battison (1980), 141. Also quoted in Maher (1996), 54.

91 *"I had come into a community":* Maher (1996), 60.

91 *I remember once when one of the old-line teachers:* Ibid., 63–64.

92 *he had studied Latin, Greek, French and German:* Ibid., 45.

93 *"I'd rather have novelty and intelligence":* Ibid., 46.

93 *Stokoe once spent the better part of a year deciphering:* Ibid., 41.

93 *deaf education in America had become an extensive commercial enterprise:* Lane, Hoffmeister and Bahan (1996), 28ff.

93 *"He earned the nickname Stubborn Stokoe":* Eric Nagourney, "William Stokoe Jr., Sign Language Advocate, Dies at 80," *New York Times,* April 11, 2000, B10.

93 *one of his boyhood electric train sets:* Maher (1996), 89.

94 *ICE-CREAM YOU WANT WHICH?:* This example is from Humphries et al. (1994), 88.

94 *"It looks to me":* Maher (1996), 54.

94 chien *or* canis *or* Hund *or* kelev: "Dog," respectively, in French, Latin, German and Hebrew.

94 *"The linguistic sign is arbitrary":* Ferdinand de Saussure, *Course in General Linguistics* (1916), English translation by Roy Harris, edited by Charles Bally and Albert Sechehaye (Chicago: Open Court, 1986), 67.

95 *"RINGO: John thought of the name Beatles":* Interview at the Plaza Hotel, New York City, Feb. 10, 1964, *The Beatles Tapes II: "Early Beatlemania, 1963–64"* (Seattle: Jerden Records, 1993).

95 *in most languages, these words, like "splat" and "squish" and "tintinnabulation":* Some spoken languages, like Bantu and Japanese, have many more onomatopoetic words than English does. Susan Fischer, personal communication.

95 *essential design properties of human language:* The notion of "design properties" of human language is generally credited to the structural linguist Charles Hockett. See, e.g., Charles F. Hockett, *A Course in Modern Linguistics* (New York: Macmillan, 1958).

95 *This ability to attach meaning:* W. F. Bolton, "Language: An Introduction," in Virginia P. Clark, Paul A. Eschholz and Alfred F. Rosa, eds., *Language: Introductory Readings,* 3rd ed. (New York: St. Martin's, 1981), 5.

97 *Any utterance in a language consists:* Hockett (1958), 574–75.

98 *"None before [the Abbé de l'Épée] and all too few after him":* Stokoe (1960), 14.

99 *Just as we know that the two English words:* Robbin Battison, "Signs Have Parts: A Simple Idea," in Baker and Battison (1980), 42, italics in original.

99 *If you hold one hand sideways, all five fingers spread:* I am indebted to Susan Fischer for this example.

100 *The sign* SUMMER *is made:* Klima and Bellugi (1979), 41.

100 *The signs* COFFEE, WORK *and* YEAR*:* This example was furnished by Jody Gill.

100 *In all, Stokoe identified:* Stokoe (1960), 41ff. Later researchers have disagreed on the precise number of handshapes, locations and movements, with some linguists arguing for as many as forty-five different handshapes and twenty-eight locations, but only a dozen movements, in ASL; see, e.g., Kyle and Woll (1985), 89.

100 *While some languages employ a larger number of discrete handshapes:* For the number of handshapes in Finnish, Taiwanese and Providence Island Sign Languages, see Van Cleve (1987), Vol. 3, 72–73, 116, 103.

100 *In Taiwanese Sign Language,* BROTHER*:* Van Cleve (1987), Vol. 3, 116. Extended middle finger in British Sign: Kyle and Woll (1985), 103.

101 *"ASL signers learning Chinese Sign Language":* Carol A. Padden, "American Sign Language," in Van Cleve (1987), Vol. 3, 47.

102 *About 60 percent of the signs of ASL:* Klima and Bellugi (1979), 48.

102 No two-handed signing in the car!: Carol Padden points out that for most deaf signers, safe signing while driving presents no difficulty. "In my family we don't take our hands off the wheel," she wrote me in an e-mail message in response to this passage. "We just drop the weak hand, or we sign close to the wheel, with one hand on."

102 *"There are restrictions on what is physically possible":* Klima and Bellugi (1979), 76.

103 *To most native English speakers, "shtr" at the start of a word:* In some dialects of English, among them Hawaiian English, "s" is pronounced "sh" before the consonant cluster "tr"—"straight," for instance, is pronounced "shtraight." Susan Fischer, personal communication.

103 *"The tendency toward symmetry":* Klima and Bellugi (1979), 77.

104 *First identified by the linguist Robbin Battison:* Robbin Battison, *Lexical Borrowing in American Sign Language* (Silver Spring, Md.: Linstock, 1978).

104 *The particular set of strictures they impose:* Dominance constraint in ASL: Klima and Bellugi (1979), 64; in British Sign Language: Rachel Sutton-Spence and Bencie Woll, *The Linguistics of British Sign Language: An Introduction* (Cambridge: Cambridge University Press, 1999), 162.

105 *in England, there are descriptions of British Sign:* Mid-seventeenth-century descriptions of British Sign include Bulwer's *Chirologia* of 1644. Van Cleve (1987), Vol. 3, 62.

105 *There is also a marvelous cache of motion picture footage:* Van Cleve (1987), Vol. 3, 279–80. This film archive, named the George W. Veditz Film Collection, after the NAD president who spearheaded the initiative, is now housed in the archives of Gallaudet University.

105 *"from the two highly transparent ASL signs":* Klima and Bellugi (1979), 28.

105 *Over time, however,* HOME *changed:* In colloquial ASL, HOME is signed in a single location, rather than moving between two locations on the cheek. Susan Fischer, personal communication. The analysis of HOME as a historical compound is from Nancy Frishberg, "Arbitrariness and Iconicity: Historical Change in ASL," *Language* 51:3 (1975), 696–719.

105 *The current merged sign:* Klima and Bellugi (1979), 29–30.

106 *"In general," Klima and Bellugi write:* Ibid., 70.

106 *"Within a short period of time, however":* Ibid., 11–12.

107 *The work so far accomplished:* Stokoe (1960), 67, italics added. The "famous definition" to which Stokoe refers is that of the structural linguists Bernard Bloch and George Trager, who wrote, "A language is a system of arbitrary vocal symbols by means of which a social group cooperates." Bernard Bloch and George L. Trager, *Outline of Linguistic Analysis* (Baltimore: Linguistic Society of America, 1942), 5.

107 *Stokoe coined the term "chereme":* Stokoe (1960), 30.

108 *"With the exception of . . . one or two colleagues":* Quoted in Sacks, Foreword to Maher (1996), xiii.

108 *"The worst crime the white man has committed:":* Quoted in Charles E. Silberman, *Crisis in Black and White* (New York: Random House, 1964), 68.

108 *"My colleagues and I laughed at Dr. Stokoe":* Gilbert C. Eastman, "From Student to Professional: A Personal Chronicle of Sign Language," in Baker and Battison (1980), 18.

108 *In 1965, he and two deaf co-authors:* William C. Stokoe, Jr., Dorothy C. Casterline and Carl G. Croneberg, *A Dictionary of American Sign Language on Linguistic Principles* (Washington: Gallaudet College Press, 1965).

109 *"It was unique to describe 'Deaf people'":* Quoted in Sacks, Foreword to Maher (1996), xiii.

109 *In one of a series of indignities:* See, e.g., Maher (1996), 155, for closing of Stokoe's Linguistic Research Laboratory.

109 *It reached a highly public apex in the spring of 1988:* A similar victorious protest was waged at Gallaudet in 2006, after I. King Jordan announced his retirement and Jane K. Fernandes, then the university's provost, was named as his successor. (Although Fernandes was deaf, many students, faculty and alumni objected to her leadership style.) After months of protest during which students shut down the campus and attracted headlines worldwide, the Gallaudet board of trustees withdrew Fernandes's selection.

110 *in May of 1988:* Maher (1996), 161ff.

CHAPTER SEVEN: THE HOUSE OF BLUE ROSES

Page

112 *It has been said that in Afar tradition:* This belief is rejected in Wilfred Thesiger, "The Awash River and the Aussa Sultanate," *Geographical Journal* 85:1 (1935), 1–19.

112 *"When people are aware that their speech is being investigated":* Dennis R. Preston, "A Renewed Proposal for the Study of Folk Linguistics," in Joy Kreeft Peyton, Peg Griffin, Walt Wolfram and Ralph Fasold, eds., *Language in Action: New Studies of Language in Society. Essays in Honor of Roger W. Shuy* (Cresskill, N.J.: Hampton, 2000), 120, italics in original. The term "observer's paradox" was coined by the eminent sociolinguist William Labov in *Language in the Inner City: Studies in the Black English Vernacular* (Philadelphia: University of Pennsylvania Press, 1972).

115 *Although linguists believe that every region:* Dennis R. Preston, "They Speak Really Bad English Down South and in New York City," in Laurie Bauer and Peter Trudgill, eds., *Language Myths* (New York: Penguin, 1998), 140.

116 *He asked a group of nearly 150 people:* Ibid., 139–49. These results are also summarized in Dennis R. Preston and Gregory C. Robinson, "Dialect Perception and Attitudes to Variation," in Martin J. Ball, ed., *Clinical Sociolinguistics* (Oxford: Blackwell, 2005), 133–49.

116 *"Preston has taken this to indicate":* Preston and Robinson (2005), 144.

117 *"Just as one might have suspected":* Ibid., 145.
117 *"Like all groups who are prejudiced against":* Preston (1998), 148.
118 *from the third generation on:* Shifra Kisch, "Negotiating (Genetic) Deafness in a Bedouin Community," in John Vickery Van Cleve, ed., *Genetics, Disability and Deafness* (Washington: Gallaudet University Press, 2004), 148–73.
119 *in Israel, as in the United States, the incidence of deafness:* Van Cleve (1987), Vol. 1, 251ff.; Vol. 2, 102.

CHAPTER EIGHT: EVERYONE HERE SPEAKS SIGN LANGUAGE

Page

123 *It is also what happened in Nicaragua:* See, e.g., Ann Senghas and Marie Coppola, "Children Creating Language: How Nicaraguan Sign Language Acquired a Spatial Grammar," *Psychological Science* 12:4 (2001), 323–28.
123 *a combined student body of more than four hundred:* L. G. Polich, "Social Agency and Deaf Communities: A Nicaraguan Case Study," (Ph.D. diss., University of Texas, 1998), quoted in Senghas and Coppola (2001), 324.
123 *"For the first time":* Senghas and Coppola (2001), 324.
124 *"As they started to communicate with each other":* Ann Senghas, Marie Coppola, Elissa L. Newport and Ted Supalla, "Argument Structure in Nicaraguan Sign Language: The Emergence of Grammatical Devices, in Elizabeth Hughes, Mary Hughes and Annabel Greenhill, eds., *Proceedings of the 21st Annual Boston University Conference on Language Development* (Somerville, Mass.: Cascadilla, 1997), Vol. 2, 550.
124 *an MIT-trained linguist who wrote her doctoral dissertation:* Judy Anne Shepard-Kegl, "Locative Relations in American Sign Language: Word Formation, Syntax and Discourse" (Ph.D. diss., Massachusetts Institute of Technology, 1985).
125 *This new sign language, Kegl, Senghas and Coppola write:* Kegl et al. (1999), 184.
125 *"The youngest members of the second cohort":* Senghas and Coppola (2001), 327.
125 *"Children surpass adults at learning languages":* Ibid., 323. For this observation, the authors cite J. S. Johnson and E. L. Newport, "Critical Period Effects in Second Language Learning: The Influence of Maturational State on the Acquisition of a Second Language," *Cognitive Psychology* 21 (1989), 60–99, and E. L. Newport, "Maturational Constraints in Language Learning," *Cognitive Science* 14 (1990), 11–28.
126 *Linguists call these formative years the "critical period":* See, e.g., Lenneberg (1967), 175ff.

126 *In the rare documented cases of "feral children":* See, e.g., Harlan Lane, *The Wild Boy of Aveyron* (Cambridge: Harvard University Press, 1976); Susan Curtiss, *Genie: A Psycholinguistic Study of a Modern-Day "Wild Child"* (New York: Academic Press, 1977).

127 *"Deaf individuals left in their homesigning environment":* Kegl et al. (1999), 206.

127 *Over their first several years together:* Senghas and Coppola (2001), 328.

127 *Among the new pupils, Senghas and her colleagues found:* Ibid., 326–27.

128 *the children's signing was accompanied by raised eyebrows:* Kegl et al. (1999), 184.

129 *We believe this use of a common location:* Senghas and Coppola (2001), 324–27.

130 *"marks the beginning of the linguistic use of gesture":* Kegl et al. (1999), 195.

131 *"The speech of pidgin speakers":* Bickerton (1984), 174.

131 *It is hypothesized that creole languages:* Ibid., 173.

132 *"Mi kape bai, mi chaek meik":* Ibid., 174–75. These examples are also quoted in Pinker (1994), 33.

132 *as Bickerton writes, they "have no recognizable syntax":* Bickerton (1984), 174.

132 *"Wan dei haed pleni av dis mauntin fish":* Ibid., 175. The first of these examples is also cited in Pinker (1994), 35.

134 *"The languages traditionally identified as creoles":* John H. McWhorter, "Identifying the Creole Prototype: Vindicating a Typological Class," *Language* 74:4 (1998), 791.

134 *The paucity of inflection in creoles:* Ibid., 793–95.

134 *"Dei gon* get *naif* pok *you":* Bickerton (1984), 175, italics added.

135 *"how subjects and objects are linked":* Ann Senghas, et al. (1997), 550.

135 *"at least points to the possibility":* Kegl, et al. (1999), 215.

135 *The linguist Robert Wilson recorded:* Quoted in Bickerton (1984), 185–86.

135 *"At the time," Bickerton writes:* Bickerton (1984), 185–86.

136 *"the normal generation-to-generation transmission":* Ibid., 176.

136 *The innovative aspects of creole grammar:* Ibid., 173.

136 *Like signed languages, creoles appear:* Susan Fischer noted the linguistic and social parallels between sign languages and spoken creoles as early as 1978. She argued that because the sign-language input to the deaf child is often deficient (as in the poor signing of hearing parents, for example), sign languages are essentially "recreolized" with every new generation of signers. Susan D. Fischer, "Sign Language and Creoles," in Siple (1978), 309–31.

137 *"He was a good neighbor":* Groce (1985), 1.

138 *"He was considered a very wealthy man":* Ibid., 1–2.

138 *I had already spent a good part of the afternoon:* Ibid., 2–3.

139 *"The entire community," Groce writes:* Ibid., 53.

139 *There has never been any attempt made: Boston Sunday Herald,* "Mark of Chilmark, Deaf and Dumb in the Village of Squibnocket," Jan. 20, 1895, quoted in ibid., 77–78.

140 *"Perhaps the best description":* Groce (1985), 5.

140 *The first known deaf Vineyarder:* Ibid., 23ff.

140 *The origin of a trait for deafness:* Ibid., 22. To be homozygous for a particular genetic trait means to possess identical mutational forms of the gene at corresponding chromosomal locations.

141 *"Barnstable continued to grow":* Ibid., 34.

141 *"Because marriage between cousins was permitted":* Ibid., 40–41.

142 *"almost 85 percent of the second cousins":* Ibid., 41.

142 *"the chances of deaf children being born":* Ibid., 41.

142 *"In all," Groce writes:* Ibid., 42.

142 *You make a neighborly call: Boston Sunday Herald* (1895), quoted in ibid., 53.

143 *"My informants remembered signs":* Groce (1985), 74.

143 *Martha's Vineyard Sign Language appears to have resembled British Sign:* Reported in Lane et al. (2000), 86. For the cognate figures, the authors cite Ben Bahan and J. Poole-Nash, "The Signing Community on Martha's Vineyard," unpublished address to the Conference on Deaf Studies 4, Haverhill, Mass., April 1995.

143 *The last deaf signer died in 1952:* Groce (1985), vii.

143 *My first sight of this, indeed:* Oliver Sacks, *Seeing Voices: A Journey into the World of the Deaf* (Berkeley: University of California Press, 1989), 35–36.

143 *This old lady:* Ibid., 36.

145 *During the mid-1960s, thousands of children:* Between 1963 and 1965, some eight thousand children were deafened as the result of prenatal rubella, also known as German measles. Van Cleve (1987), Vol. 2, 23.

145 *There are many forms of hereditary deafness:* Groce (1985), 22; Van Cleve (1987), Vol. 2, 20ff.

145 *But when it does, as Harlan Lane and his colleagues have discovered:* Lane et al. (2000).

146 *it does so, as Groce writes, "seemingly at random":* Groce (1985), 106.

146 *"deafness was viewed as something that could happen":* Ibid., 106–7.

147 *"The traditional method of making babies immune to scorpion bites":* What follows is the English translation of the scorpion story, originally told entirely in Al-Sayyid Bedouin Sign. The translation was part of a presentation given by Irit Meir at the workshop "Sign Language in Village Communities," Nijmegen, the Netherlands, April 2006:

There was a woman in a house. It was not a house, it was a cloth house—a tent. Once we didn't have houses; we had tents. The goats went out grazing. We had many goats back then. The woman put the baby in a tent. She laid him in a cradle on two wooden beams. She breast-fed the little one. After about an hour or two, she went outside and walked around. She spotted a scorpion on the ground. She took a stick and killed the scorpion. She put it in fire. She squeezed the scorpion and put the liquid on her nipple. Then she breast-fed the baby. Why did she do that? Later, when the baby grows up, if he gets stung by a scorpion, nothing will happen to him. He won't need any injections, and he'll be strong and healthy.

147 *In Al-Sayyid, too, the deafness is recessive:* Sandler et al. (2005), 2661.

CHAPTER NINE: HYSSOP

Page

150 *It was an eventful visit:* Interview with Carol Padden in New York City, June 25, 2004.

151 *From the mid-1800s on:* Barbara C. LeMaster and John P. Dwyer, "Knowing and Using Female and Male Signs in Dublin," *Sign Language Studies* 20:73 (1991), 361–96.

152 *The male sign* GREEN, *for instance:* Ibid., 367.

153 *"The issue of 'male' and 'female' language status":* Ibid., 393.

CHAPTER TEN: THE WEB OF WORDS

Page

155 *"unwoodpeckerish":* Jonathan Franzen, "My Bird Problem," *The New Yorker,* Aug. 8, 2005, 59.

155 *Mark made his reputation:* Mark Aronoff, *Word Formation in Generative Grammar* (Cambridge: MIT Press, 1976).

157 *"At that time," Bellugi and her husband:* Klima and Bellugi (1979), 244.

158 *Since the words of a language can consist:* Victoria A. Fromkin, "Slips of the Tongue," *Scientific American* 229 (1973), 114.

158 *"While one might expect any communication system":* Sandler and Lillo-Martin (2001), 543.

160 *First, the meaning of the compound often differs:* Clayton Valli and Ceil Lucas, *Linguistics of American Sign Language: An Introduction,* 2nd ed. (Washington: Gallaudet University Press, 1995), 57.

160 *Most of these compounds are unique to the language:* Ibid., 57ff.; Klima and Bellugi (1979), 205.

161 *As a later generation of linguists:* See, e.g., Ronnie B. Wilbur, "Why Syllables? What the Notion Means for ASL Research," in Susan D. Fischer and Patricia Siple, eds., *Theoretical Issues in Sign language Research* (Chicago: University of Chicago Press, 1990), 81–108; Scott K. Liddell, "THINK and BELIEVE: Sequentiality in American Sign Language," *Language* 60:2 (1984), 372–99; Wendy Sandler, *Phonological Representation of the Sign: Linearity and Nonlinearity in American Sign Language* (Dordrecht: Foris Publications, 1989).

162 *If this were the case, it would make sign language radically different:* Charles F. Hockett, "The Problem of Universals in Language," in J. H. Greenberg, ed., *Universals of Language* (Cambridge: MIT Press, 1963).

163 *In the 1970s, Ted Supalla:* Ted Supalla and Elissa L. Newport, "How Many Seats in a Chair? The Derivation of Nouns and Verbs in American Sign Language," in Siple (1978), 91–132.

163 *They found the noun TYPEWRITER:* Ibid., 128–31.

164 *In Samoan:* Fromkin and Rodman (1998), 102.

164 *In Tagalog:* Fromkin et al. (2000), 64.

164 *As the linguist Susan Fischer had already discovered:* Susan D. Fischer, "Two Processes of Reduplication in American Sign Language," in *Foundations of Language* 9 (1973), 469–80.

164 *including GUN and SHOOT; SCISSORS and CUT:* Supalla and Newport (1978), 128–31.

165 *the verb GET, made with repeated, restrained movement:* Klima and Bellugi (1979), 201.

165 *"Another remote possibility":* Ibid., 244, italics added.

166 *Looking again at the videotaped stories:* Ibid., 245, italics in original.

166 *The meaning 'became red' was often coded:* Ibid., 260.

166 *It carried the meaning of "apparent incessant duration":* Ibid., 257.

166 *a grammatical device first noted in ASL:* Fischer (1973), 469–80.

166 *"the onset, duration, frequency, recurrence":* Klima and Bellugi (1979), 247.

167 *"Tense refers to anchoring in time":* Andrew Spencer, "Morphology," in Aronoff and Rees-Miller (2001), 218, italics in original.

167 *These included the intensive aspect:* Klima and Bellugi (1979), 246–70.

167 *The ASL sign SLOW is made:* Ibid., 270–71.

167 *"(a) whether a specific act presents itself":* Ibid., 284.

168 *DIPLOMA, PRINCIPAL GIVE:* Adapted from ibid. It is important to note, however, that not every verb in ASL can be inflected in as many different ways as GIVE can.

168 *"HOUSE, (ME) MEASURE:* Adapted from ibid., 288.

168 *In ASL, multiple aspects can be layered:* Klima and Bellugi (1979), 312–13.

169 *"The existence of such elaborate formal inflectional devices":* Ibid., 314.

CHAPTER ELEVEN: THE HOUSE BUILT FROM THE SECOND STORY DOWN

Page

173 *I TIRED WHY, STUDY ALL-NIGHT:* Adapted from Valli and Lucas (1995), 140.

174 *SNOW, CLASS CANCEL:* Karen Emmorey, *Language, Cognition, and the Brain: Insights from Sign Language Research* (Mahwah, N.J.: Lawrence Erlbaum, 2002), 46–47.

174 *"When these two facial expressions accompany the same verb":* Ibid., 48.

174 *Other facial adverbs in ASL:* Ibid., 49–51.

174 *"Linguistic and emotional facial expressions differ":* Ibid., 46.

175 *"A signer who does not make use":* Fischer (1972), 193.

175 *different sign languages conscript the face:* Nicaraguan Sign Language: Ann Senghas, personal communication; Chinese Sign Language: Jun Hui Yang and Susan D. Fischer, "Expressing Negation in Chinese Sign Language," *Sign Language & Linguistics* 5:2 (2002), 173; Japanese Sign Language: Susan D. Fischer and Harry van der Hulst, "Sign Language Structures," in Marc Marschark and Patricia Elizabeth Spencer, eds., *Oxford Handbook of Deaf Studies, Language, and Education* (Oxford: Oxford University Press, 2003), 326.

175 *the sign-language linguist Sherman Wilcox:* Sherman Wilcox, personal communication.

CHAPTER TWELVE: GRAMMAR IN MIDAIR

Page

178 *"It seems very pretty":* Lewis Carroll, *Alice's Adventures in Wonderland* and *Through the Looking-Glass* (Cleveland: World, 1946), 177, italics in original.

179 Puer videt puellam: Susan D. Fischer, "An Orientation to Language," in Sims et al. (1982), 17.

179 *"Inflection seems to compensate with word-order":* Charles Osgood, "Language Universals and Psycholinguistics," in Greenberg (1963), also quoted in Susan D. Fischer, "Sign Language and Linguistic Universals," in Christian Rohrer and Nicolas Ruwet, eds., *Actes du Colloque Franco-Allemand de Grammaire Transformationnelle* (Tübingen: Max Niemeyer Verlag, 1974), 194.

181 *some spoken languages, including the Algonquian languages:* See, e.g., Kiel Tobias Christianson, "Sentence Processing in a 'Nonconfigurational' Language" (Ph.D. diss., Michigan State University, 2002), for one such language, Odawa.

182 *In many Semitic languages, the root* k-t-b: The Arabic examples are from Wendy Sandler, "Temporal Aspects and A.S.L. Phonology," in Fischer and Siple (1990), 11.

184 *One of the first linguists to study verb agreement seriously:* Carol A. Padden, *Interaction of Morphology and Syntax in American Sign Language* (New York: Garland, 1988).

184 *ASL verbs, as Carol discovered:* Ibid., 25.

184 *The first, which she called agreeing verbs:* Ibid., 242.

184 *The second class, which Carol called spatial verbs:* Ibid., 244.

185 *The third class, which Carol called plain verbs:* Ibid., 243.

185 *Carol called this curious subclass:* Ibid., 176.

185 *Even the emerging sign language of Nicaragua:* Kegl, et al. (1999), 191.

186 *One of the linguists to look deeply at these questions:* See, e.g., Irit Meir, "Motion and Transfer: The Analysis of Two Verb Classes in Israeli Sign Language," in Valerie Dively, Melanie Metzger, Sarah Taub and Anne Marie Baer, eds., *Signed Languages: Discoveries from International Research* (Washington: Gallaudet University Press, 2001), 74–87.

186 *All of these verbs, Irit found, denote some type of* transfer: Meir (2002), 81.

186 *By contrast, the endpoints of spatial verbs:* Ibid., 81.

186 *a phenomenon she called "facing":* Ibid., 76–77.

187 *the facing of the hands is always toward the* object: Ibid., 80.

187 *Irit also examined the curious case of backwards verbs:* Ibid., 79–80.

188 "(1) My uncle *realizes that I'm a lousy cook":* Adapted from George Lakoff, "Presupposition and Relative Well-Formedness," in Danny D. Steinberg and Leon A. Jakobovits, eds., *Semantics: An Interdisciplinary Reader in Philosophy, Linguists and Psychology* (Cambridge: Cambridge University Press, 1971), 332, italics added. Also quoted, in part, in Andrew Radford, *Syntax: A Minimalist Introduction* (Cambridge: Cambridge University Press, 1997), 164.

191 *"By unraveling the factors that determine this classification:* Meir (2002), 74.

191 *"a certain Chinese encyclopedia":* Jorge Luis Borges, "The Analytical Language of John Wilkins," in Jorge Louis Borges, *Other Inquisitions, 1937–1952,* translated by Ruth L. C. Simms (New York: Washington Square Press, 1966), 108. This passage is also quoted in Lakoff (1987), 92.

191 *"One of the basic questions in the study of language":* Gunter Senft, "What Do We Really Know About Nominal Classification Systems?," in Gunter Senft, ed., *Systems of Nominal Classification* (Cambridge: Cambridge University Press, 2000), 12.

192 *"It is more felicitous to include generics":* R. M. W. Dixon, *Where Have All*

the Adjectives Gone? And Other Essays in Semantics and Syntax (Berlin: Mouton, 1982), 185. Also quoted in Alexandra Y. Aikhenvald, "Classifiers in Spoken and in Signed Languages: How to Know More," in Karen Emmorey, ed., *Perspectives on Classifier Constructions in Sign Languages* (Mahwah, N.J.: Lawrence Erlbaum, 2003), 87.

193 *It is common for the grammars of languages:* Lakoff (1987), 91–92.

193 *"five round-things of oranges":* Adapted from Karen L. Adams and Nancy Faires Conklin, "Toward a Theory of Natural Classification," in Claudia Corum, T. Cedric Smith-Stark and Ann Weiser, eds., *Papers from the Ninth Regional Meeting of the Chicago Linguistic Society* (Chicago: University of Chicago, 1973), 1.

193 *To convey the notion "I bought three pencils":* The Japanese data are courtesy of Susan Fischer.

194 *In Dyirbal, every noun in the language:* Dixon (1982), 178ff. Also quoted in Lakoff (1987), 92–93.

195 *In Diegueño:* Margaret Langdon, *A Grammar of Diegueño: The Mesa Grande Dialect* (Berkeley: University of California Press, 1970), cited in Colette Grinevald, "A Morphosyntactic Typology of Classifiers," in Senft (2000), 68.

195 *In Cayuga:* Adapted from Marianne Mithun, "The Convergence of Noun Classification Systems," in Colette Craig, ed., *Noun Classes and Categorization: Proceedings of a Symposium on Categorization and Noun Classification, Eugene, Oregon, October 1983* (Amsterdam: John Benjamins, 1986), 388. Also quoted in Mark Aronoff, Irit Meir, Carol Padden, and Wendy Sandler, "Classifier Constructions and Morphology in Two Sign Languages," in Emmorey (2003), 64.

196 *"MONEY **SMALL-ROUND-SHAPE**-BE-LOCATED":* Sandler and Lillo-Martin (2001), 546.

197 *The sign A-COIN-IS-LYING-THERE is identical:* Ibid., 547.

198 *In his doctoral dissertation, written in 1982:* Ted Supalla, "Structure and Acquisition of Verbs of Motion and Location in American Sign Language" (Ph.D. diss., University of California, San Diego, 1982).

198 *For one thing, young deaf children acquiring ASL:* Ibid., 64–124.

199 *In an earlier experiment, from the late 1970s:* Carol Schwartz, "Discrete Versus Continuous Encoding in American Sign Language and Nonlinguistic Gestures" (Unpublished manuscript, University of California, San Diego, 1979). A version of this experiment, with similar results, was repeated more recently by Karen Emmorey and Melissa Herzig, described in their paper "Categorical Versus Gradient Properties of Classifier Constructions in A.S.L.," in Emmorey (2003), 221–46.

199 *If indeed the producing subjects:* Supalla (1982), 126.

201 *"In the course of his fieldwork":* Lakoff (1987), 93.
203 *The four linguists compared the classifier systems:* Aronoff et al. (2003), 53–84.
204 *"Although we have found entity classifiers like* LEGGED-ANIMAL*":* Ibid., 67.
204 *one he called the "hull" classifier:* Supalla (1982), 28–29.

CHAPTER THIRTEEN: HASSAN'S HOUSE

Page
210 *"The deaf children we study":* Susan Goldin-Meadow, *The Resilience of Language: What Gesture Creation in Deaf Children Can Tell Us About How All Children Learn Language* (New York: Psychology Press, 2005), 62.
210 *The children, who at the start of her work:* Ibid., 60, for children's ages.
211 *"The gestures the deaf children use to communicate:"* Ibid., xvii.
211 *"For example," Goldin-Meadow writes, "David is telling us":* Ibid., 74.
212 *David makes a flutter gesture:* Ibid., 76–77.
213 *"For example, if using a twist gesture as a noun":* Ibid., 130.
213 *"Importantly," Goldin-Meadow writes, "the children do not displace":* Ibid., 112.
214 *When one child, Karen:* Ibid., 111.
214 Snack *[David makes a pointing gesture]:* Adapted from ibid., 108.
214 *"the deaf children's gestures form a* linguistic system": Goldin-Meadow (2005), 81, italics in original.
215 *"Neither the way the parents respond":* Goldin-Meadow (2005), 106–61.
216 *"What I am suggesting," Goldin-Meadow writes:* Ibid., 94.
216 *"important empirical data":* Ibid., 197.
216 *"the deaf children's gestures are structured":* Ibid., 218.
217 *"I have often wondered how far":* Ibid., 222, italics in original.

CHAPTER FOURTEEN: A SIGN IN MIND

Page
219 *Our capacity for immediate memory:* Klima and Bellugi (1979), 88.
219 *"The form in which words are encoded":* Ibid., 88.
219 *"The comparison of the errors with the items originally presented":* Ibid., 89.
220 *"For hearing people," Klima and Bellugi write, "short-term memory for words":* Ibid., 89.
220 *Deaf parents tell us:* Ibid., 89, italics in original.
221 *"The nature of the . . . errors in each group":* Ibid., 96–97.
221 *For "noon," a subject recalled "noun":* Adapted from ibid., 99.

221 *For* NOON, *a subject recalled "tree":* Adapted from Klima and Bellugi (1979), 99.

222 *"There was no overlap whatsoever":* Klima and Bellugi (1979), 98.

222 *"If this were the nature of the errors":* Ibid., 99.

222 *The sign* TEA, *as it happens, is nearly identical:* In many dialects of ASL, VOTE and TEA are actually homophones, "pronounced" exactly alike. Susan Fischer, personal communication.

223 PEAS *and* THEN: Several different ASL signs can be glossed with the English word "then." The one that is formally similar to PEAS is the sign that is also glossed as the conjunction OR.

223 *"The majority of the . . . errors":* Klima and Bellugi (1979), 101.

224 *For these subjects . . . errors do not at all reflect:* Ibid., 111.

225 *"She's marked with a big scarlet R":* Victoria A. Fromkin, ed., *Errors in Linguistic Performance: Slips of the Tongue, Ear, Pen, and Hand* (New York: Academic Press, 1980), 4–5.

225 *"'Taddle tennis'":* Fromkin (1973), 112.

225 *"John dropped his cuff of coffee":* Victoria A. Fromkin, "The Non-Anomalous Nature of Anomalous Utterances," *Language* 47 (1971), 30–31. Ibid. for the next two examples in the list.

225 *Among the utterances with which Spooner is credited:* Quoted in Fromkin (1973), 110.

225 *most of the slips ascribed to Spooner are apocryphal:* See, e.g., John M. Potter, "What Was the Matter with Dr. Spooner?," in Fromkin (1980), 13–34.

225 *"Don't throw your cigarette down":* Fromkin (1980), 6–7. Ibid. for the next two examples in the list.

225 *"Fash and tickle":* Fromkin (1971), 31. Ibid. for the next example in the list.

226 *his collection, first published in 1895:* Rudolf Meringer and C. Meyer, *Versprechen und Verlesen: Eine Psychologisch-Liguistiche Studie* (Stuttgart: Göschense Verlagsbuchhandlung, 1895).

226 *"the most unpopular man at the University of Vienna":* Fromkin (1971), 28, paraphrasing an observation by E. H. Sturtevant.

226 *"whether the mechanisms of this . . . disturbance:* Sigmund Freud, *Zur Psychopathologie des Alltaglebens,* 10th ed. (Leipzig: Internationaler Psychoanalytischer Verlag); English version in A. A. Brill, ed., *Basic Writings of Sigmund Freud* (New York: Modern Library, 1938), quoted in Fromkin (1971), 27.

226 *"I wouldn't buy* kids *for the* macadamia nuts*":* Fromkin (1971), 45.

227 *"A grammar," she writes, "must represent in some way":* Fromkin (1980), 9–10.

227 *"When do you heave the louse?"*: Ibid., 6.

227 *"odd hack"*: Fromkin (1971), 31.

227 *most of the errors Fromkin recorded were plausible but nonconcurring words:* Fromkin (1980), 6.

227 *"Although 'slips of the tongue' can be incorrectly uttered"*: Fromkin (1973), 113.

228 *"Until quite recently . . . the pervasive iconicity of signs"*: Don Newkirk, Edward S. Klima, Carlene Canady Pedersen and Ursula Bellugi, "Linguistic Evidence from Slips of the Hand," in Fromkin (1980), 165–66.

228 *"As two deaf people were conversing"*: Ibid., 169.

229 *Over time, the linguists observed sign-language errors of every kind:* Klima and Bellugi (1979), 125ff.

230 *If signs were, as some previous investigators have thought:* Newkirk et al. (1980), 173.

230 *"Such slips," the four authors write:* Klima and Bellugi (1979), 145, in a chapter written in collaboration with Don Newkirk and Carlene Canady Pedersen.

230 *"If we find that the same kinds of errors occur"*: Fromkin (1980), 9.

232 *For MCE, although the sign* IMPROVE*:* Samuel J. Supalla, "Manually Coded English: The Modality Question in Signed Language Development," in Siple and Fischer (1991), 87.

232 *"SEE 2's nonspatial grammatical devices"*: Ibid., 101.

233 *"These spatial modifications," Supalla writes:* Ibid., 105.

233 *"Instead of acquiring and mastering MCE"*: Ibid., 85.

233 *ASL signers produce about two signs per second:* Bellugi and Fischer (1972), 180.

234 *"The subjects were producing underlying sentences at a comparable rate"*: Ibid., 199.

234 *If we wanted to say "may I ask you a question?"*: Fischer (1982b), 91.

234 *"there may be a common underlying temporal process"*: Bellugi and Fischer (1972), 184.

235 *"The structure of a language is shaped"*: Fischer (1982b), 91.

235 *"John likes Mary"*: Fischer (1972), 186.

235 *Most sign languages have far richer systems of pronouns:* In a personal communication, Susan Fischer writes: "In English, we use third-person pronouns like 'he,' 'her,' etc., not only to shorten discourse, but to help make it cohere. Pronouns like 'he' alert the listener to the fact that we're still talking about the same character that was mentioned earlier. Many languages, including Japanese and Italian, use what linguists call 'zero' pronouns for the same purpose. So for example, in those languages if A asks B, 'Did Bill see the movie?' B could respond simply, 'Yes, saw,' and

that would be equivalent to English 'Yes, he saw it.' . . . ASL works like Japanese and Italian, as Diane Lillo-Martin has demonstrated. So in ASL, if A asks B, 'B-I-L-L FINISH SEE MOVIE?,' B could reply ,'[headnod] FINISH SEE.'"

236 *But as the psycholinguist Laura Petitto discovered:* Laura Ann Petitto, "From Gesture to Symbol: The Relationship Between Form and Meaning in the Acquisition of Personal Pronouns in American Sign Language" (Ph.D. dissertation, Harvard University, 1983).

236 *When they are about two, many deaf children go through a period:* Ibid., 152ff.

CHAPTER FIFTEEN: THE HOUSE OF TWENTY CHILDREN

Page

241 You make a neighborly call: *Boston Sunday Herald* (1895), quoted in Groce (1985), 53.

CHAPTER SIXTEEN: THE SIGNING BRAIN

Page

246 *"As early as the time of Hippocrates":* Poinzer et al. (1987), 35.

246 *"fell presently to forget his letters only":* C. Plinius Secundus, *The Historie of the World, Book VII,* translated by Philemon Holland (1601), Chapter 23, quoted in Fromkin and Rodman (1998), 44.

246 "If I forget thee, O Jerusalem": Psalm 137, King James Version, cited in Fromkin and Rodman (1998), 37.

247 *Despite this severe handicap:* David Caplan, *Neurolinguistics and Linguistic Aphasiology: An Introduction.* (Cambridge: Cambridge University Press, 1987), 44.

247 *"the first truly scientific paper":* Ibid., 46.

247 *This man, Lelong:* For the Lelong case history, see, e.g., Malcolm Macmillan, *An Odd Kind of Fame: Stories of Phineas Gage* (Cambridge: MIT Press, 2002), 191.

248 *"he said he knew of more than twenty-five cases":* Ibid., 192.

248 *"Broca publicly announced his view":* Ibid., 193. Many left-handed people, as is now known, are also left-hemisphere-dominant for language.

248 *"Nous parlons avec l'hemisphere gauche":* Quoted in Fromkin and Rodman (1998), 36.

248 *"the first to call the attention of the neurological community":* Caplan (1987), 46.

249 *EXAMINER: Can you tell me about why you came back to the hospital?:*

Harold Goodglass, *Understanding Aphasia* (San Diego: Academic Press, 1993), 105.

250 *I feel very well:* Ibid., 86.

251 *Until recently, nearly everything learned about the human capacity for language:* Poizner et al. (1987), 1.

252 *"Sarah M. clearly is not aphasic":* Ibid., 140.

252 *Gilbert G.'s poststroke signing:* Ibid., 146.

253 *The difference between the mother and her children:* Ibid., 61.

254 *EXAMINER: What's happening there?:* Ibid., 66.

255 *Cookie . . . Okay, . . . the cookie jar:* Goodglass (1993), 139.

256 *"Although the modality is different":* Poizner, et al. (1987), 77.

256 *"Virtually all her sublexical errors":* Ibid., 82.

256 *"The rule-governed nature of Karen L.'s errors":* Ibid., 85.

257 *I have never liked splinter groups:* Ibid., 94.

257 *I walked toward the Capitol:* Ibid., 94.

258 *PAUL D: AND HAVE ONE *WAY-DOWN-THERE:* Ibid., 98.

259 *Karen L.'s aphasia, because of the location of her lesion:* It is important to note that in cases of sign-language aphasia, as with aphasia for spoken language, the type of aphasia a patient manifests—Broca's or Wernicke's—is rarely completely clear-cut. Depending on the location of the lesion, an aphasic's symptoms can suggest an admixture of both types. This appears to be the case for the left-hemisphere-damaged patient known as Karen L., who displayed problems in both the production and the comprehension of ASL.

259 *the signing difficulties of these three patients did not stem:* Poizner et al. (1987), 161–72.

259 *"This* separation between linguistic and nonlinguistic functioning": Ibid., 172, italics in original.

259 *Even more remarkable was the fact:* Poizner et al. (1987), 173–91.

260 *"The congenitally deaf patients are exactly the ones":* Ibid., 191.

261 *"These data suggest that the neural organization":* Gregory Hickok, Ursula Bellugi and Edward S. Klima, "The Neural Organization of Language: Evidence from Sign Language Aphasia," *Trends in Cognitive Sciences* 2:4 (April 1998), 135.

262 *"Research investigating the neural organization":* Ibid., 136.

262 *In his influential book of 1983:* Jerry A. Fodor, *The Modularity of Mind: An Essay on Faculty Psychology* (Cambridge: MIT Press, 1983).

263 *"we can't help but hear linguistic input as language":* Diane Lillo-Martin, "The Modular Effects of Sign Language Acquisition," in Marc Marschark, Patricia Siple, Diane Lillo-Martin, Ruth Campbell and Victoria S. Everhart, eds., *Relations of Language and Thought: The View from*

Sign Language and Deaf Children (New York: Oxford University Press, 1997), 67.

263 *"a characteristic pace and sequencing":* Ibid., 67.

264 *the remarkable case of a man they called W.L.:* David P. Corina, Howard Poizner, Ursula Bellugi, Todd Feinberg, Dorothy Dowd and Lucinda O'Grady Batch, "Dissociation Between Linguistic and Nonlinguistic Gestural Systems: A Case for Compositionality," *Brain and Language* 43 (1992), 414–47.

264 *Its gestures are global, variable and analogue:* For an opposing view of hearing people's pantomime, see the work of the psychologist David McNeill.

265 *There are major differences between sign languages and communicative pantomimic gesture:* Corina et al. (1992), 420–21, italics added.

265 *Here is his signed description of the Cookie Theft picture:* Corina et al. (1992), 428.

265 *"This mixture of signs and mimes is very unusual":* Ibid., 429.

266 *W.L. produced a sequence of mime descriptors:* Ibid., 436.

266 *"In response to a picture of a pair of scissors":* Ibid., 435–36.

266 *"This case provides a powerful indication":* Ibid., 415.

266 *"The separation in brain systems for signs and for gestures":* Ibid., 421.

266 *In 2004, a group of researchers in London:* Jane Marshall, Jo Atkinson, Elaine Smulovitch, Alice Thacker and Bencie Woll, "Aphasia in a User of British Sign Language: Dissociation Between Sign and Gesture," *Cognitive Neuropsychology* 21:5 (2004), 537–54.

267 *"In the face of his linguistic difficulties":* Ibid., 547.

267 *a powerful argument for the modularity of human language:* In linguistics, as in philosophy and psychology, the issue of modularity is still hotly contested. Not every sign-language linguist believes that data from sign language offer evidence of modularity. One of these is Wendy Sandler, who in her article "Sign Language and Modularity," *Lingua* 89:4 (1993), 315–51, invokes evidence from sign language to argue *against* Fodor's theory of the modularity of language.

268 *"There is now overwhelming evidence":* Corina et al. (1992), 420, italics in original.

268 *The differential disruption:* Corina et al. (1992), 444, italics in original.

268 *as Susan Fischer points out in a review of these studies:* Susan D. Fischer, "The Study of Sign Language and Linguistic Theory," in Carlos P. Otero, ed., *Noam Chomsky: Critical Assessments* (London: Routledge, 1994), Vol. 4, 582–99.

269 *"If moulding and active teaching":* Ibid., 591.

269 *"If non-human primates are capable of language":* Ibid., 593.

270 *BRUSH-HAIR, BOUNCE-BALL, ERASE-BOARD, SCRUB-BY-HAND:* Karen Emmorey, Thomas Grabowski, Stephen McCullough, Hanna Damasio, Laurie Ponto, Richard Hichwa and Ursula Bellugi, "Motor-Iconicity of Sign Language Does Not Alter the Neural Systems Underlying Tool and Action Naming," *Brain and Language* 89 (2004), 27–37.

270 *"is made with a grasping handshape":* Ibid., 28.

270 *"canonical tool use":* Ibid., 29.

270 *"The sensory-motor iconicity of ASL signs":* Ibid., 33–34.

271 "Even when the form of a sign is indistinguishable": Ibid., 36, italics added.

CHAPTER SEVENTEEN: IN A WET PLACE

Page

273 *"sitting around for two hours":* Ann Senghas, personal communication.

273 *"One signer for example, describing his personal history":* Sandler et al. 2662.

273 *The [nouns] could either be objects:* Ibid.

275 *the team had proposed that the world's signed languages be classed together:* Mark Aronoff, Irit Meir, Carol Padden and Wendy Sandler, "Morphological Universals and the Sign Language Type," in Geert Booij and Jaap van Marle, eds., *Yearbook of Morphology* (Dordrecht: Springer, 2004), 19–39.

276 *there was no verb agreement whatsoever in Al-Sayyid Bedouin Sign Language:* This appears to be true also of Kata Kolok, the Balinese village sign language. Susan Fischer, personal communication. The language of Kata Kolok has been discussed by I Gede Marsaja, "Kata Kolok 'Deaf Talk': A Village Sign Language from North Bali," paper presented at the workshop "Sign Language in Village Communities" workshop, Nijmegen, the Netherlands, April 2006.

276 *Aminah signed it this way:* Sandler et al. (2005) and M.F. interviews with team members.

277 *As a well-documented case of the emergence of an inflectional category:* Aronoff et al. (2005), 306.

278 *"In the space of one generation from its inception":* Sandler et al. (2005), 2661.

278 *"We have found that one of the most important organizing principles":* Ibid.

278 *SHEEP SLAUGHTER:* Sandler et al. (2005) and M.F. interviews with team members.

279 *MAN GATHER; TALK:* Ibid.

279 *"The robust word-order pattern exhibited":* Sandler et al. (2005), 2664.

281 *"so over-determined and buffered in humans":* Goldin-Meadow (2005), 62.

281 *At the start of 2005, the team published its findings:* Sandler et al. (2005).

281 *The paper generated a flurry of media attention:* Nicholas Wade, "A New Language Arises, and Scientists Watch It Evolve," *New York Times,* Feb. 1, 2005, F3.

281 *Of greater significance to us than any particular word order:* Sandler et al. (2005), 2664–65.

282 *adjectives are comparatively rare commodities:* Mark Aronoff, personal communication.

284 In the beginning was the word: Mark Aronoff used this as the title of his presidential address to the annual meeting of the Linguistic Society of America, Albuquerque, N.M., January 2006.

284 *an international convocation of sign-language researchers:* "Theoretical Issues in Sign Language Research" (TISLR) 8, Barcelona (Sept. 30–Oct. 2, 2004). The TISLR convocation is held every two years.

AFTERWORD: IT TAKES A VILLAGE

Page

286 *On a bright spring day in 2006:* "Sign Language in Village Communities," workshop at the Max Planck Institute for Psycholinguistics, Nijmegen, the Netherlands, April 4–6, 2006.

286 *Irit was there, representing the team:* Irit Meir, "The Development of Argument Structure in Al-Sayyid Bedouin Sign Language," paper presented at "Sign Language in Village Communities" workshop, Nijmegen, 2006.

287 *One, a linguist from Indonesia:* Marsaja, 2006.

287 *Kata Kolok is at least eight generations old:* Branson et al., in Lucas (1996), 42.

287 *Another scholar reported on Bhan Khor Sign Language:* Angela Nonaka, "Establishing Speech Community Size and Membership of Undocumented Village Sign Languages: An Anthropological Heuristic from the Ban Khor Case Study," paper presented at "Sign Language in Village Communities" workshop, Nijmegen, 2006.

287 *There were also presentations on Country Sign:* Keren Cumberbatch, "Country Sign: The Dying Indigenous Sign Language of Jamaica," paper presented at "Sign Language in Village Communities" workshop, Nijmegen, 2006.

287 *on Kajana Sign Language:* Beppie van den Boaerde, "Kajana Signs," paper presented at "Sign Language in Village Communities" workshop, Nijmegen, 2006.

287 *on Adamorobe Sign Language:* Nyst (2006).

287 *a Mayan community in Mexico:* John A. Lucy, "Sign Language in a Yucatec Maya Community in Mexico," paper presented at "Sign Language in Village Communities" workshop, Nijmegen, 2006.

287 *on Russell Island in Papua New Guinea:* Stephen C. Levinson, personal communication.

288 *Inuit Sign Language:* See, e.g., J. C. MacDougall, "Access to Justice for Deaf Inuit in Nunavuk: The Role of 'Inuit Sign Language,'" *Canadian Psychology* 42:1, (February 2001), 61–73.

Acknowledgments

There is no known language, signed or spoken, whose lexicon contains powerful enough words of thanks with which to express my gratitude to the four scientists whose work is at the heart of this book. I thank them all for the rigor of their scholarship and the pleasure of their company. My deepest thanks go to Wendy Sandler, the project's director, for her extraordinary willingness to take on what must have seemed an albatross in journalist's clothing. Her grace in the face of my repeated entreaties to be allowed to visit Al-Sayyid; her keen intellect; and her patience with my relentless questions before, during and after our journey are beyond measure.

I am indebted to Irit Meir, Wendy's colleague at the University of Haifa, for essential pointers on Hebrew; for her stimulating research on the workings of verbs in Israeli Sign Language; and for a lovely, long-ago dinner in her leafy garden.

Profound thanks to Carol Padden, of the University of California, San Diego, who was an invaluable resource on American Sign Language and deaf culture. She was also kind enough to sit frequently for interviews when she passed through New York City. I am grateful to her and to Dr. Sandler for their kind permission to reproduce the photographs of the team, and of Al-Sayyid, that appear in *Talking Hands.*

Last, but by no means least, my deep gratitude to Mark Aronoff, of Stony Brook University, for nearly three decades of putting up with my relentless misdeeds; for sharing with me his wonderful family; and, above all, for saying, a half-dozen years ago, over lunch amid the clangor of Times Square, "Come with us to the desert."

Two other members of Dr. Sandler's Sign Language Research Laboratory, Shai Davidi and Svetlana Dachkovsky, gave me much-needed assistance. Many thanks also to the friends and colleagues who read all or part of the manuscript and offered valuable suggestions: Susan D. Fischer, C. Claiborne Ray, Ann Senghas and Charles Strum.

I am also profoundly grateful to the men and women of Al-Sayyid, in particular the man I call Hassan, for welcoming me into their homes and their lives.

In addition, I am indebted to the following scholars, researchers and others who graciously answered questions, hunted down obscure bibliographic references and provided invaluable assistance of all kinds: James J. DeCaro, Karen Emmorey, Elisabeth Engberg-Pedersen, Mike Eslea, Susan D. Fischer, Bernard Fradin, Kenji Harahata, Thomas R. Harrington, Paul Kay, Lorraine Leeson, Jane Maher, Joan Naturale, Angela Nonaka, Victoria Nyst, Michael J. Olson, Ann Peters, Gila Reinstein, Margaret Reynolds, Ann Senghas, Samuel Supalla, Ted Supalla, Robert Vago, Ronnie B. Wilbur, Sherman Wilcox, Jun Hui Yang and Ulrike Zeshan.

Thanks also to my colleagues past and present at *The New York Times* for their stimulating company, warm encouragement and keen editorial eyes: Michael Anderson, Jude Biersdorfer, Alida Becker, D. J. R. Bruckner, Elsa Dixler, Sarah Ferrell, Tom Ferrell, Barry Gewen, Sylviane Gold, Robert R. Harris, Steven Heller, Dennis Hevesi, Julie Just, Peter Keepnews, David Kelly, Eden Ross Lipson, Douglas Martin, William McDonald, Charles McGrath, Pat O'Conner, C. Claiborne Ray, Wolfgang Saxon, Charles Strum, Sam Tanenhaus, Scott Veale and Tim Weiner.

I have been dazzled by the extraordinary care lavished on this book by the members of the Simon & Schuster editorial team, chief among them my wonderful editor, Bob Bender; his assistant, Johanna Li; the copy supervisor, Gypsy da Silva; the copyeditor, Fred Chase, who attended the manuscript with the skill of a neurosurgeon; and Nancy Wolff, the indexer. Victoria Meyer, Rebecca J. Davis and the staff in the Simon & Schuster publicity department also deserve special praise. My literary agent, Katinka Matson, of Brockman, Inc., has my thanks in perpetuity for her deep understanding and skillful handling of this book from its inception.

The photographs of ASL signs that illustrate *Talking Hands* were taken and produced digitally by the brilliant and ever-patient Ivan Farkas. The model is Jody Gill.

Finally, my thanks to my family, in particular my sisters, Robin Fox and Erica Fox, for their extraordinary patience with the prolonged absences from family life this book entailed. Above all, measureless and abiding gratitude to George Robinson, my close reader and boon companion these twenty years and more.

Index

3 3277 00231 7746